Global Perspectives on Legal Challenges Posed by Ridesharing Companies

Zeynep Ayata · Işık Önay
Editors

Global Perspectives on Legal Challenges Posed by Ridesharing Companies

A Case Study of Uber

Springer

Editors
Zeynep Ayata
Law School
Koç University
Istanbul, Turkey

Işık Önay
Law School
Koç University
Istanbul, Turkey

ISBN 978-981-15-7034-6 ISBN 978-981-15-7035-3 (eBook)
https://doi.org/10.1007/978-981-15-7035-3

This Springer imprint is published by the registered company Springer Nature Singapore Pte Ltd.
The registered company address is: 152 Beach Road, #21-01/04 Gateway East, Singapore 189721, Singapore

Acknowledgements

The volume provides analysis of legal challenges regulators faced in nine jurisdictions. It aims to establish a dialogue between jurisdictions facing the same challenges, as it seems that regulators do have a lot to learn from each other. Legal frameworks applicable to Uber's activities and Uber's strategies to navigate within these are in a constant change, and the legal issues are far from being resolved.

The idea for preparing an edited book on legal issues concerning Uber came to us years ago as we were discussing various fields of law, where legal issues could arise pertaining to Uber's activities. We have suggested it as a common subject of study to the Business Law Research Group organized within the auspices of the Law Schools Global League (LSGL), and it was welcomed enthusiastically by the members of the group. Preliminary findings of research were presented in the annual LSGL meetings held in Mexico City in the summer of 2017 and in the summer of 2018 in Madrid. Since then contributors from other countries joined our group and made it possible for us to cover nine jurisdictions in this volume.

We are indebted to the Law Schools Global League for bringing together legal experts from various jurisdictions and making the publication of this book possible. We would like to thank Mr. H. Bahadır Çolak, research assistant at Koç University Law School, for his able assistantship during the formatting of the chapters. We are also grateful to Ms. Leslie Demir for improving the text and her useful comments.

Zeynep Ayata
Işık Önay

Contents

1 **Introduction** 1
Işık Önay

2 **A Conceptual Overview of Legal Challenges Posed by Uber** 7
Zeynep Ayata

3 **Ridesharing Regulation in the USA** 35
James B. Speta

4 **Deregulation of Public Transportation Services: Can Uber Accomplish the Task?** 55
Rosa M. Rojas Vértiz C.

5 **Uber in Brazil: Glory and Consequence** 85
Paulo Doron R. de Araujo, Wanderley Fernandes,
Maria Lucia Pádua Lima, and Paulo C. Goldschmidt

6 **Regulation of Uber in the UK** 101
Margarita Amaxopoulou, Mateja Durovic, and Franciszek Lech

7 **The Legal Framework of Uber in Spain** 137
Francisco de Elizalde and Fernando Pastor-Merchante

8 **The Legal Framework for Ridesharing Businesses and the Case of Uber in Germany** 163
Michael Nietsch and Gregor Schott

9 **Über Alles or not? the Italian Perspective on the "Uber Case"** 185
Eva R. Desana, Federico Riganti, and Silvana Secinaro

10 **Disruptive Technologies and Taxi Rides in South Africa: What Is the '*Uber*' Uproar About?** 199
Sylvia Papadopoulos and Stefan van Eck

11 A Legal Perspective on Uber's Activities in Turkey 231
Işık Önay and Emek Toraman Çolgar

12 Policy Implications of the Comparative Findings 259
Işık Önay and Zeynep Ayata

13 Looking Ahead... 281
Zeynep Ayata

Editors and Contributors

About the Editors

Zeynep Ayata is an assistant professor at Koç University. Zeynep's expertise and research interests are in European Union law, competition law, law and economics. She holds a BA in Philosophy, Politics and Economics from the University of Oxford, an LLB from Université Paris 1 Panthéon Sorbonne, an LLM from College of Europe (Bruges) and a PhD in private law from Ankara University. She was a visiting scholar at the Max Planck Institute for Competition and Innovation, at the British Institute of International and Comparative law and at the University of Cambridge. She was a review panel member for COST Action for two years. She conducted a Seed Fund Project at Koç University on the regulation of collaborative platforms in the EU and its member states. She is the chair of the Law Schools Global League Business and Law Working Group.

Işık Önay is an assistant professor at Koç University and the coordinator of the LLM program in Private Law. He holds an LLB from Koç University, an LLM from Queen Mary University of London and a PhD from Istanbul University and was a visiting scholar at the Max Planck Institute for Comparative and International Law in Hamburg. His areas of interest and expertise are contract law, tort law and civil law. He was the chair of the organization committee for the 6th Annual Conference of Younger Comparativists Committee of the American Society of Comparative Law in 2017, which was hosted by Koç University.

Contributors

Margarita Amaxopoulou is a visiting lecturer and Ph.D. in Law candidate at the Dickson Poon School of Law, King's College London. She hold an LLM in Transnational Law (Distinction) from King's College London, as well as an LLB (9.1/10; Valedictorian) from the Aristotle University of Thessaloniki. She is currently reading for a Ph.D. (Law Research) at King's College London, and she is the recipient of the Professor Anthony Guest Ph.D. Scholarship. She is conducting lectures and tutorials in business law, in the context of the LLB module "Consumer Protection; Advising Global Businesses and Their Customers" at the Dickson Poon School of Law.

Emek Toraman Çolgar is an assistant professor of commercial law at Koç University Law School. She completed her LLB at Istanbul Bilgi University Faculty of Law in 2004, and after graduation worked as an intern lawyer for one year. She holds an LLM in Business Law from Istanbul Bilgi University (2008) and received her Ph.D. degree in private law from Istanbul University in 2015. During her doctoral research, she spent thirteen months at Max Planck Institute for Comparative and International Private Law, Hamburg, as a guest researcher. Her research focuses on commercial law, company law, capital markets law and banking law. She is an executive committee member of Dr. Nüsret-Semahat Arsel International Business Law Implementation and Research Center (NASAMER).

Paulo Doron R. de Araujo is a professor of private law at DIREITO GV SP (Brazil). He has an LLB degree and Ph.D. in private law (*summa cum laudae*) from the University of São Paulo (USP). He is a former lawyer with the City Attorney's Office of Guarulhos. He was a visiting scholar at Universitá di Torino (2019) and at Instituto Tecnologico Autonomo de Mexico (2017). He is Chair of the Arbitration and Mediation Committee of Instituto Brasileiro de Direito Imobiliário (IBRADIM) and Vice-chair of the Negligence and Damages Committee of International Bar Association (IBA). He has been recognized by The Legal 500, Leaders League and other international publications as a reference dispute resolution and arbitration lawyer in Brazil.

Francisco de Elizalde is a professor at IE University, Law School (Spain). He focuses on comparative private law, especially contracts and the law of property. He is a visiting professor at Koç University (Turkey) and has lectured at the City University of Hong Kong and FGV Sao Paulo (Brazil). Professor Elizalde was a visiting scholar to the University of Cambridge. He practised law at Garrigues Litigation and Arbitration Department during several years. He is a member of the Madrid Bar Association, the American Society of Comparative Law and the European Law Institute. Prof. Elizalde is the head of the EU-financed Jean Monnet Module "Liability of Robots: a European Vision for a New Legal Regime".

Eva R. Desana is a full professor of business law, bankruptcy law and European company law at the University of Turin Department of Law. She is an arbitrator appointed by the Piedmont Chamber of Arbitration and by the Milan Chamber of Arbitration. She is the founder and the senior partner of Musumeci, Altara, Desana and Associati Legal Firm (Turin and Milan). She is an expert in financial markets and listed companies, and she has authored monographs on the concept and evolution of undertakings, takeover bids and debt securities. She is also author of many articles on financial markets and corporate governance, with particular attention to gender balance issues.

Mateja Durovic is Reader in Contract and Commercial Law at the Dickson Poon School of Law. He is Deputy Director of the Law School's Centre for Technology, Ethics, Law and Society (TELOS) and Academic Director of the Executive Programme on Consumer Law. He is Visiting Professor of Law at the University of Torino, University of Macerata, UC Lyon, and the International Training Centre of the International Labour Organization (ITCILO). He has worked as assistant professor (2015–2017) at the School of Law, City University of Hong Kong. He holds a Ph.D. and LLM degrees from the European University Institute, Florence, Italy; LLM degree from the University of Cambridge, UK; and an LLB degree from the University of Belgrade, Serbia, where he graduated as the first and best student of his class. He was Post-doc Research Associate at the European University Institute (2014–2015), Visiting Scholar at Stanford Law School, USA (2011), and at the Max Planck Institute of Private International and Comparative Law, Hamburg, Germany (2010). He worked for the Legal Service of the European Commission and for the law firm Gide Loyrette Nouel and was also a consultant for the European Commission, BEUC (European Consumer Organization) and the United Nations.

Wanderley Fernandes is a guest professor of the specialization program in contracts of Fundação Getúlio Vargas of Rio de Janeiro (since 2003); and a professor of graduation, master and specialization program of the law school of Fundação Getúlio Vargas in São Paulo (GV Direito SP), since 2000. He has graduated from the Universidade de São Paulo Law School (1986). He holds an LLM by University of Illinois—School of Law at Urbana Champaign (1997). He has completed the Program of Management Development from Harvard Business School—PMD-76 (2001). He holds a Ph.D. from Universidade de São Paulo (2011). He has taught at Universidade de São Paulo, Koç University and University of Cape Town. He is Associate Coordinator of the professional master program, member or the diversity committee and of the Ethical Commission of FGV DIREITO SP. He is a member of Brazilian Arbitration Committee and of Instituto de Direito Privado. He is a partner of Nascimento e Mourão—Sociedade de Advogados (since 2009), and arbitrator at the ICC, CCBC—Center of Arbitration of Brazil-Canadá Chamber or Commerce and Center of Arbitration of the Fundação Getúlio Vargas.

Paulo C. Goldschmidt is Senior Professor at Fundação Getulio Vargas—FGV/SP. He has a degree in Business Administration from Universidade Federal de Minas Gerais—UFMG (1966), masters in marketing from Michigan State University (1970) and Ph.D. in business administration from Fundação Getulio Vargas (1982).

Franciszek Lech is a KURF research assistant at King's College London. He holds an LLB from King's College London, where he graduated as he was the recipient for the Dickson Poon Scholar for Excellence in Studies.

Maria Lucia Pádua Lima is Professor at Fundação Getulio Vargas and Coordinator of International Affairs of the São Paulo Law School of Fundação Getulio Vargas (DIREITO SP). She holds a degree in business administration, Fundação Getulio Vargas—SP (1977), a masters (1985) and a Ph.D. in economic science from Universidade Estadual de Campinas (1995). She was postdoctoral fellow at Georgetown University Law Center (2008). She has experience in economics with emphasis on Brazil and G-20, balance of payments and international finance. She has done research on WTO, multilateralism and regionalism, economic development, Doha Development Round and trade negotiations.

Michael Nietsch holds the chair for private law, company law and securities regulation at EBS Law School in Wiesbaden, Germany. Previously, he was Associate Professor at Johannes Gutenberg-University of Mainz (Centre for German and International Laws of Financial Services). He is also Director of the Centre for Corporate Compliance at EBS Law School. His research and publications deal with topics of German and international corporate law giving emphasis to requirements of legal compliance and liability of companies and their directors and officers. He also works extensively in the field of banking and financial regulation. Main areas of interest here are the prevention of market abuse, in particular insider dealing and consumer finance contracts. Increasing attention is given to sustainable finance and digital transformation. He is a frequent rapporteur to congresses and has taught nationally and internationally. He is a member to numerous associations of legal professionals and legal scholars.

Sylvia Papadopoulos is a full-time senior lecturer in the Department of Mercantile Law at the University of Pretoria. She holds the degrees BLC, LLB, LLM (*cum laude*) and LLD from the University of Pretoria. Her thesis was entitled "Selected Aspects of E-Commerce, Digital Content and Consumer Protection in South Africa". She has also been admitted as an advocate of the High Court of South Africa. She teaches in the fields of payment methods and law and technology. She has published many peer-reviewed publications, presented at both national and international conferences and has made regular appearances on television and radio. She is also an author and editor of books, such as Cyberlaw @ SA III: The Law of the Internet in South Africa (2012), Cyberlaw @ SA IV: The Law of the Internet in South Africa (2020) published by Van Schaiks and advised the Parliamentary Portfolio Committee on limited aspects of the Protection of Personal Information Act 4 of 2013. She is also the current chair of the LSGL New Technologies and the Law Working Group and has attended by invite sessions with the United Nations Commission on International Trade Law (UNCITRAL) Working Group IV (Electronic Commerce) 51st session New York 2015.

Fernando Pastor-Merchante is Assistant Professor of Law at IE University (Madrid and Segovia, Spain), where he teaches constitutional law, administrative law and EU law. His research interests lie in the field of EU administrative law, with a special focus on state-aid governance. He holds a bachelor's degree in law and political science (Universidad Autónoma de Madrid), an LL.M. (Columbia University School of Law) and Ph.D. in law (European University Institute).

Federico Riganti is Post-doctoral Fellow of business law at Department of Law and Honorary Fellow in business law at the Department of Management at the University of Turin. He graduated summa cum laude in 2012, and in 2016, he obtained a Ph.D. in corporate law and capital markets regulations at the University of Bologna. In 2014, he was Visiting Research Fellow at Fordham Law School in New York. In 2012, he studied at The Hague Academy of International Law. He is a member of the Editorial Board of several Law Journals (such as Giurisprudenza Commerciale, Giurisprudenza Italiana, Il Nuovo Diritto delle Società and Giurisprudenza Arbitrale) and author of a monograph on Corporate Governance of Banks. He is also author of many articles on corporate law and corporate governance. His current research interests are corporate governance of banks, listed corporations, capital markets regulations, institutional shareholders and comparative corporate law.

Rosa M. Rojas Vértiz C. is a part-time professor of business law and property law at ITAM (Instituto Tecnológico Autónomo de México) and Ph.D. candidate at the Institute of Legal Research of Universidad Nacional Autónoma de México (IJJ-UNAM). She was Chevening Scholar at the London School of Economics and Political Science, where she has completed her LL.M. on corporate and commercial law with merit. She holds a law degree with honors from Escuela Libre de Derecho (Mexico City). She was certified on Amparo Proceedings by Universidad Panamericana (Mexico City). Rosa joined ITAM after practicing extensively as a commercial lawyer with leading firms and after having joined the Supreme Court of Mexico. She was a member of the Banking and Finance Group of a leading Mexican firm dealing with lending and secured transactions, real estate financing, structured cross-border financing, restructurings and workouts. Later she joined the First Chamber of the Supreme Court of Justice of Mexico, where she drafted judgments and contributed to the development of legal precedents dealing with civil, commercial, finance and insolvency matters. Formerly, Rosa was also Chief Compliance Officer of a multinational insurance company. She is Next-Gen member of the Execute Committee of the International Insolvency Institute and member of the Mexican Bar Association. She is also the coordinator in Mexico of the Ibero-American Institute for Law and Finance. She has participated as speaker in many conferences and seminars dealing with business and insolvency law as well as in several publications in Mexico and abroad.

Gregor Schott is a Ph.D. candidate at EBS Law School, Wiesbaden, and works in an international law firm in Frankfurt. He has degrees in law (first state examination) and general management (M.Sc.).

Silvana Secinaro is Associate Professor in Business Administration and Accounting at University of Turin. She is member of several groups of study and author of papers focused on Public Sector Accounting. She has been included as External expert to support the implementation of structural reforms in Member States in the European Union Commission.

James B. Speta is Elizabeth Froehling Horner Professor of Law and Vice Dean at the Northwestern University Pritzker School of Law, in Chicago, Illinois. He has been on the faculty since 1999. His articles have appeared in the Antitrust Law Journal, the Duke Law Journal, the Yale Journal on Regulation, the Transportation Law Journal and other outlets. He is a co-author of Internet and Telecommunication Regulation, the leading US casebook on regulation in the telecom space. His research interests include telecommunications and Internet policy, antitrust, administrative law and market organization. As a 1991 graduate of the University of Michigan Law School, he joined the Northwestern faculty following five years of practice at Sidley Austin LLP and a one-year visit at Northwestern. He had previously clerked for Judge Harry T. Edwards on the United States Court of Appeals for the D.C. Circuit. He is of counsel to the law firm Eimer Stahl LLP.

Stefan van Eck is Professor in labour law at the University of Pretoria, Vice President (Africa region) of the International Society of Labour and Social Security Law and President of the African Labour Law Society. He specializes in national and international comparative labour law and teaches at undergraduate and postgraduate levels. He has lectured at universities abroad, including the University of Sydney, Monash University in Melbourne and the University of Paris (Sorbonne). He has contributed chapters to scholarly books and has published articles in national and international academic law journals. He is a National Research Foundation (NRF)-rated researcher. He is an admitted attorney, has acted as an *ad hoc* member of the former Industrial Court and as an assessor of the former Labour Appeal Court.

Chapter 1
Introduction

Işık Önay

The growth of the sharing economy[1] is one of the most significant economic and social phenomena of the last decade. At an almost global scale, people are increasingly choosing sharing economy platforms for the supply and demand of services. Reports show that this growth will continue; for example, a study by Juniper Research stated that the sharing economy accounted for more than 18 billion US dollars in 2017 and was expected to double and reach more than 40 billion by 2022.[2] Another study by PricewaterhouseCoopers predicted that by 2025, sales revenues will reach 335 billion US dollars.[3]

The sharing economy can be defined as the sharing of services and assets between private individuals for a fee or free of charge, mostly through the use of a digital platform or generally the Internet. As Sundararajan puts it, "sharing isn't new",[4] but the use of such platforms has created a new phenomenon. The use of digital platforms has facilitated the low-cost expansion and commercialization of sharing economy companies. It has also allowed them to run their operations on a global scale by enabling subscribers to use one account in one application in hundreds of different countries.

One of the most important characteristics of sharing economy platforms is their flexibility. The platforms are conceived for private individuals who wish to utilize

[1]The terms "collaborative economy," "gig economy," "on-demand economy," "peer-to-peer economy," and "human-to-human economy" are also used to describe the business model developed by Uber and similar companies. It is referred to as the sharing economy in this book as that appears to be the most commonly used term in the literature.

[2]Juniper Research (2017).

[3]PwC (2015).

[4]Sundararajan (2016).

I. Önay (✉)
Koç University Law School, Istanbul, Turkey
e-mail: ionay@ku.edu.tr

Z. Ayata and I. Önay (eds.), *Global Perspectives on Legal Challenges Posed by Ridesharing Companies*,
https://doi.org/10.1007/978-981-15-7035-3_1

their idle assets or unused skills. These individuals may simply be seeking additional income, or the services they provide through the platforms may be their principal employment. Either way, they merely have to be in possession of the necessary tools and/or have the necessary skills to become a provider in the system. This presents an understanding of work, employment, and income that is radically different or opposed to traditional definitions.

The services provided by sharing economy platforms generally do not correspond exactly to existing norms or definitions. In fact, not only is sharing an old phenomenon, but the services provided are also not particularly creative: Sharing economy companies provide transportation, accommodation, cleaning services, and so on. The innovation in this sharing economy is not the product or the service but the business model itself. Sharing economy platforms rely on private individuals, and thus, the system is called peer-to-peer. The sale of goods or services takes place between peers and not between a professional and a buyer or a consumer. The existing norms in markets such as transportation or accommodation are based on contracts between a professional and a non-professional. The terms applicable to such contracts assign different roles and duties to these parties that are usually not considered equal. Furthermore, for the purpose of protecting the weak party (the consumer) or public interest, these norms provide a range of rules that should be applied to the relationship between parties. In other words, they regulate them. Sharing economy companies present a challenge, at least from a legal point of view, at precisely this point. If the users, providers, and recipients of the goods and services are peers, the existing legal norms often become inapplicable.

The business models of the new sharing economy present a case of disruptive innovation as they create a new model that does not fit into the definitions, terms, and processes of the traditional or common models. The disruptive effect is undoubtedly seen on economic and social levels. However, it also has a disruptive effect for law enforcement. The new relations construed by these companies thrive in a regulatory loophole where few or none of the existing norms are applicable. The loophole is usually at the heart of the system: The lack of regulation is what provides the flexibility and the low costs that are desirable for the companies and the users. The challenge for regulators then becomes the striking of a balance among the economic benefits generated by these companies, the need for protection of individuals and the public, and the creation of a level playing field between providers of similar services.

Uber is perhaps the most emblematic company of the sharing economy. According to Schwab, the "tipping point" of the sharing economy is "globally more trips/journeys via car sharing than in private cars".[5] Uber is therefore the tipping point and definitely one of the symbols of the sharing economy. The emblematic nature of Uber is also evidenced by the use of the term "uberization" in the literature,[6] referring to the transformation of the economy by the increase in sharing economy companies that make use of digital platforms.

---

[5] Schwab (2016).

[6] Daidj (2018, pp. 2345–2355), Eder (2017, pp. 159–203).

Founded in San Francisco, the ride-sharing company now provides peer-to-peer transport services in 890 cities in 71 countries.[7] The company provided 6.9 billion rides in 2019 worldwide.[8] The same year, it generated net revenue of about 14 billion US dollars.[9] The estimated value of Uber as of May 2018 was 72 billion US dollars.[10]

Uber is not only emblematic as a success story; for the past few years, it has also been a magnet of sorts for legal controversy. Uber has faced many hundreds of lawsuits in its home country and others. Interestingly, the lawsuits are initiated by various stakeholders, such as local authorities, competitors who are mostly taxi companies and their drivers, and also the Uber users and drivers themselves. The reason why Uber faces so many legal challenges and is in itself a legal challenge is because Uber definitely operates in a regulatory loophole.

Uber owes its success to its ride-hailing smartphone app, UberCar, re-named Uber in 2011. The co-founders introduced UberX in 2012, allowing anyone to drive for Uber using their own cars. Finally, UberPool, an app matching riders with other riders traveling in the same direction and stepping into the territory of public transportation, was launched in 2014. Uber does not provide all of these types of services in all cities of operation. All of the apps/services mimic taxis, but as the co-founder and former CEO of the company has stated on numerous occasions, Uber does not provide a taxi service.

The above outlined features of Uber justify its selection as the object of a case study on the sharing economy. This book furthermore adopts a comparative approach by addressing legal problems with the contributions of legal experts from different jurisdictions. The need for such an approach is obvious as all jurisdictions are dealing with the same problems created by a ride-sharing company operating within a regulatory loophole. This study aims to initiate legal dialogue between different jurisdictions and perhaps in the long term pave the way for a harmonized approach to regulating Uber.

The selection of jurisdictions to be covered in this book was done in such a way as to get the most out of a comparative inquiry on Uber. First, all of the selected countries are major markets for Uber, as it operates in the largest cities of these countries. Sao Paolo and Mexico City, for example, are considered as cities that constitute the largest markets for Uber.[11] The selection also reflects the dichotomy between common law and civil law jurisdictions. Although most of the selected countries follow the civil law tradition, the UK and the USA represent common law approaches, whereas South Africa has a rare hybrid system of law with influences from both the British and the Dutch. Four of the countries were selected from among developed countries (Germany, Italy, Spain, and the UK), whereas the remaining four are representatives of newly industrialized countries (Brazil, Mexico, South Africa,

---

[7]https://uberestimator.com/cities. *Accessed 24 May 2020.*

[8]https://www.statista.com/statistics/946298/uber-ridership-worldwide/. *Accessed 24 May 2020.*

[9]https://www.statista.com/statistics/550635/uber-global-net-revenue/. *Accessed 24 May 2020.*

[10]https://www.statista.com/statistics/729049/ride-hailing-gross-revenue-by-key-operator-glo bally/. *Accessed 24 May 2020.*

[11]Valencia (2017).

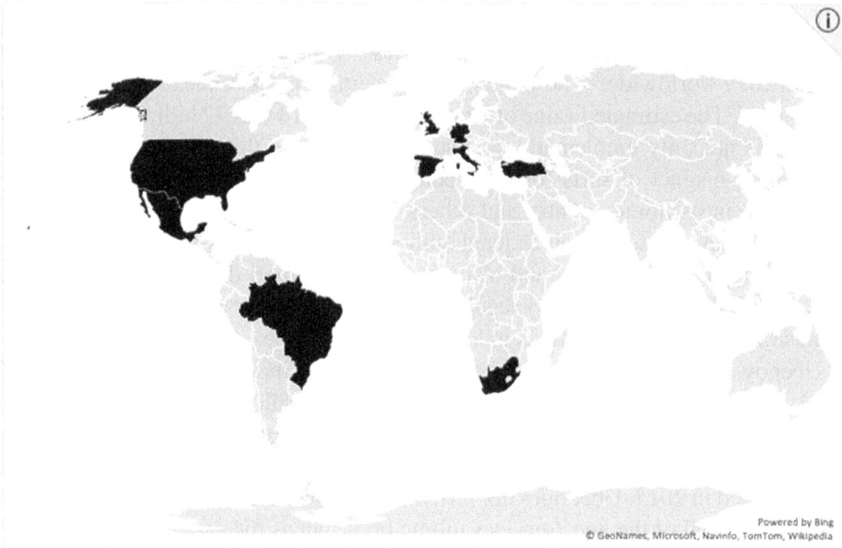

Fig. 1 Geographical scope of the study

and Turkey). Last but not least, it is important to note that the selection includes both federal (e.g., Brazil, Germany, Mexico, the USA) and unitary systems (e.g., Italy, Turkey) (Fig. 1).

The legal challenges posed by Uber are diverse and perhaps the most significant one pertains to market access. The drivers of UberX/UberPOP are private individuals providing transport services with their private vehicles. The vehicles are not registered for commercial use, and the drivers are not professionals who have to abide by certain regulations. The service itself is the same as any taxi service, but legally speaking it is certainly not a taxi service. Hence, the first problem that arises in the context of services provided by Uber is defining the market. The norms and rules applicable to any transaction depend on the definition of it. If Uber is not a taxi service, and it clearly claims that it is not, then how do we define the market and identify the rules applicable to it? How does each jurisdiction tackle this problem? What are the current rules in place for taxi/transportation services? Did Uber's entry into the market lead to a change of regulations regarding transportation services? Is Uber being held subject to these regulations? If so, how does the jurisdiction react when Uber fails to follow the rules? Is it simply banned, or are the drivers being fined for not abiding by the rules? These are the types of questions that each chapter will answer with regard to the concerned jurisdiction.

Many of the lawsuits against Uber have been initiated by Uber drivers. UberX or UberPOP drivers are by definition private individuals. They become service providers when they log on to Uber and transport passengers from one location to another using their personal vehicle or the vehicle of another private person. The relationship that they have with Uber, however, is that of user/provider of service. Uber claims that it does not enter into an employment relationship with its drivers, depriving them of economic and social benefits and protection. Hence, another legal problem that has been raised in debates and lawsuits about Uber is one pertaining to labor law. Does the concerned jurisdiction see Uber's relationship with its drivers as an employment relationship based on the rules in place? If not, did the legislator take action to include these relationships within the scope of employment contracts, or does it plan to? Would doing so not kill the model's flexibility advantage, or should we think in new and perhaps more creative terms when looking at this relationship?

Uber's operations bear the potential for civil liability. There have been unfortunate incidents in the past where accidents have caused severe harm and injury to passengers, drivers, and third parties. In such cases, numerous questions arise with regard to Uber's liability: Would Uber be liable for damages suffered in such cases? If the answer is affirmative, what would be the basis of liability? Could contractual liability be established, or do we need to resort to rules on extra-contractual liability? Is or should there be a limit to Uber's liability? Are the provisions pertaining to limitation of liability in Uber's terms and conditions valid?

This book starts with a conceptual overview of the legal challenges posed by Uber and concludes with comparative findings based on individual case studies. The remaining chapters are reserved for selected jurisdictions, where the authors deal with the legal issues pertaining to Uber that are most relevant in their respective jurisdictions. As one might expect, the legal challenges faced in different countries are similar. Legal issues tackled throughout the book in addition to those mentioned above include consumer protection, unfair competition, antitrust, and taxation.

Bibliography

Daidj N (2018) Uberization (Uberification of the economy). In: Khosrow-Pour M (ed) Encyclopedia of information science and technology, vol 3, 4th edn. IGI Global, Hershey, pp 2345–2355

Eder M (2017) Digitale evolution: Wie die digitalisierte ökonomie unser leben, arbeiten und miteinander verändern wird. Springer, Berlin, pp 159–203

Juniper Research (2017) Sharing economy revenues to double by 2022, reaching over $40 billion. https://www.juniperresearch.com/press/press-releases/sharing-economy-revenues-to-double-by-2022. Accessed on 24 May 2020

PwC (2015) Sharing or paring? Growth of the sharing economy. https://www.pwc.com/hu/en/kiadvanyok/assets/pdf/sharing-economy-en.pdf. Accessed on 24 May 2020

Schwab K (2016) The fourth industrial revolution. Penguin Random House, London

Sundararajan A (2016) The sharing economy: the end of employment and the rise of crowd-based capitalism. MIT Press, Cambridge

Valencia J (2017) Uber wants to double its presence in Mexico, its third largest market. https://fronterasdesk.org/content/10754/uber-wants-double-its-presence-mexico-its-third-largest-market. Accessed on 24 May 2020

Chapter 2
A Conceptual Overview of Legal Challenges Posed by Uber

Zeynep Ayata

1 Introduction

In 2009, two entrepreneurs, Garett Camp and Travis Kalanick, in San Francisco founded a company called Ubercab. The main aim of the company was to provide cheap private transportation. The following year they established an app which allowed people to share rides. The app was officially launched the following year. Eight years later, the platform was estimated to have 75 million users globally.[1] Ever since its official launch, the company's name, the services provided, its structure and many other of its essentials have evolved and transformed. However, the infamous Uber is still perceived as the emblematic company of what is called the sharing economy. So much so that the expansion of such platforms has been at times referred to as the *Uberization* of the economy. This phenomenon is a combination of many things such as the rise of platforms, transformation of service provisions, transformation of employment and even new understandings of trust. Of course, the business model created by Uber has also been described as innovative. Innovation is often associated with disruption: The old or the classic is replaced by the new, and the latter has disruptive effects on the former. Whether Uber may be considered as an innovator from an economic perspective or whether it has had such disruptive effects on markets may be contested. However, the most important effect of Uber has often been on the legal order, and it is certainly possible to say that Uber has had significant disruptive effects on law and regulation. It has led regulators across the globe to question rules or to adopt new ones. Uber has also been the subject of numerous controversial legal proceedings and court decisions in various fields of law. The purpose of this chapter is to discuss the existing and possible disruptive

[1] Uber (2020).

Z. Ayata (✉)
Koç University Law School, Istanbul, Turkey
e-mail: zayata@ku.edu.tr

Z. Ayata and I. Önay (eds.), *Global Perspectives on Legal Challenges Posed by Ridesharing Companies*,
https://doi.org/10.1007/978-981-15-7035-3_2

effects caused by Uber's business model that has triggered an economic, social and most importantly legal phenomenon. The economic meaning of the sharing economy and crowd-based capitalism will thus be explained with a specific focus on Uber as a ride-sharing company. In the second part of the chapter, the regulatory issues and challenges induced by Uber's business model will be scrutinized. This part will therefore lay out the conceptual framework of the legal challenges that will be examined in the following case-study chapters of this book. The chapter aims to display why Uber should be seen as a legal challenge for market regulation and for various fields of law such as labor law and civil law.

2 The Platform Economy: A Child of the Fourth Industrial Revolution

Uber, Airbnb, Lyft and TaskRabbit are all companies that are considered as part of the sharing economy. One concept is key to understanding sharing economy companies: the platform economy. In order to understand the rise of the platform economy, we must first turn to the notion of matchmaking. Matchmaking in the market may be defined as an operation of intermediation whereby a profit seeking private person matches two parties that may meet each other's needs. A second pivotal concept in analyzing the platform economy is multi-sided markets. It is the combination of this business model with the expansion of the internet and mobile applications that has led to the rise of the platform economy.

2.1 The Platform Economy

In their seminal work, Evans and Schlamensee display how matchmaking is, as a matter of fact, a very old business model.[2] Basically, matchmakers build a business model where an intermediary brings together two groups of buyers and/or consumers. The intermediary is neither the producer of a product or the provider of a service nor the consumer or the buyer. Many traditional business models such as agents or commissioners fulfill the same function. The intermediary therefore only facilitates the exchange of goods or services.

Matchmaking, which is an old business model, has seen a tremendous boost with a relatively new means of sales of goods and services, namely the Internet and the possibility of e-commerce. At a very basic level, the Internet connects people regardless of space. The Internet provides a platform on which matchmakers can remotely match the providers and the buyers. It also offers the possibility to do this on a cross-border or global scale; hence, space no longer constitutes an impediment for the transaction either. On the other hand, the spread of wireless Internet combined

---

[2]Evans and Schlamensee (2016).

with the technology of smart phones has led to the development of applications, commonly referred to as apps. Apps in turn have become the embodiment of the business model of platforms. Through the use of wireless Internet and app technology, platforms have been able to reach millions or even billions of users on a global scale through devices such as smart phones and tablets.

Platforms present a significant variety in terms of the services they offer and their strategies. However, apart from the use of wireless Internet, smart devices and apps, their business strategy entails certain common basic features. First of all, the business model presents a complex structure as it does not simply aim to link the producer to the buyer. Platforms create two-sided or multi-sided markets. Tirole and Rochet, who have coined the theory of multi-sided markets, define them as "the presence of two distinct sides whose ultimate benefit stems from interacting through a common platform."[3] The key to the multi-sided platform is the connectedness of the different sides. As a matter of fact, the service or product provided in such markets is only meaningful or valuable in so far as there are various different groups of users of the platform. Hence, demand from different sides of the platform is inter-dependent. The platform can be considered as the mere organizer of this interaction.

According to Evans, this inter-dependent demand is the raison d'être of a platform.[4] The number of users on each side of platform and their inter-dependent demand determines the appeal of the platform. The success of one side depends almost entirely on the success of the other. In economic theory, this effect is termed network effects. The network effect is the benefit brought by each user added to the network. The benefit gained by each additional user on the same side of the platform is referred to as the direct network effect. The indirect network effect is the benefit gained on one side of the platform when an additional user joins the other side. Providers of a product or service would have more incentive to join the platform if there are enough buyers on the other side. On the other hand, buyers will have a tendency to use the platform if they know that there is a variety of suppliers available. Hence, indirect network effects are more vital for the platform as they create and strengthen the inter-dependent demand. All platforms operate within a two-sided or multi-sided logic where their main strategy is to increase indirect network effects. The platform is construed on a complex structure that creates almost simultaneously a benefit for different participants.

Platforms may generate revenues through different models. The various models that have been developed have one crucial element in common: Every platform will have one side, where at least some users do not have to pay a fee or a price for using the platform or subscribing to it. The non-paying users are essential to the platform as they will be at the core of the platforms' indirect network effects. By providing usage at zero price, the platform will easily reach a very large community of users on one side which will create incentives for users/providers on the other side. On the other hand, the increase in numbers of paying users will allow the platform to subsidize the non-paying side. This system can support different types of revenue

[3] Tirole and Rochet (2003, pp. 990–1029).

[4] Evans (2003, pp. 325–382).

models. For instance, the platform may choose to charge subscription fees on one side of the platform or for certain types of users such as professionals. This model is, for example, adopted by Netflix or Amazon Prime where users have to pay a subscription fee in order to gain access. An alternative and very common model is generating revenue through advertisements. This is a business model adopted by some of the largest platforms such as Google or Facebook. Such platforms aim to increase a critical number of non-paying users in order to make the platform attractive for advertisers. Finally, the platform may charge a commission based on the price demanded by the supplier. This is the model adopted by Airbnb, where the platform collects a certain percentage of the fee charged by the host. All these models rely on indirect network effects and in order to achieve a critical mass they will allow access to the platform free of charge to certain users.

The most important advantage that platforms provide for providers or entrepreneurs is low transaction costs. Platforms offer reduced transaction costs in two ways: by matching users with different demands at lower costs and by providing easier and perhaps better access to information. Digital platforms are capable of operating without space limitations. Successful platforms easily reach a global community of users by use of advanced technology. Apps or Web sites that are accessible and are not constrained by space allow buyers to find providers by the simple use of mobile devices or the Web. Furthermore, sophisticated algorithms and artificial intelligence tools increase the precision of the search and of the match. The transaction cost of the search and the finding of a buyer for the provider is therefore significantly reduced.

The other characteristic of platforms which lowers transaction costs is perhaps the more novel use of feedbacks. According to Coase,[5] every deal entails a pre-deal, a deal-making and post-deal phase. The cost of each phase is increased due to information asymmetry. In traditional markets, especially the buyer has to undertake the cost of acquiring knowledge with regard to the product or the service that is being offered. This transaction is very costly, and the information asymmetry may never be completely overcome. Platforms have introduced user feedbacks. Each user is allowed and encouraged to review the providers, and the information is then made public. The feedback system diminishes the information asymmetry between the provider and the buyer. This in turn helps reduce the transaction cost of the pre-deal and the deal-making phases. It is a very important step towards dealing with lower transaction costs and also towards increasing consumer satisfaction through transparency.

The use of artificial intelligence and algorithms in digital applications not only ensures better matching at low transaction costs but also leads to precision in matching and in pricing of the products or services provided. Algorithms can rapidly learn the searches of users and adapt the results provided by the app or the Web. The algorithms' learning and adapting capacity will be enforced through the feedback system. This capacity immediately enables better precision in terms of search results. The precision can encompass the quality, quantity, type, etc. of product or service,

[5] Coase (2013, pp. 837–877).

but it can also prioritize prices that are affordable for the searcher. The app or the Web will therefore better suit the demand of users. This in turn proffers the supplier the possibility to adapt its production or provision. Hence, supply may meet demand with better precision by use of digital platforms.

Another important characteristic of platforms in digital markets is their capacity to grow to scale more easily than other businesses. According to Parker, Alstyne and Choudary, this capacity is mainly due to the fact that platforms do not need to "deploy capital and manage physical assets"[6] which are significant constraints for traditional business models. Digital platforms can be established with no physical asset and require very limited capital. A majority of the most successful digital platforms like Facebook or Google were launched by the development of a Web site which necessitated very little human capital and the acquisition of a domain name. The lack of capital and physical assets is not an impediment for growth. On the contrary, if the platform is successful in reaching a critical network effect, it can grow to scale at a greater speed than traditional business models. This in turn will feed the network effects of the platform creating incentive for more users to join.

The lack of physical assets or capital owned by the platform itself brings us to another important characteristic of these platforms which holds particularly in the context of sharing economy platforms. The emergence of this business model in digital markets also blurs the traditional distinctions between producers, consumers and owners. As a matter of fact, most platforms do not produce or provide the services they have created, nor do they deploy their own physical assets in the production or provision of what they offer. The platform may be the meeting point of an actual producer and a buyer, but it may also be the matcher of a person who is not necessarily a producer or a professional provider with a buyer. Sharing economy platforms in the true sense are the perfect example of platforms that allow for the commodification of private goods or property that is otherwise an idle asset. Private property owners or non-professional private persons that we normally qualify as consumers may become providers once they join the platform. This according to Lobel "radically changes the traditional equilibria of supply and demand."[7] The traditional dichotomy of associating the professional/producer with the supplier does not necessarily hold in the context of platforms. What is personal or private often becomes part of what is accessible or even commercial.[8] The blurring or disappearance of these dichotomies leads to important shifts in economic analysis as it changes production cycles and the behavior of economic actors. It also renders norms based on traditional business models and economic framework obsolete or inapplicable. The emergence and rise of platforms beg for the questioning of traditional economic and legal understanding of markets.

---

[6]Parker et al. (2016).

[7]Lobel (2016, pp. 87–166).

[8]Ibid., p. 90.

2.2 Impact of the Platform Economy

Many of the common characteristics of the platform economy have had disruptive and transformative effects on traditional markets. These effects present both economic and legal aspects. Disruption at the legal level is mostly due to the fact that existing legal norms have been grounded on definitions and parameters set by traditional economics. When those parameters are shaken, the legal norms are naturally also questioned. It is therefore necessary to examine the transformative and disruptive effects of the platform economy in order to understand why companies such as Uber have created such legal controversy.

The most crucial disruptive effect of the platform economy is the change and transformation of the supply and demand relations. Traditional economic analysis relies on the assumption that for each transaction, the supplier and the consumer can be clearly separated. This assumption also entails that the consumer is the non-professional party of the transaction, meaning that it is the party that does not have full information. Furthermore, the analysis supposes that the goods or services that are exchanged are commercial. Finally, the transaction entails a transfer of property, particularly in the case of goods, or generally a user right.

The platform economy, especially in the context of the sharing economy, changes these old assumptions. As stated earlier, the platform enables non-professional private parties to sell goods or services that were not designed or perceived as commodifiable. The goods that are offered on these platforms are often the private property of individuals who have bought them for their personal use. Similarly, individuals may offer certain services for which they are not fully professionally qualified. Such use of idle assets may of course generate additional income and contribute to economic efficiency. If such transactions are not done on a regular basis, they may be seen as singular one-time sales and purchases.

However, if the transactions follow a recurring pattern and become at least half regular, we may start to see a shift in our traditional understanding of the demand and supply relation. Economic analysis that looks into these relations in the context of the sharing economy may have to be more flexible and adaptive. Analysis of multi-sided markets may also lead us to adopt a more complex rather than linear understanding of the value created in the supply of goods and services.[9] It would perhaps be necessary to look at each particular transaction to see the source of supply and demand and their relation rather than generalizing market relations.

Whether such flexibility and adaptation would be possible for legal norms is another question. Legal norms are usually more rigid than economic factors. Moreover, legislation is a slow and complicated process. Rules aim to be general rather than particular. It is therefore difficult to envisage rules that allow enforcers to look at each transaction as a specific case and provide flexible solutions for each legal problem.

From an eco-legal point of view, this difficulty draws our attention to the diminishing of information asymmetry. Many legal rules that govern market relations and

---

[9]Parker et al. (2016, p. 9).

often constrain the behavior of professionals/sellers are designed to protect the party that has less information. The consumer is an actor who is always assumed to be at a disadvantaged position due to a lack of information. Indeed, all free market economy countries have extensive legal norms that seek to protect the consumer as the weak/weaker party. Platforms change this presumption in two ways. Firstly, they allow the consumer to be the provider. A person who does not produce becomes able to sell idle assets or skills. This sale may become somewhat regular without the person being considered a qualified professional provider of the service or the product. It therefore creates a new type or chain of supply. For such transactions, the person who is normally considered a consumer may become the supplier. Evidently, the consumer, who is now a seller, would have more information than the other party with regard to the good or the service provided and would have lost the weak party entitlement. On the other hand, buyer feedback provided in the platforms gives the consumer immediate and experience-based information on the good or the service that is offered. As already explained, the feedback system significantly reduces information asymmetry which is at the heart of consumer protection policies. When the most important reason for consumer protection, the weakness of the consumer, is no longer applicable, policies and rules developed for this purpose may become obsolete. These rules generally rely on the separation between the professional and the consumer. It may then be argued that the consumer who is not a professional but has more and better information on the good or service should not be entitled to protection. Transactions and exchanges within platforms may therefore challenge the system of such protections by leading us to question the qualification of a person as a consumer.

There may also be significant changes in ownership in the context of platforms. In our traditional understanding of market transactions, a producer who produces and therefore has ownership of a good sells it to a buyer by transferring ownership rights. Platforms, however, are not the supplier or the owner of the good. They act as intermediaries between the supplier and the buyer. Transfer of ownership rights may happen through the platform but usually the platform does not acquire the good at any point during the transaction. On the other hand, owners of the goods are users of the platform and so they gain another identity through it. Most legal frameworks would provide rules applicable to agents or commissioners that act as intermediaries. However, there is an ongoing debate as to whether digital platforms should be considered intermediaries in terms of the provision of goods and services. If they are mere intermediaries, determining their obligations is a rather easy task. However, many platforms also have control over essential elements of the sales transaction such as price or terms of delivery. If platforms set some of the essential elements of the contract, they can no longer be considered an agent in the pure sense. Although platforms are not owners of the goods offered, they allow access to the goods.[10] Hence, the value created by the platform is not the transfer of the ownership but the access to the good or the service. Then, the critical question also shifts: instead of determining who the owner is, law makers will have to look at the transaction and

[10]Lobel (2016, p. 110).

the value of providing access. The problem would become more complicated when factoring in the fact this value, which may be close to the concept of usufruct, is not created by the owner but by the platform. Hence, platforms may be creating a new form of transaction and value which may not be defined precisely in a legal norm or framework.

3 The Sharing Economy: Innovation, Disruption and Transformation

The sharing economy is a business model that is growing rapidly throughout the globe. It has also become a significant economic development across the globe. Its growth is estimated to continue in the future and reach 335 billion US dollars within the next five years.[11] It is a business model that presents economic and societal benefits as it provides new services, creates creative and flexible employment and therefore generates new income. However, the sharing economy also entails new legal challenges as it renders traditional legal rules insufficient and/or inadequate.

3.1 Understanding the Sharing Economy

The sharing economy is a term used to characterize digital platforms that allow their users to exchange goods or services. At the heart of the sharing economy lies the motivation to put to use idle assets. Sharing economy companies set up platforms where private persons are enabled to share, exchange their idle assets or skills. Sharing economy platforms are very diverse; however, they all aim to build a community where private persons may offer their personal skills or products in return of another good or service or a remuneration. The sharing economy therefore creates new markets and new services. Furthermore, it encourages private persons to use their property, their belongings or their skills to their full capacity. The purpose is to generate further economic efficiency and at times to provide additional income. It may also create other positive externalities such as energy and resource efficiency, encouraging socialization and building trust. However, it should be noted that in its current form, sharing is not mere exchange of goods or services. Its commercial and revenue generating aspects have become dominant.

Like other digital platforms, sharing economy companies rely on network effects. The platform has to reach a critical mass of providers on side for there to be incentives for other users to join and vice versa. Hence, sharing economy companies are often associated with crowdsourcing. Crowdsourcing entails gathering information or revenue for a specific service or task from large numbers of people. It is widely used for project financing or for start-ups. Sharing economy platforms aim to create

---

[11]Rinne (2019).

"crowd-based networks"[12] that comprise diverse users. Certain platforms, like Uber, may focus on one type of service, while others, like TaskRabbit, may offer a variety of different services under the same terms. This business model is very different from the traditional firm structure which often has a centralized and possibly hierarchical structure.[13] As Sundararajan argues, sharing economy companies adopt a decentralized structure where the platform operates with crowds that are not constrained by space or time. The platform does not exercise a strict hierarchical control over the activities of the users. The control mechanism may be embedded in the feedback system which would suggest self-regulation rather than a top-down approach.[14] Hence, sharing economy platforms emerge as community-based decentralized structures.

An important effect of the sharing economy is lowering barriers to market entry.[15] This may be valid for many platforms as they require very little initial capital and usually no physical asset. However, as far as the sharing economy is concerned, there are low barriers to entry not just for the platform but also for the users who supply. It is normally rather difficult to find buyers for a good or service if you are not a professional provider in that sector. This difficulty may have its roots in various reasons such as licenses, inability to find buyers, space and time constraints, etc. which all constitute transactional or financial costs. Sharing economy platforms allow private persons to offer their products and services to an in-built community at low cost and little or no additional charge. It can therefore be argued that these platforms contribute to product diversification and consumer choice in the market. Expansion of choice does not only apply to consumers; it is also equally true for the suppliers. Platforms provide flexibility and choice as to when, what and how much the users are going to supply.[16] Traditional labor markets, for instance, are evidently more rigid and entail stricter rules. Sharing economy platforms allow for more flexible work and commerce, which is why they are often described as on-demand economy platforms.

3.2 *The Disruptive Effects of Sharing Economy Platforms*

The most important reason why traditional markets are more rigid and costly is regulation. Rules are designed to protect a weak party such as the consumer or the worker or to protect public interest. All these rules come at a financial or transactional cost for the provider. However, in order for the rules to apply, the activity that is being provided has to fit into the definition that is provided in the norm. The definition of the consumer, the worker, the professional is set by a norm. Though the norm may change and evolve over time, the essence of the definition will remain the same. Most sharing

[12] Sundararajan (2016).

[13] Ibid., p. 27.

[14] Ibid.

[15] Lobel (2016, p. 110).

[16] Prassl (2018).

economy companies notoriously deny that the products or services they provide fit into the existing normative definitions. Airbnb, for example, claims that it does not provide an accommodation service; the platform merely matches private persons who are looking for an accommodation with those who can offer one. Refusing to accept the applicability of the regulatory structure leads to the lowering of costs. As Lobel argues "even when we recognize the economic logic of reducing transaction costs, we still need to answer whether a platform company is either competing within an existing industry or carving out a new market."[17] Such platforms are thus said to develop, operate and thrive in regulatory loopholes. An important debate that emerges from this claim is whether regulatory loopholes stimulate innovation or whether platforms use and abuse regulatory loopholes in order to lower their costs and increase their profits. Proponents of the former would be inclined to argue that platforms should not be regulated, they should be allowed to operate at low transaction costs for the sake of innovation, efficiency and employment they create. Proponents of the latter would maintain that not applying existent rules to these platforms leads to economic and legal uncertainty, creating risks and inequality.

Indeed, the disruptive effect of sharing economy platforms in the regulatory context lies in the defiance of legal definitions. These platforms claim that they are intermediaries and should therefore not be legally qualified as a producer, an employer or a provider. The intermediary is not bound by many rules that the producer, employer and provider have to abide with. These norms are deemed necessary for the protection of private and public interests; but they undeniably raise costs. When Airbnb refuses to associate itself with the hotel business, it does not have to follow the safety measures that are provided by local administrations. When Uber does not qualify itself as an employer, it does not have to cover the security and insurance costs of the drivers. Hence, platforms generally and sharing economy platforms specifically reduce costs also by evading regulations. This problem is at the heart of the legal controversies created by companies such as Uber and Airbnb.

Fleischer defines this behavior as regulatory arbitrage which is "the manipulation of the structure of a deal to take advantage of a gap between the economic substance of a transaction and its regulatory."[18] According to Fleischer, companies face a trade-off between transaction costs in the Coasean sense and regulatory costs.[19] When establishing their business, parties can plan their corporate model or business model to minimize regulatory costs. This strategy, Fleischer argues, does not create any new value in the market.[20] If platforms develop business strategies that rely on such regulatory arbitrage, then we would have to accept that although they lower transaction costs, they evade regulatory costs. They undermine or deny antitrust rules, tax laws, consumer protection regulations and employment laws. This evasion further reduces transaction costs and lowers barriers to entry, but this economic efficiency is created at the cost of challenging private and public interests.

[17]Lobel (2016, p. 112).

[18]Fleischer (2010, pp. 227–290).

[19]See Footnote 18.

[20]Ibid., p. 234.

In that case, platforms may be increasing what Prassl refers to as social costs.[21] Prassl explains how platforms ignore the time lost or the cost incured by the users. As they do not accept any liability for the users by refusing to qualify them as workers or to own the service that is provided. They do not cover the loss that is endured by the users when they are staying connected and looking for a match for their good or service. For example, in the case of Uber, the drivers that are connected to the app have to drive around the city and look for a matching customer. During this time however, they are consuming time and petrol. This loss has to be covered entirely by the driver. It furthermore increases pollution in the city.

The business model adopted by the platforms based on creating network effects may also have adverse effects on the market and on the users. Digital platforms generate and feed on data more than anything else. Every user of any digital platform, whether they consume the good or service or provide them, constantly creates data, the new most valuable commodity in the world. This process of collecting and using data, has led, over the last decade, to a shift in our understanding of market structure and market power. Digital platforms can aggregate large quantities of data very rapidly, and they do so every second. This creation of Big Data has changed dramatically the market structure in every industry. Data-based platforms such as Google, Facebook and Amazon are creeping up in the lists of companies with highest revenues. Data in itself is considered a commodity, and maintaining and using Big Data is increasingly considered as a dominant position in the sense of competition law. If holding data constitutes market power, use of data may therefore constitute an abuse of dominant position (monopolization). It is often argued that digital platforms, as a result of low transaction costs, are able to charge lower prices leading to consumer efficiency. However, once they reach a monopoly power based on data, they may also charge monopoly prices. As a matter of fact, dynamic pricing through sophisticated algorithms allows both for price discrimination and for increasing prices to almost monopoly levels when demand is high.

Data has also become an important factor in understanding consumer behavior and thus an important concern for legislators. Data privacy terms, especially with the entry into force of the General Data Protection Regulation in the European Union (EU), is perceived as an essential element of the good or service that is provided by digital platforms. Data privacy is a non-price element but can be considered as part of the quality of the product. The use of data by the firm and the terms of privacy that are being offered can constitute the quality of the product. If the platform chooses to offer inadequate or little data protection or if it chooses to evade such regulations through regulatory arbitrage, the quality of the product or the service will be affected. This problem could of course occur in other fields of law and types of regulation. If the platform evades rules that are designed to protect the buyer or the consumer, the terms of sale and the product or service itself may be deemed of lower quality. However, problems relating to data protection are particularly pertinent as digital platforms could easily be undermining their users' privacy through invasive data collection.

---

[21] Prassl (2018, pp. 21–22).

In conclusion, the gray areas in which sharing economy platforms operate present a true dilemma in economic, societal and legal terms. On the one hand, many argue that the sharing economy thrives in these regulatory loopholes and it owes its flexibility to the lack of applicable norms that would increase the costs or perhaps even bar the activities of the platform altogether. On the other hand, the absence of regulation creates many legal challenges that endanger the rights of product and service providers and consumers alike, and perhaps even public interest. Uber as one of the first and largest sharing economy companies embodies all of these controversies.

4 Uber: The Emblematic Sharing Economy Company

Uber and its business model have become such a controversy that it can be seen as a historical success story or a notoriously evil machinery. Its impact is so significant that many commentators and authors are using the term "uberization" of the economy to refer to changes and trends in markets and business models. This section is dedicated to analyzing this company, its business model and its place in the world of digital sharing economy platforms. It will also look at Uber as part of the crucial legal challenge of the new platform economy in order to understand the controversy it has created.

Uber operates as a digital platform. The service that users provide or buy on Uber is rides or ride sharing, i.e., transportation. The initial service provided by Uber claims to provide an intermediation service between drivers who are willing to drive a person from one location to another in a city and customers who need transportation at a given time. The drivers are not professional drivers who possess the necessary administrative and/or commercial licenses. The drivers are private persons who can drive and have spare time during which they can transport other private persons. The drivers do not even have to own the car they are driving; they simply have to have legitimate access to it. Persons who are willing to offer their services as drivers have to register with the Uber application. Depending on the country or region, the platform may request and verify certain information with regard to the qualifications of the driver (methods by which the information is verified may also differ in each country or region). Once they are registered, the drivers connect to the app when they are available and wait for a match. Customers on the other hand, have to download the app, create an account and determine the means of payment. Once they have an account, they log on to the app when they need a ride and the application will show them the available nearby riders. If there is match, the app will give an estimate for the price of the ride. If the customer accepts, he/she is provided with information (name, picture, rating) about the driver. The customer can view the location of the car on a map before its arrival and during the ride which may help him/her feel safer.

Since its establishment, Uber has introduced new services such as UberXL, UberEats, etc. However, the basic elements remain unchanged. Uber allows for private persons to provide transportation services to other private persons through its application. From the point of view of platform markets, a few characteristics of

Uber's business model are worth examining. First of all, Uber operates as a two-sided platform. One side is constituted by drivers who provide the transportation service, and the other is constituted by customers who need a ride. Each additional user on the customer side creates incentive for drivers who wish to join as they will see the service as lucrative. On the other hand, new customer will be inclined to join if they are convinced that the app is able to provide a critical number of drivers at all times. The indirect network effect will thus be ensured for both sides.

Secondly, it is most certainly free to join Uber for the customers, and as far as publicly available information is concerned, it is also free for the drivers. The free usership creates a significant advantage for the indirect network effects and for the purposes of crowdsourcing. As Uber does not own the cars or employ the drivers, it can easily and rapidly grow to scale. However, free usage also means that the platform does not generate revenues from subscriptions. Uber generates income by collecting a commission from each driver for each ride. Indeed, Uber's business model's most creative element is the notorious price surge system. For every demand for a ride, Uber's algorithm determines a price. The algorithm takes into account many elements such as the total distance of the journey or the traffic situation, but most importantly it sets the price based on the demand for a driver at one given location and time. If there are few drivers available and there is high demand, the price will increase. Hence, Uber's use of dynamic pricing optimizes the remuneration of the driver as well as generating more income for the platform.

Uber does not own any physical assets. For instance, the cars that are used for the services are not Uber's property. Furthermore, the drivers are not employees of the company. The platform qualifies them as self-employed. This qualification has significant consequences as it allows Uber to evade any norm that is applicable to an employment contract. It also releases Uber from any duty such as providing social security, insurance, sick leave, etc. Hill states that such businesses that only work with ""non regular" employees reduce labor costs by as much as 30%."[22] Therefore, the qualifications that are adopted by the platform or the lack of normative pressures allow Uber to significantly reduce its regulatory costs.

Another significant normative framework that Uber refuses to accept is that of taxi services. Taxi services are one of the most well-defined and regulated services, especially in large cities. The legal framework is usually decentralized; local authorities have considerable discretion in terms of licenses and even pricing rules. Taxi service providers are not only subject to extensive rules, but they also have to face high barriers to entry in the form of costly licenses. Uber can avoid the costs of these legal barriers to entry by defining itself as an intermediary platform. If the services provided by Uber are defined as intermediation rather than transport in the sense of taxi services, very few norms or perhaps even no regulatory framework will encompass its activities. Uber can then enter a market with very low barriers to entry in every additional country or city and can easily grow on a larger scale.

It is therefore possible to argue that Uber's business model and its activities display a good example of regulatory arbitrage. The platform appears to defy many normative

[22] Hill (2016).

definitions and the regulatory framework applicable to similar or close services. The question that must be addressed and answered then is whether it would be more beneficial for the markets, individuals and the public concerned to regulate Uber and its activities through existing norms or by establishing new ones.

5 Regulating Uber

Platforms create and develop new business models. These models may be considered as process innovation. If sharing economy platforms such as Uber are truly innovative, they may be creating new markets which in turn may be leading to disruption. We can then contemplate on whether the lack of regulation provides an environment that is favorable for innovation. Another approach could also lead us to adopting innovative regulation that would adapt to new markets. Instead of forcing Uber to fit into existing normative frameworks, we would then try to establish new and perhaps more flexible norms that would cover Uber's activities. However, if we do not accept that there is genuine innovation and therefore creation of a new value, we have to question whether Uber and its activities should be subject to existing regulations. This section firstly discusses legislative reactions and approaches to Uber from a conceptual point of view. It then looks at the stance of the EU in terms of sharing economy platforms and Uber through the EU Commission's (Commission) approach and the case-law of the Court of Justice of the European Union (CJEU).

5.1 Uber: Novelty and Flexibility

Uber may only be considered an innovator in so far as it creates a new business model. Establishing a digital platform that connects two different types of users and growing through network effects was not truly innovative in 2009 when Uber was established. Hence, it is not the platform model that hints at the presence of a newly created value. It can only be argued that allowing a transportation service provided by private persons on an irregular basis is innovation. If we accept this argument, we have to question whether this is a disruptive innovative model in order to then contemplate on if and how it should be regulated.

Markides defines business model innovation as redefining "what an existing product is and how it is provided to customers."[23] He argues that such innovators may use different characteristics or offer different dimensions of a product or service that is not used or emphasized by the incumbents.[24] If the firm sets out to enter a market with such a strategy, it needs to support it with activities that are specifically

[23] Markides (2006, pp. 19–25).

[24] Ibid., p. 20.

designed for the new model.[25] According to Markides, these business models grow very rapidly but usually do not overtake the market; they tend to co-exist in the market with traditional business model companies.[26] Thus, there is little incentive for the incumbents to transform their business and adopt the same or a new model. Markides finds that one significant exception to this conclusion is the case where the new business model enters "a new market where entrenched competitors have first mover advantages" and thus "the new entrant must attack by breaking the rules."[27]

Uber's business model fits into many aspects of the broad structure suggested by Markides. Uber redefines not only urban transportation services generally but also taxi services specifically. It allows private persons who do not have the necessary licenses or other requirements to almost become taxi drivers on an irregular basis. Thus, it could be argued that it focuses on different and new dimensions of a service. It uses a digital platform, a rating system and the price surge which altogether support its business model's activities. Uber has grown very rapidly, but it has not been able to replace taxi services entirely. The only question that remains is whether it has succeeded in being a disrupter.

Looking at the reaction of incumbent taxi service providers to Uber leads us to believe that it is indeed a disrupter. It has managed to attract consumers in so far as it often offers a service that is cheaper[28] than regular taxis and customers who find taxis expensive may find Uber more affordable. It has also proven to have the capacity to grow more rapidly than taxi services using the network effects of the platform. As a matter of fact, unlike urban taxi services, it is not constrained by space and has a global outreach. The consumers are exposed to a new experience and they are given the opportunity to rate it. It can therefore be argued that consumers have more control and power over the service they are getting.

Uber also offers a new and more flexible type of work. Perhaps, this part-time or irregular work opportunity requires more attention than other advantages created by the platform. Uber takes pride in creating an opportunity for private persons to use their idle skills (driving) and property (cars). Indeed, through this model, Uber has created a new employment format which is at the root of the term "Uberization" of the economy. This new format is on-demand, irregular work which was previously offered as part of the informal economy. Uber has perhaps developed a way of formalizing and easing the informal economy through the use of digital platforms. However, this formalization is also the re-definition of a service and a transformation or radical change in the market. Whether it has positive innovatory effects or not, this re-definition is disruptive for the incumbents in the market.

---

[25]Ibid., p. 21.

[26]Ibid.

[27]Ibid., p. 22.

[28]This advantage may not always hold true because the price of an Uber ride varies according to demand and may at times be more expensive than taxi rides.

5.2 The Legal Problem with Uber's Disruption

The departure from the traditional taxi service has a significant disruptive effect on the legal framework. Labor law norms almost universally define the employer–employee relationship based on the level and type of control exercised by one over the other. Although Uber has extensive control over the relationship between the driver and customer, it claims that the driver is not under its control and that there is no subordination. This situates Uber drivers outside the labor law contract, but it also signifies that they are not self-employed in the true sense as they are not free to determine their remuneration. From a legal point of view, this implies that Uber is introducing a new type of work relationship in which drivers are neither employees nor self-employed.

This means that drivers are not employees of Uber and are not entitled to legal rights and benefits provided for workers such as minimum wage, sick leave, etc. Although the work they accomplish while connected to Uber is formalized and digitized, their status remains precarious. For those who work part-time or those who truly work for extra income, this may not be a serious problem. However, for drivers whose only source of income is Uber, the prospects are not much better than informal work. These drivers need to stay connected to the app while constantly driving and only get paid for the rides that are matched. They do not benefit from the protection provided by labor law. They also drive at their own risk as Uber does not accept liability as an employer for damages that may occur during the ride.

Another significant legal problem that arises not only in the context of Uber's activities but with all digital platforms is the use of data. Digital platforms constantly collect data and this data is, to a certain extent, used and stored by the platforms. Uber, for instance, collects several categories of data. First of all, when the customer or the driver connects to the app as users of the platform, the app collects information. Presumably, more detailed data is required for the driver. Then, as soon as the driver is connected to Uber, even when the driver does not have a passenger aboard, Uber collects data. Uber also collects data on the habits or the travels of the passenger and on the payments made to every driver. However, most importantly Uber collects data on the ratings and the feedback of the drivers and sometimes of the passengers. A great majority of all this information in the form of digital data is relevant for regulators. However, Uber can easily claim that it cannot disclose the data which is personal. If the data is classified as commercial data, then it may not be protected under personal data protection rules. On the other hand, Uber, who claims to be a mere intermediary platform, may refuse to provide data that should clearly be classified as commercial to the competent authorities.

This problem creates another crucial legal challenge by Uber and similar companies: tax evasion. By defining itself as a provider of intermediation service, Uber refuses to pay taxes that are applicable to potentially competing industries. For instance, taxis, depending on the city where they operate, may have to pay certain local taxes. There is also the issue of how the revenues of the drivers should be taxed. In order to ensure full tax cohesion, the state may need Uber's collaboration. There is of course also the problem of the corporate tax. The most important advantage of the digital world is that, without any physical assets, you may conduct your activities anywhere in the globe. Uber provides its services through one single app. This technical advantage created by digitalization allows platforms to be incorporated in one or few countries while generating income in tens or hundreds of countries. As a company incorporated in Netherlands, Uber has been accused of evading EU tax rules and moving its accounts from Dutch banks to offshore subsidiaries.[29] The most important reason why Uber could avoid transfer its income so easily is the global nature of its operations. It can centralize incorporation and its financial assets in one country where there are favorable rules and evade taxes in countries with stricter rules.

5.3 The Promises and the Perils of Self-regulation

The platform economy has introduced many novelties, and the most significant one is the rating system. Digital technology has allowed platforms to provide in-built feedback systems whereby users rate their experience almost immediately after use. The ratings are made public. They provide a mechanism of control in several different relationships within the platform which can be illustrated through the example of Uber. When they use the app, the customers have to rate their experience as a passenger. They mostly give feedback on the driver, and that is how the passenger controls the driver. In order get high ratings, the driver has to make sure that the passenger is satisfied. On the other hand, the same ratings are going to allow Uber to control the drivers. Those that do not get satisfactory reviews may be warned or even excluded from the platform. Finally, Uber may also allow drivers to give feedback on passengers, in which case customers that misbehave will be known and drivers may eventually have the opportunity to deny their request for a ride.

It has been argued that this system of rating or feedback bears a form potential self-regulation. Parker, Van Alstyne and Choudary draw attention to the large number of users of platforms and claim that "today's biggest platforms businesses resemble nation-states."[30] According to the authors, platforms are creating value for consumers, but the challenge they face in order to achieve good governance is to ensure a fair distribution of the wealth they create. Sundararajan writes that "the new peer-to-peer marketplaces have sophisticated controls naturally built in,"[31] and this system is a contender for good governance. The solution is then "to delegate more regulatory responsibility to the marketplaces and platforms."[32] Although he

[29]Browning and Newcomer (2019).

[30]Parker et al. (2016, p. 159).

[31]Sundajaran (2014). https://economix.blogs.nytimes.com/2014/03/03/trusting-the-sharing-economy-to-regulate-itself/?smid=tw-share. Accessed May 2020.

[32]Ibid. (2014).

does not argue that we should entirely abandon government control and regulation, he claims that the platforms' control mechanisms should be trusted enough to limit state interference.

When it comes to innovative markets or models, in addition to discussions on whether there should be a regulatory framework, there are also questions concerning how regulation should be adopted. The underlying premise here is that these markets present dynamics that may require a different method or approach in regulatory processes. Ayres and Braithwaite have argued that regulatory authorities can use mechanisms of consultation and develop more inclusive processes of rulemaking.[33] This process, referred to as responsive regulation, will allow congruence of relevant parties not only because of enforcement mechanisms but also because they have been part of the process and they agree with the rules on an ethical level.[34] Such processes would lead to internalization of applicable rules and ensure better compliance. Gunningham and Graboski developed the concept of smart regulation, exploring the idea that not only public authorities but also stakeholders could willingly establish rules which would lead up to self-regulation.[35] This process would thus rely on actors of the market as rule makers and enforcers to a certain extent.

Evidently, platforms can be conceived not only as intermediaries or suppliers but also, unlike traditional market actors, as controllers in the market. Furthermore, differently from state control, platforms are more inclusive in so far as they give more power to stakeholders such as customers or providers. Users can immediately see the response and effect of their feedback. They display a more sophisticated and an improved use of technology than state regulators. Their algorithms are capable of storing large amounts of data and can retrieve the information when necessary. Their control is decentralized; they operate at a global scale but their control mechanism functions and generates results at local scale. This almost ironic proximity to stakeholders can help them offer better suited solutions for problems encountered by passengers or drivers. Thus platforms can be seen as serious contenders for self-regulation.

On the other hand, it is dubitable whether platforms can replace the state in terms of control and regulation. It should first of all be noted that platforms are interest and profit seeking entities. Even if they are well intentioned, they will always be inclined to put the interest of the company before the users' protection. Platforms generally deny certain normative frameworks and resist their applicability to the services they provide. Under such circumstances, it is also difficult to argue that platforms can be trusted to enforce the necessary control mechanisms to protect the passengers, the drivers and the public interest. Lobel draws a distinction between hard cases, where regulation aims to protect public welfare, and easy cases, where regulation should be considered a barrier to entry thereby constrain competition.[36] For the former, we

[33]Ayres and Braithwate (1991, pp. 158–159).

[34]See Footnote 33.

[35]Gunningham and Graborski (1998).

[36]Lobel (2016, p. 93).

should be wearier of platforms as they may not be well placed to assess or protect public welfare.

There is also evidence that sharing economy platforms may fail to enforce their own control mechanisms. Airbnb usually does not require proof of identification from the house owner. It also does not have any means to verify that the accommodation that is being offered matches the reality. There is the highly mediatized case where an Uber driver hit a six-year-old girl and her mother, killing the girl and severely injuring the mother.[37] Uber claimed that the driver had, at the time of the accident, disconnected from the app and therefore refused to accept any liability. However, allegedly the driver had a reckless driving record which Uber failed to uncover. Such extreme examples set aside, sharing economy companies raise many safety, liability, consumer protection, data privacy concerns that may not be addressed or remedied by the ranking system. Rules and regulations that are often rendered obsolete by the platforms are designed to protect weak parties and public welfare. Such purposes may not always be heard through rankings or the aggregate of the provided feedback may not amount to public welfare. It may therefore be argued that we must turn to the state who has the authority to investigate, inspect and require information to protect the public interest.

6 Dealing with Uber: The Example of the EU

Despite the advantages and novelties provided by the feedback systems, a few years of experience has shown that a certain level of public intervention on sharing economy platforms is necessary. Furthermore, there is an ongoing tension between rule enforcers and sharing economy companies, especially Uber. The following chapters of this book will provide detailed analysis of such tensions in several countries. This section will display the policy attempts and case law of the EU as an example of regional regulatory response to these challenges.

The EU comprises 27 member states,[38] each with their own legal traditions. These member states are all part of the internal market where goods, services, workers and capital are allowed to move freely. The EU has also a strong strategy for establishing a Single Digital Market. Hence, all the activities of Uber fall under the scope of issues regulated by the EU. Therefore, the EU's reaction to Uber and similar services provides an interesting example. The approach of the EU is twofold: firstly, there is the work of Commission who is the policy initiator and secondly, there is the case law of CJEU which has rendered a crucial judgment on how Uber's services should be considered at the EU level.

[37] CBS SF (2015).

[38] As of January 31st, 2020, after Brexit.

6.1 Policy Building Attempts at the EU Level

Before looking at the specific legal problems created by the collaborative economy, the significance of rules and regulations applicable to provision of services under EU law should be explained. The internal market of the European Union is founded on four freedoms: free movement of goods, free movement of workers, free movement of capital and free movement of services. The latter, which is also the most relevant freedom with respect to the collaborative economy, comprises the free movement of service providers, free movement of the recipients of services and the freedom of establishment (Articles 49, 56 and 57 of the Treaty on the Functioning of the European Union (TFEU)). Free movement in the context of the internal market refers to a general prohibition of legal impediments to market access and of discrimination against nationals of other member states. In the context of services, the member states therefore have a duty not to adopt any measures that would render legally or practically impossible the provision of service by a provider established in another member states. They should equally not restrict service recipients from moving from one member state to another in order to receive a service. These restrictions are usually in the form of legal requirements such as authorizations, licenses, etc. imposed by the national or local authorities. The requirements may be directly or indirectly discriminatory and limit the access of the service provider to a national or local market. These restrictions are considered to be a severe violation of Internal market Law and essentially contrary to the overarching principles of market integration. As it is one of the four fundamental elements of the internal market, provision of services is largely and heavily regulated at the EU level. The definition and regulation of collaborative economy services are therefore of significant importance for this jurisdiction. Given that almost all sharing economy platforms provide a type of service, the legal qualification of their output may have consequences under EU law.

In order to face the legal challenges created by the sharing economy platforms, the EU Commission launched in 2015 the "European agenda for the collaborative economy," comprising a public consultation procedure and a series of projects and events with the purpose of better understanding and discussing the benefits and the challenges of the collaborative economy. As a result of this process, the Commission published a communication in June 2016.[39] Although it does not have a binding effect, the communication is an important source for legal policy as it provides guidance for EU member states and identifies existing and potential legal controversies that require attention.

Later on, in 2017 the Commission launched a series of workshops in order to collaborate with authorities of EU member states. At this stage, the Commission aimed to provide guidance for the member states and enhance cooperation. The most important goal was to avoid a fragmented set of rules across member states and to prevent a fragmentation of the internal market. The Commission particularly focused on tourism accommodation sector, more specifically on Airbnb. In 2018, the Commission held a conference entitled "Collaborative economy: opportunities,

[39] European Commission (2016).

challenges, policies." This conference brought together policy-makers, academics and stakeholders in order to discuss policy solutions for the legal challenges that member state authorities had to face with sharing economy platforms.

The Commission defines the sharing economy in the 2016 Communication as "business models where activities are facilitated by collaborative platforms that create an open marketplace for the temporary usage of goods or services often provided by private individuals." The Communication also indicates that there are three categories of actors in the collaborative economy: the actual service providers who may be private individuals or persons acting in their professional capacity, the users of these services and the platforms which connect these actors online. According to the Commission, the collaborative economy has many benefits and should be seen as an economic opportunity by EU authorities. It also has positive societal impacts as it incentivizes asset sharing and social interaction.

However, like other authorities around the world, the Commission is also weary of collaborative platforms. In the European agenda for the collaborative economy, the Commission has identified five main legal areas that need to be addressed when dealing with collaborative platforms: market access requirements, liability regimes, consumer protection, workers' rights and taxation. Thus, the Commission also sees that, in the context of these critical issues, the services provided under these new models do not fit within the existing rules. According to the Commission, some collaborative platforms provide services that are innovative. For instance, in many EU member states, there are collaborative platforms that allow individuals to spontaneously share their home cooked meal with other users of the platform in their household. In cases where the platform dispenses a new or an atypical service, existing rules become inapplicable as the service in question does not fit within a definition envisaged in a legal norm. Other services simply facilitate the provision of a traditional service by reducing costs with the platform acting as intermediary between users. An example of such a traditional service would be transportation by car of passengers within a city. However, these collaborative platforms may also fall in a gray area in terms of regulation. Although the service itself fits within a traditional definition, it is usually provided by a person who is not a professional, a trader or a worker. The problem therefore arises not from the service, but from the users of the platform and the business model that is established.

As the Commission's definition indicates, sharing economy companies are primarily a platform and therefore an actor of the digital economy. This finding evidently affirms that the sharing economy platforms must abide by a number of rules and regulations that are applicable to operators of the digital economy. For instance, in the EU, e-commerce and information society services is regulated under the Directive 2000/31/EC[40] (Directive on electronic commerce) that provides rules for established service providers in the internal market. Certain rules envisaged by the

[40]Directive 2000/31/EC of the European Parliament and of the Council of 8 June 2000 on certain legal aspects of information society services, in particular electronic commerce, in the Internal Market ('Directive on electronic commerce'). http://eur-lex.europa.eu/legal-content/EN/ALL/?uri=CELEX:32000L0031. Accessed May 2020.

Directive on electronic commerce are definitely applicable to collaborative platforms. However, the Directive on electronic commerce is mainly designed for professional service providers and traders of goods. As the definition adopted by the Commission clearly indicates, the providers of the collaborative economy are not necessarily professionals or traders. On the contrary, the main characteristic of the collaborative economy is that it allows for private individuals to provide services by connecting to a platform. Moreover, the services are usually provided temporarily and/or their provision is not the main occupation of the service provider. Hence, most elements of the services provided by collaborative platforms are outside the scope of the Directive on electronic commerce.

Another EU policy area which may be relevant for sharing economy companies is online platforms and especially efforts for improving services provided by platforms at EU level. Over the past few years, the EU Commission has undertaken significant efforts to further market integration in digital services and enhance consumer protection. The "Regulation on promoting fairness and transparency for business users of online intermediation services,"[41] which is part of the Commission's initiative to regulate platform services at EU level, entered into force on April 26, 2019. It expired one year after its entry into force. The Regulation aimed to establish a common legal framework that ensures a more transparent and fair provision of services while trying to increase the effectiveness of digital intermediary services. It focused on improving the terms and conditions of services by platforms by precluding possible arbitrary behavior of the providers.[42] It also attempted to improve transparency by including a set of rules that would apply to the ranking system of platforms.[43] It required platforms to make certain information with regard to the ranking of their search results public.[44] Furthermore, it increased efficiency in complaint mechanisms and redress for users.[45]

However, the regulation did not capture the activities of Uber and similar sharing economy platforms. The scope of the Regulation covered online intermediation services to business users whom were defined as professionals. The Regulation therefore targeted B2B businesses and excluded B2C and C2C intermediation. Thus, Uber's intermediation model which entails private persons providing a service to consumers was not regulated by the Regulation. The scope of this legislation seems to indicate that the Commission is not yet inclined to regulate Uber and similar companies at the EU level. Furthermore, unlike other sharing economy companies like Airbnb, Uber's exclusion from EU norms is also in line with the approach of the CJEU.

---

[41] Regulation of the European Parliament and of the Council on promoting fairness and transparency for business users of online intermediation services. https://eur-lex.europa.eu/legal-content/EN/TXT/PDF/?uri=CELEX:32019R1150&from=EN. Accessed May 2020.

[42] Regulation 2019/1150 Article 1.

[43] Regulation 2019/1150 Article 5.

[44] Regulation 2019/1150 Article 9.

[45] Regulation 2019/1150 Articles 11, 12, 13.

6.2 Judicial Response: The CJEU's Uber Ruling

One important issue concerning Uber's legal activities is market access. Market access requirements comprise all legal authorizations including business authorizations, licensing requirements or quality standard requirements. The present-day regulatory picture of market access requirements for sharing economy platforms in the EU Member States is mixed. One pattern, however, can be clearly identified: the lack of appropriate and special rules leads to fragmented implementation and disparate results. Certain platforms such as UberPop are banned outright in certain member states. Other platforms such as BlaBlaCar are left entirely unregulated. There are also initiatives to develop new rules for certain collaborative platforms. The most common example of this trend seems to be Airbnb for which many member states have established a regulatory framework on the basis of thresholds (usually the owner is allowed to rent his/her property for a maximum number of days per year).

This fragmented and diverse situation is due to the fact that EU regulators have not yet adopted a harmonized approach to sharing economies. The Communication has no legally binding effect and it is merely a document that may guide member states when adopting new rules or implementing existing ones. Although the Commission clearly states that market access requirements may only be justified under public interest objectives, the current legal structure gives member states complete discretion for regulating sharing economy platforms.

This fragmentation is also now somewhat justified by the CJEU in its ruling on Uber.[46] In 2014, a taxi drivers association from Barcelona Spain brought an action before a Commercial Court claiming that Uber's activities were amounting to misleading practices and unfair competition. The taxi association claimed that Uber's activities should be qualified as taxi services and that they should therefore be subject to the same licensing, etc. requirements as them. The Spanish Court than asked the CJEU to determine whether the activities of Uber fell under the scope of information society services as defined by article 56 TFEU and Article 1 of Directive 98/34,[47] Articles 2, 3 and 4 of Directive 2000/31[48] or whether it should fall into the exception defined in the Recital and the Articles 2 and 9 of Directive 2006/123[49] as transport services such as urban transportation and taxi services. In 2017 the Court

[46]Case C-434/15 Asociación Profesional Elite Taxi v Uber Systems Spain SL.

[47]Directive 98/34/EC of the European Parliament and of the Council laying down a procedure for the provision of information in the field of technical standards and regulations.

https://eur-lex.europa.eu/legal-content/EN/TXT/PDF/?uri=CELEX:31998L0034&from=EN. Accessed May 2020.

[48]Directive 2000/31/EC of the European Parliament and of the Council on certain legal aspects of information society services, in particular electronic commerce, in the Internal Market.

https://eur-lex.europa.eu/legal-content/EN/TXT/PDF/?uri=CELEX:32000L0031&from=EN. Accessed May 2020.

[49]Directive 2006/123/EC of the European Parliament and of the Council on services in the internal market https://eur-lex.europa.eu/legal-content/EN/TXT/PDF/?uri=CELEX:32006L0123&from=EN. Accessed May 2020.

decided, as advocate Spuznar had suggested in his opinion,[50] that Uber is a platform which provides transportation services.

The CJEU's decision has two significant consequences. The first is highly but only relevant in the EU context. When the Court ruled that the services provided by Uber were transport services within the meaning of Directive 2006/123, it implied that such services did not benefit from the free movement rights recognized in Article 56 TFEU nor did it fall under the scope of protections provided by Directives 98/34 and Directive 2006/123. Uber therefore could not claim that it had the freedom to provide its information services anywhere in the internal market as a legitimately established service provider in one of the member states. More importantly, because of general EU provisions on competence combined the exception provided in Directive 2006/123 on urban transport services, Uber's activities could not be regulated at the EU level. According to the distribution of competences provided in the relevant legislation, member states would have the competence to regulate Uber and to provide the legal conditions under which it could operate.

Secondly, the CJEU rejected the claim according to which Uber should be seen merely as a platform which provides a service of intermediation. Prior to this decision, many courts around the globe may have reached the same conclusion. However, as a decision that has a binding effect for the entire internal market and for some of the largest economies in the world, the CJEU's ruling is of great significance. The fact that Uber provides urban transportation services may have a variety of legal consequences. The immediate effect of this case will be on the relationship between Uber and traditional taxis. After this decision, many member states of the European Union would be inclined to require Uber to, at the very least, apply for the necessary licenses. It could also lead many national courts to conclude that Uber is infringing upon fair competition rules by not abiding with rules applicable to taxis and thus misleading users. However, the ramifications could reach many other areas of law such as taxation rules, labor law and consumer protection.

7 Concluding Remarks

Uber has been at the center of attention and controversy for almost a decade. As this chapter has tried to portray, many of the problems associated with Uber are pertinent for all digital platforms. However, Uber is emblematic. This may be due to the fact that Uber is one of the first and largest growing sharing economy companies. Uber has provoked significant disruption in many areas of law such as labor law, consumer protection, tax law, data privacy, unfair competition and antitrust. It has faced legal challenges originating from local authorities, passengers and even its own drivers.

---

[50]Opinion of Advocate General Szpunar delivered on 11 May 20171 Case C-434/15 Asociación Profesional Elite Taxi v Uber Systems Spain SL. https://eur-lex.europa.eu/legal-content/EN/TXT/PDF/?uri=CELEX:62015CC0434&from=EN. Accessed May 2020.

This economic and social unease and these legal actions are evidence of the disruptive effects of Uber.

From a legal point of view, the most important question is how to respond to this disruption. There is a common conception according to which innovation and innovators thrive in regulatory loopholes.[51] Accordingly, creativity is triggered or made possible by the flexibility and boundlessness that is found in these spaces. If that is the case, we should perhaps allow for the loopholes to exist and to be found. However, the more critical question is how regulators should react once the innovation led disruption has occurred. Should the policy makers then fill in the gap that has been discovered? How far should they go in regulating? When does regulation start killing incentives to innovate? How can we detect over-regulation? And most importantly, how should we weigh and balance the value created by innovation and the values that are protected by normative frameworks?

Perhaps the most significant contribution of sharing economy companies in the form of digital platforms like Uber has been these discussions. Similar debates are being held today on artificial intelligence, biomedical innovation research or Internet of Things. Whichever field or type of innovation we look at, we will face similar disruptive effects and we will face the same questions from a legal point of view. Governments across the globe are confronted with the pressure of incentivizing and keeping up with the innovation race on the one hand and protecting their citizens and their societies' welfare on the other. Individuals and societies enjoy the benefits of technological advancement and innovation almost at the same time as its negative externalities. The most crucial debate is therefore the legal one, as it will design the framework and scope of protection against the threats of this world of rapid change. The legal responses to one child of the fourth industrial revolution such as the sharing economy provide food for thought for regulating others.

References

Ayres I, Braithwate J (1991) Responsive regulation: transcending the deregulatory debate. Oxford University Press, New York

Browning L, Newcomer E (2019) Uber Created a $6.1 billion Dutch Weapon to avoid paying taxes. Bloomberg. https://www.bloomberg.com/news/articles/2019-08-08/uber-created-a-6-1-billion-dutch-weapon-to-avoid-paying-taxes. Accessed on May 2020

CBS SF (2015) Family of 6-year-old girl killed by Uber driver in San Francisco Settles Lawsuit. https://sanfrancisco.cbslocal.com/2015/07/14/uber-lawsuit-sofia-liu-san-francisco/. Accessed on May 2020

Coase RH (2013) Problem of social cost. J Law Econ 56(4):837–877

European Commission (2016) Communication from the Commission to the European Parliament, the Council, the European Economic and Social Committee and the Committee of Regions: A European agenda for the collaborative economy. http://ec.europa.eu/DocsRoom/documents/16881/attachments/2/translations. Accessed on May 2020

[51] Tirole (2019).

Evans DS (2003) The antitrust economics of multi-sided platform markets. Yale J on Reg 20(2):325–381
Evans DS, Schlamensee R (2016) Matchmakers. Harvard Business Review Press, Boston
Fleischer V (2010) Regulatory arbitrage. Texas Law Rev 89(2):227–290
Gunningham N, Graborski PM (1998) Smart regulation: designing environmental policy. Oxford University Press, New York
Hill S (2016) The California challenge. Friedrich Ebert Stiftung. https://steven-hill.com/wp-content/uploads/2016/10/Hill-FES-paper-California-Challenge-How-not-to-regulate-disruptive-business-models.pdf. Accessed on May 2020
https://economix.blogs.nytimes.com/2014/03/03/trusting-the-sharing-economy-to-regulate-itself/?smid=tw-share. Accessed on May 2020
Lobel O (2016) The law of the platform. Minnesota Law Rev 101(1):87–166
Markides C (2006) Disruptive innovation: in need of better theory. J Prod Innov Manag 23:19–25
Parker GG, Van Alstyne MW, Choudary SP (2016) Platform revolution: how networked markets are transforming the economy and how to make them work for you. Norton, London
Prassl J (2018) Humans as a service: The promise and perils of work in the gig economy. Oxford University Press, Oxford
Rinne A (2019) 4 big trends for the sharing economy in 2019. World Economic Forum. https://www.weforum.org/agenda/2019/01/sharing-economy/. Accessed on May 2020
Sundajaran A (2014) Trusting the 'sharing economy' to regulate itself. The New York Times
Sundararajan A (2016) The sharing economy: the end of employment and the rise of crowd-based capitalism. The MIT Press, Massachusetts
Tirole J (2019) Regulating the disrupters. Live Mint. https://www.livemint.com/Technology/XsgWUgy9tR4uaoME7xtITI/Regulating-the-disrupters-Jean-Tirole.html. Accessed on May 2020
Tirole J-C, Rochet J (2003) Platform competition in two-sided markets. J Eur Econ Assoc 1(4):990–1029
Uber (2020) Much needed 10 April 2020 Uber by the numbers: Users & drivers statistics, demographics, and fun facts. https://muchneeded.com/uber-statistics/. Accessed on May 2020

Cases

CJEU Case C-434/15 Asociación Profesional Elite Taxi v Uber Systems Spain SL
Opinion of Advocate General Szpunar delivered on 11 May 20171 Case C-434/15 Asociación Profesional Elite Taxi v Uber Systems Spain SL. https://eur-lex.europa.eu/legal-content/EN/TXT/PDF/?uri=CELEX:62015CC0434&from=EN. Accessed on May 2020

Legislative Materials

Directive 98/34/EC of the European Parliament and of the Council laying down a procedure for the provision of information in the field of technical standards and regulations
https://eur-lex.europa.eu/legal-content/EN/TXT/PDF/?uri=CELEX:31998L0034&from=EN. Accessed
Directive 2000/31/EC of the European Parliament and of the Council of 8 June 2000 on certain legal aspects of information society services, in particular electronic commerce, in the Internal Market ('Directive on electronic commerce'). http://eur-lex.europa.eu/legal-content/EN/ALL/?uri=CELEX:32000L0031. Accessed on May 2020

Directive 2006/123/EC of the European Parliament and of the Council on services in the internal market https://eur-lex.europa.eu/legal-content/EN/TXT/PDF/?uri=CELEX:32006L0123&from=EN. Accessed on May 2020

Regulation of the European Parliament and of the Council on promoting fairness and transparency for business users of online intermediation services. https://eur-lex.europa.eu/legal-content/EN/TXT/PDF/?uri=CELEX:32019R1150

Chapter 3
Ridesharing Regulation in the USA

James B. Speta

Modern ridesharing began in the USA in 2010, when Uber released its app-based platform in San Francisco. Its growth, nationally and internationally, has been stratospheric. Initially, ridesharing faced the very real argument that the service was entirely illegal, for it was simply unlicensed taxi service. States and municipalities had long regulated taxis under a common carrier model, with limited licensing, rate regulation, and extensive service requirements. Claiming that it was a "technology company," Uber simply ignored those limitations, and as consumers rapidly adopted ridesharing, U.S. jurisdictions quickly turned to permit them.

Ridesharing is now legal throughout the USA, after myriad legal attempts to forestall ridesharing's entry have been rejected. This regulatory transformation has mirrored the prior waves of deregulating transportation and utility markets. Indeed, that deregulatory background provided a new, general model for modern regulation: eliminating economic controls while focusing on safety issues. Creating a new category of operators, "transportation network companies," states and cities now regulate drivers and cars, require insurance, and take other steps, but rates and number of drivers are no longer limited. The transition has, of course, created new problems, such as traffic congestion and determining the status of drivers as employees or independent contractors. These issues, and others such as disability access and privacy, are still being resolved, and they demonstrate a tension between general laws and new, specific contexts. But, on the whole, the USA and its flexible approaches have rapidly accommodated themselves to the new driving economy.

J. B. Speta (✉)
Northwestern Pritzker School of Law, Northwestern University, Chicago, IL, United States
e-mail: j-speta@law.northwestern.edu

Z. Ayata and I. Önay (eds.), *Global Perspectives on Legal Challenges Posed by Ridesharing Companies*,
https://doi.org/10.1007/978-981-15-7035-3_3

1 Background: U.S. Taxi Regulation Before Ridesharing

Prior to ridesharing's debut, taxi services in the USA were reasonably heavily regulated, under the traditional common carrier model that historically had applied to most transportation services. Local regulation prevailed, instead of the federally led structures of railroad, air, bus, and truck (and other) transportation regulation. But the overall scheme was similar, and similar to state and federal regulation of public utilities such as electricity, natural gas, and water. Taxi markets arguably differed in their underlying structure, and should have been more amenable to deregulation and competition. But, in fact, regulation survived in taxi markets long after it had been dismantled in other transportation industries.

Public ownership has never played a dominant role in transportation and public utilities in the USA. Unlike the history of most European and many other countries, even the national rail, telephone, and pipeline networks were privately owned, while being subject to extensive government regulation.[1] Starting in the late 1880s, under the so-called Progressive Movement, and continuing through the 1930s "New Deal" explosion of the federal administrative state, what began as a state and local movement to regulate grew to include federal leadership.[2] The Interstate Commerce Act of 1886, which came first and addressed the railroads, was copied into statute after statute, subjecting most transportation services and utilities, as well as adjuncts such as stockyards, to regulation by federal commission (while usually preserving a state role for the regulation of local services). At its peak, the regulatory state included rail, truck, bus, maritime, and many warehouse services; telegraphs and telephone networks; electric, gas, water, and sewer companies; and myriad others.[3]

As a result of this legislative uniformity, the regulatory schemes across industries were more or less consistent, and this model can be labeled either the "common carrier" or "public utility" model. First, government limited entry into and exit from territories and service markets, either through franchising or licensing. Second, government controlled the terms and conditions of service. Rates were regulated, to ensure both that excess profits were not earned and that the service-provider received sufficient revenue to continue to provide quality service. The providers were forbidden to engage in unreasonable price and service discrimination, which usually meant that regulators had to approve any such differentials. And, third, government usually pursued some kind of universal service policy, either by simply requiring companies to provide service to all those who requested it or, more expansively, by requiring companies to provide certain services at below-cost prices (or for no price) while allowing them to recover additional revenues on other services in order to be made whole.[4] This regulation was effected by federal and state commissions, usually under a tariff-filing regime, in which the companies proposed terms of service and sought approval, and involved comprehensive ratemaking and other supervisory

---

[1] *See, e.g.*, Helm and Yarrow (1988).

[2] Schwartz (1973).

[3] Kearney and Merrill (1998), pp. 1333–1334.

[4] Ibid., (pp. 1331–1335).

proceedings. Indeed, the statutes almost always granted to the commissions extraordinarily broad authority, calling for "just and reasonable" rates and other regulation to be based on the "public interest, convenience, and necessity."[5]

In many markets, the common carrier model corresponded to an industry structure that did not permit or that at least severely limited the possibility of competition. At the extreme, telephone, electric, gas, and several other markets were sometimes considered to be "natural monopoly" markets, in which demand could be served most efficiently (or perhaps only) by a single company. In these markets, usually involving very high capital costs and very low marginal costs of service, competition would be undesirable as well as difficult, for it would result in duplicative investment.[6] In oligopolistic markets, the dual (but conflicting) concerns of coordinated pricing and destructive competition similarly gave rise to economic arguments for government control.[7] But it would be a mistake to say that, in the USA, common carrier regulation was restricted to noncompetitive industries. Some of the network industries, notably telephony, were competitive at the outset, and others, such as airlines, stockyards, and bus service, were probably never subject to monopoly or oligopoly concerns. Rather, regulation arose in some cases due to concerns over discriminatory pricing or due to industry preference for regulation. And, in other cases, regulation of subsequent industries flowed, both politically and economically, from earlier instances. For example, truck and water carrier regulation flowed in part from pressures by the regulated railroads for consistent treatment and in part from protectionist impulses. For another example, airlines eventually sought government regulation to ensure adequate pricing, and government, which feared for airplane safety, complied.[8]

Taxi regulation largely followed these characteristics, although a few significant differences obtained. In general, municipalities and not state or federal governments controlled licensing. A person could not provide taxi service without government permission, usually through "medallion" ownership or lease. (A medallion was the physical badge that had to be bolted to an automobile to publicly indicate permission to provide taxi services.) Municipalities also set rates, usually a combination of time and distance served. Service was required, in the sense that taxis were required to provide service to all of those who requested it, to any destination within the service territory. This requirement was often breached in practice, as concerns about taxis refusing to serve minorities and poor communities were widespread. But the formal requirement nevertheless obtained. And municipalities sought to assure some universal service, by requiring disability access and providing some service subsidies.[9]

Taxi markets, of course, even more than busses and airlines, were in no way natural monopolies. Once the government provides streets, the only capital cost of taxi service is the modest cost of an automobile, and most urban markets could support

[5]Ibid., (p. 1334).

[6]*See generally* Sharkey (1982), Posner (1969).

[7]Kahn (1970), pp. 4–5.

[8]Kearney and Merrill (1998), p. 1333.

[9]*See generally* Speta (2016), pp. 105–108, Dempsey (1996).

thousands or tens of thousands of taxi drivers. Some modest economies of scale could obtain through affiliation and the sharing of dispatch services, and similarly network effects might be generated by accumulating dedicated bases of riders and drivers. But these were relatively small gains, and multiple companies and individual drivers could compete with one another—as borne out by actual practice throughout the country. Indeed, the structure of taxi markets could support competition rather easily.

Regulation of taxi markets, therefore, had a number of different motivations, and understanding those motivations helps to situate the deregulatory response that eventually occurred in the USA when ridesharing entered. One of the principal drivers of taxi regulation did not relate to the economics of the industry, or at least not directly, and that was the problem of congestion. England regulated carriages to address congestion, and in many cities, taxi services were blamed for significant traffic problems. To limit congestion, government acted to limit the number of authorized taxi drivers, setting up the industry for the balance of common carrier regulation—control of rates and service.[10]

Beyond congestion, however, the customary justifications for taxi regulation did have some economic components. Concerns over consumer exploitation were common—exploitation by the exercise of local monopoly power in the hail market. That is, a consumer who hails a cab in the street and then attempts to negotiate a price may experience the localized monopoly that comes with the first cab to arrive, bolstered by the uncertainty that the consumer could reach a better price with a subsequent cab. On the flip side, in circumstances in which a consumer could negotiate with multiple cabs, for example at cab stands, the concern was that cabs would engage in destructive competition. Under this scenario, cabs would bid down their prices to just their gasoline costs, which would be too low to maintain service. Pricing in the so-called dispatch market, where consumers placed orders for taxis in advance, might behave more rationally, as consumers could get prices from multiple companies and companies could build reputations for good service. But the dispatch market, because it required advanced planning, did not constrain the pricing anomalies that could arise in hail and stand markets.[11]

Given these pressures, governments adopted price regulation, and price regulation then reinforced the other parts of the common carrier model. With prices regulated, the only way for taxi drivers increase their revenues is to increase the percentage of total time in which they are carrying a passenger, as opposed to driving empty. Thus, taxis will provide service primarily to densely populated areas (the airport, train station, and central business district) and will refuse to pick up or drop off customers in instances in which they risk a "dead head"—an empty return. As a result, regulators imposed "duties to serve," adopting the regulatory rule referenced earlier that taxis must accept all customers and take those customers where they wish to go. And this also reinforced the limitation on the number of licenses, because by now limiting competition, the regulators could assure taxi drivers that if they lost

[10] Speta (2016), p. 115.

[11] Speta (2016), pp. 110–115, Shrieber (1975), Williams (1980), p. 106.

money on some trips (because they had to return empty) they would make it up on other, more valuable trips. In this manner, the internal cross-subsidies common to other utility industries—telephone, electric, gas, and others—were replicated in taxi markets.[12]

To be sure, taxi regulation also had other motivators. Taxis are transportation, of course, and most transportation services were regulated as common carriers. The power of legal analogy mandated similar treatment, and sometimes competitive parties lobbied for regulation. And sometimes, the government itself had an economic incentive to limit taxi service, to protect publicly owned bus and other transport services. Moreover, taxi regulation always had a safety dimension—concern for safe cars and safe drivers—that was entangled with the regulation. Drivers, for example, had to pass background checks as well as have satisfactory driving records. Suffice to say that, for all of these reasons, the scheme of licensing, rate control, and service regulation, was relatively stable until ridesharing's disruptive entry into the market.[13]

2 The U.S. Deregulatory Context Preceding Ridesharing

Ridesharing's entry into the U.S. taxi market was, in some sense, unique, in that its entry followed an Internet commerce model, notwithstanding that the service was physical transportation. But, in other regards, ridesharing's entry and the subsequent regulatory reaction resembled transitions that have occurred in other industries. Over the past 40 years, the USA has substantially deregulated both utility and transportation markets, and has relied more on competition law oversight, either by general antitrust authorities or as applied by specialist agencies. At the one extreme, deregulation ended some administrative agencies' existences—as with the federal Civil Aeronautics Board (airlines) and Interstate Commerce Commission (railroads), which were disbanded in 1978 and 1996, respectively. At the other extreme, agencies came to rely much more on competition law concepts, largely permitting entry and evaluating markets with competitive results as both a goal and a baseline. In the USA, the Federal Communications Commission, from the 1980s forward and particularly after the Telecommunications Act of 1996, is the leading model of an agency that retained sector-specific authority but largely shifted its thinking to open markets and competition law principles.[14]

Indeed, airline regulation and telecommunications regulation are two particularly illuminating examples of industry deregulation, and they provide an important part of the intellectual context for U.S. regulatory reaction to the entry of ridesharing. Airlines, as part of the nation's transportation services, were initially regulated as common carriers in 1938, and subject to entry limits and price and service regulation.

[12] *See* Gallick and Sisk (1987), pp. 118–120.

[13] Speta (2016), pp. 108–110, 115–116.

[14] *See generally* Kearney and Merrill (1998), pp. 1335–1342.

The airlines eventually lobbied for the regulation, arguing that regulation was necessary to keep sufficient revenues, and that "financial starvation" could "could lead to traffic competition of such intensity that the accident ratio might accelerate instead of decline."[15] Under common carrier regulation, price competition among airlines was largely eliminated, although nonprice competition continued, with airlines offering larger seats, better food, and more elaborate service. But federal price regulation did not encompass flights that were wholly within a single state, and both Texas and California were large enough that local airlines began to thrive by offering much lower prices. The lower prices offered by these intrastate airlines were concrete and persuasive proof that regulation was having a perverse effect; in the late 1970s, Congress rolled airline deregulation into its broader fight against price inflation.[16]

When Congress eliminated price regulation, airlines were not completely deregulated. Instead, Congress created the Federal Aviation Administration and charged it with comprehensive safety regulation of airplanes and air service. Entry was still limited, in the sense that FAA certification was required before planes and service could be offered (particularly in commercial service), but the FAA did not directly limit the number of airlines or control routes. Under traditional regulation, the CAB had controlled airlines to the route level, requiring permission both to begin and to cease service. The available evidence suggests that safety actually improved under the FAA.[17] Similarly, Congress created an alternative universal service regime for air service. Under common carrier regulation, airlines were required to service some small communities, and permitted to make up any losses through the general rate-setting process. At the same time it passed airline deregulation, Congress allocated funds for Essential Air Service. These funds were raised by fees on airline tickets generally and used to subsidize service to small, usually rural communities.[18]

In the USA, telephony was also regulated as a common carrier service, beginning at the federal level with the Interstate Commerce Commission in 1910 and then the independent Federal Communications Commission in 1934.[19] The economic rationale for regulating was more customary, as telephone networks were thought to be natural monopolies, both due to high network costs and due to network effects—although in the early days significant local competition developed and might have been maintained through interconnection regulation instead of the full blown utility model. But the American Telephone and Telegraph Company ("AT&T"), the nation's dominant carrier, also lobbied for continuing regulation, under its slogan of "one nation, one network, universal service." The market began to shift in the 1970s, with the development of microwave communications technologies, which allowed lower-cost construction of long-distance links. New companies, such as MCI and Sprint, showed that that lower prices and higher quality service was possible, and many companies sought to interconnect their new, partial networks with AT&T's

[15]Kelly (1963); *see* Levine (1965).

[16]Morrison and Whinston (1988).

[17]*See generally* Rose (1992), Barnett and Higgin (1989).

[18]Hall et al. (2015).

[19]Speta (2002), pp. 251–258.

local networks, which were harder to duplicate, in order to provide comprehensive services. The FCC, however, moved slowly, permitting only limited entry over many years.[20] The turning point was antitrust litigation, and in particular a government civil case that resulted in the negotiated breakup of the Bell System and established competitive long-distance markets.[21]

In 1996, Congress acted to further open telecommunications markets to competition, by banning any legal restrictions on entry and requiring incumbent local carriers to interconnect with and provide unbundled service to new competitors.[22] Some local competition had developed, particularly for business services in dense urban markets, and consumer wireless service was also growing across the country. Although not anticipated by the 1996 Act, the beginnings of the broadband Internet together with digital convergence also increased the competitive horizon, by bringing cable television companies and others into data markets that soon competed with traditional voice. As to universal service, the FCC had begun, following the AT&T breakup, to shift from implicit cross-subsidies that supported residential and local service to explicit support mechanisms. In general, the FCC approved access fees that long-distance carriers paid to local companies and that, because they were set far above costs, had the effect of subsidizing local services. The FCC, working with the states, also expanded universal service funding for high-cost areas and for low-income individuals. In the 1996 Act, Congress reiterated its commitment to universal service and specifically required "equitable and nondiscriminatory contributions" to be formulated in a "competitively neutral" manner, to support both traditional and advanced telecommunications services.[23] Under this regime, the FCC moved to an explicit "tax and spend" model, under which all telecommunications carriers were taxed and funds were distributed to low-income consumers, high-cost carriers, and certain targeted industries such as education and health care.[24]

Airlines and telecommunications are but two of the leading examples of a general trend of U.S. deregulation of transportation and utility industries. As Professors Joseph Kearney and Thomas Merrill, two of the leading commentators, have put it: The USA from the late 1970s through the present day has experienced a shift from viewing these markets "as best served by a limited number of service providers that would be overseen by a regulatory commission concerned with maintaining standardized packages of services and prices ... to a new paradigm emphasizing, to the maximum degree feasible, consumer choice among multiple competing providers."[25] In surveying the reasons for these changes, both legal and social, Kearney and Merrill conclude that no single institutional driver—Congress, the courts, or the administrative agencies—played a consistent leading role, such that a single legal or political explanation for change is sufficient. Rather, "the transformation is being driving

[20] Robinson (1988).

[21] United States v. Western Elec. Co., (1984).

[22] Krattenmaker (1996).

[23] 47 U.S.C. § 254.

[24] Prieger (1998).

[25] Kearney and Merrill (1998), p. 1329.

by deep-seated economic and social forces—forces that affect all the industries under consideration and transcend the particular historical episodes in any particular industry."[26]

In particular, Professors Kearney and Merrill identify four forces as the key drivers toward deregulation across industries and markets. First, in some industries, technological change created the possibility of "significant efficiency gains to be obtained in moving from a monopolistic or oligopolistic industrial structure to a competitive market structure."[27] Although they conclude that this explanation did not apply to all industries and that deregulation often preceded innovation, they do ascribe it some power and identify airlines and telecommunications as two markets in which innovation and new entrants demonstrated the possibilities of competition.[28] Second, and relatedly, they identify "chain reactions," in which deregulation in one industry leads to deregulation in other, related industries due to the adjacent, newly created competitive pressures. While this cannot explain change in the first industry, "the phenomenon ... helps explain why regulatory change has occurred simultaneously or nearly simultaneously in so many industries."[29] Third, Kearney and Merrill identify important instances of interest group politics, although the source of the political pressure varied. In some industries, consumers pressed hard for changes that they believed would lower prices. In others, the incumbents pushed for deregulation, fearing that they would lose out to new entrants. And, in still others, powerful user groups, representing industrial customers and business purchasers, coalesced to push for change.[30] Finally, Kearney and Merrill identify an important intellectual evolution, characterized by "changing ideas about the relative merits of markets and governments."[31] Influenced by several leading economists, elite opinion began to worry less about the persistence of natural monopoly and to worry more about the effectiveness of government. Government was costly, ineffective, and, in the worst telling, captured by industries that actually used the regulatory process to protect themselves and to garner additional profits.[32] They conclude that "[t]his transmission of ideas [from the academic community to the political sphere] unquestionably has had a pronounced effect on the shape of public policy."[33]

This wave of deregulation had occurred even before 2000. And it was into this world that ridesharing entered to disrupt one of the last tightly controlled transportation markets.

---

[26]Ibid, (p. 1383).

[27]Ibid., (p. 1384).

[28]Ibid., (pp. 1389–1390).

[29]Ibid., (p. 1393).

[30]Ibid., (p. 1397).

[31]Ibid.

[32]Ibid., (pp. 1399–1400).

[33]Ibid., (p. 1403).

3 Ridesharing's Growth

Ridesharing began its modern era in 2010, when Uber first launched public service in San Francisco, and it has become the dominant ground transportation service across most of the USA. After its debut, Uber rapidly expanded to other U.S. cities, opening in New York and Chicago in 2011, and began its international expansion in 2014. Although first started as an app-based limousine service (and therefore priced higher than taxi services), Uber in 2012 launched the UberX product, where private drivers could use their production cars to offer paid rides. UberX was the revolutionary product that accelerated Uber's growth. Uber quickly became a "unicorn," attracting significant financing and expanding at an explosive rate. By the first few months of 2013, Uber was operating in 35 different cities, on its way to its current footprint of 785 metropolitan areas and 110 million worldwide users. Uber's entry was followed closely in the USA and elsewhere by other ridesharing services, such as Lyft.[34]

Uber's ridesharing services offered a number of advantages over traditional taxi services. First, within a short time after entry, ridesharing operated much more quickly than taxi dispatch services, with wait times sometimes indistinguishable from hail times. A survey conducted in December 2014 put wait times in New York City between 2 minutes in Manhattan and 3 minutes in the outer boroughs. In Washington D.C., Atlanta, Chicago, Austin, Los Angeles, San Francisco, and Seattle, average Uber wait times were all below 4 minutes.[35] Second, Uber offered service at much cheaper prices than taxis. A different survey conducted in late 2014 found Uber's rates to be below taxi charges in 19 of 21 large U.S. cities.[36] Even more importantly, Uber provided significantly cheaper service on the highest value routes—between the central business district and the airport. For example, in Los Angeles, Uber was \$34 cheaper; in Chicago, \$28; in Dallas, \$22; and Washington DC (Dulles) \$30.[37] To be sure, notwithstanding its high enterprise valuations, Uber has long lost money, and its low prices may simply reflect a significant transfer from investors to riders and drivers and not actually lower costs than taxi services, although we will return to this question below. But, in either event, Uber's lower prices (and the lower prices of its principal competitors) have pushed almost exponential growth.

Ridesharing has become one of the most popular local transportation options. Precise data is difficult to develop, as taxi data and ridesharing data are not shared in widely compatible formats. But estimates from reimbursed ground travel surveys have demonstrated ridesharing's dominance. The company Certify began tracking these reimbursements in 2014, and in the first quarter of that year, ridesharing represented only 8% of the market (which included, in addition to ridesharing, taxi charges and car rentals). In the middle of 2018, ridesharing had risen to 72% of the market, with car rentals second at 22%, and taxis at only 5% of reimbursements.[38] Uber, of

[34]Cetin and Deakin (2019).

[35]Mosendz and Sender (2014).

[36]Silverstein (2014).

[37]Bender (2015).

[38]Richter and Street (2018).

course, was the dominant company in the USA throughout this period, but recently Lyft, which also operates in most U.S. cities, has risen to be approximately 35% of the ridesharing market. (No other national competitor has significant market share.)[39]

4 Specific Regulatory Challenges

Ridesharing has created significant regulatory challenges, from those internal to traditional ground transportation regulation to several associated regulatory problems, such as congestion, employment, and privacy. The ridesharing platforms themselves have long maintained that they were not transportation services at all, but rather were simply technology companies. And they have similarly claimed that they neither employed their drivers nor were responsible for their drivers' quality of service. In part, these claims were necessary because the system of taxi regulation did not permit the offering of services by companies or drivers that were not approved by municipal authorities. Indeed, in some cities in the USA, ridesharing was banned or at least forbidden from operating at airports and train stations, although the extent of its market exclusion was never as great as in some other countries.

Relatively quickly, municipalities moved to allow ridesharing services to operate, typically under new legislation directed at "transportation network companies." The statutes offered largely parallel regulation to taxi services, although without price and other economic controls. The more interesting disputes came when taxi companies fought back through antitrust litigation and as states and cities sought to grapple with the difficult questions of traffic congestion, safety, employment status of drivers, and other issues. In each of these areas, the tension between regulation specific to ridesharing and the application of more general legislation was highlighted, with important evolution still continuing in a number of areas.

4.1 Entry and Competition

Overall, the U.S. response followed that in prior instances of deregulation, discussed above in Part II, although over a much-compressed time frame. Uber and other ridesharing services presented a technological shock to the market, demonstrating that a service functionally similar to taxis could be offered at a lower price and with higher quality. Consumers reacted by adopting the service, and, combined with the thousands of drivers who joined the service, created a political base that would oppose significant restrictions. Finally, elites and policymakers were primed by earlier examples of deregulation, and a general suspicion of nonmarket solutions, to be receptive to arguments for deregulating ground transportation markets to accommodate these new services.

[39]Bosa (2018).

The initial reaction to ridesharing was mixed, but U.S. state and local governments moved reasonably quickly to permit them under new legislation. The California Public Utility Commission initially issued cease and desist orders to many ridesharing companies.[40] In 2013, however, California become the first state to pass rules governing "transportation network companies," defined as companies using an "online-enabled app or platform to connect passengers with drivers using their personal vehicles."[41] Some resistance at the state and city level continued through 2016,[42] although more states and cities also began to permit ridesharing,[43] often adopting similar legislation. In some cases, municipalities sought initial compromises, permitting ridesharing to operate generally but restricting their entry into the most high-value areas such as airports. In mid-2016, for example, ten of the busiest 40 airports in the USA still did not allow Uber to enter to pick up passengers.[44] Even into 2019, some U.S. airports have preferential pickup arrangements for traditional taxi services, moving rideshare pickups to more remote garages or less convenient areas.[45] Nevertheless, despite some lingering instances of unequal treatment, U.S. markets are now more or less open to ridesharing generally.[46]

Taxi drivers, having made a substantial investment in their licenses and facing new competition, fought against ridesharing's entry, not just politically but also through litigation. These efforts arose in large part from a significant decline in the value of a taxi medallion, a reaction to the competitive pressures from ridesharing. According to the Report of the New York City Medallion Task Force, taxi medallions there had traded in the early 2010s for between $1 million and $1.3 million.[47] In other words, a significant investment was required to enter the taxi market, which had to be serviced through fares or leases to drivers earning fares. The medallions themselves had substantial value, and that value was rapidly lost to competition. In New York, "[t]he average price of one of the city's 13,711 medallions has fallen from an average of $1 [million] during the summer of 2014 to $690,000 [in mid-2015], an aggregate loss of some $4 billion in value."[48] By January of 2018, a New York City medallion traded for only $188,000,[49] a further aggregate loss of nearly $7 billion. The same occurred in other cities in which medallion scarcity had caused significantly high prices.[50]

---

[40] Geron (2012).

[41] California Public Utility Commission Decision 13-09-045 (2013).

[42] *See* Posen (2015), pp. 423–433.

[43] Sloan (2016).

[44] McCartney (2016), Tierney (2015) at B1.

[45] McNicholas (2019).

[46] *See* Cetin and Deakin (2019), Spicer et al. (2018), pp. 149–150, Perritt (2019), pp. 105–121.

[47] Report of the New York City Taxi Medallion Task Force (2020) at 12–13.

[48] Taxis v. Uber: Substitutes or Complements (2015).

[49] Report of the Taxi Medallion Task Force (2020) at 13.

[50] Maidenberg (2016).

Taxi companies and drivers pursued a number of different claims, without success. The most aggressive claims were against governments that permitted, by regulation or default, ridesharing entry, claiming that the change effected an unconstitutional taking of property.[51] These claims had some precedent in earlier deregulatory episodes. Incumbent telecommunications companies had similarly challenged the 1996 Act, which eliminated their local monopolies and required them to provide network services to competitors at low prices, as takings of their property. As Professor Daniel Spulber and J. Gregory Sidak put it more generally, "The takings issue arises because those utilities assumed obligations to serve in return for the regulator's assurance that the utilities would earn a competitive return on invested capital, along with compensation for the full cost of providing service."[52] The Supreme Court denied the telecom companies' claims, although largely on the ground that the companies had been unable to show that they were not adequately compensated for the use of their property.[53] And, in any event, the notion that government either made a perpetual promise not to permit competition or could be liable for a change in regulation runs up against both legal and political realities.[54]

The taxi companies' takings claims were similarly rejected. Two opinions written by the famous U.S. appellate judge (and former law professor) Richard Posner are emblematic.[55] The court first notes that, had the cities "confiscated taxi medallions, which are the licenses that authorize the use of an automobile as a taxi," the takings claims "would have had merit."[56] But, "'[p]roperty' does not include a right to be free from competition."[57] For example, a city does not incur any liability if it rezones property or otherwise issues a business permit that increases the competition that an existing business faces.[58] Judge Posner, of course, was one of the leading figures in U.S. law and economics, and had written articles strongly questioning natural monopoly (and other forms of) regulation.[59] And this general attitude is reflected in the court's opinion: "Were the old deemed to have a constitutional right to preclude the entry of the new into the markets of the old, economic progress might grind to a halt. Instead of taxis we might have horse and buggies; instead of the telephone, the telegraph; instead of computers, slide rules. Obsolescence would equal entitlement."[60] The court also ruled against the taxi companies' equal protection claims,

[51]The Fifth Amendment to the United States Constitution, which applies equally to federal, state, and local governments, provides in part that "private property [shall not] be taken for public use, without just compensation." US Const amend V.

[52]Sidak and Spulber (1997). Sidak has written that takings claims by taxi companies do not fit this model. Sidak (2016).

[53]Verizon Comm, Inc v. FCC, 535 U.S. 467, 524 (2002).

[54]*See* Baumol and Merrill (1997), Baumol and Merrill (1998).

[55]Illinois Transp Ass'n v. City of Chicago, 839 F.3d 594 (7th Cir. 2016); Joe Sanfelippo Cabs, Inc. v. City of Milwaukee, 839 F.3d 613 (7th Cir. 2016)

[56]Illinois Transp Ass'n v. City of Chicago, 839 F.3d at 596.

[57]Ibid.

[58]Ibid., (p. 597).

[59]Posner (1969).

[60]Illinois Transp Ass'n, 839 F.3d at 597.

brought because the new city regulations were somewhat lighter than traditional taxi regulation.[61] And, the court concluded by explicitly tying the entry of ridesharing to the broader deregulatory context.

> Beginning in the 1970s, a deregulation movement swept the country, powered by the belief that competition is often a superior alternative to regulation. Entire agencies vanished, such as the Civil Aeronautics Board, which had greatly limited competition in the airline industry. Many cities loosened the regulatory limitations on taxi services—and this well before there were any [transportation network providers]. The deregulation movement has surged with the advent of the TNPs. Chicago ... has chosen the side of deregulation, and thus of competition, over preserving the traditional taxicab monopolies. That is a legally permissible choice.[62]

Taxi drivers also sued under antitrust laws, for example, claiming that Uber's entry into Philadelphia, which was permitted by state and local law, constituted an attempt to monopolize, through predatory conduct and otherwise.[63] In the Philadelphia case, the appellate court rejected the claim, noting that Uber was simply *increasing* competition. Uber's fast entry with many drivers and its lower prices "bolstered competition by offering customers lower prices, more available taxicabs, and a high-tech alternative to the customary method of hailing taxicabs and paying for rides."[64] At a minimum, the court found, even if taxis would suffer from Uber's entry, the ground transportation market more generally did not demonstrate significant barriers to entry, making it unlikely that Uber could monopolize the market. In other words, traditional taxis might be out, but other ridesharing companies could enter to compete with Uber.[65]

4.2 Safety

Ridesharing of course raises many of the same safety concerns as taxi services, and taxi companies as well as some regulators and consumers initially resisted ridesharing's entry by arguing that Uber and other companies failed to provide safe services. Initially, ridesharing services contended that market effects, such as feedback from riders on their drivers, would provide sufficient safety, together with screening done by the companies.[66] But, as states and cities began to regulate, they extended safety regulation to transportation network companies. In so doing, they replicated the transition in airlines and other industries, replacing economic supervision of an industry with regulation focused on safety.

State regulation generally addresses both vehicle and driver qualifications, as well as setting other safety requirements. By 2016, most states had required a driver

---

[61] Ibid., (p. 598).

[62] Ibid., (p. 599).

[63] See Philadelphia Taxi Ass'n v. Uber Technologies, Inc., 886 F.3d 332 (3d Cir. 2018).

[64] Ibid., (p. 340).

[65] Ibid., (p. 342).

[66] *See* LaFrance and Eveleth (2015).

application and background check,[67] although the depth of the background check was still the source of some dispute.[68] States or cities also set vehicle safety standards, although in many cases these were delegated to the companies to ensure that the cars were in good working order and compliant with federal safety standards.[69] Additional safety requirements present in some statutes included drug and alcohol policies, insurance requirements, driver training, and informational rules.[70]

The regulations for ridesharing and the regulation for taxi services, however, have not achieved complete parity, as should be expected for competitive neutrality. Taxi regulation often requires that the vehicles used for taxi service meet safety standards that go beyond those of typical production vehicles.[71] Given that taxi and ridesharing services are virtually identical, neither type of service should have a competitive advantage due to differential regulation. The optimal level of safety regulation, of course, may be difficult to determine. But the better result might be to reduce the regulation of taxi services to mirror that of ridesharing.

4.3 Congestion

Ridesharing's meteoric rise has now raised concerns over increased congestion and other attendant externalities, such as increases in pollution[72] and traffic fatalities.[73] Some studies have shown that ridesharing substitutes for the use of private cars, while other studies have shown an increase in total traffic as riders were using the services for trips that previously would have been taken by public transportation, on foot, or by bicycle.[74] Initially few cities acted, although New York imposed temporary caps on the number of ridesharing drivers, in an attempt to study the congestion problems.[75] More recently, several cities have announced congestion fees, applied either to all traffic or specifically to ridesharing platforms. New York City, for example, has passed an ordinance that will require a fee of between $11 and $14 for trips into central Manhattan, beginning in 2021.[76] Chicago has already imposed fees of $1.25 for all ridesharing trips, and $3 for all trips that reach or begin in the downtown core. Although the fees are slightly lower for shared rides, the new charges are expected to total $40 million annually.[77]

---

[67] Moran and Lasley (2017), p. 167.

[68] *See* Nelson and Reyes (2015).

[69] Moran and Lasley (2017).

[70] Ibid.

[71] LaFrance and Eveleth (2015).

[72] *See* Bliss (2017).

[73] Barrios et al. (2020).

[74] Bliss (2017).

[75] Fitzsimmons (2018).

[76] Hu (2019).

[77] Grossman (2020).

Congestion pricing is not, of course, an entirely new idea. In the USA, California and a few other places had already instituted congestion pricing on tollways.[78] Several cities around the world have implemented or experimented with congestion pricing in the core.[79] And a 2006 survey of the literature found a "strong consensus among economists on how to reduce traffic jams"—through congestion pricing.[80] To be sure, as Professor Ronald Coase has noted in the context of broadcast regulation, economists' bedrock belief is "that the allocation of resources should be determined by the forces of the market rather than as a result of government decisions."[81] And the corollary is that scarcity is ubiquitous and does not usually require regulation. Rather, "the way this is usually done in the American economic system is to employ the price mechanism."[82]

Congestion pricing is another example of separating health and safety regulation from the economic control of an industry. Here, congestion pricing (or even congestion regulation) attacks an externality of ridesharing directly, instead of limiting competition in the market. The key, of course, to maintaining an innovative market is to apply externality regulation in an even-handed manner. Only then will market forces seek the least costly way to comply. In the context of ridesharing, this means of course that congestion fees or regulation should apply to all traffic equally, including taxis, private cars, trucks, and other users of the streets, where "equally" means in a way equal to their contribution to congestion (or pollution or traffic fatalities, as the case may be). Without minimizing the difficulty of making these calculations, which are in part why congestion fees have not been adopted widely,[83] congestion fees on ridesharing services alone do not meet this requirement.

4.4 Employment

A third difficult issue raised by the expansion of ridesharing services is the employment status of the drivers, and this area has seen relatively recent action in the USA. Although precise numbers are difficult to come by, one industry source estimates that as of 2019 there were between 1.5 million and 2 million Uber and Lyft drivers in the USA alone.[84] As members of the so-called gig economy, a significant percentage of these drivers only work part-time, and many hold other employment.

---

[78] *See* Bribbin (2019).

[79] Brown (2011).

[80] Lindsey (2006), p. 292.

[81] Coase (1959), p. 18.

[82] Ibid., (p. 14).

[83] Lindsey (2006), p. 296 ("In short, economists do agree that highway congestion should be solved by pricing. Beyond that primary insight, however, there is much disagreement. Economists disagree over how to set tolls, how to cover common costs, what to do with any excess revenues, whether and how 'losers' from tolling previously free roads should be compensated, and whether to privatize highways").

[84] Berry (2019).

Consistent with their view that the ridesharing platforms are technology companies, the providers' clear position is that drivers are independent contractors and not employees. Under U.S. law, this generally means that the companies need not pay minimum wages, make contributions to social security, provide unemployment insurance, or offer other benefits and protections. Additionally, the drivers' status as independent contractors puts them outside certain other employment protections, such as some antidiscrimination laws. As two commentators summarized the stakes: "Employees are more expensive than independent contractors because businesses are responsible for, among other things, payroll taxes, workers' compensation insurance, health care, minimum wages, overtime, and the reimbursement of business-related expenses. If saddled with those costs, the on-demand business model might not survive, at least not in its current form."[85]

Reflecting its federal structure as well as the multiple statutory schemes under which the question of "employee or independent contractor" might arise, the USA has yet to give a dispositive answer on the status of ridesharing drivers. At the federal level, the most contentious issue has been coverage under the National Labor Relations Act which, among other things, protects workers' rights to unionize. In April 2019, the General Counsel of the National Labor Relations Board, the administering agency, issued an "Advice Memorandum," stating that both "UberX and UberBLACK drivers were independent contractors."[86] The memorandum, which is not the definitive position of the agency but is nevertheless persuasive authority, considered the usual common-law factors in determining agency/employment status. The General Counsel concluded that drivers controlled the principal conditions of their employment—when they worked, where they worked, and for whom they worked (noting in this regard that Uber drivers often worked simultaneously for Uber and Uber's competitors). As a result, Uber did not have the sufficient degree of "control" necessary to find an employment relationship.[87] And, while "control" is typically the most important factor, the General Counsel also found that other aspects of the relationship, such as the drivers' provision of their own cars, weighed against finding an employment relationship.

Standing in direct opposition to the NLRB counsel opinion are decisions, both judicial and legislative, coming from California, the largest U.S. ridesharing market (and largest state economy generally). In 2018, the California Supreme Court, in a lawsuit brought by delivery drivers who had been reclassified as independent contractors, certified a class action to determine whether they must be considered employees for the purposes of California wage law.[88] In so doing, the court noted that California law was broader than the common-law agency tests applied at the federal level and in many other states, and it strongly suggested that the breadth of that interpretation leaned in favor of finding employment relationships. "The adoption of the exceptionally broad … standard in California wage orders finds its justification in

---

[85] Means and Seiner (2016), pp. 1513–1514.

[86] Office of the General Counsel (2019).

[87] Ibid., (p. 6).

[88] Dynamex Operations West v. Superior Court, 416 P.3d 1 (Cal. 2018).

the fundamental purposes and necessity of the minimum wage and maximum hour legislation in which the standard has been embodied. Wage and hour statutes and wage orders are adopted in recognition of the fact that individual workers generally possess less bargaining power than a hiring business and that workers' fundamental need to earn income for their families' survival may lead them to accept work for substandard wages or working conditions."[89] Although the court's decision did not end the litigation, the California legislature soon stepped in. The new law, passed in 2019 and now in effect, codified the employment test the court had advanced and would classify all rideshare drivers as employees of the platforms on which they work.[90] Uber and Lyft and others have, so far, refused to comply and have sued to prevent the law's going into effect, but these matters are currently unresolved.[91]

Adding to the current uncertainty, some cities, acting independently, have passed or are considering legislation to mandate minimum wages to rideshare drivers.[92]

5 Conclusion and Further Issues

As a significant economic force, ridesharing services will continue to create legal issues in the USA. In addition to those already mentioned are several others that are even more unsettled. For example, the tort liability of rideshare platforms follows, in large part, the unsettled question of the relationship—employee or independent contractor—between the driver and the company.[93] Similarly, whether the platform must provide disability access also depends on whether it is, itself, providing the transportation. Although some state and local statutes have begun to address this issue and a federal statute might apply, we are still far from a resolution.[94] And some commentators and jurisdiction have begun to worry about the personal data that ridesharing companies accumulate, not just from rides but from the other businesses such as food and package delivery that they are beginning.[95]

In each of these areas, the law will continue to confront the need to tune general standards to the specifics of the new economic context. As the regulatory transition has shown, however, ridesharing creates a new competitive horizon and the opportunity for innovative services and lower prices.

---

[89] Ibid., (pp. 32–33).

[90] Hawkins (2019).

[91] Rodd (2020).

[92] Nelson (2019), Oxley (2019), Eidelson (2019).

[93] McPeak (2016).

[94] Reed (2016).

[95] Rogers (2015), Thomas (2018).

References

U.S.C. § 254

Barnett A, Higgin M (1989) Airline safety: the last decade. Mgmt Sci 35:1–21

Barrios J, Hochberg Y, Yi H (February, 2020) The cost of convenience: Ridehailing and traffic fatalities. NBER Working Paper No. 26783. https://www.nber.org/papers/w26783

Baumol W, Merrill T (1997) Deregulatory takings, breach of the regulatory contract, and the telecommunications Act of 1996. NYU L Rev 72:1037–1067

Baumol W, Merrill T (1998) Does the constitution require that we kill the competitive goose? Pricing local phone services to rivals. NYU L Rev 73:1122–1148

Bender A (April 10, 2015) Uber's astounding rise: Overtaking taxis in key markets. Forbes http://www.forbes.com/sites/andrewbender/2015/04/10/ubers-astounding-rise-overtaking-taxis-in-key-markets/. Accessed 20 Jan 2020

Berry M (June 1, 2019) How many uber drivers are there? Ride share guy. https://therideshareguy.com/how-many-uber-drivers-are-there/. Accessed 20 Jan 2020

Bliss L (October 12, 2017) The ride-hailing effect: More cars, more trips, more miles. CityLab.com. https://www.citylab.com/transportation/2017/10/the-ride-hailing-effect-more-cars-more-trips-more-miles/542592/. Accessed 20 Jan 2020

Bosa (May 14, 2018) Lyft claims it now has more than one-third of the US ride-sharing market. CNBC.com, May 14, 2018. https://www.cnbc.com/2018/05/14/lyft-market-share-051418-bosa-sf.html. Accessed 20 Jan 2020

Bribbin D (October 16, 2019) Congestion pricing is all around us. Why is it taboo on our roads? Brookings.edu. https://www.brookings.edu/blog/the-avenue/2019/10/16/congestion-pricing-is-all-around-us-why-is-it-taboo-on-our-roads/ Accessed 20 Jan 2020

Brown T (August 22, 2011) Five cities with congestion pricing. This big city. http://doi.org/thisbigcity.net;five-cities-with-congestion-pricing/. Accessed 20 Jan 2020

California Public Utility Commission decision 13-09-045 (2013)

Cetin T, Deakin E (2019) Regulation of taxis and the rise of ridesharing. Transport Pol'y 76:149–158

Coase R (1959) The Federal communications commission. JL Econ 1:1–40

Dempsey P (1996) Taxi industry regulation, deregulation and reregulation: the paradox of market failure. Transp LJ 24:73–120

Eidelson J (February, 2019) Uber and lyft raise prices in New York City, citing wage law. Bloomberg Bus Wk. https://www.bloomberg.com/news/articles/2019-02-01/uber-raises-prices-in-new-york-city-citing-new-minimum-wage-law. 20 Jan 2020

Fitzsimmons E (August 8, 2018) Uber hit with cap as New York City takes lead in crackdown. N.Y. Times. https://www.nytimes.com/2018/08/08/nyregion/uber-vote-city-council-cap.html. Accessed 20 Jan 2020

Gallick E, Sisk D (1987) A reconsideration of taxi regulation. JL Econ Org 3:117–128

Geron T (October 8, 2012) Ride-sharing startups get California cease and desist letter. Forbes.com. https://www.forbes.com/sites/tomiogeron/2012/10/08/ride-sharing-startups-get-california-cease-and-desist-letters/#4345f18851d3. Accessed 20 Jan 2020

Grossman (January 6, 2020) Lyft, Uber congestion tax in Chicago starts Monday. Wgntv.com. https://wgntv.com/news/lyft-uber-congestion-tax-in-chicago-starts-monday/. Accessed 20 Jan 2020

Hall J, Ross A, Yencha C (2015) The political economy of the essential air service program. Public Choice 165:147–164

Hawkins A (September 18, 2019) California Just dropped a bomb on the gig economy—What's next? The Verge. https://www.theverge.com/2019/9/11/20860578/california-ab5-bill-passage-uber-lyft-drivers-union-techlash. Accessed 20 Jan 2020

Helm D, Yarrow G (1988) The assessment: the regulation of utilities. Oxford Rev Econ Pol'y 4:i-xxxi

Hu W (April 24, 2019) Confused about congestion pricing? Here's what we know. NY Times. https://www.nytimes.com/2019/04/24/nyregion/what-is-congestion-pricing.html. Accessed 20 Jan 2020

Kahn A (1970) The economics of regulation 1:2. Wiley, New York
Kearney J, Merrill T (1998) The great transformation of regulated industries law. Colum L Rev 98:1323–1409
Kelly C (1963) The sky's the limit: the history of the airlines 101. Coward-McCann, New York
Krattenmaker T (1996) The telecommunications act of 1996. Fed Comm LJ 49:1–49
LaFrance A, Eveleth R (March 3, 2015) Are taxis safer than Uber? The Atlantic. https://www.theatlantic.com/technology/archive/2015/03/are-taxis-safer-than-uber/386207/. Accessed 20 Jan 2020
Levine M (1965) Is regulation necessary? California air transportation and national regulatory policy. Yale LJ 74:1416–1447
Lindsey R (2006) Do economists reach a conclusion on road pricing? The intellectual history of an idea. Econ J Watch 3:292–379
Maidenberg M (February 25, 2016) Taxi lender: Chicago Uber-clueless on ride-bookers' impact. Crain's Chicago Bus. https://www.chicagobusiness.com/article/20160225/NEWS10/160229928/a-banker-at-new-york-based-signature-bank-none-too-happy-with-the-city-s-taxi-regulators. Accessed 20 Jan 2020
McCartney S (July 6, 2016) You can't take an Uber home from these airports. The Wall St J. https://www.wsj.com/articles/you-cant-take-an-uber-home-from-these-airports-1467829592. Accessed 20 Jan 2020
McNicholas T (October 29, 2019) As other airports ban curbside rideshare pickups, O'Hare has a solution of color-coded zones. CBSChicago.com. https://chicago.cbslocal.com/2019/10/29/ohare-color-coded-rideshare-pickups/. Accessed 20 Jan 2020
McPeak A (2016) Sharing tort liability in the new sharing economy. Conn L Rev 49:171–225
Means B, Seiner J (2016) Navigating the Uber economy. UC Davis L Rev 49:1511–1546
Moran M, Lasley P (2017) Legislating transportation network companies. Transp Res Record: J Transp Res Bd 2650:163–171
Morrison S, Whinston C (1988) Air safety, deregulation, and public policy. Brookings, DC, Rev 6:10–15
Mosendz P, Sender H (2014) Exclusive: Here's how long it takes to get an Uber in U.S. cities. Newsweek (December 14, 2012). http://www.newsweek.com/exclusiveheres-how-long-it-takes-get-uber-across-us-cities-289133. Accessed 20 Jan 2020
Nelson L (October 16 2019) Should Uber and Lyft drivers earn $30 per hour? Los Angeles will study a minimum wage. LA Times. https://www.latimes.com/california/story/2019-10-16/uber-lyft-drivers-pay-minimum-wage-los-angeles-ab5. Accessed 20 Jan 2020
Nelson L, Reyes E (August 20, 2015) Uber's Driver Screening practices fuel political debate on rider safety. LA Times. https://www.latimes.com/local/cityhall/la-me-uber-criminal-drivers-20150821-story.html. Accessed 20 Jan 2020
Office of the General Counsel, NLRB Case No. 13-CA-163062, at 3 (April 16, 2019). https://www.laborrelationsupdate.com/files/2019/05/NLRB-Uber-memo.pdf. Accessed 30 May 2020
Oxley D (November 18, 2019) Seattle begins effort to establish minimum wage for Uber, Lyft drivers. KOMO News. https://komonews.com/news/local/seattle-begins-effort-to-establish-minimum-wage-for-uber-lyft-drivers. Accessed 20 Jan 2020
Perritt H (2019) Don't burn the looms: regulation of Uber and other gig labor markets. SMU Sci Tech L Rev 22:51–149
Posen H (2015) Ridesharing in the sharing economy: Should regulators impose Uber regulations on Uber? Iowa L Rev 101:405–433
Posner R (1969) Natural monopoly and its regulation. Stanford L Rev 21:548–643
Prieger J (1998) Universal service and the telecommunications act of 1996. The fact after the act. Telecomm Pol'y 22:57–71
Reed R (2016) Disability rights in the age of Uber. Ga St U L Rev 33:517–551
Report of the New York City Taxi Medallion Task Force (2020). https://a860-gpp.nyc.gov/bitstream/gpp/24346/1/Taxi%20Medallion%20Task%20Force%20Report%20-%20January%202020.pdf. Accessed 20 Jan 2020

Richter W, Street W (July 30, 2018) Uber and Lyft are gaining even more market share over taxis and rentals. Business Insider. https://www.businessinsider.com/uber-lyft-are-gaining-even-more-market-share-over-taxis-and-rentals-2018-7. Accessed 20 Jan 2020
Robinson G (1988) The Titanic remembered: AT&T and the changing world of telecommunications. Yale J on Reg 5:517–545
Rodd S (January 4, 2020) Uber, Lyft, Postmates refuse to comply with California gig economy law. NPR. https://www.npr.org/2020/01/04/793142903/as-california-tries-to-make-contract-workers-employees-industries-push-back. Accessed 20 Jan 2020
Rogers B (2015) The social costs of Uber. U Chi L Rev Dialogue 82:85–102
Rose N (1992) Fear of flying? Economic analyses of airline safety. J Econ Persp 6:75–94
Schwartz B (1973) The economic regulation of business and industry: a Legislative history of U.S. regulatory agencies. Chelsea House, New York
Sharkey W (1982) The theory of natural monopoly. Cambridge, New York
Shrieber C (1975) The economic reasons for price and entry regulation of taxicabs. J Transport Econ Pol'y 9:268–279
Sidak J (2016) Is Uber unconstitutional? Criterion J Innov 1:179–195
Sidak J, Spulber D (1997) Deregulatory takings and the regulatory contract: The competitive transformation of network industries in the United States 4. Cambridge, New York
Silverstein S (October 16, 2014) These animated charts tell you everything about Uber prices in 21 cities. Business Insider. http://www.businessinsider.com/uber-vs-taxipricing-by-city-2014-10. Accessed 20 Jan 2020
Sloan S (2016) State regulation of rideshare companies. Cncl of State Govts. https://knowledgecenter.csg.org/kc/content/state-regulation-rideshare-companies. Accessed 20 Jan 2020
Speta J (2016) Southwest Airlines, MCI, and now Uber: lessons for managing competitive entry into taxi markets. Transp LJ 43:101–136
Speta J (2002) A common carrier approach to internet interconnection. Fed Comm LJ 54:225–279
Spicer Z, Eidelamn G, Zwick A (2018) Pattern of local policy disruption: regulatory responses to Uber in ten north merican cities. Rev Pol'y Res 36:146–167
Taxis v. Uber (August 10, 2015) Substitutes or complements. The economist. http://www.economist.com/blogs/graphicdetail/2015/08/taxis-v-uber. Accessed 20 Jan 2020
Thomas C (2018) Ride oversharing: privacy regulation within the gig economy. Cardozo Arts Ent LJ 36:247–276
Tierney M (May 26, 2015) Uber's final frontier: Airports. NY Times, at B1
US Const amend V
Williams D (1980) The economic reasons for price and entry regulation of taxicabs: a Comment. J. Transport Econ Pol'y 14:105–112

Cases

Dynamex Operations West v. Superior Court, 416 P.3d 1 (Cal. 2018)
Illinois Transp Ass'n v. City of Chicago, 839 F.3d 594 (7th Cir. 2016)
Joe Sanfelippo Cabs, Inc. v. City of Milwaukee, 839 F.3d 613 (7th Cir. 2016)
Philadelphia Taxi Ass'n v. Uber Technologies, Inc., 886 F.3d 332 (3d Cir. 2018)
United States v. Western Elec. Co., 552 F. Supp. 131 (D.D.C. 1982), aff'd mem., Maryland v. United States, 460 U.S. 1001 (1984)
Verizon Comm, Inc v. FCC, 535 U.S. 467, 524 (2002)

Chapter 4
Deregulation of Public Transportation Services: Can Uber Accomplish the Task?

Rosa M. Rojas Vértiz C.

Mexico City is the first and the largest city in the world, outside the USA, to approve an innovative regulation for Transport Network Companies. These regulations imposed an original approach by categorizing TNCs' services as private transportation services as opposed to the public transportation services provided by taxis. This has resulted in a different treatment to services rendered by TNCs. This chapter will look at the legislative and adjudicatory developments to examine if this different treatment is justified and will identify certain loopholes in this regulation which can lead to conclude that the purported differences are inexistent. The chapter also addresses the civil liability that Mexican law imposes on TNCs and the reasons why drivers have not been considered employees under Mexican labor law. Finally, this chapter discusses the benefits disruption by TNCs have caused in public transportation services and the challenges that this new service industry poses for regulators.

1 Background of Uber Services in Mexico

1.1 Background of Individual Public Transportation Services (Taxis)

Mexico is a Federal Republic formed by 32 local entities. Local entities have the authority to regulate transportation services.[1] As it can be cumbersome to address

[1] Article 124 of the Federal Constitution.

R. M. Rojas Vértiz C. (✉)
Instituto Tecnológico Autónomo de México (ITAM), Mexico City, Mexico
e-mail: rosa.rojasvertiz@itam.mx

Z. Ayata and I. Önay (eds.), *Global Perspectives on Legal Challenges Posed by Ridesharing Companies*,
https://doi.org/10.1007/978-981-15-7035-3_4

the regulations of all 32 entities, we will focus on the regulatory environment of Mexico City, and only to the extent deemed convenient, refer to the regulation of other local entities. Mexico City is the largest city of the country. Its population in 2015 consisted of 8,918,653 inhabitants.[2] If we include all people living in *Valle de Mexico*, this is, the conurbation around Mexico City, the population adds up to over 20,000,000 inhabitants.[3] According to the statistics published by the National Institute of Statistics and Geography (INEGI), by December 31, 2018, there were 134,375 public vehicles in Mexico City, excluding buses, motorcicles and official vehicles.[4]

Under Mexican law, taxis provide a public transportation service. Therefore, they need a concession to operate, which is granted by a local government. Taxis are regulated in Mexico City by the Law of Mobility,[5] which defines public transportation services as an activity by which the public administration must satisfy the transportation needs of passengers; on the understanding that the service has to be provided to the *general public* in a continuous, regular, permanent and uniform way. The law distinguishes public from private transportation services by specifying that the former is offered to the "general public." This is, to any person, and not only to persons belonging to a specific group, as could be the case of certain private transportation services, such as school buses or employer transportation services.

The Law of Mobility does not limit the number of taxis that may operate within the city. It provides that technical studies based on supply and demand should determine the necessity to award more concessions.[6] However, it limits the number of concessions that may be held by the same individual to boost competition.[7] Concession notices are rare. Generally, a person interested in a concession award must purchase it in the market at a price higher than the one stated in the law. Transfer of a concession award requires the previous authorization of the government.[8]

There is a big range of taxi services in Mexico. Some taxis may only pick up customers on the go; however, others—such as, radio taxis—are not allowed to do so and must have a base for operations. The latter may receive customers at the dispatch station or pick them up at the address specified by the customer. Taxis may also be hired for one or more days, or for a couple of hours.

Fares are determined by the local government.[9] They usually consist of a minimum fare plus an additional amount determined by time and distance. Fares are usually

[2]INEGI (2015).

[3]OECD (2015a, b).

[4]INEGI (2018).

[5]Ley de Movilidad de la Ciudad de México (Law of Mobility of Mexico City). The most recent amendment was published on April 23, 2020. Please be advised that all laws and regulations cited in this chapter were accessed and in effect on May 16, 2020. They may be changed afterward.

[6]Articles 99 and 100 of the Law of Mobility of Mexico City.

[7]Ibid., Article 95. Although it is not difficult to obtain concessions in the name of a relative or close friend.

[8]Ibid., Article 104.

[9]Ibid., Articles 163 and 164.

paid in cash. Taxis do not customarily accept credit cards. The minimum fare of taxis taken on the street is lower than the minimum fare charged by radio taxis. Taxis should have a taximeter that shows the fare that is being generated during the trip, and customers pay upon arrival of their destination. Exceptionally, taxis may have a fixed fare, such as taxis taken at the airport. The service rendered at the airport fixes a different fare for each area of the city. Customers pay the fixed fare to the company when they request the service.

The Law of Mobility and its regulations set forth many requirements to obtain and maintain a concession award.[10] Regulations typically address issues such as: the type and appearance of vehicles, requirements and tests drivers must approve, registration of the vehicle and the driver, periodical revisions, payment of fees and the issuance and exchange of licenses, as well as permits and other documents required to render the service. Vehicles are generally required to have four doors and a trunk, and they must be replaced when the model is ten years old.[11] Vehicles must also be labeled pursuant to the rules issued by the local government, and drivers must have a liability insurance policy.[12]

Concession holders are bound to provide the service continuously and permanently, and to train drivers.[13] Drivers must fix, on the window of the taxi, a large identification card with their picture, name, authorization and a phone number for complaints.[14]

To conclude, the strong regulations to which taxi services are subject to have put a burden on taxi owners and have hindered competition among them. Taxi drivers and owners are not allowed to increase or decrease their fare.[15] Moreover, completion with all regulatory issues is expensive. Regulations require the payment of many different types of fees. If we add to those payments, the cost of insurance policies and regular expenses, such as, gas and regular car maintenance services, then it is not surprising that concession holders do not invest resources in the maintenance of their vehicles or exchange their vehicles more regularly. They do not have an incentive to do so. Especially considering that as fares are controlled, consumers were captive and did not have other choices. In addition, the lack of transparency by authorities in the management of the fees collected also has a deterring effect on taxi drivers and concession holders. The authorities do not publish any statistics or information regarding public transportation services.

[10]Ibid., Articles 94, 110 and 118.

[11]This information was confirmed by Julio Romero, Manager of Sitio 197, and Juan O'Gorman Merino, businessman in public transportation services, on June 18, 2018.

[12]Article 90 of the Law of Mobility of Mexico City.

[13]Ibid., Article 110.

[14]Ibid., Article 82.

[15]Ibid., Article 115, subsection VIII.

1.2 TNCs and Private Transportation Services

In such an environment Transportation Network Companies (hereafter, "TNCs") started operations in Mexico.[16] Uber started operations in Mexico in 2013, and it was the first TNC to connect consumers with private drivers willing to provide transportation services. Uber's services became very popular quickly among a sector of the population. We conducted a small survey among 52 people in Mexico City in June 2018.[17] The results showed that only 2 out of the 53 persons that answered the survey had not used Uber services, but only 8 out of those 53 had used other TNCs.

Generally, people that answered the survey answered that they liked Uber more than taxis for the following reasons:

- Vehicles are of more recent models and are cleaner;
- Drivers are friendlier;
- Passengers feel more security: as soon as the driver accepts the ride, customers are provided with (a) the name and picture of the driver, and (b) the model and license plates of the vehicle. The possibility to track the route and asses the driver contributes to security.
- It is easier to find an Uber vehicle, and they arrive faster;
- Quality is standardized;
- A few mentioned as an advantage the possibility to pay with banking cards and receipt of an invoice.

Most people that answered had the opposite complaints about taxi services: vehicles are usually dirty, old and not in a good condition, drivers are not friendly, they feel more insecure in taxis, occasionally the taximeter may be altered, sometimes they are not easy to find or may deny the service. Only one person mentioned cost as a reason to prefer Uber. Few persons complained about the timing for Uber's arrival. The time showed in the application for arrival when the trip is accepted may increase twice or more in certain cases. Another complaint by Uber customers is that taxi drivers usually know the city much better and may take shorter and more convenient routes. In contrast, Uber drivers only follow the GPS, which sometimes may lead through longer routes.

---

[16]Transportation Network Companies are companies that connect passengers with drivers through an electronic platform that may be downloaded in a mobile phone. In Spanish, TNCs are called: Empresas de Redes de Transporte (ERT).

[17]The survey was conducted among 52 people from different ages and in different environments. The group was comprised of ladies from a sports club and the trainer, women lawyers that work in big firms and multinational companies in Mexico City, moms with kids in a middle class school in Mexico City, and students of a social sciences methodology course at UNAM (the biggest public university in Mexico). No random sample was made. People that answered the survey were available at the place and time the survey was being made, or chose to answer the survey when they received the link through a WhatsApp chat to which they belong.

The foregoing shows why Uber has extended its services nowadays to 56 cities within Mexico,[18] and has over 250,000 drivers in the country.[19]

2 Regulation of TNCs. The Categorization of Uber Services

To the same extent support in favor of Uber grew in Mexico, opposition from taxi drivers increased. They argued Uber was providing public transportation services without having a concession or complying with the regulations. They disputed an unfair competition and required the government to take action. However, Uber services continued to grow. Consumers were not discouraged by the actions of taxis drivers. The strong support consumers gave to Uber services forced the government to look for solutions to harmonize the conflicting interests of technology-based platforms with public transportation services.

One of the steps local governments took in finding a solution was to request an opinion from the Federal Competition Commission (hereafter, the "Commission").[20] The Commission issued its opinion on June 4, 2015.[21] By then, many TNCs were already operating in Mexico: Uber, Cabify, Easytaxi and Yaxi. Easytaxi is a Brazilian company that started operations in Mexico at the same time as Uber, but Easytaxi only connected consumers with registered taxi drivers, this is, with holders of a concession to offer *public* transportation services. Similarly, Yaxi was a Mexican company that started operating in 2014 and only connected consumers with taxi drivers.[22] For such reason, the Commission classified Easytaxi and Yaxi as *complementary platforms*. Cabify started operations in 2014. Both Uber and Cabify were classified by the Commission as *independent platforms*, because they connected consumers with drivers that were not registered nor had a concession and therefore offered *private* transportation services.

---

[18]Uber (2020). Aguascalientes, Campeche, Cancún, Celaya, Chihuahua, Ciudad de México, Ciudad Juárez, Ciudad Obregón, Ciudad Victoria, Colima, Cuautla, Cuernavaca, Culiacán, Dolores Hidalgo, Durango, Gomez Palacio, Guadalajara, Guanajuato, Guasave, Guaymas, Hermosillo, Irapuato, La Paz, León, Los Cabos, Los Mochis, Manzanillo, Mazatlán, Mérida, Mexicali, Monclova, Monterrey, Morelia, Navojoa, Nogales, Nuevo Vallarta, Piedras Negras, Puebla, Puerto Vallarta, Querétaro, Salamanca, Saltillo, San Juan Del Rio, San Luis Potosí, San Luis Rio Colorado, San Miguel de Allende, Tampico, Tehuacán, Tepic, Tijuana, Tlaxcala, Toluca, Torreón, Uruapan, Villahermosa y Zacatecas.

[19]Number of drivers obtained from the information Uber publishes in its web page: https://www.uber.com/es-MX/newsroom/todos-los-viajes-realizados-en-la-aplicacion-de-uber-seran-asegurados-por-axa-seguros-y-seguros-sura/.

[20]Comisión Federal de Competencia Económica.

[21]Opinion OPN-008-2015.

[22]Chavez (2018). Easytaxi purchased Yaxi in 2018. Accordingly, Easytaxi changed its name to EasyYaxi. Eventhough both companies started connecting consumers only with taxi drivers, they have extended their services to connect consumers also with drivers that offer private transportation services.

The Commission considered that the services provided by TNCs benefited the population in Mexico, as they filled a gap that existed with public transportation services. It argued that the services provided by TNCs granted: quality, security, transparency, a good price and certainty. The Commission asserted that, among other benefits, TNCs:

(a) allowed passengers to know before the beginning of the trip: (i) the amount they would pay, (ii) the name and identity of the driver, and (iii) the quality and license plate of the vehicle;
(b) provided an automatic route that would avert drivers from deviation to charge greater fees;
(c) implemented a dynamic fee that varied in accordance with supply and demand of transportation services in actual time, which increased supply during rush hours;
(d) allowed transparency on the fares to be charged; and
(e) allowed customers to assess drivers and the other way around.

The foregoing decreased uncertainty and provided transparency. The Commission also stated that electronic platforms reduced coordination problems, as drivers would know where to pick up customers avoiding over or under-supply of drivers in certain places. It insisted in the fact that the demand of TNCs' services came from certain segments of the population with access to electronic payments and intelligent devices.

The Commission concluded by recommending the authorities to *create a new category of service* with a flexible and transparent regulation. This regulation should privilege competition and a free market and should be limited to the main provisions required to protect the security of passengers, such as the obligation to hire liability insurance policies and to implement a system to review the background and abilities of drivers. Also, the regulation should avoid the following issues: control of fares, the requirement to register every vehicle or to limit the number of operating vehicles—matters that should be determined by supply and demand—, or the imposition of special license plates.

In Mexico City, public transportation services are generally paid in cash, which makes it difficult to have a clear accountability of the number of trips or passengers that used the service, and accordingly, to tax each service. That has led to charge fees on regulatory matters instead of taxing the services.

It was clear to the government that imposing on Uber the regulation applicable to taxis would very possibly have ended Uber's services, as many of the benefits it offered to consumers were possible because it was not paying so many fees and it did not have to comply with many regulations that could be deemed unnecessary. The end of Uber's services would have caused disappointment among the population. On the other hand, it was easier to tax the transportation services rendered by Uber drivers as the platform allowed a control of all trips and payments made by users.

Accordingly, the Mexico City government faced an important challenge in trying to reconcile the interests of consumers and taxi concession holders, and decided to start negotiations with TNCs. The results of these negotiations were published in the Official Gazette of Mexico City on July 15, 2015 (hereafter, "TNCs' Ruling"). The TNCs' Ruling created a registry for companies that operate digital platforms through which, either *taxi* services, or *private* transportation services with a driver may be hired in Mexico City.[23] It acknowledged benefits digital platforms provide to transportation services, such as: being friendlier with the environment by reducing contaminants as there is no need to drive around to look for passengers, more efficient management, and a higher standard of security for passengers because those systems allow passengers to identify the driver, the license plates and model of the vehicle in advance.

However, the fundamental issue of the TNCs' Ruling was to classify the services provided by Uber and Cabify as *private* transportation services with a driver hired through a digital platform. By doing that, such companies do not have to comply with all regulations applicable to taxis. They were provided with a different treatment. The ruling distinguished between the companies managing digital platforms that connect passengers with registered taxis from those that connect passengers with private drivers. The first ones only need to register and pay the corresponding fees. Upon registering, they must identify in the registry each taxi that is added to their platform. However, all regulations applicable to public transportation services must be fulfilled by the taxi drivers or taxi owners, who hold a concession and have acquired all those obligations with the authorities. Registry of the platform is only for control purposes.

In the case of platforms that connect passengers with private drivers, such as Uber and Cabify, the situation is different: drivers are not previously registered with the authority, they have not been awarded a concession, and they have not assumed obligations before the authorities. Therefore, the TNCs' Ruling imposes more obligations on the companies that operate with private drivers than on those that only operate with registered taxis. The TNCs' Ruling has been amended twice. The last reform was published on April 25, 2019. In the first place, to be registered, all companies that manage digital platforms for transportation services must: (a) be duly incorporated under Mexican law; (b) have a domicile in Mexico City and provide the name, address, phone numbers, e-mail and an ID of a legal representative in Mexico; (c) be registered with Mexican tax authorities and provide the Federal Tax Registry Number; and (d) provide the name and general information on the functioning of the application to be used. In addition to that, companies that connect passengers with private drivers must also comply with other obligations: pay a registration fee, register each vehicle and each driver that has been incorporated into the platform, pay annual fees for the registration of each vehicle, contribute with 1.5% of the fare paid per trip to a Fund for Taxis, Mobility and Pedestrians,[24] and commit to share with the regulatory authority information on the number of vehicles and drivers registered with the company, and on the origin, destiny, distance and length of trips made.[25]

[23]Registry of Companies that Operate or Administrate Applications and Digital Platforms for the Control, Programming and/or Geolocation in Fixed or Mobile Devices, through which persons may hire a private transportation service with a driver with Mexico City.

[24]Fondo para el Taxi, Movilidad y el Peatón.

[25]The last requirement was incorporated in the amended TNC's Ruling published on April 25. 2019.

The Fund for Taxis, Mobility and Pedestrians was created to achieve two targets. On the one hand, it would be equivalent to the tax local authorities have had difficulties in charging. On the other hand, it was an important tool to stop, or at least diminish, the strong opposition that Uber and Cabify were receiving from taxi drivers. The proposal was to have TNCs that do not work with taxis contribute to a fund that would improve services rendered by taxis. The plan worked: since the publication of the TNCs' Ruling, strikes and opposition to Uber or similar platforms declined within Mexico City.[26] Uber used to publish in its website contributions made to such a fund. Up to April 2020, Uber has contributed over $530,000,000.00 Pesos.[27] However, as the obligation to make contributions was included in the TNCs' Ruling and not in a law, such contributions were not deemed taxes. Moreover, contributions were made in a trust. Such scheme revealed lack of transparency in the control of the funds. On December 23, 2019, it was finally included in article 307 Bis of the Mexico City Tax Code as a tax contribution. The provision has been in effect since January 2020 and provides that the contribution will be decreased from 1.5 to 1% per trip when the driver is a woman or when the car is hybrid. Drivers of electric vehicles are exempt from the contribution. Amounts collected must be applied to (a) do research for the innovation and improvement of public transportation services; (b) improve infrastructure and technology in public transportation services, including taxis; (c) design policies and programs addressed to improve the security of pedestrians and bikers; and (c) enforce policies to improve mobility within the city.[28]

The TNCs' Ruling also imposed a couple of restrictions on the vehicles that may be used and on the payment method used by customers.[29] As aforesaid, each vehicle must be registered, but the TNCs' Ruling does not limit the number of cars that may render the service. The number is determined by supply and demand. All drivers must have a liability insurance policy and must have passed the training course authorized by the Ministry of Mobility. However, the governor that took office on December 2018 in Mexico City has hardened the rules applicable to TNCs. She has expressed an aim to equal the treatment of taxi drivers and TNCs. Customarily, annual revisions to vehicles registered with TNCs were done randomly.[30] The new TCNs' Ruling

[26]Pursuant to interviews with taxi drivers, they continue to think that Uber constitutes unfair competition, as they operate without a concession and do not have to comply with all the regulation applicable to public transportation services. But they have focused on trying to improve their services.

[27]In an interview held on February 14, 2018, at the offices of Uber located in Mexico City, an officer of the Company informed that from 2016 up to December 2017 Uber had contributed $212,649,549.00 pesos. In an email dated May 5, 2020, the officer informed Uber has contributed over $530,000,000.00 pesos, equivalent to over US$22'000,000.00 Dollars according to an exchange rate of 23.95 pesos per dollar. BANXICO (2020).

[28]Código Fiscal de la Ciudad de México. Taxes are paid directly to the Treasury of the Mexico City government, and therefore, contributions are no longer paid to a trust.

[29]In Mexico City, vehicles must have a minimum invoice price of at least $200,000.00 Pesos, equivalent to approximately US$8,361.20 Dollars, according to an exchange rate of 23.92 pesos per dollar published by Banco de Mexico.http://www.banxico.org.mx/portal-mercado-cambiario/ Accessed 2 May 2020.

[30]According to officers of Uber, in interview held on February 14, 2018, in the offices of Uber Mexico, vehicle revisions were made randomly. Uber, as many other companies in Mexico, may

provides that failure to make an annual revision of vehicles registered with TNCs would cause the company's registry to be canceled.[31]

The TNCs' Ruling also provides that private drivers must not accept payments in cash or wait in a dispatch station for passengers. These prohibitions appear to have been essential to the special treatment received by TNCs that operate with private drivers, as the original TNCs' Ruling stressed that the private transportation service with a driver is addressed to an *exclusive sector* of the population and is not granted to the general public. This exclusive sector of the population is characterized by having access to digital applications, being interested in paying with bank cards and receiving invoices for tax purposes. In other words, the service has been categorized as a specialized private service. This categorization distinguishes them from public transportation services and justifies the different treatment.

Upon publication of the original TNCs' Ruling in the Official Gazette of Mexico City on July 15, 2015, Uber published an article on its website entitled "Uber stays in Mexico City."[32] The article explained that Mexico City was the largest city in the world that had approved a vanguard regulation for digital platforms as Uber. It added that Mexico City was being a pioneer in acknowledging a law that accepts supply must correspond to demand and to the free choice of consumers. This regulation reduced the strong opposition by taxi drivers and allowed Uber to freely operate within the city; although we point out that Uber's vehicles do not have any sign or label in Mexico. It is not possible for third parties to identify Uber's vehicles.

On September 15, 2017, a new Regulation of the Law of Mobility was published in the Official Gazette of Mexico City (hereafter, the "Law of Mobility Regulation").[33] This regulation incorporated what was stated in the original TNCs' Ruling, and a little more. It continued to classify services provided by Uber and Cabify as private transportation services with a driver hired through a platform. It repeated that the companies managing the digital platforms should register with the Ministry of Mobility through the same process detailed in the TNCs' Ruling. However, it added the following: models of vehicles registered with the platform should not exceed ten years; vehicles should pass the annual revision process and should have an identity label determined by the Ministry of Mobility.[34]

After the regulation in Mexico City, many other states of Mexico published special regulations for TNCs. This section does not intend to present a comprehensive study of the features of all regulations implemented by the local states of Mexico, but only

challenge the regulation by filing an *amparo* suit against any law or legal provision that binds them to do anything they deem is against the Constitution. By filing the complaint, the company may cease to comply with the law until a final judgment is issued.

[31] Rule 9 of TNCs' Ruling published on April 25, 2019, in the Official Gazette of Mexico City.

[32] Uber (2015).

[33] Reglamento de la Ley de Movilidad del Distrito Federal (Law of Mobility Regulation), amended on April 24 and 26, 2019.

[34] Articles 58 and 59 of the Regulation of the Law of Mobility for the Federal District.

to discuss the main issues that have been incorporated. On May 2020, Uber is operating in 56 cities.[35] located within 27 states of the country.[36] Up to May 2020, 17 of such states have issued special regulations for TNCs.[37] The content of these regulations is similar to the regulations approved in Mexico City. All of them require TNCs to obtain an authorization to operate. For such purposes, they must register with the local authority. Many laws also require registration of each vehicle and each driver incorporated into the platform prior to payment of the corresponding fees. Generally, only companies incorporated under Mexican law with a legal representative, a domicile in the state where they are operating, and with a tax registry number may be suitable for registration. All drivers must have a liability insurance policy. Regulations also generally state that the transportation service may only be hired through the digital platforms; therefore, drivers must not pick up passengers on the street nor wait for them on dispatch stations. In addition, regulations generally restrict the rendering of the service to vehicles with the following features: recent models—not over 4–10 years old—with a minimum invoice value, regularly from 5 to 7 seats, air conditioning, air bags in front, radio and security belts for all passengers.

Certain states, such as Aguascalientes, Colima, Sonora, San Luis Potosí, Nayarit, Nuevo León and Coahuila, also require TNCs to contribute to the local authorities with 1.5% of the fees received per trip.[38] The same applies to Tijuana.[39] Aguascalientes, Quintana Roo, Sonora, Querétaro and San Luis Potosí forbid payments in cash.[40] Aguascalientes states that vehicles used by the platforms must have a special label.[41] Quintana Roo, Coahuila, Puebla and Sonora increased restrictions on the vehicles that may be used, as platforms may only register models of vehicles with

[35]See above note 18.

[36]Uber (2020). States of Mexico where Uber operates: Aguascalientes, Baja California, Baja California Sur, Campeche, Ciudad de México, Coahuila de Zaragoza, Colima, Chihuahua, Durango, Estado de México, Guanajuato, Jalisco, Michoacán, Morelos, Nayarit, Nuevo León, Puebla, Querétaro, Quintana Roo, San Luis Potosí, Sinaloa, Sonora, Tabasco, Tamaulipas, Tlaxcala, Yucatán y Zacatecas.

[37]Aguascalientes, Guanajuato, Querétaro, Jalisco, Yucatán, Sonora, Puebla, Coahuila, CDMX, San Luis Potosí, Tijuana (the State of Baja California authorizes cities to regulate transportation services), Estado de México, Colima, Nayarit, Nuevo León, Tamaulipas and Quintana Roo.

[38]Article 209 of Law of Mobility of Aguascalientes (hereafter "Law of Aguascalientes"), article 177 of the Sustentable Mobility Law of Colima, article 18 of the Regulation of services for the Transportation of by Electronic Means of Sonora (hereafter "the Law of Sonora"), article 101 of the Law of Transportation and Sustainable Mobility for the State of Coahuila de Zaragoza (hereafter "the Law of Coahuila"), article 370 of the Law of Mobility of Nayarit, article 106 of the Law of Sustainable Mobility and Accessibility for the state of Nuevo León (hereafter "the Law of Nuevo León") and article 71 Bis of the Public Transport Law of the State of San Luis Potosí (hereafter "the Law of San Luis Potosí").

[39]Article 293 of Regulation of the Public Transportation for the Municipality of Tijuana, state of Baja California (hereafter "the Law of Tijuana").

[40]Article 134 of the Law of Aguascalientes, Article 4 of the Law of Sonora, Article 158 Mobility Law of Quintana Roo (hereafter, "the Law of Quintana Roo"), article 105 Quinquies Decies of Law of Mobility for the Transport of Querétaro (hereafter "the Law of Querétaro") and article 71 Septies of the Law of San Luis Potosí.

[41]Articles 134, 135, 208–216 of the Law of Aguascalientes.

no more than 4 or 5 years.[42] Tijuana requires that pre-formulated standard contracts used by TNCs should be previously approved by the Bureau of Consumer Protection. Estado de México holds a similar position; as it also considers that the contracts used by TNCs are subject to the authority of the Bureau of Consumer Protection.[43]

Moreover, Uber claimed by the end of 2017 that the bill of the Transportation Law of Puebla violated the human right to privacy because it allowed authorities to have access to Uber's technology system in real time to surveil drivers and users.[44] However, the amendment made to the Transportation Law of Puebla in November 2017 only provides in article 92 Quarter, subsection VI, that TNCs must assist the authorities by allowing access to the technology of smart mobiles, GPS and technological platforms they use to render their services if required by the authorities in order to obtain the necessary information to fulfill their investigation role for security reasons. Such provisions, which may seem reasonable, could also be deemed necessary considering that on such state in September 2017, a young woman was apparently murdered by the driver of a TNC.[45] Very possibly for the same reason, the following subsection of the law provides that TNCs must verify that all trips terminate where they should end, and in the event of any inconsistency, they must immediately notify the authorities.[46] The same article provides that TNCs must enable mechanisms of alert in case of risk and the possibility to share their trip, including the name and picture of the driver and license plates of the vehicle.[47]

Uber has been challenging many of the restrictions that local laws have imposed on TNCs providing private transportation services. The outcome of many of the trials is unknown; however, it is fair to ask to what extent are states allowed to impose any type of restrictions on private transportation services? This question was posed to the Supreme Court of Mexico.

Under Mexican law, in addition to the claims that TNCs may file, a minority of the lawmakers in a legislature that approved a law may challenge portions of the approved law as unconstitutional.[48] The claim must be resolved by the Supreme Court of Justice. On July 21, 2016, a small group of lawmakers of the state of Yucatán filed a claim at the Supreme Court arguing that the amendments made to the Transportation Law of Yucatán violated the right of equality and free competition, freedom of commerce and freedom to choose an occupation. On May 23–25, 2017, the Supreme Court of Justice of Mexico discussed if the regulation applicable to

[42] Article 163 of the Law of Quintana Roo, article 100 of the Law of Coahuila, article 16 of the Law of Sonora and article 36 Bis of Law of Transport of the State of Puebla (hereafter "the Law of Puebla").

[43] Article 293 of the Law of Tijuana and article 7.880 Quarter of the Civil Code of Estado de México (hereafter "the Civil Code of Edomex").

[44] Uber (2017).

[45] Animal Político (2017). According to the stories that were published in the news, Mara Castilla took a cabify in the state of Puebla from a club to go home before the dawn of September 8, 2017, but she never got home.

[46] Article 92 Quater, subsections VI and VII of the Law of Puebla.

[47] The Uber application allows users to share their trip with a third party.

[48] This proceeding is called "Acción de Inconstitucionalidad."

TNCs in Yucatán violated the constitution.[49] The Supreme Court of Mexico has 11 justices, but two were absent. Therefore, the discussion took place only among nine justices.

The first issue the justices had to discuss was if the government of Yucatán had the authority to regulate the services rendered by TNCs. Although that issue was not posed by the lawsuit, it was a crucial issue to be determined due to the following: under the Mexican Federal Constitution, authorities not granted to the federal branches of government are granted to the local entities.[50] The federal congress has the authority to regulate commercial matters, but it does not have the authority to regulate transportation services. Accordingly, the legislative bodies of each of the 32 local entities have the authority to regulate transportation services but not commercial matters. Then, it was crucial to determine if the services regulated by the state of Yucatán were commercial services or transportation services. If they were only commercial services, the whole amendment would be void as the state of Yucatán did not have the authority to regulate commercial services. But if the regulation concerned transportation services, then Yucatán had the authority to issue such a regulation and it was possible to go to the second step: review whether the regulation was in agreement with the Federal Constitution or not.

Unfortunately, the discussion on this crucial issue was slight. Only one of the justices.[51] insisted on the fact that if TNCs only connect service providers with customers, then they are performing a commercial service and not a transportation service. All other justices considered that it was not a matter of *e-commerce*,[52] but a matter of transportation. They asserted that the government of Yucatán was creating a new category of transportation service, and some of them mentioned that it was not possible to segregate the platform from the way in which the transportation service was being rendered. On this important issue, eight out of nine justices concluded that the regulation was of transportation services, and therefore, the Government of Yucatán had the authority to regulate the issues subject-matter of the controversy.

The following argument posed by the claimants was that the regulations violated the right of equality and free competition because they imposed more restrictions to the operation of TNCs than to the operations of taxis, such as: forbidding payments in cash and imposing many special features in the vehicles. However, again eight out of nine justices considered that it was not possible to attend such argument because the services rendered by TNCs and taxis are different, and therefore, not comparable; so, it was not advisable to make such a comparison.

Afterward, the justices debated the provision that bans payments in cash and requests that all payments be made with bank cards. The claimants argued that it was a violation of freedom of commerce. On this topic five out of nine justices deemed such a measure unconstitutional. They considered that only the federal congress had authority to rule on the use of cash and financial services, and that such a measure

[49] Acción de Inconstitucionalidad 63/2016.

[50] See Footnote 1.

[51] Justice Norma Lucía Piña Hernández.

[52] Transcription (versiones taquigráficas) of the discussions held on May 23–25, 2017.

would only exclude from the TNCs market consumers with no access to banking services. However, none of the issues discussed gathered the eight votes required to void the provisions, so all of them had to be upheld at the end of the debate.

The account of the discussion would not be complete without adding that most of the justices frequently argued in favor of the benefits this new transportation service brings to the population. Although they acknowledged the difficulties it poses to regulators, many of them insisted that imposing unnecessary restrictions to the service would only discontinue a service that had filled a gap and favored consumers. One of the justices stressed that technology has turned the current public transportation system obsolete,[53] and many agreed that supply and demand, as well as, free competition and self-regulation would determine the requirements vehicles should have.

Although the portion of the law that was challenged could not be voided, this decision turned out to be very satisfactory to TNCs. Despite that it is not binding on other states, the decision has encouraged TNCs, like Uber, to challenge prohibitions for payments in cash and requirements that could be deemed as unnecessary. In fact, payments in cash are not prohibited in all states of Mexico, so Uber started in 2017 a campaign to advertise the possibility to pay in cash. In such case, Uber uses an alternative system to identify the user. Uber identifies the user through the user's Facebook account.[54] According to Uber's tutorials, the user may choose the payment form and the application will record the amount charged. Many stories in the newspapers report that many drivers of Uber have been challenging in courts the prohibition to receive cash.[55] Uber also informed that it has challenged that prohibition in several states of Mexico,[56] which nowadays must include Mexico City as the Law of Mobility Regulation and the TNCs' Ruling—both applicable in Mexico City—continue to prohibit TNCs to receive payments in cash.[57] Notwithstanding the foregoing, since approximately 2018 Uber advertises the possibility to pay in cash in Mexico City and provides the option to pay in cash in the mobile application. This means Uber may have obtained a judgment allowing payments in cash, or it has challenged the prohibition and obtained an injunction that allows payments in cash until a final judgment is issued.

Uber initially had refrained to challenge the prohibition to receive payments in cash as it appears to have been part of the negotiations that led to the issuance by the government of Mexico City of the TCNs' Ruling—that regulated TNCs as private transportation services with lighter obligations than those imposed on taxis and other persons providing public transportation services. However, the resolution of the Supreme Court of Justice of Mexico that was discussed, and a new resolution issued on October 16, 2018, where the Supreme Court of Justice of Mexico—with the vote of 8 justices—invalidated the prohibition to receive payments in cash stated

[53] Dissenting vote (voto particular y concurrente) of Justice Arturo Zaldívar Lelo de Larrea.

[54] Uber (2018).

[55] Fuentes (2017); Cerbón (2019).

[56] Interview with officers of Uber held on February 14, 2018, in the offices of Uber Mexico.

[57] In May 2020.

in the Mobility Law of the state of Colima,[58] encouraged Uber to challenge the prohibition to receive payments in cash. Uber's argument is that such prohibition limits the right of consumers to access technology by discriminating the sector of the population that does not have access to banking services.[59] Nonetheless, the possibility to receive payments in cash weakens one the main arguments that sustained the different treatment in the regulation of private transportation services with a driver and public transportation services because the regulation of the former has been distinguished from public transportation services arguing that they are specialized services for an exclusive sector of the population with access to bank cards; and therefore, it is not a service offered to the general public.

To the extent that the private transportation services offered by TNCs resemble more to public transportation services, or in other words, to the extent the differences between the two type of services are narrowed; then, the weak arguments that have sustained that Uber do not offers transportation services for the general public will fall. In such a situation, authorities will no longer be able to justify a different treatment to taxis. The central problem will be the same dilemma that has not been thoroughly resolved today: either the regulation applicable to TNCs is extended to taxis, or vice versa. If all taxis start using a digital platform to accept trips,[60] authorities may have no other choice but to apply the same regulations to both types of services. Hopefully, the target is deregulation. The system applied to TNCs that connect passengers with a private driver brings along more transparency and efficiency, facilitates control and the taxing of transportation services, and avoids unnecessary bureaucratic procedures and fees. But will those advantages remain if drivers use cash?

The question that remains open is if all these measures TNCs are taking to increase their market will contribute to the efficiency of these transportation systems, and eventually lead to a deregulation of taxis; or if they will only end up impairing the service.

3 Why Uber Drivers Have not Been Deemed Employees Under Mexican Law?

This section discusses the relationship between TNCs and drivers. Technology and digital media have changed traditional ways of doing business. Accordingly, features

---

[58]The Supreme Justice of Mexico resolved *Acción de Inconstitucionalidad 13/2017* on October 16, 2018. In such case, lawmakers of the legislative body of the state of Colima challenged certain provisions of the Law of Mobility of Colima that they deemed unconstitutional. The Supreme Court of Justice resolved that the local authorities could not forbid the use of cash in transportation services as it was a federal matter; and accordingly, the Supreme Court invalidated the legal provision that prohibited payments in cash.

[59]Uber (2018).

[60]Redondo (2018). According to several news sites, taxis are working in an app to compete with TNCs' services.

that typically belong to a labor relationship or to an independent professional service do not properly fit when dealing with technology. In the relationship held between a TNC and the owners of vehicles registered with the platform, many features that typically belong to a labor relationship or to the rendering of independent services appear, such as the following:

- Materials required to render the service are not provided by TNCs. Persons interested in rendering the service pays with their own means all expenses incurred, such as: price of the vehicle, gas, repairs, service maintenance, license plates, driver's license and other periodical fees or services that may be required by local authorities including the smart phone and the web service.
- TNCs do not impose a schedule to render the service.
- TNCs do not provide a place for performance of the service.
- The service must not necessarily be continuous. Although drivers may obtain advantages—some of them economic—if they connect more regularly, TNCs allow drivers to perform other economic activities. Drivers may work for different TNCs or may perform any other job. In other words, drivers may be employees in another company or have their own business and connect eventually to the platform to render a transportation service; or drivers may choose to allot most of their time to render transportation services under a TNC platform. Therefore, it is the drivers' choice what determines the amount of time allotted to perform transportation services under a platform, and not an imposition by a TNC.
- The drivers' compensation is not a fixed amount but varies in accordance with the services rendered.

All such features are traditionally attributed to independent professional services; however, there are other features in the relationship that are usually linked to a labor relationship, such as:

- TNCs determine the way in which the transportation services will be rendered: the transportation services should only be hired and conducted through a platform that is managed and provided by TNCs to drivers.
- TNCs determine the payment method by users, and the payment method to drivers.
- TNCs determine the amount to be paid for the service; and consequently, the compensation the driver will receive.
- Except for payments in cash, TNCs generally collect the payment for the service and decide when and how to distribute the corresponding fees to drivers.
- TNCs set forth the criteria to select the vehicles and drivers and recruit the latter. Generally, TNCs substitute the authorities in the registration process of both: vehicles and drivers.
- TNCs concentrate the full names and contact information of drivers and users—the drivers' clients—, which is not shared among them.

Under Mexican law, labor law is a federal subject. Then, the federal congress is the legislative body with authority to regulate labor matters.[61] The federal congress issued the Federal Labor Law to regulate employees working in the private sector.[62] Federal courts specialized in labor matters have resolved that the name of the contract is not relevant to determine the nature of a labor relationship. In other words, the fact that a person enters into an independent professional services agreement is not enough to elude a labor relationship. According to these courts, there are many issues that must be considered. A *non-labor relationship* takes place: if the professional pays with its own means the materials required to render the services and has liberty to determine its schedule and the terms of the services. In contrast, a *labor relationship* generally takes place if: the person rendering the service is ordered how and when to provide the service, the means to develop the service are provided by the employer, and the rendering of the service is continuous, in the place and under the schedule specified by the employer in exchange for a monetary compensation.[63]

We will focus first on owners of a vehicle registered with a platform that are also drivers. Their situation does not properly fit in any of the foregoing categories because although they are not provided with the means to render the services and they may arrange their own schedule, the TNCs exercise some control over the terms of the services. TNCs may not determine "when" the service is rendered, but they do determine "how." On the other hand, drivers may not decide the amount to be charged for their services, and not even the payment method. Unless payments are made in cash, they do not collect the fare from users, but are compensated weekly by the TNC. Therefore, it is debatable whether persons that register their vehicles with a TNC platform and render transportation services may be deemed employees. However, an important factor to make a decision is the level of control exercised by the TNC over the driver.

The Federal Labor Law enhances "subordination" as an essential element of a labor relationship.[64] "Subordination" exists when a person is under the authority or control of another. Judicial precedents have also insisted that subordination is a requirement of a labor relationship under Mexican law.[65] Drivers that register their vehicle with a TNC platform to render transportation services are not subordinated to the TNC. The TNC does not exercise control or authority over them. It is possible to hold that they are independent service providers because it is entirely up to them to decide how many hours and how many days to render the service. It is true that TNCs set forth the conditions for the rendering of the service, but that may also be true of any professional who is hired by a client for a service. In other words, if the professional wants to keep the client, it may have to adjust to the clients' conditions.

[61] Articles 73, section X, and 123 of the Federal Constitution.

[62] Ley Federal del Trabajo.

[63] Tesis 2ª. /J.20/2005, with Registry number 178849; Tesis I.7o.T. J/25, with Registry number 172794; Tesis: I.9o.T. J/51, with Registry Number 172688; Tesis I.10.T.J./52, with Registry number 174925.

[64] Article 20 of the Federal Labor Law.

[65] Registro: 242682. RELACION LABORAL, CARACTERISTICAS DE LA.

In the case of drivers that register their vehicles with TNCs, they get to choose if they want to connect to the platform and render the services or not.

It is arguable if the outcome should remain the same in the event drivers only render services to one TNC. This is, when all their income derives from the services rendered under only one platform. Although it continues to be the sole decision of the driver, in this situation there is an additional economic argument that could tilt the balance to a labor relationship. However, subordination may have to be proved to a certain extent, as an economic dependency alone may not be enough to be construed as a labor relationship.

The situation may be different when drivers are not the owners of the vehicles. In this case, the relationship between the vehicle owner and the TNC is clearly not a labor one, as the vehicle owner is not rendering any service. However, the relationship between the vehicle owner and the driver could be deemed a labor relationship. Again, subordination may be the clue. The arrangement between the vehicle owner and the driver is crucial. If drivers have the liberty to choose how many hours to work and they even perform a different activity, then it would not be possible to speak of subordination. But to the extent: drivers are bound to deliver a fixed percentage or amount per day/week to the vehicle owner, drivers render their services exclusively to one vehicle owner, and all income drivers receive come from one vehicle owner, it may be considered that drivers are subordinated to such vehicle owner and that a labor relationship exists.

What remains to be discussed is the relationship between the driver that does not own the vehicle and the TNC. Generally, this is not a labor relationship because the driver is hired by the vehicle owner, and not by the TNC. Moreover, it is the vehicle owner who agrees with the driver the frequency of the services and the compensation the driver will receive. However, exceptionally, TNCs could be deemed subsidiary employers. According to article 13 of the Federal Labor Law, if the vehicle owner is condemned to indemnify the driver and the vehicle owner does not have sufficient means to fulfill such order, then fulfillment of the judgment may be requested from the TNCs. Also exceptionally, the TNC could be deemed an employer of the drivers if it is construed that both the vehicle owner and the driver were hired by the TNC to render services in the terms requested by the TNC and under the surveillance of the TNC to the extent the work to be performed is not specialized.[66]

Nonetheless, by conversations with 7 drivers from Uber in Mexico City,[67] it was confirmed that drivers like and use in their benefit the flexibility Uber grants to drivers. Four of these drivers said they are owners of the car they drive; they have a personal business other than the transportation services, and for that reason, they only connect to the Uber platform occasionally or for a couple of hours per day. Another driver said he also owns the car he drives, and he combines that service with being a student. Only one driver mentioned that he does not own the car, and that he works full time providing transportation services for a vehicle owner; although

[66] Article 15-A of the Federal Labor Law. Also see: Amador and Riquelme (2015).

[67] Conversations held between February and June 2018 with José Manuel, José Luis, Héctor, Gustavo, Carlos, Luis and Emanuel when using Uber for transportation.

he mentioned he works for two different platforms. Finally, the last driver, who was quite young, mentioned he owns the car he drives, and he does not have another job because he lives out of a pension he receives because he was declared with permanent disability due to a strong disease that forced him to leave the executive job he had previously. He cannot be seated for too many hours, and he likes Uber because he can increase his income by only sitting for a few hours.

The foregoing shows that the schemes offered by TNCs are suitable for many different types of persons, and that flexibility is a very important tool to be productive.

4 Why the General Disclaimer from Civil Liability Is not Enforceable Under Mexican Law?

This section discusses the relationship between the TNC and the consumer, as well as, the relationship between the driver and the consumer. We will start with the relationship between the TNC and the consumer.

TNCs have insisted that they do not render a transportation service, but only a service of intermediation. In other words, they argue that they only connect drivers with consumers. Naturally, they charge a fee for their services. Typically, they do some other things than just connecting the service provider with the consumer. They organize the whole transportation system. Among their duties are the following:

- TNCs determine the fare that will be charged for the service;
- TNCs collect the fare from the consumer, and then hand it over to the vehicle owner after retaining their corresponding fee and certain taxes and contributions—except in payments in cash;
- TNCs also determine the type of vehicles that may be used, as well as, the number of vehicles to be registered in the platform;
- TNCs design the selection process for drivers, accept or remove drivers from the platform;
- TNCs even offered to find drivers when a person had a spare vehicle that would like to incorporate into the platform[68];
- TNCs also develop and manage the application used for the transportation services, and have direct or indirect ownership rights over the application and related materials; and
- TNCs decide when to give promotions to the drivers or the customers and design the promotions to be available.

Then, it is at least debatable whether TNCs provide a transportation service or not. However, the purpose of this section is not to arrive to a unique conclusion, but rather to determine whether TNCs may incur in civil liability under Mexican law.

[68]Uber (2018), Uber (2020).

Under Mexican law, civil liability may be incurred due to a breach of contract, or tort. Civil liability is generally regulated in the civil codes. However, there are 32 civil codes in Mexico because each of the 32 states has authority to regulate civil matters. Civil law is not a federal subject, as opposed to commercial law. In addition, there is a federal civil code issued by the federal congress that is only applicable to the loopholes of the commercial code when dealing with commercial matters.[69] Therefore, to identify the civil code that will resolve the issue the first step is to determine whether the civil liability arises from a breach of contract or from a tort. If it arises from a breach of contract, it is necessary to determine if the contract is governed by commercial law or not.

Pursuant to the commercial code, there is an assumption that companies incorporated under Mexican business laws perform commercial acts in their ordinary course of business; and that such acts may be governed by Mexican commercial laws to the extent they are performed or have effects within the country. Moreover, incorporation under Mexican law is not required for commercial purposes.[70] Also commercial acts performed within the country by foreign companies or branches of foreign companies are governed by Mexican commercial laws.[71] TNCs perform commercial acts within the country. Even pretending that TNCs do not render transportation services, connecting service providers with customers and charging a fee for such service may be construed as a commercial service. The goal of TNCs is to render a good service and to obtain a revenue in return. Then, they may qualify as a service provider under the Federal Consumer Protection Law (hereafter the "Consumer Protection Law").[72]

One of the main purposes of the Consumer Protection Law is to protect the interests of consumers. Providers are bound by the law, and its provisions may not be waived.[73] Only providers that render financial services are excluded from the application of the law, as well as, labor matters and non-business professional services.[74] According to article 10, which was amended on January 2018, providers must not apply unfair commercial practices, or include abusive clauses in the rendering of their services. On January 2018, Chapter VIII Bis of the Consumer Protection Law—concerning rights of consumers in transactions made through electronic, optical media and any other technology—was amended.[75] According to article 76 Bis, providers must furnish consumers—before entering into the transaction—a domicile in Mexico, including telephone numbers and other contact information that may be convenient for filing complaints. In addition, the newly added article 76 Bis1 states that providers that offer goods or services through electronic, optical media or any other technology

[69] Article 2 of the Commercial Code (Código de Comercio).

[70] Ibid., Articles 3, 4 and 75.

[71] Articles 6, 12 and 13 of the Federal Civil Code (Código Civil Federal).

[72] According to article 2, subsection II, of the Consumer Protection Law, a Mexican or foreign company that customarily offers or renders services in Mexico is a "provider."

[73] Articles 1 and 6 of the Consumer Protection Law (Ley Federal de Protección al Consumidor).

[74] Ibid., Article 5.

[75] Ibid., Chapter VIII Bis.

must follow the rules established by the Ministry of Economy in NMX-COE-001-SCFI-2018, which is in effect since May 1, 2019.[76] This ruling imposes several obligations to providers of goods and services to consumers and is applicable to "intermediary providers".[77] Moreover, the Consumer Protection Law states that pre-formulated standard contracts to be valid must be in the Spanish language and must not impose disproportionate, unfair or abusive obligations on consumers.[78] According to article 90, clauses with the following features are not deemed valid:

(a) Clauses that allow the provider to unilaterally modify the contract, or to withdraw from its obligations;
(b) Clauses that release the provider from civil liability, excepting a default by the consumer;
(c) Clauses that transfer to a third party the provider's civil liability;
(d) Clauses that bind the consumer to waive the protections granted by the Consumer Protection Law or that submit the consumer to foreign courts.

Most TNCs have in their applications a pre-formulated standard contract that intends to regulate the legal relationship between the TNC and the consumer. These contracts are sometimes only drafted in the English language, which would render them invalid under Mexican law. When translated into Spanish, the translation is often not accurate, and they introduce legal issues that may not enforceable in Mexico. Most contracts: provide that the TNC in question does not render transportation services but only acts as an intermediary or agent, contain a general disclaimer from civil liability, are vague in the description of the TNC's obligations, allow TNCs to determine certain things unilaterally, and submit consumers to a different jurisdiction. Most of these features could be voided by a court under Mexican law.

As an example, Uber has a pre-formulated standard contract in the application used in Mexico, which is a translation to Spanish of an agreement that is governed by Dutch law. The party entering the contract with the Mexican customer is Uber B.V., a Dutch company. The contract states that it must be construed pursuant to Dutch law, and that any controversy arising therefrom must be solved through mediation or arbitration in Amsterdam. This contract breaches many of the rules established by the Consumer Protection Law and by the NMX-COE-001-SCFI-2018, so it could be rendered invalid if a customer challenges its clauses in Mexico. Clauses of the Uber's contract are clearly addressed to avoid liability in Mexico: they provide in capital letters that the user acknowledges that Uber is not providing transportation services, Uber does not guarantee the quality, suitability, security or ability of the

---

[76] Normas Oficiales Mexicanas, also called NOMs, are binding technical rules that have been issued under article 40 of the Federal Law on Metrology and Standardization (Ley Federal sobre Metrología y Normalización). Such law which will be replaced by the Quality Infrastructure Law as from August 30, 2020.

[77] The NMX-COE-001-SCFI-2018 defines "intermediary providers" as a person that operates an information system which connects third party providers with consumers for a commercial transaction or service, on the understanding that the system may facilitate payment or the performance of the service.

[78] Article 85 of the Consumer Protection Law.

drivers and the user accepts all risks arising from the services and agrees to indemnify Uber. Moreover, the contract says that Uber's liability will in no event exceed 500 euros. On July 2018, the Bureau of Consumer Protection imposed a fine on Uber and other TNCs for including abusive clauses in their contracts and for using misleading advertising. However, although amendments have been made to the Uber contract afterward, many breaches to the applicable law remain, including the fact that Mexican consumers continue to contract with a Dutch company and must submit to Dutch law and to an arbitration in Amsterdam.

Uber is rendering services in Mexico and collecting many revenues from doing so. According to Uber's figures, in four years, it has contributed to the government approximately US$20'000,000.00 dollars, which is equivalent to only 1.5% of the fare charged per trip.[79] Then, if to operate in Mexico Uber had to incorporate a Mexican company that pays taxes in Mexico and is registered as a TNC with the authorities, why do consumers must contract with a Dutch company? It appears that the fine imposed on Uber and other TNCs was too low to encourage such service providers to adjust their contracts to the law. Stronger measures must be taken by Mexican authorities to force these companies to delete abusive clauses.

Moreover, to make it clear that the Consumer Protection Law applies to TNCs and their pre-formulated standard contracts, on October 24, 2017, a senator presented a bill to add a chapter to the Consumer Protection Law with the following purposes:[80]

(a) To expressly authorize the Bureau of Consumer Protection to review the pre-formulated standard contracts used by TNCs to verify they have no abusive clauses. Also, to register such contracts with the Bureau and to make sure their terms are subject to Mexican law and Mexican courts;
(b) To expressly provide that TNCs must guarantee the suitability, security and ability of drivers, and are responsible jointly with the drivers for any tort that may be caused; and
(c) To request registration of TNCs and their drivers with the Bureau of Consumer Protection.

Even if such bill is not approved, the services that TNCs render fit within the authority of the Bureau of Consumer Protection, who may sue these companies to invalidate abusive clauses in their contracts. Conclusively, the pre-formulated standard contracts TNCs contain in their applications will not be useful to avoid civil liability when it can be fairly attributed to them. But when can it be fairly attributed to them? To answer this question, we will switch to the relationship between the driver and the consumer.

The relationship between the driver and the consumer is clearly a transportation service. Under Mexican law, transportation agreements do not have to be in writing. So, every time drivers take persons to their chosen destination, a transportation agreement takes place. Transportation agreements may be governed by commercial law if

[79] See above note 28.

[80] Senator José de Jesús Santana García. https://www.senado.gob.mx/64/gaceta_del_senado/documento/76375. Accessed 14 May 2020. However, up to May 14, 2020, the bill has not been approved.

they are performed by a company.[81] If they are performed by an individual, the individual rather renders a professional service. Non-business transportation agreements are governed by a civil code. Generally, the civil code of the state where the service was rendered will be applicable. Each civil code has conflicts of law rules to help determine the applicable code when the service has contact with the laws of more than one state. Anyhow, the provisions relating to civil liability are very similar in all civil codes of Mexico. For purposes of this study, we will focus on the regulation of the Civil Code for Mexico City.

Civil liability arising from the rendering of a transportation service may also derive from a breach of contract or from a tort. Civil liability arising under a breach of contract may be regulated by the parties.[82] However, this does not happen when a consumer hires the transportation service through a TNC because the agreement TNCs have in the applications pretend to regulate the services provided by TNCs to consumers, not the transportation service provided by the driver. There is no written agreement between the driver and the consumer; so in the absence of a special clause, provisions from the civil code apply.

Drivers that breach a transportation agreement incur in civil liability; and therefore, they are liable to indemnify the user for any damage and future loss the breach may have caused. However, if the driver is not the owner of the vehicle, the vehicle owner may be jointly liable with the driver.[83] Neither the driver nor the vehicle owner are liable if the breach was caused by an act of God or *force majeure*.[84]

As aforesaid, torts may also cause civil liability. Under Mexican law, civil liability arising from torts is generally classified in two main items:

(a) *Personal liability:* is based on fault or negligence of the wrongdoer, who must have caused a damage to a third party[85]; or
(b) *Impersonal liability or liability based on dangerous devices:* does not require fault or negligence, but may only take place if the damage was caused by the use of a dangerous device.[86] Motor vehicles are deemed dangerous devices; then, the driver may be liable even if no fault is involved except when it is proved that the damage was caused by the unjustifiable negligence of the victim.[87]

If the driver commits a tort, in most cases, both the driver and the vehicle owner will be jointly liable for the damages and loss of profit caused to the injured party.[88]The

[81] Articles 3, subsection I, and 75, subsection VIII, of the Commercial Code.

[82] Article 2,117 of the Civil Code for Mexico City.

[83] Articles 2,647, 2,650 and 2,654 of the Civil Code for Mexico City provide that the carrier is responsible to pay damages and loss of profit if drivers cannot pay. The articles may assume a labor relationship.

[84] Article 2,111 of the Civil Code for Mexico City.

[85] Article 1,910 of the Civil Code for Mexico City.

[86] Devices or substances that are dangerous in themselves, due to the velocity they may reach, explosive nature or similar causes. Article 1,913 of the Civil Code for Mexico City.

[87] Article 1,913 of the Civil Code for Mexico City.

[88] Articles 1,917, 1,924, 1,928, 1,935 of the Civil Code for Mexico City regulate civil liability arising from tort. Article 1,917 provides that persons that have jointly caused a damage are jointly liable.

law may extend such responsibility to the owner of the vehicle if the latter may be attributed any fault, such as: not having an insurance policy or not having checked the background of the driver.[89] The owner of the vehicle will also be liable if the driver is deemed an employee.[90]

The statute of limitations to claim civil liability from a transportation service expires in six months as from the date the damage was caused.[91]

What about TNCs? Can they also be held liable under Mexican law? It is debatable whether TNCs may be liable for a breach of contract, as it may be argued that TNCs have entered into no transportation agreement with the passenger. However, they may certainly be held liable for having implemented abusive commercial practices toward consumers and for breach of the Consumer Protection Law provisions; and they may also be held liable for torts in the event a fault may be attributed to them. Article 1,917 of the civil code provides that persons that have jointly caused a harm are jointly liable to the injured party. Accordingly, TNCs cannot elude liability for the bad selection of drivers or for not having enough controls, among many other things. This has been acknowledged in judicial precedents issued by the First Chamber of the Supreme Court when dealing with medical negligence: rights that may affect public interest may not be waived, and a disclaimer in an agreement will not release the wrongdoer from negligence or fault.[92]

In addition to the foregoing, many laws issued by the local entities of Mexico to regulate transportation services hired through a TNC within its jurisdiction have expressly stated that TNCs are liable in case of tort. Such is the case of the Law of Mobility of Quintana Roo, the Law of Sustainable Mobility and Transportation for Baja California and the Civil Code of Estado de México, which impose on TNCs a subsidiary liability for any tort incurred by the driver.[93] Other laws, such as the laws of Sonora, Coahuila, Yucatán, Jalisco, Querétaro, San Luis Potosí and Tijuana, impose on TNCs a *joint liability* for any tort incurred by the driver.[94]

It may be argued that the vehicle owner contributed to the damage by providing the vehicle to a negligent driver. The remaining 3 articles presume a labor relationship.

[89] For example: it the driver is under 18 years old or has a disability for driving a vehicle.

[90] Articles 1,911, 1,924, 1,936 and 2,647 of the Civil Code for Mexico City.

[91] Article 2,657 of the Civil Code for Mexico City.

[92] First Chamber of the Supreme Court of Justice of Mexico, Tesis: 1a. CCXXXVI/2014 (10a.), Registry: 2006738, DAÑOS POR NEGLIGENCIA. SI SE OCASIONAN, NO PUEDEN TENERSE POR ACEPTADOS CON BASE EN UN CONTRATO DE PRESTACIÓN DE SERVICIOS.

[93] Article 156 of the Law of Quintana Roo, article 214 of the Law of Sustainable Mobility and Transportation for Baja California and article 7.880 Ter of the Civil Code of Edomex.

[94] Article 43 of the Law of Sonora, article 291 of the Law of Tijuana, article 83 Ter of Law of Mobility and Transport of Jalisco, articles 38 and 105 Undecies of the Law of Querétaro and article 71 Sexties of the Law of San Luis Potosí. Article 101 of the Law of Coahuila imposes on NTCs the obligation to contract an insurance policy to cover jointly with the driver any damages that may be caused by the driver. Articles 104 of the Law of Nuevo León, 36 Sexties of the Transportation Law of Yucatán and 36 Sexties of the Transportation Law of Tamaulipas provide TNCs will be liable if the driver does not have an insurance policy.

Apparently, Uber has understood the foregoing well, as by the end of 2017 it announced a full coverage insurance policy.[95] The insurance policy taken out by Uber covers drivers, passengers and third parties only for as long as the driver is connected to Uber's application. In other words: drivers and third parties will be covered only when the driver is rendering transportation services using Uber's application, and passengers will be covered from the moment they enter the vehicle until they get out. The insurance policy taken out by Uber covers civil liability for injuries, medical expenses, accidental death, total and permanent disability. It is also a contingent policy for theft and material damage with coverage in excess of the policy held by the driver. Drivers must additionally have an insurance policy that will cover them when they are not connected to the application. According to the announcement, no deduction is applicable for civil liability, and a deduction of 10% of the commercial value of the vehicle is applicable on the coverage for material damage and theft. This policy started operating on October 2017 in Mexico City and in the state of Mexico and should have been extended gradually to all other cities during 2018.

Likewise, Uber has informed on its website that it has implemented several controls to incorporate drivers into the platform, such as the following[96]:

- In addition to reviewing the driver's documentation (the driver's ID and license) and the vehicle's documents, it requires a lack of criminal record in Mexico and makes a no criminal check in six states of the USA (California, Texas, Illinois, Florida, Nuevo México and Arizona);
- Through a third party performs psychometric exams to the drivers, as well as, aleatory psychological and toxicology exams;
- Check of driving records;
- Aleatory periodical interviews.

Uber informs that it has implemented additional security tools for passengers, such as:

- To see the first name and picture of the driver in the application, as well as the model and license plates of the vehicle;
- The possibility to share the trip with up to five people;
- Assessment of the driver. The passenger may evaluate the driver with 1–5 stars. If the passenger grants only one star to the driver, the passenger will no longer be connected with such a driver;
- A chat to contact the driver upon acceptance of the trip (this feature is to avoid sharing telephone numbers);
- Panic button to call the authorities during an emergency;
- Follow up of the whole trip through GPS to detect any unusual stop.

Uber has also instrumented security tools for the drivers, such as:

---

[95] Uber (2020).
Uber (2017).

[96] Uber (2020). https://www.uber.com/mx/es/ride/safety/ Accessed 16 May 2020.
Uber (2018).

- The personal information of the driver cannot be accessed by the passenger, except for the first name and the driver's picture;
- The driver may also assess the passenger with the same star system implemented for passengers;
- The identity of passengers that want to pay in cash is verified through the passenger's Facebook profile.

5 Conclusions

TNCs have disrupted public transportation services in Mexico. They have imposed a different way to render transportation services, and consumers have welcomed innovation. This disruption created awareness of the general dissatisfaction that existed with individual public transportation (taxis). Before Uber, taxis were the best choice to move from one place to another, although also being the more expensive one. Consumers that used taxis did not have a different choice because all taxis are controlled by the government. As they render a public service, the government sets forth: the fares, the types of vehicles, and the requirements drivers must comply with, among many other things. There was very little space for competition as all taxi companies had to comply with the same requirements. In addition, over regulation increased expenses and reduced revenues, which created little incentive for innovation and investment.

TNCs have changed the foregoing. They entered the market with the opposite condition: self-regulation and a desire for innovation. Consumers immediately compared the services and showed open preferences for TNCs. Naturally, taxi drivers argued unfair competition. The government was forced to issue a minimum regulation for TNCs. Regulation should basically ensure registration for control purposes, and, to some extent, consumer protection.

Conclusively, TNCs have brought several benefits. Among them, we can mention the following: reduced costs and at the same time reduced prices for consumers, they are friendlier with the environment by reducing contaminants, vehicles are generally in better shape and more recent models are used, they help customers feel more comfortable because they know in advance who is picking them up and receive an approximate cost for the service, customers may follow the route in the GPS, may evaluate the driver, share the trip with third parties, receive invoices, have the possibility to pay with cards, and have a registry of all trips made.

TNCs have also improved self-employment, pushed taxi drivers to improve their services and contributed to progressively shift transportation services to formal economy. In Mexico, public transportation services have generally been paid in cash. Most taxi drivers would not accept a payment method other than cash. However, since Uber started operating in the Mexican market, it required all persons that wished to render the transportation service to have a Tax Registry Number. It forced drivers to use an electronic system to report payments, to account for every peso received and to pay all applicable taxes for the services rendered. TNCs pay federal and local taxes and contributions as any other Mexican company. Persons rendering the transportation service must pay income tax and value added tax. An invoice is issued in favor of the customer every time a trip is completed. In order to simplify accounting and tax filings to drivers and vehicle owners, Mexican tax authorities have regulated a special regime, under which TNCs may withhold monthly 2–8% for income tax payment and 8% for value added tax payments out of the earnings received for the transportation services. Drivers that submit to such scheme do not have to do monthly filings with tax authorities and must only file their annual tax return.[97]

Nonetheless, there are issues that require improvement. Uber has not distinguished itself for punctuality. The application usually provides that the driver will arrive in 4 minutes, but very frequently drivers arrive very much behind the time scheduled. Also, they are not expected to wait for customers. If customers are not ready upon arrival, they are free to accept another trip and move right away. In contrast, radio taxis usually arrive ahead of time and wait for customers for as long as required. Moreover, although radio taxis may usually be a little more expensive than Uber services, all types of taxis can also be sometimes cheaper—and not necessarily during rush hours. Difference in cost has narrowed. Uber carries a fare that is called "dynamic," which takes place in rush hours. When the dynamic fare takes place, the cost of the trip may double or even go higher.[98] This works as an incentive to attract more drivers to the areas that require more services and avoids to run out of vehicles. However, in such cases, the fare shown at the beginning of the trip does not reflect the final price. Another complaint by Uber customers is that taxi drivers usually know the city much better and may take shorter and more convenient routes. In contrast, Uber drivers only follow the GPS, which may sometimes lead to longer routes being taken.

Services by TNCs have grown dramatically in Mexico. In only six years, Uber managed to operate in 56 cities and has over 250,000 drivers in the country. However, growth has carried a couple of problems. Taxis have learned the lesson. Nowadays, many taxi drivers: accept credit card payments, issue invoices, carry a GPS, may be hired through an electronic platform, have seat belts for all passengers, and some of them have changed their vehicle to a more recent model and care to show a cleaner vehicle. In other words, TNCs have awaken competition. But competition does not only takes place with certain taxi services, competition among Uber and other TNC's—especially when the Chinese Didi entered the market—has caused TNCs to lower fees charged to users, leaving many drivers with a very low compensation. Such situation has discouraged many of the features that originally provided an exceptional service: affected drivers have less interest in improving their vehicles, and as they need to work more hours to obtain a reasonable compensation they are less concerned with the satisfaction of the customer. Social media show frequent complaints from customers and even from drivers claiming standards for hiring drivers has lowered, and that less attention is given to the quality of the service. It appears that the hustle to win the race and to increase earnings could be reducing the

[97]Rule 3.11.11 of *Miscelánea Fiscal para 2020*.

[98]Uber (2020).

quality standards that people praised at the beginning. Careful consideration should be given to such complaints.

Moreover, the interest Uber has shown to accept payments in cash will only continue to narrow the purported differences between public and private transportation services. The main reason to distinguish both type of services is that private services are not offered to the *general public*, but only to persons belonging to a certain group. For that reason, they do not need a concession award to operate and their regulation is lighter. Is that really the case of TNCs? They have made it clear that they want to reach all sectors of the population. The new phenomena TNCs have introduced will require a reformulation of traditional concepts. Should transportation services offered to the *general public* only be satisfied by the public administration through an award of a concession—as it currently takes place—, or should the role of the public administration limit itself to regulate the minimum conditions the services should meet and to assure that private parties that offer the services comply with consumer protection? Disruption by TNCs forces an adjustment on the principles applicable to transportation systems offered to the general public. Facts show that TNCs have arrived to stay. Accordingly, modern regulation should eliminate unnecessary requirements and focus on ensuring the continuity of the service, minimum standards, consumer protection and accountability.

References

Animal Político (2017) Confirman asesinato de Mara Castilla, la joven que desapareció tras tomar un taxi Cabify. Animal Político. https://www.animalpolitico.com/2017/09/mara-castilla-muerte-chofer-cabify/. Accessed 8 Jun 2018

Amador A, Riquelme E (2015) Uber: patrón o socio ¿Le hablo de Tú o de Usted? Revista de la Barra Mexicana, Colegio de Abogados 96:27–30

BANXICO (2020) Sistema de Información Económica. http://www.banxico.org.mx/portal-mercado-cambiario/. Accessed 15 May 2020

Cerbón M (2019) Gana Chofer de uber primer amparo contra ley de movilidad. https://newsweekespanol.com/2018/06/gana-chofer-de-uber-primer-amparo-contra-ley-de-movilidad/. Accessed 2 May 2020

Chavez G (2018) Easy Compra Yaxi para competir en movilidad. Expansion. https://expansion.mx/tecnologia/2018/03/13/easytaxi-compra-yaxi-para-competir-en-movilidad. Accessed 8 Jun 2018

Fuentes V (2017) Impugnan choferes app por efectivo. Reforma. https://www.reforma.com/aplicaciones/articulo/default.aspx?id=1254276&v=1. Accessed 16 Jun 2018

INEGI (2015) Información Poblacional Distrito Federal. Mexico City. Mexico. http://cuentame.inegi.org.mx/monografias/informacion/df/poblacion/. Accessed 4 Jun 2018

OECD (2015a) Estudios Territoriales de la OCDE. Mexico City. Mexico. https://www.gob.mx/cms/uploads/attachment/file/56213/valle-de-mexico-OCDE.pdf. Accessed 4 Jun 201

OECD (2015b) OECD Territorial Reviews: Valle de México, Mexico. http://dx.doi.org/10.1787/9789264245174-en. Accessed 4 Jun 2018

Redondo M (2018) La revancha de los taxistas mexicanos contra Uber: operarán a través de una app. Hipertextual. https://hipertextual.com/2018/02/taxistas-mexico-nekso-app. Accessed 26 June 2018

SCT (2007) Análisis de los sistemas de transporte. México. https://www.imt.mx/archivos/Publicaciones/PublicacionTecnica/pt307.pdf

SEMOVI (2019) Plan estratético de movilidad de la ciudad de México. Una ciudad, un sistema. Mexico City. México. https://semovi.cdmx.gob.mx/storage/app/media/uploaded-files/plan-estrategico-de-movilidad-2019.pdf
Senado de la República (2020) Gaceta del Senado. México. https://www.senado.gob.mx/64/gaceta_del_senado/documento/76375
Uber (2015) Uber se queda en la Ciudad de México. https://newsroom.uber.com/mexico/uber-se-queda-en-la-ciudad-de-mexico/. Accessed 7 Jun 2018
Uber (2017) La nueva regulación para ERT en Puebla viola el derecho humano a la privacidad y limita el acceso a la tecnología de los poblanos. https://www.uber.com/es-MX/newsroom/regulacion-puebla/. Accessed 15 Jun 2018
Uber (2017) Todos los viajes realizados en la aplicación de Uber serán asegurados por AXA Seguros y Seguros Sura. https://www.uber.com/es-MX/newsroom/todos-los-viajes-realizados-en-la-aplicacion-de-uber-seran-asegurados-por-axa-seguros-y-seguros-sura/. Accessed 16 Jun 2018
Uber (2018) Conoce más información sobre el pago de Uber. https://www.uber.com/es-MX/blog/uber-pago-en-efectivo-mexico/. Accessed 16 Jun 2018
Uber (2018) Uber refuerza filtros para socios conductores, luego de la eliminación de la Carta de No Antecedentes Penales en Nuevo León. https://www.uber.com/es-MX/newsroom/seguridad-nuevo-leon/. Accessed 20 Jun 2018
Uber (2018) Administración Uber. http://www.administracionuber.com.mx/conduce-uber.php Accessed 15 June, 2018; Uber (2020) Choferes para Uber. http://www.choferes-uber.com Accessed 26 May 2020
Uber (2020) Requisitos para conducir o ser socio. https://www.uber.com/es-MX/drive/requirements/. Accessed 22 Jun 2018
Uber (2020) Todos los viajes con Uber asegurados en México. https://www.uber.com/es-MX/drive/insurance/. Accessed 22 Jun 2018 and 2 May 2020
Uber (2020) Usa Uber en ciudades en todo el mundo. https://www.uber.com/global/es/cities/. Accessed 2 May 2020
Uber (2020) ¿Que son las tarifas dinámicas? México. https://help.uber.com/es-MX/h/e9375d5e-917b-4bc5-8142-23b89a440eec. Accessed 2 May 2020

Applicable Mexican Laws and Regulations (all accessed as of May 14, 2020)

Acuerdo por el que se crea el Registro de Personas Morales que Operen, Utilicen y/o Administren Aplicaciones para el Control, Programación y/o Geolocalización en Dispositivos Fijos o Móviles, a través de las cuales los Particulares pueden Contratar el Servicio Público de Taxi en el Distrito Federal publicado en la Gaceta No. 133 Bis, 15 de Julio de 2015, Gaceta Oficial Distrito Federal
Acuerdo por el que se crea el Registro de Personas Morales que Operen y/o Administren Aplicaciones y Plataformas Informáticas para el Control, Programación y/o Geolocalización en Dispositivos Fijos o Móviles, a través de las cuales los Particulares pueden Contratar el Servicio Privado de Transporte con Chofer en el Distrito Federal publicado en la Gaceta No. 133 Bis, 15 de Julio de 2015, Gaceta Oficial Distrito Federal
Acuerdo que establece el procedimiento para obtener la Constancia de Registro y la Constancia de Registro Vehicular, por parte de las personas morales que operen, utilicen y/o administren aplicaciones y plataformas informáticas para el control, programación y/o geolocalización en dispositivos fijos o móviles, a través de las cuales, los usuarios pueden contratar el servicio de transporte de pasajeros privado especializado con chofer en la Ciudad de México publicado en la Gaceta No. 78, 25 de Abril de 2019, Gaceta Oficial de la Ciudad de México

Aviso por el que se establece el procedimiento para el trámite de validación vehicular de las unidades que prestan el servicio de transporte de pasajeros privado especializado con chofer, correspondiente al año 2019 publicado en la Gaceta No. 78, 25 de Abril de 2019, Gaceta Oficial de la Ciudad de México
Acuerdo por el que se Reforman y Adicionan Disposiciones del Acuerdo que Modifica el Diverso por el que se Crea el Registro de Personas Morales que Operen y/o Administren Aplicaciones y Plataformas Informáticas para el Control, Programación y/o Geolocalización en Dispositivos Fijos o Móviles, a través de las Cuales los Particulares Pueden Contratar el Servicio Privado de Transporte con Chofer en el Distrito Federal, publicado en la Gaceta Oficial de la Ciudad de México, el 12 de Agosto de 2016, publicado en la Gaceta No. 389 Bis, 17 de Agosto de 2018, Gaceta Oficial de la Ciudad de México
Código Civil del Estado de México
Código Civil de la Ciudad de México
Código de Comercio
Constitución Política de los Estados Unidos Mexicanos
Código Fiscal de la Ciudad de México
Iniciativa con Proyecto de Decreto por el que se adicionan diversas disposiciones de la Ley Federal de Protección al Consumidor en las transacciones efectuadas a través de personas morales que operan utilizan o administran aplicaciones informáticas para el control, programación y/o geolocalización en dispositivos fijos o móviles a través de las cuales los particulares contratan el servicio privado de transporte con chofer, presentada el 24 de Octubre de 2017 por el senador José de Jesús Santana García
Ley Federal de Metrología y Normalización
Ley Federal de Protección al Consumidor
Ley Federal del Trabajo
Ley de Movilidad de Aguascalientes
Ley de Movilidad de Ciudad de México
Ley de Movilidad de Nayarit
Ley de Movilidad de Quintana Roo
Ley de Movilidad Sustentable de Colima
Ley de Movilidad Sostenible y Accesibilidad para el Estado de Nuevo León
Ley de Movilidad Sostenible y Transporte de Baja California
Ley de Movilidad y Transporte del estado de Jalisco
Ley de Transporte del Estado de Puebla
Ley de Transporte de Tamaulipas
Ley de Transporte de Yucatán
Ley de Transporte Público del Estado de San Luis Potosí
Ley de Transporte y Movilidad Sustentable del Estado de Coahuila de Zaragoza
Norma Mexicana: NMX-COE-001-SCFI-2018. Comercio Electrónico – Disposiciones a las que se sujetarán aquellas personas que ofrezcan, comercialicen o vendan bienes, productos o servicios
Reglamento de la Ley de Movilidad para el Distrito Federal
Reglamento de Servicio de Transporte de personas por Medios Electrónicos del Estado de Sonora
Reglamento de Transporte Público para el Municipio de Tijuana, Baja California
Resolución Miscelánea Fiscal 2020 y sus Anexos

Relevant Judgements

Acción de Inconstitucionalidad 63/2016 (Suprema Corte de Justicia de la Nación)
Acción de Inconstitucionalidad 13/2017 (Suprema Corte de Justicia de la Nación)

INEGI (2018) Datos. Transporte. Parque Vehicular. Tabulados. Vehículos de Motor Registrados en Circulación del año 2018. https://www.inegi.org.mx/temas/vehiculos/default.html#. Accesed June 4, 2018.

Chapter 5
Uber in Brazil: Glory and Consequence

Paulo Doron R. de Araujo, Wanderley Fernandes, Maria Lucia Pádua Lima, and Paulo C. Goldschmidt

1 After the Glory, Come the Consequences

The disruption movement in Brazilian passenger transportation industry was led by Uber. Initially working on an alleged lack of regulation, Uber provoked local regulators in many cities around the country, resulting in different approaches, a lot of protests and some violent reactions from the traditional players (such as the taxi drivers). Courts intervened in most of the cases and considering the prevailing interpretation the conclusion was that federal general regulation was necessary according to Brazilian Constitution. So, in 2018 a federal law was passed (Federal Law n. 13.240, published in May 26, 2018). Although the new law has addressed the main issue, stating the legality of activities such as Uber, it let the local regulators to dispose of specific requirements and rules, resulting in a new round of negotiations, discussions and accommodation of interests in each Brazilian major city.

The struggle with local regulators has taken Uber to Brazilian Supreme Court. In May 2019, the country's highest Court has decided that although local governments

[1] ADPF 449, Tribunal Pleno, Rapporteur: Justice LUIZ FUX, available at: https://jurisprudencia.stf.jus.br/pages/search/sjur409361/false. Accessed Apr 2020.

P. D. R. de Araujo (✉) · W. Fernandes · M. L. P. Lima · P. C. Goldschmidt
Fundação Getulio Vargas (FGV), São Paulo, Brazil
e-mail: paulo.araujo@fgv.br

W. Fernandes
e-mail: wanderley@nascimentomourao.adv.br

M. L. P. Lima
e-mail: marialucia.padualima@fgv.br

P. C. Goldschmidt
e-mail: Paulo.Goldschmidt@fgv.br

Z. Ayata and I. Önay (eds.), *Global Perspectives on Legal Challenges Posed by Ridesharing Companies*,
https://doi.org/10.1007/978-981-15-7035-3_5

have authority to regulate Uber-like companies' activities in their territories, they cannot forbid their operations or implicitly ban their services.[1]

It was, indeed, a tough battle, but it paid off. Brazil became the second most important market for the ride-sharing company, where it has more than six hundred thousand assigned drivers, twenty-two million users and revenues close to US$1 billion in 2018, according to documents disclosed when the company was preparing for its initial public offer (IPO) on the New York Stock Exchange.[2] If Brazil is important for Uber, the city of São Paulo is the main reason. The city is one of the five metropolitan areas in the world that together represent 24% of Uber's ride-sharing gross bookings in 2018. After São Paulo, Uber is also present in more than one hundred Brazilian cities.

But as the song says, "Every battle has its glory and its consequence."[3] The first consequence is the creation of a new market. Although Uber is still the leader, other world giants as Lyft and Cabify came to claim their share aside with more than ten local Brazilian apps. The largest among them is 99, acquired by a Chinese group in 2018, supposedly for US$1 billion.[4]

Because of its immense and rapid growth, Uber also started playing important social roles. Transportation and delivery applications—such as Uber, 99, iFood and Rappi—became the largest "employer" in the country. Almost 4 million self-employed workers use platforms as a source of income. If they were combined on the same payroll, it would be 35 times longer than that of Correios (the Brazilian Post Office), the largest state-owned company in terms of number of employees, with 109 thousand employees.[5]

The consequence after that glory is that Uber is now a very frequent defendant before Brazilian labor courts. Only in the State of São Paulo, there were 178 ongoing labor suits against the ride-sharing company in 2019, according to a survey performed by a specialized Web site on the legal field.[6] The main subject under debate is whether Uber is considered an employer according to Brazilian Labor Law.

Another glory is that ride-sharing companies are transporting three times more people than taxi drivers in Brazil every day. A study conducted by researchers at Federal University of Rio de Janeiro revealed that applications like Uber, 99 and Cabify transport almost 750 thousand passengers a day in Rio against just over 233 thousand by taxis.[7]

The consequence in this case can be noted by the number of ongoing civil lawsuits against Uber in the State of São Paulo in 2019: 622. Almost 60% of these cases are about compensation for damages,[8] pointing out how important it is, in Brazil, to

[2]For more: McKenna (2019).

[3]HARPER, Ben. *Glory and Consequence*.

[4]Lunden (2018).

[5]Estadão Conteúdo (2019).

[6]Valente (2019).

[7]Magalhães (2019).

[8]Valente (Valente 2019).

define if Uber-like platforms are liable or not for damages experienced by passengers, drivers and third parties.

The purpose of this report is to offer an overview of how some of these subjects are currently developing in Brazil, considering specifically Uber and how its activities are being regulated in Brazilian territory by governmental authorities and courts. The study departs from the assumption that in Brazil, Uber does not own the vehicles used to transport people or goods on its platform. Cars and motorbikes belong to the drivers, who join Uber or Uber Eats after a quick and non-disclosed background check and who are ranked by users after each ride.

Considering the context and these assumptions, we will approach regulatory, labor and civil liability issues according to actual Brazilian state of art regarding platform economy regulation.[9]

2 The Regulatory Struggle and Its Outcome

As a federative republic, Brazil has three levels of regulatory powers: federal, state and municipal. The distribution of authority is determined by the Federal Constitution. Regulation of transportation is defined depending on the type of services, as for instance, aviation is a typical federal concern, and state roads are regulated by the state where they are located. Following this rational, taxi and individual terrestrial transportation is a municipal issue.

Individual or shared transportation are usually regulated by municipal authorities under licenses granted directly to individuals or companies authorized to provide services in a specifically determined area. The number of licenses is limited, what has created in some cities a real black market with benefits to companies that have close connections with driver unions.

Taxi services are deemed as public interest recognized by Brazilian authorities, despite its private character. Therefore, it is regulated nationally and locally. Federal laws provide a general framework that is detailed and regulated by Municipal law. This general treatment is provided by Federal Law n. 12.587/2012, stating that taxi services are submitted to municipal public rules in three aspects: (i) market entry, (ii) rates and (iii) quality.

Uber started its operation in Brazil in 2014, and, therefore, at that time, the company, as many innovative businesses, relied on a regulatory gap. The 2012 law was changed in 2018 exactly to regulate this new activity that brought an enormous controversy with taxi drivers as this category complained that there was unfair competition. Taxi drivers were subject to regulatory and taxation control, whereas Uber drivers were not subject to any bureaucracy, except the platform's own procedures.

---

[9]Authors thank DIREITO GV SP undergraduate students Marcella Penhalber, Mariana Trotta and Lucas Pinatti Marina for their valuable collaboration with the research necessary to the elaboration of this report.

On the federal level, Law n. 12.587/2012 requires that taxi drivers have to obtain a permit from municipal authorities. Municipalities must establish form and conditions under which taxi services must be provided and monitored. On the municipal level, taxis are regulated by local authorities, especially regarding the maximum value to be charged to passengers. In addition, local authorities must issue and enforce rules to ensure minimum standards of vehicle maintenance, safety and inspection of the meters and the drivers.

It is clear, thus, that taxi market in Brazil is highly regulated. Taxi drivers and companies organized to provide taxi services are not free to establish or to fix their fares by themselves and must be submitted to regular inspections conducted by public agents. Nevertheless, taxis are considered precarious in many locations, registering complaints about quality of the service, drivers' inappropriate behavior and high charges.

Uber first started in São Paulo and Rio de Janeiro in 2014. In 2019, the platform was offering services in more than one hundred Brazilian cities, not only focusing in passenger individual transportation, but also delivering goods under, for example, the Uber Eats application.

To fill the regulatory gap at the time, Uber argued to be a different animal from a traditional taxi provider because it would be only a platform providing peer-to-peer communication to bring together available private drivers and passengers willing to pay for a ride. They always argued that they did not provide transportation services, but a sort of brokering activity, putting together private drivers and passengers. Since there would be no legal prohibition on hitchhiking and this activity was not even regulated, Uber activities would be allowed and should not be state regulated by any means. Taxi drivers, on the other hand, have argued that Uber is nothing more than a form of unfair and dangerous competition as it is not subject to ordinary entry barriers and to the scrutiny of public agents.

Since taxi drivers' labor unions are politically influent, they have been putting local governments under pressure to ban Uber-like services or at least to restrict them by imposing permits, bureaucracy, and municipal taxes. Hence, judicial courts were triggered both by Uber and taxi representatives.

The Brazilian courts have then handed down injunctions favorable to Uber, allowing services to continue, even in places where local laws have been passed prohibiting this sort of activity. Mainly, these judicial decisions were based on the rule of article 21, paragraph XX, of the Federal Constitution, which establishes exclusive competence of the Union to create guidelines for urban development, including housing, basic sanitation and urban transportation. Thus, as long as there was a lack of federal law disciplining transportation services such as Uber, the activity should remain.

This scenario changed substantially in 2018 when Federal Law 13.640 dated as of March 26, 2018, introduced changes in the 2012 federal regulation to contemplate the new ride-sharing industry. The new law was very synthetic. Basically, it provided that individual and shared transportation is a local issue and it must be regulated by the Federal District (city of Brasilia) and municipal governments.

The law provided a definition of the new modality of services with the following language:

> Remunerated transportation of individual private passengers: remunerated transport services of passengers, not open to public, for individual or shared services called exclusively by users previously registered in applications or other platforms of web communication.

It sets forth the minimum requirements that should be followed by local regulation. Therefore, local laws should comply with the following guidelines:

1. activity should be subject to local taxation upon services revenues;
2. service providers must hire personal injury insurance policies for passengers and pay mandatory insurance for victims of accidents; and
3. drivers must be enrolled in the social security program.

In addition to these basic requirements, drivers must meet the following conditions:

1. they must have driver's licenses with the information that they perform remunerated activity of individual transportation;
2. cars must not have an age of usage above the limit determined by local regulation;
3. vehicles must be properly licensed; and
4. drivers must provide a clearing certificate of criminal practices.

The other important fact on federal level was the already referred Brazilian Supreme Court decision issued in May 2019, by which many local laws and regulations were considered unconstitutional on the grounds that instead of regulating locally, they implicitly banned or forbade Uber and similar services from operating in their respective territories. The country highest court ruled that although local regulators may have jurisdiction to impose duties and taxes to the ride-sharing companies, they do not have the authority to prevent Uber and its competitors from working.

Coming back to the local level, as mentioned above, Uber has been developing its activities in many Brazilian municipalities and the Supreme Court decision reinforced its position in all these places. It would be impossible, however, in the size of this report to review each local regulation. Since São Paulo is the biggest city in the country and a leading reference as a pioneer in regulatory initiatives, we will use it as a first illustration of what happened locally in Brazil, followed by examples from other cities.

Even before the federal regulation referred to above, the city of São Paulo, in 2016, started regulating the ride-sharing initiatives by requiring the enrollment of companies to legally provide these services. Local authorities created a specific category of service provider called Registered Transportation Technology Operator. It is interesting to note that the local regulator did not define the services as transportation, but operation of transport technology.

After federal regulation of 2018, the city of São Paulo issued detailed regulation on the activity, establishing requirements in a few broad categories:

1. local registration: car, driver and Registered Transportation Technology Operator must be legally registered in the city hall. Additionally, to the federal requirements mentioned above, drivers must be approved in driving training and also be committed to work only though registered applications and platforms;
2. conditions of cars: cars cannot be older than eight years and they must be inspected every year after one year of manufacturing.
3. regional restrictions: services within the city limits can be provided only by cars with plates registered in the city of São Paulo.
4. inspection: cars must be inspected every year according to a schedule based on the final number of the plate;
5. trip reports: for safety reasons and for the purpose of tax collection, the service providers must submit to local authorities a detailed monthly report of all trips made in the previous month.

In Rio de Janeiro, initially, the city passed a regulation forbidding Uber services. However, the state court allowed the operation based on the ground that the local law was unconstitutional. Despite the judicial discussion, the local government passed regulations on the matter in 2019. Some provisions simply follow federal requirements and have similar rules as the city of São Paulo, but Uber drivers should be subject to some restrictions: drivers cannot be informed about final destination until meeting the passenger, they cannot use exclusive path for public and taxi transportation, and they cannot remain in a collective space to wait for potential passengers.

Following the line of the city of São Paulo, Brasilia's Governor signed a law regulating private individual transportation applications. According to the Governor, the rules aim to simplify the platforms' activities. Besides that, the sanctioned bill provides several demands that drivers must follow to ensure ultimate comfort for the passenger.

As Brasília, the city of Porto Alegre sanctioned the law n. 12.162/2016 regulating individual private transport of passengers services. According to the law, companies must file a request for grant of authorization for the execution of the service that will be valid for 18 months. There are requirements to be fulfilled by drivers and fees and taxes to be periodically paid. After the federal law and the ruling coming from the Supreme Court, the State Court of Rio Grande do Sul have considered the local regulation partially unconstitutional, revoking parts of the municipal law. Even so, this is still the law regulating ride-sharing activities in the Brazilian most southern state capital.

Considering the reality where Uber and other similar services are working in a great number of Brazilian cities, it is safe to say that these platforms came to stay. Still, it is beyond doubt that their services will be subject to regulation, especially because of the risks involved and the profits they produce. Nevertheless, the struggle remains in the regulatory field, but with a different trend. If in the last four or five years Uber-like companies fought and conquered relevant market share that monopolistically belonged to taxi drivers, in the years to come the battle will likely be against the hunger of local regulators to create or raise up taxes on the ride-sharing services and against taxi drivers and unions lobbying to impose more bureaucratic duties and sunk costs to their apps competitors.

3 Ride-Sharing Companies Under Brazilian Labor Law: Victory in Courts and Battles in Congress

The Consolidation of Labor Laws (CLT) regulates the individual and collective employment relationships in Brazil. It is a protective statute issued by the populist government of Getúlio Vargas in 1943, effective until present day. The second and third articles of the "CLT" provide the elements of an employment agreement:

1. Personal connection, that is, the services are performed by a specific professional and not by any professional as in a regular services agreement;
2. Continuous work, not an occasional performance of services;
3. Subordination, the employee renders its services under the supervision of the employer;
4. Reciprocal obligations, meaning that the employee must be paid for his/her work.

CLT sets forth these thresholds to determine if a service agreement should be deemed as a labor contract and, consequently, the employee would be entitled to all the labor and social security regarding labor relationships. In general, labor burdens may reach about 70% of the amount of the wages.

Another important implication regards to occupational accidents that impose strict liability to the employer, including compensation for personal injury, moral damages and loss of profits. The liability in this case is allocated by the "risk theory." The employer creates the risks of its economic activity and takes the benefit of it (theories of "created risk" and "risk-benefit"). If the employer creates the risks and obtains the profits of the business, it is fair to allocate the risks on the entrepreneur.

That being said, it is not a surprise that labor law is a battlefield for Uber-like companies in Brazil. On the one side, some drivers see themselves as employees of ride-sharing companies, aiming all the related benefits and safeguards. On the other side, Uber and its competitors feel goosebumps when someone says they might be considered employers according to Brazilian law, arguing that if the costs of labor relations were imposed to the transportation apps it will simply derail their business model, causing them to stop operating in the country.

As in the regulatory chapter of the story, this discussion was taken to the courts. But in Brazil there is a singularity: The judiciary system has a branch specialized only in labor cases. And it is not rare that labor judges, especially in lower courts, decide under some kind of bias in favor of employees.

The battle has begun showing some contradictory court decisions. For matters of concision, we will briefly refer to two of them, issued by the same Brazilian labor appealing court:

Artur Soares Neto v. Uber Do Brasil.[10] The decision was taken on January 30, 2017. The plaintiff claims compensation for an alleged abusive dismissal, payment of overtime work, and all labor rights not paid during the employment.

Uber does not acknowledge the existence of an employment relationship with the driver, arguing the lack of all the elements of a labor contract (personal connection, continuity, and subordination). The court considered some factual items: Uber (a) controls the transportation services provided by the drivers to the passengers; (b) determines the prices to be charged; (c) receives the amount paid by the client, and (d) pays the driver, retaining 25–30% of the tariff.

Uber argued that the company does not provide any transportation service, but, instead, the drivers are the ones that hire their services as they use the platform to connect with the final users. Moreover, Uber alleged that the risk of the transportation activity is taken directly by the driver. The company simply provides to the "users", that is, the drivers, a digital platform to improve their ability to attract more passengers. The standard of behavior is not mandatory, without any control by Uber, and there are no monitoring instruments of working hours.

The court decided in favor of Uber, mainly based on the following assumptions: there is no subordination and Uber does not provide transportation services, but just digital technological services.

Eustáquio Da Paixão Dias v. Uber Do Brasil.[11] The decision was taken on July 19, 2019. The court analyzed an appeal by a driver who claimed recognition of employment relationship with the ride-sharing app. According to the driver, he was hired by the company in June 2016 to provide driver services, transporting passengers in the city of Belo Horizonte. The contract was unilaterally and abusively terminated in February 2017 without prior notice. Changing the first instance judge's decision that had not recognized the plaintiff's employee condition, the appealing court stated that in order to characterize the employment relationship, it is necessary to demonstrate an *intuitu personae* service rendering relationship, in which employee depends on employer and is paid for it. Once, in the view of the judges, all the elements were present in the specific relation between Uber and the driver, they recognized the labor relationship and granted the plaintiff the rights arising therefrom.

Just like these two opposing decisions from the same labor court from the State of Minas Gerais, many others were issued by the twenty-four different appealing labor courts in the country, creating an environment of legal uncertainty and a feeling of lottery for drivers willing to have their day in court.

Cases were, then, taken by Uber to the high courts, whose constitutional role is precisely to avoid that disputes referring to similar facts may be decided differently depending on the regional or state court's opinion about the applicable law. It is important to highlight that there is always risk in taking cases to the high courts, because once they are decided, it is likely that all the similar ongoing cases will be ruled according to the same line of reasoning. Nevertheless, Uber strategy of taking labor cases to the high courts has been successful, at least until now.

---

[10] *Artur Soares Neto v. Uber Do Brasil* (2017) TRT-3rd Region, Procedure n. 0011863-62.2016.5.03.0137.

[11] *Eustáquio da Paixão Dias v. Uber do Brasil* (2019) TRT-3rd Region, Procedure n. 0010806-62.2017.5.03.0011.

Both Superior Tribunal de Justiça (STJ)[12] and Tribunal Superior do Trabalho (TST)[13] have ruled in favor of the ride-sharing industry. In the STJ decision issued in August 2019, Justice Moura Ribeiro, rapporteur of the case, has written that application drivers do not maintain a hierarchical relationship with Uber because their services are provided eventually, without pre-established schedules. Also, drivers do not receive a fixed payment, which mischaracterizes an employment relationship.[14]

The other case, decided by the Superior Labor Court (TST) in February 2020, went in the same direction. Justice Breno Medeiros, rappoteur of the case, stated that the claimant expressly admitted the possibility of staying offline without time limits, a circumstance that indicates the complete absence of services rendered under a hierarchical relationship. This fact alone translates in practice the claimant's ample flexibility in determining his routine, his working hours, places where he wants to work and the number of clients he wants to serve per day. The court has found, then, that such self-determination is incompatible with the recognition of an employment relationship under the Brazilian law, which has the concept of subordination as its basic premise.[15]

Although decided by Brazilian high courts, the debate around the relationship between Uber-like companies and their drivers is not close to its end. The recent rulings have brought light to an already ongoing debate about the actual definition of subordination. For some scholars and authorities, simply saying that Uber drivers are not employees is not the right thing to do.

As in many other parts of the planet, the discussions vary from the necessity of creating a new legal category of workers[16] to the idea of reading the legal concept of subordination in a more contemporary context.[17] According to this last view, the control of the workers' activities may not be exercised directly by the employer, but it is still exercisable through electronic systems, algorithms, users' reputational control and evaluation of services, making it possible to characterize an employment relationship.

Following the discussions in the academic and economic fields, the General Attorney's Office for Labor and Employment created a task force in 2016 to study the subject and present their conclusions.[18] According to the published study, when

---

[12]Superior Court constitutionally responsible for standardizing the interpretation of Federal Law in general, according to article 104 of the Brazilian Federal Constitution.

[13]Superior Labor Court constitutionally assigned for standardizing the interpretation of federal Law over the twenty-four Regional Appealing Labor Courts, according to article 114 of the Brazilian Federal Constitution.

[14]Full text of decision available in Portuguese at https://ww2.stj.jus.br/processo/revista/documento/mediado/?componente=ITA&sequencial=1857953&num_registro=201900799520&data=20190904&formato=PDF.

[15]Full text of decision available in Portuguese at http://aplicacao4.tst.jus.br/consultaProcessual/consultaTstNumUnica.do?consulta=Consultar&conscsjt=&numeroTst=1000123&digitoTst=89&anoTst=2017&orgaoTst=5&tribunalTst=02&varaTst=0038&submit=Consultar.

[16]Harris and Kruger (2015).

[17]Sachs (2015).

[18]Oitaven et al. (2018).

analyzing subordination in Uber-like relations, emphasis should not be placed on the traditional dimension of direct orders, but on the verification of command, control and supervision through electronic or computational means, what is already considered by Brazilian labor law to characterize an employment relationship (CLT: article 6).

Based on that study and other scholar articles and opinions, labor public prosecutors around the country have initiated investigations or have filed civil actions not only against Uber-like companies, but also against delivery services like Uber Eats, Loggi and others, based on the argument that the transportation apps are refusing to comply with Brazilian labor regulations and should be condemned to grant their drivers all the rights and benefits applicable to a traditional employee.

One of these civil actions was decided by the judge of the 27th Labor Court of São Paulo in January 2020.[19] The decision was one more time in favor of companies, on the grounds that it was demonstrated during the process that the workers are available to work on the day they choose to work, starting and ending the journey at the moment they decide, choosing the delivery they want to make and choosing to which application they will make themselves available, at the same time, for as many applications as they want. The labor public prosecutor in charge has appealed, and the case waits for a decision by the Labor Court of Appeals of the 2nd Region, in São Paulo.

As in the regulatory chapter of the story, Uber victories in court lead to a second battle field: the legislative power. In 2019, a bill was presented by Brazilian congressmen[20] proposing to modify federal law regulating ride-sharing services in the country in order to establish that application drivers must be considered employees. The bill waits for evaluation and so far does not have a date to be voted by the Congress.

As a conclusion to this topic, it is possible to say that there is a clear trend in Brazilian judiciary to deny the recognition of an employment relationship to transportation application drivers, especially because of the concepts of subordination and workers self-determination according to Brazilian labor law. It can be considered an important conquer of Uber in favor of its business model. However, Brazil is not immune to influences coming from abroad and the recent law passed in California[21] stating that gig economy workers might be considered employees is expected to bring new energy to the already ongoing discussions and legislative initiatives in favor of entitling Uber drivers to labor rights.

[19]Full text of the judicial award in Portuguese available at https://www.conjur.com.br/dl/decisao-ifood-vinculo-empregaticio.pdf. Accessed Apr 2020.

[20]Bill n. 5.756/2019. Full text in Portuguese and status available at https://www.camara.leg.br/proposicoesWeb/fichadetramitacao?idProposicao=2227685. Accessed Apr 2020.

[21]Full text available at: https://legiscan.com/CA/text/AB5/2019. Accessed Apr 2020.

4 Injuries, Damages, Harassment … the Challenges in Establishing Clear Boundaries to Civil Liability of Uber-like Companies Under Brazilian Civil and Consumer Codes

Brazil's civil liability system is governed by multiple laws although the Civil Code is the main and primary basis when it comes to responsibility for damages. As widely known, Brazilian civil legislation is based on the Napoleonic Code and other European systems like Germany, Italy and Portugal. Therefore, according to the Brazilian Civil Code, one who causes damages to someone else is obliged to indemnify such damages, what may include immediate material damage, loss of profits and, in some cases, moral damages.

In the Brazilian system, the paradigm of liability based on fault of the offender lives together with strict liability rules. In this second scheme, in circumstances where the activity normally carried out by the party who caused the damage entails, by its nature, risk to the rights of others, civil liability will arise regardless of fault. The same applies to the liability of the employer due to action or omission of its representatives, employees or subcontractors.

Transportation contracts have a specific chapter in Brazilian Civil Code, where articles 734 and 735 define transporter's strict liability for damages caused to passengers and third parties. Writing about these rules, commentators have concluded that, in Brazil, transporter's liability for damages is equivalent to full responsibility, with very few hypothesis of avoidance, often related to causal link breakdown. In fact, it is possible to collect from Brazilian Superior Court of Justice (STJ) case law precedents that have considered traditional transportation companies liable for cases involving robbery,[22] misusage by other passengers,[23] interference of third parties[24] and others.

Parallel to the Civil Code liability provisions, there is also the Consumer Protection Code (federal law n. 8.078/1990, known as "CDC"). The CDC establishes that the consumers will be protected against consumption defects and accidents (articles 12, 14, 18 and 20). This protection lies over a broad sense of liability, meaning that supplier will be accountable for the damage caused to the consumer irrespective of its fault, no matter if it is a producer, distributor, dealer, intermediary, etc. The aim is to make the whole supply chain liable, regardless of who has effectively caused

---

[22]STJ, AgRg no AREsp 218.394/RJ, Rel. Ministro Antonio Carlos Ferreira, Quarta Turma, Dje 16/10/2015 and STJ, REsp 1083023/MG, Rel. Ministro Marco Buzzi, Rel. p/Acórdão Ministro Raul Araújo, Quarta Turma, Dje 08/05/2015, full text available in Portuguese at http://www.stj.jus.br/SCON/jurisprudencia/doc.jsp?livre=transporte+e+responsabilidade+e+objetiva+e+roubo&b=ACOR&p=true&t=JURIDICO&l=10&i=3. Accessed Jun 2019.

[23]REsp 1.645.744/SP, Rel. Ministro Ricardo Villas Bôas Cueva, Terceira Turma, Dje 13/06/2017; full text available in Portuguese at http://www.stj.jus.br/SCON/jurisprudencia/toc.jsp?livre=1645744&&tipo_visualizacao=RESUMO&b=ACOR. Accessed Jun 2019.

[24]EREsp 1318095/MG, Rel. Ministro Raul Araújo, Segunda Seção, Dje 14/03/2017, full text available in Portuguese at http://www.stj.jus.br/SCON/jurisprudencia/doc.jsp?processo=1318095&b=ACOR&p=true&t=JURIDICO&l=10&i=1. Accessed Jun 2019.

the damage, in order to enable the consumer to easily obtain compensation for the damages suffered. There is a difference, though, between how law is applicable to suppliers of goods and to suppliers of services. To the first ones, there are two express rules (articles 12 and 13) establishing supply chain participants' liability. As to the services suppliers, law is not express about liability of others than the ones who effectively render the service to the client.

Consumer protection provisions are applicable to transportation contracts since passengers are considered consumers according to law requirements (i.e., the final intended party that acquires goods or services). All the court decisions referred to above depart from this premise.

Uber, on the other hand, does not seem to consider itself a transporter. As matter of fact, it does not seem to consider itself liable for damages incurred by passengers during transportation, since it is expressly written in Uber terms of usage for Brazil that the platform will not be accountable for any damages, of any nature, incidentally or consequentially related to the use of its services, even if Uber has been advised of the possibility of such. However, it can also be read in the same section of Uber's terms of use that the limitations and denial of warranties proposed do not have the objective to limit or alter consumer rights that under applicable law cannot be limited or changed.[25]

Although subject to some debate in the beginning of its operations in Brazil, local courts have not shown any difficulty in considering Uber liable for damages under Brazilian Civil or Consumer Protection Code.

Only in the State Court of São Paulo, we can refer to decisions condemning Uber to pay compensation for damages to passengers in cases of (i) accidents resulting harm to passengers,[26] (ii) disappearance of personal items left in the car by passengers,[27] (iii) aggressions and robbery of passengers' items by drivers,[28] (iv) verbal or written offenses perpetrated by drivers against passengers,[29] (v) missed flight due to taking the wrong way or delay by driver,[30] (vi) abandonment of passenger's minor children on the sidewalk by driver while passenger went to meet his wife inside the hospital[31]

[25]Uber alleged that it should not be considered a transportation company and therefore should not be considered liable for damages suffered during transportation and this position can still be read in capital letters right at the beginning of Uber's Terms of Service for Brazilian jurisdiction (text in Portuguese available at https://www.uber.com/legal/terms/br/. Accessed in Apr 2019).

[26]Case n. 1003697-74.2019.8.26.0348, decided on 31.01.2020, full text in Portuguese available at: http://www.tjsp.jus.br/.

[27]Case n. 1023043-82.2018.8.26.0562, decided on 16.12.2019, full text in Portuguese available at: http://www.tjsp.jus.br/.

[28]Case n. 1004878-78.2019.8.26.0100, decided on 24.10.2019, full text in Portuguese available at: http://www.tjsp.jus.br/.

[29]Case n. 0006100-14.2018.8.26.0010, decided on 19.09.2019, full text in Portuguese available at: http://www.tjsp.jus.br/.

[30]Case n. 0020122-56.2018.8.26.0405, decided on 22.08.2019, full text in Portuguese available at: http://www.tjsp.jus.br/.

[31]Case n. 0007052-45.2018.8.26.0704, decided on 03.05.2019, full text in Portuguese available at: http://www.tjsp.jus.br/.

and (vii) passenger and child obliged by driver to get out of the car in heavy rain at the wrong address.[32] The same kind of rulings against ride-sharing platforms can be found in many other state courts around the country.

It is clear, then, that Brazilian courts do apply the Consumer Protection Code's strict liability regime to Uber in all the cases involving damages and losses suffered by passengers, not taking in consideration other risk factors as the choice of passengers for a less formal service when compared to taxi drivers or public transportation, neither accepting the argument that the platform does not exercise any kind of control on the drivers' actions during the rides. For Brazilian judges, Uber is definitely accountable for driver's misdoings related to passengers.

The situation is different, however, with damages caused to third parties. Ride-sharing companies are not considered liable by São Paulo State Court for damages caused to pedestrians in car accidents, for example.[33] All the decisions go under the line of reasoning that it is not possible to establish a direct link between the platform activities and the cause of the damages, especially if at the moment of the accident the driver was not transporting any Uber passenger.

Questions remain, though, in the cases that the driver is using the application online, going to pick-up a passenger or actually transporting a passenger. Brazilian Consumer Protection Code has, in its article 17, the rule of strict liability in case of damages to the bystander, defined as the person that is not legally a consumer, but by any reason is submitted to the risks arising of the provider's activity. Third parties in car accidents can be qualified as bystanders.

Lastly, there are the cases involving damages to the drivers. Normally, Brazilian state courts do not consider drivers to be consumers in relation to platforms. The relation is regulated only by the Civil Code. Hence, companies are not liable for losses or injuries experienced by drivers during transportation of passengers. In cases of robbery, extortion or offenses perpetrated by passengers,[34] for example, decisions are unanimous in saying that provision of security and safety to drivers is not among the contractual duties of the platforms. Drivers work at their own risk, especially because platforms do not perform any kind of background or identity check on the passengers.

Another relevant point that can be easily perceived by checking Uber case law in São Paulo State Court is that out of the approximately 160 decisions issued until

---

[32]Case n. 1040406-30.2016.8.26.0602, decided on 06.10.2017, full text in Portuguese available at: http://www.tjsp.jus.br/.

[33]See case n. 2146719-53.2019.8.26.0000, decided on 27.08.2019; case n. 1012376-75.2017.8.26.0011, decided on 15.06.2018; and case n. 0100283-92.2017.8.26.9004, decided on 29.09.2017, all full texts available in Portuguese at: http://www.tjsp.jus.br/.

[34]See case n. 1007005-80.2019.8.26.0005, decided on 31.01.2020; case n. 1024292-68.2018.8.26.0562, decided on 11.06.2019; case n. 1036565-71.2017.8.26.0576, decided on 23.09.2019; case n. 1010663-74.2018.8.26.0223, decided on 07.08.2019; and case n. 1003851-48.2019.8.26.0007, decided on 08.08.2019; case n. 1035103-24.2018.8.26.0001, decided on 30.07.2019; case n. 1024292-68.2018.8.26.0562, decided on 11.06.2019, case n. 1019691-05.2018.8.26.0114, decided on 08.02.2019; and case n. 1011405-68.2018.8.26.0007, decided on 03.12.2008; all full texts available in Portuguese at: http://www.tjsp.jus.br/.

the completion of this article regarding Uber and discussions about compensation for damages, around two-thirds of them were disputes between the company and its individual drivers, mostly about abusive contract termination by the ride-sharing app.[35] Although not very successful, drivers are frequent adversaries of Uber in court.

Therefore, the different legal solutions given to damages experienced by passengers, third parties and drivers indicate important developments on the application of strict liability regime to gig economy initiatives in Brazil. Although drivers and passengers are both users of the services provided by the platforms, their legal qualification differs considerably. Passengers were easily considered consumers in relation to the platforms just like in any other traditional business model and because of that may count on the protective rules provided by the system. On the other hand, drivers were considered mere civil contractors, having to support the burdens and the risks of the transportation activity by themselves, not being entitled to any protective rule in case of damages caused by passengers or third parties. As a matter of fact, drivers do not have better luck even in contract termination disputes against Uber.

5 Synopsis and Conclusions

Definitely Uber found glory in Brazil. The company and its similar competitors became very relevant players in the local market, and their activities created the necessity of reviewing old legal concepts and principles such as the definition of transportation and technology companies, the labor relations and even the classic civil liability schemes.

But the glory did not come without a fight. Although enjoying relative tranquility after a federal law has passed and the Supreme Court has ensured the legality of its business model, it is not possible to say that Uber-like companies have permanently won the regulatory battle in Brazil. Actually, they will have to remain vigilant to deal with local legislators' hunger for taxes and to resist the pressure of taxi drivers and unions always wanting to impose ridesharing companies and drivers the same duties and bureaucracy that shaped the taxi industry for decades.

Differently of the regulatory field where vigilance seems to be enough, the battle on the labor relation with the drivers will probably show new ups and downs in the near future. It seems the authorities' perception is that the flexibility and the freedom of today's way of working in the gig economy may be the failure of the social security system in the future. It is likely, thus, that Uber and similar companies will be called to contribute with a share in sponsoring the system by providing their workers with some labor rights and social benefits. If these rights and benefits will be equal to traditional employees or will emerge as a new category of workers, it is still early to say.

[35] List in Portuguese language of the 160 selected decisions by São Paulo State Court research-engine available at: https://esaj.tjsp.jus.br/cjsg/resultadoCompleta.do. Accessed Apr 2020.

Finally, when it comes to civil liability, our research has shown that Brazilian courts were partially convinced by the risk management policy proposed by Uber when it first arrived to the country. We say partially because for the passengers few risks were assigned although it was the company's first intention not to have them qualified as Uber consumers. But for the drivers, the narrative built by Uber was quite successful and the main risks were kept with them.

But the merits in Uber strategy do not lie on its effective sales pitch. Actually, there is an important bias to be considered. Judges are much more likely to see themselves as passengers than drivers. Therefore, it is expected that case law may tend to build a more protective legal regime to the former instead of the latter, and our results reveal it at least on labor and civil liability matters.

If we look at the future, it is possible that this might create a perverse situation, since drivers are not entitled to employee rights and benefits and still have to manage alone the majority of transportation risks. So, to summarize it as an analysis of glory and consequence, Uber has taken all the glory and managed to transfer a good part of the consequences to the drivers. But if the song is right and every glory has its consequence, it is likely that a new battle is approaching onto the horizon for Uber and this time it will be against its own drivers.

References

Estadão Conteúdo (2019) Apps como Uber e iFood se tornam "maior empregador" do Brasil. Exame, São Paulo. https://exame.abril.com.br/economia/apps-como-uber-e-ifood-sao-fonte-de-renda-de-quase-4-milhoes-de-pessoas/. Accessed 5 Mar 2020

Harris SD, Kruger AB (2015) A proposal for modernizing labor laws for twenty-first-century work: the "independent worker". https://www.hamiltonproject.org/assets/files/modernizing_labor_laws_for_twenty_first_century_work_krueger_harris.pdf. Accessed Apr 2020

Lunden I (2018) Didi confirms it has acquired 99 in Brazil to expand in Latin America. TechCrunch. https://techcrunch.com/2018/01/03/didi-confirms-it-has-acquired-99-in-brazil-to-expand-in-latin-america/. Accessed 5 Mar 2020

Magalhães LE (2019) Pesquisa mostra que aplicativos já transportam o triplo dos passageiros de táxis. O Globo, Rio de Janeiro. https://oglobo.globo.com/rio/pesquisa-mostra-que-aplicativos-ja-transportam-triplo-dos-passageiros-de-taxis-23912389. Accessed on 9 Mar 2020

McKenna F (2019) Uber customers paid more than $6 billion in cash last year, and accounting for it isn't easy. MarketWatch, New York. https://www.marketwatch.com/story/uber-customers-paid-more-than-6-billion-in-cash-last-year-and-accounting-for-it-isnt-easy-2019-08-16. Accessed 3 Mar 2020

Oitaven JCC, Carelli RL, Casagrande CL (2018) Empresas de transporte, plataformas digitais e a relação de emprego: um estudo do trabalho subordinado sob aplicativos. Ministério Público do Trabalho, Brasília. http://csb.org.br/wp-content/uploads/2019/01/CONAFRET_WEB-compressed.pdf. Accessed Mar/Apr 2020

Sachs B (2015) Do we need an "independent worker" category? http://onlabor.org/2015/12/08/do-we-need-an-independent-worker-category/. Accessed Apr 2020

Valente F (2019) Indenização por dano moral lidera processos da Uber em São Paulo. Conjur, São Paulo. https://www.conjur.com.br/2019-mar-18/indenizacao-dano-moral-lidera-processos-uber-sao-paulo. Accessed 9 Mar 2020

Chapter 6
Regulation of Uber in the UK

Margarita Amaxopoulou, Mateja Durovic, and Franciszek Lech

1 Introduction

Uber[1] is omnipresent in the United Kingdom (UK): from Glasgow to Brighton and from Cardiff to Cambridge, through the major English cities of London, Manchester, Leeds, Birmingham and Nottingham.[2] Uber's operation in the UK is mutually beneficial: the UK is an important market for Uber globally, and, in turn, Uber is a main player in the UK market for personal transport, giving it political leverage.[3] Regulatory issues on Uber's operations, the employment status of Uber drivers, as well as uncertainty as to the possibility of Uber's liability for personal injury and property damage have been drawing significant attention in the legal and political discourse on the British Isles. This chapter grapples with the interplay of these legal

[1]By using the company's name 'Uber' in this chapter, we refer to Uber X/Uber Black, and not the UberPop and UberEats services. In the domestic context, Uber is understood as a transportation company and not as a mere intermediary between service-providers and customers using the Uber app. See *Aslam v Uber BV* [2017] I.R.L.R.4 (ET) 89, 92. This interpretation of the company's nature, legal status, purpose and obligations is in line with the interpretation of CJEU on the same matter in Case C-434/15 *Asociación Profesional Èlite Taxi v Uber Systems Spain SL,* judgment of 20 December 2017, ECLI:EU:C:2017:981.

[2]Uber (2019).

[3]Dudley et al. (2017).

M. Amaxopoulou · M. Durovic (✉) · F. Lech
The Dickson Poon School of Law, King's College London, London, UK
e-mail: mateja.durovic@kcl.ac.uk

M. Amaxopoulou
e-mail: margarita.amaxopoulou@kcl.ac.uk

F. Lech
e-mail: fransciszek.lech@kcl.ac.uk

Z. Ayata and I. Önay (eds.), *Global Perspectives on Legal Challenges Posed by Ridesharing Companies*,
https://doi.org/10.1007/978-981-15-7035-3_6

matters and Uber's rise and expansion in the domestic context. Before proceeding any further, however, two complications need to be addressed from the outset.

Firstly, the United Kingdom is no longer a part of the European Union (EU). While (at the time of writing) EU legal frameworks of relevance to Uber will be retained,[4] the UK is no longer bound to maintain them and thus may take a different regulatory approach with respect to Uber. Nonetheless, EU law leaves the Member States substantial room for manoeuvre, the Court of Justice of the EU has specified that Uber is (contrary to the company's position) a 'service in the field of transport'.[5] This conclusion means that the company's activities do not fall within the scope of Directive 2006/123 on services,[6] instead being regulated under Article 58(1) TFEU. This means that EU Member States have discretion to regulate transport activities. ([7] Whether the UK will deem it necessary to depart from the EU's approach to Uber remains to be seen.

Secondly, Uber is currently under the spotlight as TfL, London's transport regulator decided against the renewal for the company's licence to operate in London for a second time in November 2019.[8] The company has appealed this decision. [9] This turn is a ground-shaking development in the ride-hailing industry, because the outcome of the case will be highly relevant to the operations of other private hire vehicle (PHV) operators too. Specifically with regard to Uber, the outcome may influence other licensing authorities across the country on whether to provide the company with a licence or not. [10] For example, the Birmingham City Council has stated that Uber's licence in the Midlands is 'likely' to be renewed but it will be following the developments in London closely; this depicts the nationwide importance of this case.[11] A hearing is scheduled to take place at the Westminster Magistrates' Court in the summer of 2020. In the meantime, the company is allowed to operate as usual in the meantime.[12] These clarifications indicate that both transport regulation in general and Uber's regulation in London and in other UK cities are likely to change in the future. That being said, and for the purposes of this chapter, we will be drawing upon past and present developments with regard to Uber's regulation in the domestic context.

[4]By virtue of European Union (Withdrawal) Act 2018 (as amended), ss. 2, 3 and 7.

[5]Case C-434/15 *Asociación Profesional Èlite Taxi v Uber Systems Spain SL,* judgment of 20 December 2017, ECLI:EU:C:2017: 981, [39–41].

[6]Council Directive 2006/123/EC of 12 December 2006 on services in the internal market [2006] OJ L 376/36, Article 2(2)(d).

[7]n 8) [47].

[8]Topham G (2019).

[9]See our analysis below p. 8.

[10]We briefly explain the scheme of the private hire trade in the UK below, pp. 5–6.

[11]BBC News (2019).

[12]Ibid.

More specifically, the present chapter illustrates the political and legal controversy shrouding Uber's presence in the UK.[13] In order to take a closer look at these issues, we proceed in three steps. First, we provide an overview of the historical and factual background of Uber's operations in the UK. Second, we focus on emerging regulatory issues between Uber and the national regulators in the context of licensing. We argue that the fragmentation of the local experience, and the limits of both conventional and novel approaches, renders national efforts to adopt a homogenous response to regulating Uber a challenging task. Third, we demonstrate the difficulties in developing a national regulatory strategy by expanding on three specific legal fields that have been 'disrupted' by Uber's operations in the UK, namely employment law, taxation and tortious liability issues. Beyond the relevance of the present analysis for the future of regulating Uber in the UK, it is hoped that there are broader lessons to be learned about the challenges and limitations that foreign regulators are likely to grapple with.

1.1 The UK Background and the Delicate Dynamics Between Uber and Local Actors

Shedding light to the idiosyncratic legal issues emerging from the operations of Uber in the UK requires a more holistic understanding of the local context. We identify two main threads running across Uber's activities, namely (a) the tensions between Uber and the local licensing bodies and (b) the tensions between Uber and the Black Cab community. Since London is the epicentre of Uber's operations in the UK, a significant amount of the analysis will be devoted to issues that have arisen there.

1.1.1 Uber and Licensing Authorities: Carrot or Stick?

London was the first market for Uber in the UK back in 2012. Today, the UK capital is one of Uber's biggest markets (45,000 Uber drivers in the city), and is on course to become the company's second most lucrative operating location after North America.[14] The San Francisco-based ride-hailing app derives approximately 24% of all of its revenues from just five cities, of which London is one—making the city and its regulatory regime a focal point of interest for the company's management and strategy.[15]

---

[13]England, Scotland, Wales and Northern Ireland all have different systems and frameworks. While the regulatory issues addressed in this chapter are all shared by the different countries of the United Kingdom we are mostly referring to English examples.

[14]Lanxon (2019) Is This the End of the Road for Uber in London? Washington Post. https://www.washingtonpost.com/business/is-thisthe-end-of-the-road-for-uber-in-london/2019/11/25/8fab68a6-0f83-11ea-924c-b34d09bbc948_story.html. Accessed 18 Apr 2020.

[15]BBC News (2019).

Many enterprises have followed Uber's steps, and the ride-hailing scene in London is becoming too populous for Uber to claim that it has the exclusivity on providing personal transport services. The city is a battleground for the fierce competition between Uber and companies such as ViaVan[16], Kapten,[17] Bolt,[18] Ola,[19] Kabee,[20] Gett,[21] Wheely,[22] Xooox[23]. These companies do differ from Uber in some aspects: Wheely operates only luxury 'chaffeur' services, Xooox is a networking platform for existing cab drivers (not a ride-hailing service themselves), and Kabbee specialises in airport transfers, but still all of these companies have entered the market *after* Uber, and trodden the path pioneered by it. Additionally, the Black Cabs have adopted some of Uber's techniques, such as pre-booking or smartphone-based applications, which contributes to Uber's market share being squeezed from both sides—traditional taxi services, and public transport networks on one hand and competitor PHV operators on another, [24] all while Uber is engaged in a dispute with the local regulator, i.e., Transport for London (TfL).

TfL is the public authority overseeing the UK capital's transport regulation and is responsible for licensing ride-hailing enterprises.[25] TfL is legally obliged to develop and enforce 'policies for the promotion and encouragement of safe, integrated, efficient and economic transport facilities and services to, from and within Greater London'.[26] One distinction that has to be made here, is the historic differentiation between Black Cabs (or Hackney Carriages) [27]—the iconic London taxis—and private hire vehicles (PHV),[28] which are subject to a different regulatory regime,[29] even if both regimes are overseen by the TfL. In London, PHV Operators, such as

[16]ViaVan (2020).

[17]Kapten (2020).

[18]Bolt (2020).

[19]OlaRide (2020).

[20]Kabbee (2020).

[21]Gett (2020).

[22]Wheely (2020).

[23]Xooox (2020).

[24]Katwala (2019).

[25]Private Hire Vehicles (London) Act 1998, ss 2(1), 6(1) and 36, also Greater London Authority Act 1999, s 254(1) and (3) and Sch 21, para 17 which conferred the licensing jurisdiction to TfL

[26]Greater London Authority Act 1999, ss 141(1) and 154(3).

[27]As defined by the Town Police Clauses Act 1847s 38: Every wheeled carriage, whatever may be its form or construction, used in standing or plying for hire in any street within the prescribed distance, and every carriage standing upon any street within the prescribed distance, having thereon any numbered plate required by this or the special act to be fixed upon a hackney carriage, or having thereon any plate resembling or intended to resemble any such plate as aforesaid, shall be deemed to be a hackney carriage.

[28]Private Hire Vehicles (London) Act 1998, s. 1(1): "private hire vehicle" means a vehicle constructed or adapted to seat fewer than nine passengers which is made available with a driver…for hire *for the purpose of carrying passengers*, other than a licensed taxi or a public service vehicle. (emphasis supplied)

[29]For more details on the differences of taxi and PHV regulation, see Local Government Association (2017) Taxi and PHV licensing. Councillors' handbook (England

Uber, are regulated under Private Hire Vehicles (London) Act 1998, which stipulates that to provide transport services as a PHV, both the individual driver,[30] and the operator, must each hold a licence.[31] The licence is granted by the TfL if the operator is deemed *'fit and proper'*.[32] On the other hand, Black Cabs are licenced by TfL[33] under the Metropolitan Public Carriage Act 1869 and the London Cab Order 1934. The main difference is that Black Cabs can ply for hire, that is can be hired off the street, whereas PHVs must be booked *in advance* and cannot ply for hire.[34] As we shall see, thanks in no small part to Uber, this distinction has been blurred in practice.

Uber commenced its London operations in 2012 but, unlike in many other European cities, the UberX service was officially licensed by the Transport for London (TfL) from the very beginning.[35] It was the year that the Summer Olympic Games were hosted in London, and the TfL feared that there might be insufficient transport capacity for the visitors and spectators, so registering a largely unknown, tech-driven private hire vehicle company was seen as a short-term solution.[36] Soon, Uber took London by storm—by 2016 over 30,000 Londoners were downloading the app each day.[37] In 2015, the then-Mayor Boris Johnson admitted that TfL did not seek legal advice before issuing Uber with a licence. This was controversial, because the company required its drivers to agree to a clause stating that 'Uber *does not provide transportation services,* function as a transport carrier or agent for the transportation of passengers',[38] which contravenes the legal definition of a PHV,[39] thus casting doubt on the ability of TfL to provide a PHV licence in the first place.

In 2016, Sadiq Khan took over from Boris Johnson as the London Mayor, and he quickly introduced his Taxi and Private Hire Action Plan.[40] The plan seemed sympathetic to the Black Cab drivers: the number of officials enforcing PHV regulations was quadrupled, and PHV operators like Uber were required to have a London-based call centre.[41] For the TfL, this was a turning point from leniency to increasingly less covert power struggle. At the same time, Uber reached its zenith—geographically, it serviced most of the Greater London Area from Heathrow Airport to Greenwich,

and Wales). https://www.local.gov.uk/sites/default/files/documents/10.9%20Councillor%20Handbook%20-%20Taxi%20and%20PHV%20Licensing_November_2017.pdf. Accessed 18 Apr 2020.

[30] Private Hire Vehicles (London) Act 1998, s 6(1).

[31] Private Hire Vehicles (London) Act 1998, s 2(1).

[32] Ibid., s. 3(3) (emphasis supplied).

[33] Greater London Authority Act 1999, s 253 and sch 20, para 1(1).

[34] TfL (2020).

[35] Dudley et al. (2017, p.493).

[36] Ibid.

[37] Katwala (2019).

[38] Ferrari (2016).

[39] (n 30).

[40] Mayor of London (2016).

[41] Ibid., (p. 496).

while it also rolled out other services such as UberPool[42] (which challenged the London public transport network) or UberEats (food delivery).[43]

Concurrently with this expansion tensions emerged around Uber's operations. This included the issue of whether the Uber app operates as a taximeter. TfL claimed that the app effectively constitutes a taximeter,[44] breaching an express prohibition on taximeters in PHVs.[45] The High Court agreed with Uber that its app was not a taximeter.[46] The company then successfully challenged TfL's rule about the London-based call centre in courts on the basis that it was too wide in scope and disproportionate.[47]

In 2017, TfL refused to renew Uber's licence for the first time, concluding that 'Uber London Limited is not fit and proper to hold' a licence, due to 'lack of corporate responsibility' in relation to reporting criminal offences, background checks, medical certificates and use of Greyball software.[48] Uber exercised its statutory right to appeal[49] the TfL's decision to a magistrates court and won after nine months. Chief Magistrate Emma Arbuthnot granted Uber a 15-month licence in June 2018 on agreed conditions, finding that 'whilst [Uber] was not a fit and proper person at the time of the [TfL's] decision' it has since adapted and demonstrated it is 'now a fit and proper person'.[50]

The saga was far from over, with TfL rejecting Uber's application for licence renewal again in November 2019, because of a systems failure that allowed uninsured or even unlicensed drivers to pretend to be the booked drivers by uploading their photo to another driver's profile—this resulted in some 14,000 Uber rides that were uninsured and with unlicensed drivers of which the passengers were not aware.[51] Uber responded claiming that they have 'fundamentally changed' their practices and were 'setting the standard on safety', claiming that TfL's decision is 'wrong' and announcing their intention to appeal.[52] During the appeal process, the outcome of which is as of now unknown, Uber is allowed to operate normally.

---

[42]UberPool—a service that matches passengers going along similar routes and placing them in one car at a discounted rate.

[43]Dudley et al. (2017, p. 497).

[44]*Transport for London v Uber London Ltd (Transport for London v Uber London Ltd* [2015] EWHC 2918.

[45]Private Hire Vehicles (London) Act 1998, s 11.

[46]*TfL v Uber London Ltd* (n 47) [49].

[47]*R. on the Application of Uber London Limited, Mr Sandor Balogh, Mr Nikolay Dimitrov, Mr Imran Khan v Transport for London* [2017] EWHC 435.

[48]TfL (2017) Licensing decision on Uber London Limited. https://tfl.gov.uk/info-for/media/press-releases/2017/september/licensing-decision-on-uber-london-limited. Accessed 18 Apr 2020.

[49]Private Hire Vehicles (London) Act 1998, s. 7(7).

[50]Uber London Limited v Transport for London. Westminster Magistrates Court. Judgment of 26 June 2018 [40–42].

[51]TfL (2019) Uber London Limited Found To Be Not A Fit And Proper To Hold A Private Hire Operator Licence. https://tfl.gov.uk/info-for/media/press-releases/2019/november/uber-london-limited-found-to-be-not-fit-and-proper-to-hold-a-private-hire-operator-licence. Accessed 18 Apr 2020.

[52]Uber (2019).

TfL has also removed the congestion charge[53] exemption for PHVs,[54] and introduced English language requirements[55] and a basic topography test,[56] as necessary prerequisites for a PHV licence. While previously the Black Cab drivers had to pass such tests, PHV operators were not required to (contributing to the greater ease with which one could become an Uber driver). Uber has challenged those and other measures imposed by London authorities in court but has mostly been unsuccessful.[57]

Overall, Uber has rapidly achieved huge growth using innovative, though not necessarily unique, technology. Its strategy was of 'relentless pursuit of market growth through overriding or even bypassing, established interests and regulatory systems' best reflected by its founder, Travis Kalanick's, motto that it is 'easier to ask for forgiveness than permission'.[58]

Outside of the capital, the legislation—as in TfL's case—grants a discretion to the local authorities[59] to determine who is 'fit and proper' and what conditions need to be satisfied in order to receive a PHV-operating licence, with the Department of Transport issuing non-binding 'best practices'.[60] Each council has its own licensing policies, and most of the time does not regulate taximeters, meaning that PHV drivers can—unlike London—have a taximeter.[61] Generally, Uber has been capable of replicating its rapid growth in the rest of the country with a few interesting exceptions. The uniting thread has been that of calm enthusiasm and careful scrutiny in cities such as Edinburgh, Glasgow, Cambridge and Brighton.[62] York is an interesting case since the City Council refused to renew Uber's licence; the reason was personal data breaches and customer complaints, as well as the lack of basic knowledge of the topography of the region of the drivers.[63] Generally, however, Uber expanded rapidly both within and outside of London. We now turn to the relationships between Uber and the Black Cabs.

---

[53] A payment for entering the city centre on weekdays in working hours.

[54] Greater London (Central Zone) Congestion Charging Variation Order 2018, sch 1, art 6.

[55] TfL (2016), 'English language requirement' https://tfl.gov.uk/info-for/taxis-and-private-hire/english-language-requirement. Accessed 18 Apr 2020.

[56] TfL (2019).

[57] For example with regard to the English language test, the courts have upheld TfLs regulation, considering it to be of a reasonable extent in *R. on the Application of Uber London Limited* (n 51). For more details on these disputes, see Marique and Marique (2018).

[58] Dudley et al. (2017, p. 498).

[59] Local Government (Miscellaneous Provisions) Act 1976, s. 46(1).

[60] Marique and Marique (2018, p. 21).

[61] Ibid.

[62] Ibid., (pp. 21–22).

[63] Ibid., (pp. 22–23).

1.1.2 Uber and Black Cabs: Differences and Similarities that Lead to Conflict

With Uber profoundly disrupting the 'Black Cab' model, tensions between it and the UK 'Cabbies' became somewhat inevitable.[64] There is a large market overlay between taxis and PHVs, and the historic distinction between them, based on plying for hire, is increasingly blurred: Taxis now accept pre-bookings and Uber vehicles take on practically immediate bookings from event venues, airports and rail stations (where drivers wait before receiving a booking).[65]

Taxis have been regulated since the seventeenth century, when King Charles I restricted the number of hackney coaches to 50 in a, seemingly timeless, effort to fight congestion in London.[66] Hackney Carriages are defined as 'any carriage for the conveyance of passengers which plies for hire…and is neither a stage carriage nor a tramcar'.[67] Later, provisions specified that 'cab' shall be synonymous with 'hackney carriage'.[68]

In terms of modern regulation, London's taxis have been subject to statutory control continuously since 1831.[69] The legislation has introduced a licensing requirement (in force today), with the licence being available only to those who 'satisfy [the regulator] of [their] good behaviour and fitness for such a situation'.[70] Initially, the Metropolitan Police was responsible for issuing licences,[71] but, with TfL's creation, the powers related to oversight and licensing of Black Cabs (and, as we have seen, PHVs) were conferred to it.[72] TfL has the power to pass 'London Cab Orders',[73] through which the TfL regulates the activities of the black cabs in the capital.[74]

A taxi licence is not the only requirement. Taxi drivers must also pass a series of tests, the most infamous of which is "The Knowledge"—a trial requiring prospective drivers to respond to questions related to 25,000 streets, landmarks and points of interest in central London. This challenge became a rite of passage for a proud profession.[75] On the contrary, PHV drivers (initially) faced no requirements as to English proficiency or topography knowledge, meaning practically that anyone could become an Uber driver. Still, Uber was able to win a substantial market share from

---

[64]Business Energy and Industrial Strategy Committee of the House of Commons (2016).

[65]Butcher (2018).

[66]Ibid.

[67]Metropolitan Public Carriage Act 1869 (32 and 33 Vict c 115), s 4.

[68]London Cab Act 1896 (59 and 60 Vict c 27), s. 3: 'the expression "cab" shall mean any hackney carriage within the meaning of the Metropolitan Public Carriage Act 1869", see (n 57)'.

[69]London Hackney Carriage Act 1831 (1 and 2 Will 4 c 22).

[70]London Hackney Carriage Act 1843 (6 and 7 Vict c 86), s 8.

[71]London Hackney Carriage Act 1850 (13 and 14 Vict c 7), s 2.

[72]Greater London Authority Act 1999, s 253, sch 20, part 1, [1–8]

[73]London Cab Act 1968, s 4B.

[74]See for example, London Cab Order 2019 of 4 December 2019. http://content.tfl.gov.uk/london-cab-order-2019-taxi-fares.pdf. Accessed 18 Apr 2020.

[75]Dudley et al. (2017, p. 495).

taxis, thanks to the novelty of its app, and most importantly, prices—68% of black cab passengers think that the fares are 'too high' providing fertile ground for Uber to provide a cheaper service to frustrated customers.[76]

To illustrate why Uber was able to exploit the price differences, it suffices to note that taxi fares have risen by 131% (other estimates have it at 204%) between 2001 and 2016, compared to London underground fare which increased by a mere *26%*[77] over the same period. This explains the widely-held perception that Black Cabs are unaffordable.[78] During the day, the price and time difference of a taxi journey versus an Uber one is negligible, with the cab being both quicker and cheaper at times[79], but at night a Black Cab can be more than twice as expensive as an Uber ride.[80]

We compared fares in January 2020 on a 2.5 mile journey from Trafalgar Square to the Shard in London. A taxi would cost up to £24 on a weekday between 05:00am and 8:00 pm; the same journey in an Uber would be £13 on the UberX service—Bolt predicted a £8.1 fare and Kapten a £28.1 fee.[81] We can see that Uber is not the cheapest, but still overwhelmingly bests the Black Cab on price. At half past midnight, on a Friday night, a Black Cab fare for the same journey might be up to £30, while Uber's is still £12.[82] From the perspective of a Black Cab driver then, the arrival of Uber, and soon after other ride-hailing apps was no pleasant experience—their rivals faced significantly lower barriers to entry, and were and are very adept at undermining their revenues, meaning taxi drivers' huge initial investment (opportunity costs of studying and passing The Knowledge, costs of purchasing their own car, insurance, etc.) might not pay off, which led to a widely held frustration with Uber and TfL.

This frustration has externalised with open protests of the Black Cab Associations against Uber.[83] Some drivers argue that the fare discrepancy is a 'deliberate attempt to kill off' Black Cabs in London, and blame Uber for undercutting their revenues and threatening their standard of living.[84] Furthermore, the disapproval of Uber by

---

[76]Ferrari (2016, p. 26).

[77]Inflation in that period has been 50%, see ibid., (p. 31).

[78]Ibid.

[79]Wall Street Journal (2014); Topping (2014).

[80]Ferrari (2016, p. 31).

[81]The comparison was done virtually: we took the journey distance and estimated time to calculate the fare for each provider, except for the Black Cab and Uber where we used the TfL calculator for the former and the Uber app for the latter. Important variables such as surge charge and traffic coefficients are not included—in heavy traffic, a Black Cab can have the advantage of convenient shortcuts.

[82]Based on the app prediction—does not include traffic or surge coefficients.

[83]Topham (2016) Black Cab's Driver's Uber Protest Brings London Traffic To A Standstill. The Guardian. https://www.theguardian.com/technology/2016/feb/10/black-cab-drivers-uber-protest-london-traffic-standstill. Accessed 18 Apr 2020.; Grafton-Green (2018) London Taxi Protest: Black Cab Drivers Stage Demo Against TfL and Uber, Evening Standard. https://www.standard.co.uk/news/london/london-taxi-protest-traffic-chaos-at-elephant-and-castle-as-black-cab-drivers-descend-to-protest-tfl-a3740711.html. Accessed 18 Apr 2020.

[84]Bennhold (2017) On London's Streets, Black Cabs and Uber Fight For A Future. The New York Times. https://www.nytimes.com/2017/07/04/world/europe/london-uk-brexit-uber-taxi.html. Accessed 18 Apr 2020.

the Black Cab drivers is evident on the roads, with hundreds of reports of verbal abuse from taxi drivers towards Uber drivers, as well as displaying middle fingers across the windshield and not giving way on intersections.[85] Taxi drivers see Uber as killing their profession and identity, threatening the cultural heritage of their vocation; Uber drivers, in turn, see Black Cabs as entitled and abusive—relics of the past who choose to be angry with Uber drivers, rather than adapt to technological changes.[86]

In the background to this dispute, there is another less obvious tension: the tension between the immigrants and the natives, the old versus the new, the global against the national. Black Cab drivers are predominantly white, working class males, while London's Uber drivers are predominantly non-white, immigrant males.[87] A survey from 2016 found that only 20% of Uber drivers identify themselves as 'white',[88] while in the PHV sector more generally, up to 94% of drivers are from BAME backgrounds.[89] The tension between the Black Cabs and Uber stretches beyond competing business models.

In conclusion, this extensive overview serves to illustrate that these key tensions between Uber and licensing authorities on the one hand and Black Cabs on the other provide the necessary context for the analysis of regulatory and legal issues around Uber's operation in the UK. Since these local actors appeal to regulation as a necessary tool for resolution, debates about the justification, purpose and tools of different regulatory approaches towards Uber come to the forefront.

2 Uber: Regulatory Issues in the UK

2.1 The Limits in 'Command-and-Control': Constraining Uber's Ride-Booking Process in London

This section takes a closer look on regulatory issues and grapples with prescriptive and principle-based approaches to regulation[90] by referring to the interaction

[85] Ibid.

[86] Ibid.

[87] Adam and Booth (2017) In London, Black Cabs Win A Battle Against Uber. But Is The War Over? Washington Post. https://www.washingtonpost.com/world/europe/in-london-black-cabs-win-a-battle-against-uber-but-is-the-war-over/2017/10/17/8a2c1468-a395-11e7-b573-8ec86cdfe1ed_story.html. Accessed 18 Apr 2020.

[88] Ainsworth (2017).

[89] *R (on the application of Independent Workers' Union of Great Britain and others) v The Mayor of London* [2019] EWHC 1997 (Admin), [78] (Lewis J).

[90] For present purposes, suffice it to say that principle-based regulation differs from prescriptive regulation in one crucial aspect. Prescriptive regulation relies on the capacity of state authorities to create particular rules that govern the behaviour of private actors and enforce them through formal enforcement procedures. By contrast, principle-based regulation involves the establishment of broad principles by the state. Private corporations are supposed to demonstrate their compliance with these

between Uber and TfL. More specifically, it discusses how the *technological* apparatus employed by Uber creates nuances and complications for the conventional regulatory debate. The use of algorithmic decision-making systems, with which most regulators are unfamiliar, raises salient challenges for local and national regulators. As it will be argued, the fragmentation of regulatory interaction with such dynamic and complex technologies across different localities in the UK makes the design of a uniform national regulatory strategy towards Uber a tall task. To elaborate on this argument, we discuss how different localities in the UK have made use of the aforementioned regulatory approaches and highlight their different experiences and struggles in the specific 'battleground' of licensing Uber as a private hire operator.

As we noted in the introduction, TfL is known for their active and interventionist approach towards Uber, with the local department of Uber (Uber London Limited or ULL) having already lost its licence to operate in London twice.[91] In this process of revocation, the regulator has been constantly assessing Uber's conformity with specific legal standards and did not hesitate to enforce sanctions to ensure such conformity. TfL, however, faced particular difficulties in identifying whether and to what extent ULL are in breach of its legal obligations due to difficulties with grasping the operation of algorithmic technologies employed by the company within its *ride-booking* process.

Following various tensions in the early years of their collaboration as regulator and regulatee,[92] major difficulties started to arise in 2014 when TfL aimed to assess whether ULL were complying with section 2 of the *Private Hire Vehicles (London) Act 1998*.[93] This section provides that for one to be legally able to 'accept' bookings, this person should hold an operator's licence in London. In other words, it is illegal for

principles, but they are not limited in how they will achieve this. In fact, they are encouraged to develop their own rules and standards.

[91] The last time was in November 2019 due to safety concerns and before this, the company licence renewal application was rejected by Transport for London (TfL) in September 2017, Topham (2019).

In this section, since we will be only discussing Uber–TfL interactions, we will be using the term 'ULL' (Uber London Limited) to distinguish Uber's office in London from other offices in the UK as well as Uber as transnational entity.

[92] For example, TfL was informed by Metropolitan Police in 2017 that ULL had not reported a number of serious and potentially criminal allegations against its drivers to the police. ULL, when asked, argued that passengers' privacy mandates the passengers themselves report such incidents, despite TfL's relevant guidelines in place stating that it is operators' responsibility to do so. In addition, tension arose because ULL was using an unsound online system for their drivers' medical checks (Push Doctor). Another example is their disagreement over the drivers enhanced criminal records checks. ULL recommended to their drivers to use a third-party company, i.e., Onfido,, to obtain these checks, instead of the TfL appointed GBGroup (a registered body to obtain these checks on TfL's behalf). It emerged that Onfido was relying on ULL itself to conduct identification of drivers. This move was interpreted by TfL as another step 'to interfere with TfL's private hire licensing requirements'. See TfL (2017).

[93] According to this provision, 'no person shall in London make provision for the invitation or London acceptance of, or accept, private hire bookings unless he is the holder of operator's licence, a private hire vehicle operator's licence for London'. If someone acts in contravention of this, section is guilty of an offence and liable on summary conviction to a fine not exceeding level 4 on the standard scale.

individual Uber drivers to accept bookings in these legal terms, since the person who holds an operator's London licence is ULL as a company. Hence, the only entity that should accept bookings is ULL and not the drivers. The company's rhetoric of empowering individual drivers to freely choose their terms of employment and flourish as entrepreneurs clearly raised challenges from a licensing law perspective. Were the drivers or were ULL accepting the bookings?

To clarify the conformity of both of these parties with licensing law, TfL requested from ULL the disclosure of the specific data flows associated with its ride-booking process. ULL responded that booking requests are *accepted by* the *ULL*'s dispatch server, which *then* selects an available driver and forwards details of the client request to her. After that, the driver heads to the pick-up location. ULL stated that it retains full control of all dispatches and 'has full responsibility for the data stored on the dispatch servers'.[94] According to this narrative, there was no violation of the law as ULL's dispatch server *first accepts* and *then allocates* a booking to an available driver.

TfL were not content with this explanation and insisted on requesting more information from ULL, pointing out that Uber's own terms and conditions suggest that drivers are 'accepting' bookings. In response, ULL claimed that drivers 'accept' rides only for the purposes of contract law and not for the purposes of the Private Hire Vehicles (London) Act 1998.[95] Crucially, ULL stated that 'acceptance by ULL of the passenger's booking takes place *at the same time* as the relevant driver is notified of the booking. This is an *inevitable consequence of the technology used* (emphasis added)'.[96] This was a different position than the explanation originally provided to the TfL, namely that ULL's dispatch server first accepts and then allocates a booking to an available driver.

Further complications arose in the context of the 2016 *Aslam* litigation over Uber drivers' employment status. Uber's general manager for northern Europe described the ride-booking process in detail. He suggested that the booking is *not accepted* by ULL *until* a driver has confirmed that they are available and ready to take the journey. This meant that acceptance by ULL happens almost simultaneously *after* a driver's acceptance. Despite TfL's request for explanations and flow charts as well as their visit to ULL' s offices to see the booking process-real time,[97] ULL only provided TfL with some (static) slides showing that driver's confirmation precedes ULL's acceptance of a booking for 1 s.[98]

In the summer of 2017, still struggling to clarify the specifics of the ride-booking process, the TfL appointed Deloitte to 'carry out an IT systems architect review'.[99] This review 'provided TfL with a much clearer and definitive understanding of the

[94]Witness Statement of Helen Kay Chapman (2018).

[95]Ibid., [75].

[96]Ibid., [79(c)].

[97]Chapman (2018, [101]).

[98]Ibid., [105].

[99]Ibid., [47].

booking process'.[100] Specifically, it has been found that ULL's algorithms automatically 'accept' the booking only *after* a driver has accepted the trip. If the driver rejects the trip, the rider's request goes to another available driver. It was clear that until that point no booking has been accepted by ULL. This finding directly contradicted earlier ULL explanations about its booking process. Based on this finding, TfL asked ULL whether its booking process had changed since 2014. In response, the company replied that the descriptions they provided back in 2014 were 'more generic' than the detailed discussions from 2016 onwards. Uber also insisted that 'our position on acceptance of bookings has not changed (...) we are not saying anything 'different'.[101] The tension between the two parties climaxed in September 2017, when the TfL did not renew Uber' licence to operate in London.

One might argue that this case demonstrates, eventually, a triumph of prescriptive regulation over the complexities posed by tech-driven multinational operation. The reality, however, is quite the opposite. The TfL, which is a quite well-resourced regulator and finds itself at the epicentre of media attention in the UK, needed more than three (3) years to comprehend and constrain only one aspect of Uber's operation. With the opacity created by ULL's ride-booking algorithms, the regulator struggled to assess the validity of the company's claims and their conformity with prescribed legal standards. Even with TfL's significant organisational capacity, the regulator eventually needed to outsource the final assessment to another private 'giant', Deloitte, so as to eventually resolve its difficulties. In the light of this experience, it is sensible to assume that other, less well resourced in money and expertise and less experienced regulators, might be heavily discouraged from embarking on a similar *bras de fer* with Uber. Are there, then, any better alternatives for them?

2.2 Challenging the Viability of Self-regulation: Cross-Border Hiring in the UK

Do the difficulties faced by TfL suggest that principle-based approaches to regulation are preferable to manage Uber's operation? While some local councils in the UK rejected Uber's licensing requests,[102] most licensing authorities have welcomed Uber's operation in their jurisdiction[103] To facilitate this, such authorities have been interpreting and implementing liberally the requirement of a 'fit and proper' operator in licensing law.[104] While this requirement must be met for the company's

[100]Ibid., [113].

[101]Ibid., [117].

[102]Swansea is one example where Uber's application for a licence has been rejected, See: Walford (2017).

[103]London, Manchester, Bristol, Leeds, Leicester, Sheffield, Nottingham Edinburgh and Glasgow are only some of the UK cities where Uber is operating. See Uber, Find Uber in cities around the world. https://www.uber.com/global/en/cities/. Accessed 18 Apr 2020.

[104]Local Government (Miscellaneous Provisions) Act 1976, s. 55, 1(a).

operation in London too,[105] local licensing authorities in other cities often use a minimal-standards-tick box-list for the fitness and propriety of an operator.[106] These are mostly satisfied by the absence of negative elements, such as previous licence revocation, convictions, penalty notices or arrests,[107] testing which takes place at the moment of considering an operator's application. After this point, they often take a 'wait-and-see' approach, trusting the private hire operator to develop their business in the area in good faith. Establishing good working relationships with Uber has been regarded as the optimal solution in this context. This has proven instrumental to enabling the company to produce its own solutions to thorny regulatory issues, in the way envisaged by self-regulatory approaches.

A prime example is the so-called issue of 'cross-border hiring'. Currently, there are some difficulties with clearly delineating the geographical boundaries within which private hire vehicles are allowed to deliver rides within the UK. In an attempt to resolve the issue, the Law Commission noted in a 2014 report that 'a licensed PHV driver can undertake journeys starting or ending anywhere in England and Wales that (relevant) operators are allowed to accept jobs',[108] i.e., within the latter's licensing district. This can happen if the driver, their vehicle and the operator they are working for are licenced by the same licensing authority. For example, an Uber driver and their vehicle may be licensed by TfL, but this driver is constantly working in the city of Leeds. Thus, licensing authorities cannot have real-time knowledge of whether particular drivers on the streets are licensed by them or another authority.

This creates multiple complications from a regulatory perspective. Crucially, it hampers effective enforcement of licensing legislation. In essence, it allows the delivery of rides anywhere in the country, without an effective monitoring of whether the driver is licensed in the district within which a particular ride is undertaken. As a corollary to that, licensing authorities are often also unable to deal with complaints against cross-border drivers. Both law-abiding drivers and customers are unhappy and, sometimes, not quite safe due to this inability. Furthermore, this allows the emergence of a particular type of 'forum shopping' carried out by private hire operators. Since companies like Uber can choose their preferred licensing authority without substantial repercussions, it will often be the case that they register where the requirements are less onerous and then operate in places with more demanding licensing

---

[105]Private Hire Vehicles (London) Act 1998, s 3(a).

[106]While TfL, in their operators guidance documents, outline both the administrative requirements necessary for the 'fit and proper' test and the elements that an operator should show their compliance with in the event of enforcement process (inspection). See s. 4a and 4b in TfF 'A guide for applicants who are applying for a London private hire operator's licence. http://content.tfl.gov.uk/phv-102.pdf

[107]See for example Leeds City Council, Taxi and Private Hire Licensing: Standard Conditions attached to operators licence. https://www.leeds.gov.uk/docs/Private%20Hire%20Vehicle%20Conditions.pdf; Exeter City Council. New operators application form. https://exeter.gov.uk/licensing/taxis-and-private-hire/private-hire-operators-licences/apply-for-a-new-private-hire-operators-licence/. Accessed 18 Apr 2020.

[108]Butcher (2018, p. 36) citing Law Commission, Taxi and Private Hire Services. Law Com No 347 (May 2014) [7.52].

frameworks. In the light of these implications, a solution to cross-border hiring is often listed high in the local authority's priorities.[109]

The Task and Finish Group, a body established in 2017 to assess the adequacy of licensing authority powers, argued in 2018 that the way forward is *stopping* cross-border hiring.[110] The Government, responding in February 2019, agreed that 'national minimum standards for taxi and PHV licensing' should be introduced.[111] While national legislative processes have been moving quite slowly, however, local authorities welcomed the development of a solution by none other than Uber themselves. In February 2018, the company made an announcement that they change the way their app works to help local regulators deal with cross-border hiring. More specifically, they said that Uber 'drivers will only be able to receive requests from the Uber app in the region which their licensing authority is'.[112] Uber was able to offer this solution by employing an algorithmic process that precludes customer requests in another region from appearing on the drivers' Uber app. Does this mean that algorithms saved the day for legal enforcement?

While algorithmic processes, indeed, revolutionised *what can be done* in the particular case, the devil is often in the details. Uber outlined nine 'regions' in the country: North East, North West, Yorkshire, Midlands, East of England, South East, South West, Greater London and Wales. Crucially, Uber drew their *own* regions,[113] which are larger than a single licensing authority and most of the time include many of them. Various licensing authorities, however, while belonging to one of Uber's 'regions', prescribe different licensing conditions for private hire operators. They may even disagree as to whether an operator should be licensed or not in the first place. This example indicates that principle-based regulation has its own limits, much like the prescriptive approach to regulation. Should, then, the government rely on Uber's organisational capacity to define and enforce effective rules on issues like cross-border hiring or should a more prescriptive approach remain the norm?

The discussed experiences of regulatory interaction between Uber and licensing regulators in the UK indicate the difficulty of crafting an homogenous, national regulatory strategy towards Uber. Sometimes, algorithmic processes raise high barriers to rule-enforcement, whereas other times their potential to assist regulation comes at the price of accountability and 'ownership' of reforms. In both cases, the interaction between the 'global' (as in Uber's business model) with the 'local' (as in regulatory action of local authorities) creates fast-moving, dynamic interactions, with national

---

[109]Local Government Association (2017, p. 7).

[110]Task and Finish Group on Taxi and Private Hire Vehicle Licensing (2018) Taxi and Private Hire Vehicle Licensing: Steps towards a safer and more robust system' [2.4]. https://assets.publishing.service.gov.uk/government/uploads/system/uploads/attachment_data/file/745516/taxi-and-phv-working-group-report.pdf. Accessed 18 Apr 2020.

[111]Department for Transport (2019) Government response; Report of the Task and Finish Group on Taxi and Private Hire Vehicle Licensing: Moving Britain Ahead 8. https://assets.publishing.service.gov.uk/government/uploads/system/uploads/attachment_data/file/847315/taxi-task-and-finish-gov-repsonse.pdf. Accessed 18 Apr 2020.

[112]Phillips (2018).

[113]Ibid.

authorities struggling to catch up in time. The fragmentation of the local experience and the discussed limits of both prescriptive and principle-based approaches render the national effort to adopt a homogenous response to regulating Uber a challenging task. Moving forward, it will be for the government to navigate a steady, context-specific course of action between the Scylla of ineffective prescription and the Charybdis of unrestrained, privately-created technological solutions. How has, however, the UK government attempted to strike this balance in so-far practice? We now illustrate this difficulty by reference to three specific legal fields, namely employment and tax and tortious liability.

3 Uber and Employment Law

Employment status in the gig economy has been at the epicentre of public discourse in the UK. The issue has been brought to the courts, triggering media reports,[114] policy dialogue,[115] parliamentary enquiries and investigations.[116] The most attention, however, has been paid to the litigation of Uber drivers aiming to re-classify them as 'workers' instead of self-employed 'independent contractors'.[117] To provide the legal background, UK law recognises a special intermediate category between 'employees' and 'independent contractors': 'workers'.[118] The status of 'worker' is associated with less entitlements in comparison with the protection provided to 'employees'. Specifically, a 'worker' enjoys trade union rights, a minimum wage, paid holidays, automatic employer pension contributions and protection from discrimination; an 'employee' enjoys statutory sick pay, maternity/paternity leave, a minimum notice period in the case of employment termination and protection against unfair dismissal.[119]

---

[114]'Gig economy' has become an autonomous news-column; See among others BBC News. https://www.bbc.co.uk/news/topics/c45x56x82mvt/gig-economy. Accessed 18 Apr 2020; the Guardian. https://www.theguardian.com/business/the-gig-economy. Accessed 18 Apr 2020.

[115]Watts J (2018) Gig economy: Theresa May promises to improve conditions for millions of workers. Independent. https://www.independent.co.uk/news/uk/politics/gig-economy-workers-rights-theresa-may-holiday-sick-pay-contracts-a8197906.html. Accessed 18 Apr 2020.

[116]Commons Select Committee (2017) Uber, Deliveroo, Hermes and Amazon questioned on 'gig economy'. UK Parliament. https://www.parliament.uk/business/committees/committees-a-z/commons-select/work-and-pensions-committee/news-parliament-2015/self-employment-gig-economy-evidence2-16-17/. Accessed 18 Apr 2020; Coghlan (2018).

[117]Johnston (2016).

[118]Employment Rights Act 1996, s 230(b). According to this section 'worker' is a person working under a contract 'whereby the individual undertakes to do or perform personally any work or services for another party to the contract whose status is not by virtue of the contract that of a client or customer of any profession or business undertaking carried on by the individual'. The same line is followed in Working Time Regulations 1998s 2(1)(b), National Minimum Wage Act 1998s 1(2)(a), Employment Relations Act 1999s 13 (1)(a), and the Part-time Workers (Prevention of Less Favourable Treatment) Regulations 2000s 1 (2)(b).

[119]For a brief depiction of the 'employee' and 'worker' status entitlements see the UK government's guidelines on employment status. https://www.gov.uk/employment-status. Accessed 18 Apr 2020.

The first major relevant litigation in the UK was the so-called *Aslam* case. In 2015, drivers Farrar and Aslam brought a claim against Uber to the Employment Tribunal (ET).[120] The claimants argued that they were not self-employed, as the company had been asserting, but 'workers' under UK employment law.[121] Despite the opposite arguments raised by Uber, the court granted their claims, concluding that they are entitled to the national minimum wage. The Tribunal's analysis on the 'worker' question revolved around whether someone is 'operating an *independent* profession or business' (emphasis added).[122] The judges found that this was not the case with Uber drivers, finding the idea that Uber in London is a 'mosaic of 30,000 small businesses linked by a common "platform" (…) faintly ridiculous'.[123] Uber, to the Tribunal, is not a mere intermediary but a transportation service company which exerts important control over its drivers-workers.[124] This finding mainly relied on the fact that the company 'fixes the fare (…), imposes numerous conditions on drivers (such as the limited choice of acceptable vehicles), (…) (and) (has in place a) rating system (which) amounts to a performance management/disciplinary procedure'.[125][126] This 'landmark ruling'[127] was upheld after two company's appeals.[128] The reasons behind this included, among others, that the performance of the contract cannot be transferred to a third person, that Uber sets the terms and conditions, manages and receives the journey's invoices and that the burden of the risks lie on the company when someone fraudulently uses the app.[129] This conclusion was not easy to reach, due to the ambiguousness surrounding the (in)dependence of those working via platforms. Other European courts have adjudicated that gig-economy service-providers are independent contractors,[130] whereas some employment law scholars argue that existing employment status categories are not adequate to capture the realities of working via an app.[131]

Because of this divergence, the *Aslam* developments were enthusiastically celebrated by trade unions in the UK, with the general secretary of GMB saying 'Uber

---

120 *Aslam* (n 4).

121 Employment Rights Act 1996, s 230(3)(b).

122 See Footnote 122.

123 Ibid., [90].

124 Ibid., [89] and [92].

125 Ibid., [92].

126 On the reliance of similar employment law cases using the 'economic reality test' and 'control test', see, e.g., Ratti L (2017).

127 Osborne H (2016).

128 *Uber BV v Aslam* [2018] EWCA Civ 2748; *Uber BV v Aslam and Ors* [2017] UKEAT

129 Marique and Marique (2018, p. 19).

130 Di Gennaro and Pavone (2018) Italian labour court hands down landmark decision on Foodora case with potentially far-reaching implications for any company active in Italy's growing Gig economy. Global Workplace Insider. https://www.globalworkplaceinsider.com/2018/05/italian-labour-court-hands-down-landmark-decision-on-foodora-case-with-potentially-far-reaching-implications-for-any-company-active-in-italys-growing-gig-economy/. Accessed 18 Apr 2020; Bohic (2018).

131 Todolli-Signes (2017).

should just accept the verdict and stop trying to find loopholes that deprive people of their hard-won rights and hard-earned pay'.[132] The case will move forward to the Supreme Court in July 2020 and the prospect of Uber aiming to overturn the *Aslam* judgment certainly creates nervousness to regulators. The latter find themselves at a crossroads as the Government's Review of Modern Working Practices in 2017—a year after this decision—proposed the introduction of a new status category, namely 'dependent contractor' to replace the term 'worker'. The review's proposals have been criticised on multiple grounds,[133] including that its suggestions for putting more emphasis on the notion of 'control' in Aslam-like cases departs 'from the approach currently taken by the courts'.[134]

To further illustrate the regulatory difficulties in the domestic context, the following sections touch upon two other important areas affected by Uber's operations, namely tax law and liability issues. We briefly discuss the relevant complications that Uber's business model has given rise to, before articulating our concluding remarks.

4 Uber and Taxation

Uber's tax practices in the UK are an important factor in explaining public discontent with the company. In 2013 and 2014 (first two full operating years), Uber London Ltd had a reported annual turnover of £12.4 m and paid £28,796 in tax—the equivalent of the annual tax contribution of just *three* Black Cab drivers.[135] Despite the mantra repeated by Uber representatives that it 'complies with all relevant tax provisions',[136] Uber's ingenious corporate structure allows it to minimise the tax burden. Uber Technologies Inc. is headquartered in San Francisco, US, but all of its operations outside of the US are controlled by subsidiaries; in the UK, we have Uber London Ltd (**"ULL"**) and Uber Britannia Ltd (**"UBL"**) which hold the PHV licences for London and the other locations in the UK respectively—these in turn are wholly owned by Uber International Holding B.V, a Dutch corporation headquartered in Amsterdam, which holds the legal rights to the Uber app[137]. The Dutch corporation is in turn owned by a Bermuda-based parent company.[138] When you book an Uber ride in London, you accept that the service is provided by Uber BV, the Dutch company, not Uber London or Uber Britannia.[139]

---

[132]Butler (2018).

[133]Bales et al. (2018).

[134]Ibid., (p. 61).

[135]Ferrari (2016, p. 60).

[136]Ibid.

[137]See Footnote 122.

[138]Ferrari (2016, p. 60).

[139]Ibid.

This structure allows Uber to take advantage of a procedure under EU VAT rules, called 'reverse charging'. Under EU law, when a service is rendered by a business in one Member State to a business in another Member State, the place where the transaction takes place in law (and where VAT stands to be collected) is the location where the *recipient* operates.[140] This mechanism was introduced to 'cut paperwork' involved in collecting VAT, by imposing the responsibility for VAT collection on the recipient country, rather than having to trace and refund all double VAT charges made in two Member States in intra-community transactions.[141] Hence, Uber BV is providing a service to UK-registered drivers, which would ordinarily mean the UK drivers should collect and pay VAT on the Uber fees under reverse charging. However, under UK law, individuals with annual turnover of under £85,000 are not required to register for VAT.[142] As most Uber drivers do not reach that threshold, they are not required to register nor collect tax, meaning that no VAT ends up being paid on the Uber fees.[143] If instead, ULL or UBL were providing the service, VAT would be payable. A 2017 estimate showed that using this mechanism, Uber can save £40 m a year.[144]

This fuels the dissatisfaction of the public, since Uber's services are heavily reliant on the UK infrastructure, paid for and maintained by UK taxpayers, to which Uber does not contribute its *fair share*. This can be seen as Uber's operations being effectively subsidised by the taxpaying public, a vast majority of whom never use Uber.[145] These complications notwithstanding that there is little scholarly attention to how the issues of intersect with the platform business model adopted by Uber. Nonetheless, with the UK having recently departed from the EU, the UK government's capacity to depart from EU 'reverse charging' tax rules in the interest of collecting more tax revenues from Uber will soon have to be tested. It is safe to assume that more tensions are likely to emerge from this issue, not only between Uber and the government, but also the UK government and the EU in the context of negotiating the future trade deal between the two parties.

---

[140] Council Directive 2006/112/EC of 28 November 2006 on the common system of value added tax [2006] OJ L 347/1, Article 44.

[141] Bergin (2017) Exclusive—Loophole Allows Uber To Avoid UK Tax, Undercut Rivals. https://uk.reuters.com/article/uk-uber-tax-britain/exclusive-loophole-allows-uber-to-avoid-uk-tax-undercut-rivals-idUKKBN18Y1Z6. Accessed 18 Apr 2020.

[142] Value Added Tax Act 1994, s 3(2), sch 3.

[143] Bergin (2017).

[144] Ibid.

[145] Ferrari (2016, p. 60).

5 Uber and Liability

5.1 Liability in Tort

In the event of personal injury or property damage caused by careless driving, the victims may have a claim against Uber in the tort of negligence. Negligence, in English law, is a tort that involves a breach of a duty to take care, which is imposed by common law or statute.[146] The logical first step is to establish that Uber owed their client a duty, and then move on to discuss a breach thereof.

5.1.1 Direct Duty Owed by Uber to Passengers

Generally businesses have a duty to provide competent staff,[147] and the appropriate equipment.[148] By analogy, it could be argued that Uber owes a primary duty of care to its users that the drivers are licensed, trained, insured, possess safe vehicles, and that the identity of the driver as displayed in the app, and in reality, correspond. Since the 'landmark case'[149] of *Robinson,* only for novel (in the sense: outside of previous court decision) imposition of a duty of care may a general test be applied; all other instances are determined by strict application of precedent.[150] As applying this duty to Uber, would be a 'novel' case, it would be determined[151] by application of the *Caparo*[152] test. The *Caparo* test was an attempt to provide a universal[153] test that could be applied in every case to determine whether a duty of care arose. However,

[146]Walton et al. (2018).

[147]*Butler (or Black) and another v Fife Coal Company Ltd* [1912] AC 149, 154 (Earl Loreburn LC): 'there was a duty upon the mine owners to appoint and keep in charge persons competent to deal with the dangers arising in this mine, and that they did not discharge this duty, whereby this unfortunate man met with his death'. The appeal was from Scotland and so was grounded in Scots Law, but the case was considered in *Harrison v National Coal Board* [1951] AC 639 for example at 642 without confining it to Scots law. It is treated as prima facie applying also in England and Wales in Peel E, Goudkamp J (eds) (2014) Winfield and Jolowicz on Tort, 19th edn. Sweet and Maxwell, UK, [9-021]. See also *Color Quest Ltd and others v Total Downstream UK plc* [2009] EWHC 540 (Comm), [330]-[365].

[148]*Ross v Associated Portland Cement Manufacturers Ltd* [1964] 1 WLR (HL) 768, 777 (Lord Reid) considered in terms of statutory liability under Factories Act 1937 and Factories Act 1969, but see Lord Donovan at 786: 'claim against the respondents, grounded in breach of statutory duty, can yield no different result from the action at common law'. See also *McGarvey v EVE NCI Ltd* [2002] EWCA Civ 374.

[149]Tofaris S (2018).

[150]*Robinson v Chief Constable of West Yorkshire Police* [2018] UKSC 4; [2018] AC 736, [26] (Lord Reed).

[151]*James-Bowen v Commissioner of Police for the Metropolis* [2018] UKSC 40, [22] (Lord Lloyd-Jones).

[152]*Caparo Industries plc v Dickman and others* (HL) [1990] 2 AC 606.

[153]See *Robinson v Chief Constable of West Yorkshire* (CA) [2014] EWCA Civ 15, [40]: 'the *Caparo* test applies to all claims in the modern law of negligence' (Hallett LJ).

the Supreme Court has found that such reading of the case was mistaken[154]: there can be no single, universal, test applicable for every case; instead an incremental approach based on precedent must be adopted. In 'novel' cases where the *Caparo* test ought to be applied, it involves three limbs: (1) foreseeability of the harm as a consequence of the defendant's conduct; (2) a relationship of sufficient proximity and (3) the imposition of the duty of care being fair, just and reasonable in the circumstances.[155]

However, this primary duty would largely be useless to a potential claimant, and thus, such an exercise is unlikely to ever be had, because 'negligence alone does not give a cause of action, damage alone does not give a cause of action; the two must co-exist'.[156] It is implausible that a breach of this precise duty would be the actual cause of damage. An unsafe vehicle would likely result in a claim in tort under the Occupiers' Liability Act 1957,[157] while an uninsured or an unlicensed driver, or someone just pretending to be the registered Uber driver, would likely result in a contractual claim, and since claims in tort and in contract can be concurrent and independent,[158] the route in tort outlined above would remain untrodden. A contractual claim would be possible since clause 3 of Uber's Terms of Conditions (T&Cs), which provides that 'the Booking Services include…(2) Identifying suitable Transportation Providers', who in turn are defined in clause 1 as 'drivers licensed to carry out private hire bookings in accordance with the Legislation'.[159] Failure to observe such a hypothetical duty then would also constitute a breach of contract, providing a simpler litigation path to the claimant. Even if the driver was uninsured, and hence a fruitless defendant for an action for compensation, the Motor Insurer's Bureau (MIB) will ordinarily step into pay the compensation to the victims of accidents caused by uninsured drivers.[160] Any primary duty to take care owed by Uber directly to the customer is likely to be of little practical assistance for those wronged in the course of enjoying Uber's services, and so secondary liability comes to fore.

5.1.2 Uber's Vicarious Liability for Torts Committed by Its Workers

The direct duty of Uber towards the individual consumer thus presenting no satisfactory solution, can an Uber user sue the company directly in tort for personal injury or property damage sustained as a result of negligent driving? The principle vicarious

---

[154] *Michael v Chief Constable of South Wales Police* [2015] UKSC 2; [2015] AC 1732, [106] (Lord Toulson).

[155] *Caparo Industries plc v Dickman and others* (HL) [1990] 2 AC 606, 615 (Lord Bridge).

[156] *East Suffolk Rivers Catchment Board v Kent* [1941] AC 74, 86–87 (Viscount Simon LC).

[157] See below Sect. 5.1.2.

[158] *Henderson and others v Merrett Syndicates Ltd and others* (HL) [1995] 2 AC 145, 193.

[159] Uber, Terms and Conditions (updated 17 Mar 2020), available online at. https://www.uber.com/legal/en/document/?name=general-terms-of-use&country=great-britain&lang=en-gb. Accessed 22 Apr 2020.

[160] *Delaney v Pickett* [2011] EWCA Civ 1532, [38] (Ward LJ).

liability the injured person can sue Uber for tort committed by another.[161] Now, it seems evident that Uber B.V. or Uber Britannia Ltd as legal entities do not owe a direct duty to each and every Uber passenger to drive carefully as they do not have any control over that, and they are not in the driver seat. However, a tort committed by a negligent Uber driver *can* in English law be attributed to Uber. The elements that have to be present before the tort of one can be ascribed to another are: (a) a civil wrong (tort); (b) committed by someone in the position of an 'employee' or 'akin to employee' of the defendant[162] and; (c) a sufficiently close link between the relationship and the tortious act.[163] The latter two elements have recently been elaborated in two important judgments of the Supreme Court in *Barclays v VC*[164] and *Morrisons v VC*.[165] Each element of vicarious liability shall be analysed in turn.

Tort of the Driver

At common law, the driver has a duty to exercise proper care to not injure or damage persons and property on and adjoining the highway, such proper care connoting 'avoidance of excessive speed, keeping a good look-out, observing traffic rules and signals and so on'.[166] Hence, if the driver does not exercise due care and causes injury or property damage, they are *prima facie* liable to the passenger in negligence (subject to the injury or damage not being too remote, and any defence invoked by the driver). Similarly, when the hypothetical driver allows another into their car (for remuneration or otherwise), under Occupiers Liability Act 1957 they must 'take such care as in all the circumstances of the case is reasonable to see that the visitor will be reasonably safe in using the premises for the purposes for which he is invited or permitted by the occupier to be there'[167], and this duty applies equally to vehicles.[168] If the driver does not take the requisite care to ensure the car is safe, they are also prima facie in breach of his statutory duty of care arising from this legislation. So,

---

[161] *Woodland v Swimming Teachers Association* [2013] UKSC 66, [3]; *Winfield and Jolowicz* (n), [21-001].

[162] *Majrowski v Guy's and St Thomas' NHS Trust* [2006] UKHL 34; [2007] 1 AC 224, [15] (Lord Nicholls); *Fecitt and others v NHS Manchester* [2011] EWCA Civ 1190, [33]: 'Absent any legal wrong by the employee, there is no room for the doctrine to operate' (Elias LJ).

[163] *The Catholic Child Welfare Society and others* v *Various Claimants and The Institute of the Brothers of the Christian Schools and others* [2012] UKSC 56; [2013] 2 AC 1 ('*Christian Brothers case*), [21] (Lord Phillips); *Barclays Bank plc v Various Claimants* (in the Supreme Court) ('Barclays v VC') [2020] UKSC 12, [1] (Lady Hale).

[164] *Barclays Bank plc v Various Claimants* (SC) [2020] UKSC 12.

[165] *WM Morrisons Supermarkets plc v Various Claimants* ('Morrisons v VC') (SC) [2020] UKSC 11.

[166] *Bourhill v Young* [1943] AC 92, 104 (Lord MacMillan), see also *Sutherland v Glasgow Corporation* [1951] SC (HL) 1, 6 (Lord Normand): 'The drivers of public vehicles, such as tramway cars and omnibuses particularly, may reasonably be expected to have skill and quickness of decision capable of coping with all ordinary traffic emergencies without endangering their passengers'.

[167] Occupiers' Liability Act 1957 ('OLA 1957'), s 2(2).

[168] OLA 1957, s 1(3).

once the aggrieved Uber passenger can demonstrate the negligence of the driver, the first element of vicarious liability is present.

Uber Drivers: Employees or Independent Contractors?

Next, moving onto the requisite relationship. Tort law has traditionally distinguished between just two categories of contractors—employees and independent contractors. Traditionally, the employer was vicariously liable for the acts of employees, but not those of independent contractors.[169] However, to paraphrase a frequently quoted statement by Lord Phillips in the *Christian Brothers* case: the law of vicarious liability has been on the move, and the categories have been expanding;[170] vicarious liability has been hotly litigated and discussed by courts, including at the highest level.[171] Notwithstanding all the 'moving', a historical principle that one is *never* vicariously liable for the torts committed by an independent contractor[172] has been recently reaffirmed by the Supreme Court.[173] However, in Employment Law, Uber drivers have been classified as 'workers',[174] and for the purposes of Tort Law, there is no such intermediate category—they can either be seen as '*employees*' (in which case Uber would be liable in tort for the personal injury or damage they cause by negligence) or '*independent contractors*' (meaning Uber would not be liable). In a recent judgment, Lady Hale has stressed that 'it would be going too far down the road to tidiness for this court to align the common law concept of vicarious liability, developed for one set of reasons, with the statutory concept of "worker", developed for a quite different set of reasons'.[175] This means that despite the drivers being seen as 'workers' in Labour law, they can still be labeled as 'employees' or 'independent contractors' for the purposes of determining tort liability: the Employment Law and Tort Law enquiries are distinct, though they may draw on similar factual features. In the following analysis, we use 'worker' in the lay sense, without importing any consideration of the Employment Law position, but merely to describe a person who fulfils tasks for another under contract, as distinguished from an 'employee' or 'independent contractor' which bear a significant legal meaning in tort.

Hence, whether Uber is liable for the negligence of its drivers turns on whether they are in (tort) law more like 'employees' or 'independent contractors'. However, in early 2020, the answer would almost certainly be that Uber drivers are indeed

---

[169] *Barclays Bank plc v Various Claimants* (SC) [2020] UKSC 12, [7].

[170] *Christian Brothers* case (n 166), [19].

[171] *Christian Brothers case* (n 166); *Cox v Ministry of Justice* [2016] UKSC 10; [2016] AC 660; *Mohamud v WM Morrison Supermarkets plc* [2016] UKSC 11; [2016] AC 667; *Armes v Nottinghamshire County Council* [2017] UKSC 60; [2018] AC 355; *WM Morrison Supermarkets plc v Various Claimants* [2020] UKSC 11 and *Barclays Bank plc v Various Claimants* (SC) [2020] UKSC 12.

[172] *D & F Estates Ltd v Church Commissioners* [1989] AC 177, 208 (Lord Bridge).

[173] *Barclays Bank plc v Various Claimants* (SC) [2020] UKSC 12, [24].

[174] See above Sect. 3 and *Uber BV v Aslam* [2018] EWCA Civ 2748.

[175] *Barclays Bank plc v Various Claimants* (SC) [2020] UKSC 12, [29].

'employees' for the purposes of vicarious liability, this no longer seems that clear. The highpoint in the expansive development of the doctrine marked by Court of Appeal decisions in *Bellman*[176] and *Barclays Bank v Various Claimants*[177] has now seen a retreat,[178] with the former case narrowly confirmed on the facts[179] and the latter case overturned on appeal.[180] It can no longer be said with confidence that Uber drivers would be seen in law as employees of the corporation for the purposes of tort law. What follows below is a discussion of the various legal principles, the interaction of which precludes a clear answer. It is argued, however, that various legal and policy considerations point us towards finding that Uber drivers would indeed be 'employees' of Uber for the purposes of vicarious liability in tort.

To begin with, the representatives of Uber could argue that their drivers have to be seen as independent contractors. After all, the drivers are under Uber's T&Cs 'independent third-party transportation providers'[181] and so, the argument goes, independent contractors for whose torts Uber can bear no vicarious liability. This objection can be rebutted. Mere labeling of the relationship as that of 'independent contractors' by the parties, even if that is in fact their intention (and not imposed by one by virtue of their superior bargaining power), is not conclusive and so does not preclude a finding of tortious liability.[182]

The traditional method of delineating if the person is an employee or an independent contractor is the 'control test', namely: can the defendant control the method in which the tortfeasor performs their tasks?[183] While there are elements which point to Uber having control, many of which were discussed above in the context of the *Aslam* case, the control test is, however, not the only test to determine the status of the worker. In fact, case law witnessed a departure from it even before our economy became a 'gig' one.[184] A degree of autonomy in the performance of a task is not conclusive of the relationship being that of a contract for services (independent contractor). The preferred test is that to impose vicarious liability onto the defendant the tortfeasor had to be at least in a position 'akin to employment'.[185] This has been

---

[176] *Bellman v Northampton Recruitment Ltd* [2018] EWCA Civ 2214.

[177] *Barclays Bank plc v Various Claimants* [2018] EWCA Civ 1670 (in the Court of Appeal).

[178] Johnson (2020), available online at https://www.lawgazette.co.uk/legal-updates/rowing-back-on-vicarious-liability/5103876.article. Accessed 22 Apr 2020.

[179] *WM Morrison Supermarkets plc v Various Claimants* [2020] UKSC 12, [46]: 'Although in some respects the judgment in *Bellman* adopted a similar [flawed] approach to *Mohamud* to that adopted by the Court of Appeal in the present case, the conclusion reached was correct' (Lord Reed).

[180] *Barclays Bank plc v Various Claimants* (SC) [2020] UKSC 12, [30].

[181] Cl 2 Part 2 Uber's Terms and Conditions (n 196).

[182] *Ferguson v Dawson and Partners (Contractors) Ltd* [1976] 1 WLR. 1213, 1222, 1230.

[183] *Market Investigations Ltd v Minister of Social Security* [1969] 2 QB 173, 186.

[184] As early as 2012 Lord Philips noted 'Today it is not realistic to look for a right to direct how an employee should perform his duties as a necessary element in the relationship between employer and employee', *Christian Brothers case* (n 166), [36]. This was echoed recently by Lady Hale in the *Barclays* case: see Footnote 175.

[185] *Christian Brothers case* (n 166), [47], [60].

recently reaffirmed by the Supreme Court in *Barclays Bank v VC*.[186] Let us see if an application of this test brings us any closer to the answer.

The relationship can be considered as sufficiently as '*akin*' to employment where the

> harm is wrongfully done by an individual who carries on activities *as an integral part of the business activities carried out by the defendant and for its benefit* (rather than his activities being *entirely* attributable to the conduct of a recognisably independent business of his own or of a third party), and where the commission of the wrongful act is a risk created by the defendant by assigning those activities to the individual in question.[187]

In this regard, let it be said that the activities of Uber's drivers, or for that matter its delivery people for UberEats, certainly constitute an 'integral' part of Uber's business in the United Kingdom. In fact Uber's profitability, and thus presence on the market, would be impossible without it. We can refer to a number of factual findings made in *Cox* by Lord Reed and apply them by analogy: Uber drivers are incorporated into Uber's transportation services: the drivers, in transporting Uber's customers, form the core of Uber's operations and profitability; Uber puts them in a position (that of a driver) where they may commit a variety of negligent acts, including causing personal injury or property damage by negligent driving[188]; the customer pays Uber not the individual driver for the service, and Uber is then a platform through which the drivers are paid; Uber determines the fee.[189] However, there have been cases where the drivers are not exclusively working *for* Uber—they keep a multitude of PHV apps open and accept bookings from a range of them.[190] In such cases, it can be difficult to maintain that Uber in fact provided anything more than a platform for the driver to further their own business venture. Again the inquiry is not overwhelmingly resolved, though there seems to be a (relatively) strong case for making Uber's employees (in labour law) and employees (in tort law).

Nonetheless, the counterargument can be made that Uber drivers are pursuing their own business venture and so are independent contractors. Recently, the Supreme Court found evidence that being paid a fee for each assignment as opposed to a retainer, the ability to refuse an offer of work and the carrying of own insurance was indicative of an 'independent' character of the work, sufficient to sever the link of vicarious liability.[191] Yes the defendant Bank had a form that the tortfeasor had to fill, and so his work was in that sense 'directed' but that was equally the case of many traditional independent contractors such as the people who washed windows, or auditors, the Supreme Court said.[192] The activity of Uber drivers could be assimilated

---

[186] *Barclays Bank plc v Various Claimants* (SC) [2020] UKSC 12, [22].

[187] *Cox* (n 174), [24] (emphasis supplied).

[188] *Cox* (n 174), [32].

[189] Hatzopoulos (2018).

[190] Katwala (2019).

[191] *Barclays Bank plc v Various Claimants* (SC) [2020] UKSC 12, [28].

[192] Ibid.

to such a model. They *can* refuse bookings. They are paid per journey. They are free to decide when and where they begin and end employment.

This would indeed be a compelling argument; however, it has to be kept in mind that there is an element of policy involved in finding vicarious liability.[193] The impact of policy can be seen in action by comparing the outcome of *Barclays Bank v VC* in the Court of Appeal and the Supreme Court. In the same set of facts, the Court of Appeal found sufficient indicators that the Bank *is* to be held vicariously liable,[194] while in the Supreme Court the facts were seen as pointing *against* liability.[195] The remark of Lord Justice Irwin, in the lower Court, that 'changes in the structure of employment', particularly in the fields of services,[196] required by the era of the gig economy needs to be followed by a change in the law of vicarious liability, hints at the eminent role played by policy and its application to our hypothetical case of a negligent Uber driver. In the *Barclays Bank v VC* case, the Supreme Court ultimately disagreed that such gig-economy-related policy reasons were sufficient to make the Bank liable in that particular case of a classic (we can even say outdated on the modern labour market) independent contractor, but that does not preclude policy pointing to a different conclusion in a case of Uber.

Even if there has been recent criticism by the Supreme Courts that lower courts are too ready to take the policy reasons to justify extending vicarious liability outside the scope of the 'akin to employment' situation,[197] the fact remains that policy *remains* pertinent, and rightly so. Making A liable for torts committed by B is difficult to justify on the basis of justice and so policy is what we fallback on to explain making innocent A pay for B's wrong against C. Consequently, it has to be observed that there are different policy considerations underpinning a finding that a publicly listed company is to be liable for sexual assaults committed up to 60 years ago by a since-deceased (whose estate has been long distributed) independent contractor[198], as compared to ensuring that millions of passengers of Uber have access to compensation for suffering injury or harm in the course of enjoying a widely available service. Both actions seek to vindicate a profoundly important right, but one has a much more current impact in terms of policy and potentially a wider application. The policy pursued would be making Uber bear the risks of the venture they undertake. Accordingly, the findings of the Supreme Court in *Barclays* can be distinguished, and their warning on excessive use of policy to find employers liable not fatal to classifying Uber's workforce as 'employees' in tort.

---

[193] *E v English Province of Our Lady of Charity* [2012] EWCA Civ 938; [2013] QB 722 [54] (Ward LJ): 'one cannot understand how the law relating to vicarious liability has developed nor how, if at all, it should develop without being aware of the various strands of policy which have informed that development'.

[194] *Barclays Bank plc v Various Claimants* (SC) [2020] UKSC 12, [55].

[195] Ibid., [28].

[196] Ibid., [45].

[197] Ibid., [16] (Lady Hale).

[198] Ibid., [1–5].

Lord Phillips' oft-quoted formulation expressly concedes the 'number of policy reasons which make it fair, just and reasonable to impose vicarious liability…'.[199] These include the fact that: (1) the employer is more likely to have the means to compensate the victim than the employee and can be expected to have insured against that liability; (2) the tort will have been committed as a result of activity for the benefit of the employer; (3) as part of the employer's business activity; (4) by employing the employee the employer will have created the risk of the tort committed by the employee; (5) the employee will, to a greater or lesser degree, have been under control of the employer.[200]

Taking these in turn given the nature of Uber's workforce (immigrant, working class) in England,[201] it is substantially more likely that Uber will be capable of bearing the burden of paying the victims' compensation. Simultaneously, every driver ought to have been insured, and so the argument might not be the most applicable, since there ordinarily will be an insurer with deep pockets to cover the loss. Similarly, as regards the fifth factor, the case of an Uber driver or a delivery person would likely be at the 'lesser extent'-end of the scale of control. Yet, the jurisprudence of the Supreme Court is unclear as to the significance of these factors: in 2016, Lord Reed said the first and fifth elements are the least significant,[202] while in 2017 the same Lord Reed (reiterating that the first factor as not important) relied on the local council's deeper pockets to justify finding vicarious liability.[203] Notwithstanding, assuming that it is the factors (2)-(4) that are crucial, we can see that, considering Uber's revenue structure which depends on the drivers, that Uber compels these drivers to provide transport services on their behalf, consequently creating a situation where the tort can be committed (after all, without Uber, the passenger would unlikely have been in the car in the first place at the time of the accident). Interestingly, in the case of a third unrelated party (so not an Uber user, but a passerby or another commuter) being a victim of the driver's negligence, this factor could sway the finding the other way, since it can be argued that the likelihood of a driver hitting a pedestrian is not increased by the virtue of the driver's working for Uber.

In terms of policy, it is in our view right that if Uber undertakes the business of providing transportation in London and throughout the United Kingdom, they bear the risks of that activity. The public dissatisfaction, which is felt against Uber for a number of reasons, might in fact only be heightened if the tech corporation relies on nuanced technicalities of law to evade liability. Perhaps in light of the fact that there are no reported cases of Uber being sued for personal injury and damage, suggests that there are very few such accidents. The office of London's Mayor estimates that 'private hire occupant casualties make up fewer than two per cent of all casualties, which is roughly proportionate to their overall share of journeys

[199] *Christian Brothers Case* (n 166), [35].

[200] Ibid.

[201] See section I.2 above at p. 13.

[202] *Cox* (n 174), [20–21].

[203] *Armes v Nottinghamshire CC* [2017] UKSC 60; [2018] AC 355, [63] (Lord Reed).

travelled on London's roads',[204] suggesting that Uber is not abnormally prone to be causing or participating in car accidents. Perhaps still, Uber is particularly good at settling such cases internally and directly with the victims which results in an absence of litigation on this issue. Perhaps, the above discussion is moot since drivers' insurers are there to provide compensation, rendering recourse to vicarious liability unnecessary. Either way, while not conclusive, it is submitted that policy should guide us towards ascribing vicarious liability to Uber, in the event that a case where vicarious liability is pleaded against Uber.

Policy reasoning must be formidable to justify departure from an established line of jurisprudence. Let us deduce what has been the approach of English courts to like cases. This precedent-reliant approach has been endorsed by the Supreme Court in recent decisions.[205] The question is whether an historic precedent solves this Gordian knot?

In *Willard v Whiteley Ltd*,[206] the claimant who owned numerous lorries licensed one, together with the driver, to the defendants, so that the latter could move some furniture. The defendants could not dismiss the driver, and his wages were paid by the claimants. In the course of moving the furniture an accident occurred which damaged the lorry, so the claimants sued, arguing at the time the driver was an employee of the defendant. The Court of Appeal dismissed the case arguing that, the fact that the defendant had no power to fire the driver plus that the wages were paid by the claimant, clearly indicated that the driver continued to be an employee of the *claimant* not the defendant, and so no liability could be established.[207] Pointing the other way is *Hall v Lees*.[208] In that case an association which contracted to provide nurses for local healthcare establishments, and to that end issued binding regulations for the nurses, carefully selected their workers, and were responsible for paying the nurses' wages, were found not to be their employer, meaning that there was no vicarious liability for the nurses' negligence in spilling hot water onto a patient recovering from an operation.[209] It should be said, however, that in this particular case, the Master of the Rolls made extensive reference to the regulations adopted by the defendants, as well as the contractual arrangement in place,[210] meaning it can be confined to its facts and bear little influence on the Uber case.

Lastly, in *White v Steadman*,[211] the owner of a landau was liable to passengers who hired a horse, landau and driver from him, after the horse was upset and bolted causing injury to the claimants.[212] The judgment is couched in terms of 'master and servant' which is clearly not apposite for a gig-economy consideration, but still

[204] London Assembly, 'Questions to the Mayor: Uber Accidents' (May 16, 2019).

[205] See Footnote 150, and *Morrisons v Various Claimants* (n 202), [36] (Lord Reed).

[206] [1938] 3 All ER 779.

[207] Ibid., 781 (Greer LJ).

[208] [1904] 2 KB 602.

[209] Ibid., 615 (Lord Collins MR).

[210] Ibid., 612.

[211] *White and wife v Steadman* [1913] 3 KB 340.

[212] Ibid., 349 (Lush J).

it could be used to support an argument that where the person paying the driver wages arranged with the passenger for a transport service they remained liable for the accident caused by the driver. The counterargument may be to argue that liability hinged on the finding of the horse as a 'dangerous animal',[213] which imposed a primary duty owed by the owner of said dangerous beast to those who may come in contact with it. However, it is submitted that in the historical context of the case, despite the judgement using that language to impose liability was not the main ground for the decision. The court stated that a 'person who keeps for hire horses, some of which he knows may be dangerous, cannot shelter himself behind his own want of knowledge, if that arises from his indifference or carelessness'.[214] This can also point towards the underlying principle that since the defendant made a business of hiring out horses and drivers, he ought to have borne the risk and not hide behind the horses' malicious spirit—hence, he ought to be liable. The fact that this particular defendant was in the business of hiring out horse-drawn carriages meant that the risk associated with that activity was of anxious horses, which is why the judge referred to the animal's spirit. By this reasoning, why should Uber be allowed to shift the risks of their activities in the United Kingdom to the drivers they employ.

Furthermore, there is an established principle in the parallel trade of licensed taxi drivers where the legal owner of a taxi is liable for the torts committed by the taxi driver notwithstanding that their relationship *may* be that of an independent contractor.[215] The reason is not simply that ownership of the vehicle imports some moral or legal duty but simply that of policy, that the public be allowed to sue those undertaking the business venture which resulted in their harm. It seems reasonable that the same policy reasoning be applied to Uber, and that this chain of reasoning be sufficient to justify finding such liability. In any event, a judicial finding to that effect would not constitute a radical departure from the established jurisprudence in England.

Summing up this lengthy discussion, the conclusion on this preliminary point is that the law does not provide a clear-cut answer as to whether drivers of Uber can be considered 'employees' for the purposes of vicarious liability. It has, however, been considered that a sound argument, grounded in policy and law, allows us to posit that PHV drivers operating for Uber ought to be seen as the company's employees as far as vicarious liability for tort is concerned. Each case will of course turn on its facts and the particular conduct of a particular driver may have a bearing on that determination.

---

[213] Ibid., 347.

[214] Ibid., 348.

[215] *Keen v Henry* [1894] 1 QB 292, 294 (Lord Esher MR); *King v London Improved Cab Co Ltd* (1889) 23 QBD 281, 283: 'public are entitled, whether as between the proprietor and the driver the relationship of master and servant exists or not, to say that so far as the public are concerned that relationship must be deemed, to exist'. (Lord Esher MR).

Course of Employment

Lastly, let us look at the third requirement for vicarious liability, namely, whether driving falls within the 'scope of employment'. The legal test has also undergone some mutations, predominantly in the seminal cases of *Lister*[216] and *Christian Brothers*,[217] where the Courts have struggled to bring sexual abuse of children within the 'scope of employment' of child-carer. The test subsequently reaffirmed by the Supreme Court is to consider whether an act is 'so closely connected with acts [the employee] was authorised to do that, for the purposes of the liability of his employer to third parties, [employee's wrongful act] may fairly and properly be regarded as done by him while acting in the ordinary course of his employment'.[218] Once a court has found that an Uber driver is an 'employee' employed for the purposes of driving passengers around, it becomes straightforward[219] that negligent driving causing personal injury or property damage is sufficiently connected with employment as to attribute liability in tort to Uber. But what if the driver does not have passengers in the car at the time of the accident? Are they still 'in the course of employment'?

To analyse this scenario, we can turn to established precedent. Old authorities require us to ask whether the conduct of the 'employee' at the time of the tort can be considered 'a separate journey'.[220] Accordingly, it should be asked whether a driver with their app on, driving through the streets waiting for a booking has 'departed altogether from [their] master's business'[221]? The answer is in the negative. In fact, they are precisely doing what Uber requires them to do. Additionally, cases have recognised that where the employment is peripatetic, the travel from locations where it is undertaken is still within the course of employment.[222] Hence, it can safely be argued that even if the Uber driver did not have a passenger in the car at the time of the tort's commission, but was either travelling to the pick-up destination or in search of a booking, vicarious liability of Uber can still be established.

---

[216] *Lister v Hesley Hall Ltd* [2001] UKHL 22; [2002] 1 AC 215, [65].

[217] *Christian Brothers case* (n 166), [85] (Lord Phillips).

[218] *Morrisons v Various Claimants* (n 202), [32] (Lord Reed) citing *Dubai Aluminium Co Ltd v Salaam* [2002] UKHL 48; [2003] 2 AC 366, [23] (Lord Nicholls).

[219] '[Vicarious liability] plainly covers the situation where the employee does something that he is employed to do in a manner that is negligent'. *Christian Brothers Case* (n 166), [62].

[220] *Hilton v Thomas Burthon (Rhodes) Ltd* [1961] 1 WLR 705, 709 (Diplock J). Older cases use the formulation "frolic of their own" to denote the employees radical departure from the duties assigned to them for own motives which severs the link of vicarious liability, stemming from a formulation in *Joel v Morrison* (1834) 172 ER 1338, 1339: 'The master is only liable where the servant is acting in the course of his employment. If he was going out of his way, against his master's implied commands, when driving on his master's business, he will make his master liable; but if he was going on a frolic of his own, without being at all on his master's business, the master will not be liable' (Parke B).

[221] *Nottingham v Aldridge* [1971] 2 QB 739, 747.

[222] *Nancollas v Insurance Officer* [1985] 1 All ER 833, 838.

It can, however, be difficult to draw a line before the personal use of the car and use thereof 'in the course of employment'. Technically, since employment for Uber is done from the drivers' own vehicles, at any point when the driver is driving their car, they can be moving to or from a place of employment. What if they decide that they will drive to the centre of a nearby town, before activating the app, and the accident happens before they reach it? Should they be seen as in the 'course of employment' in such a case? It becomes evident that a clear-cut answer which would apply in every case is impossible to prescribe, but that the determination of whether the tort occurred in the 'course of employment', provided that such 'employment' is found in the first place, will turn on the facts relevant to each driver, including evidence relating to their intention.

If our hypothetical victim got this far down the legal rabbit hole and establishes that Uber is vicariously liable for the harm that befell them, Uber can still turn around and recover all, or a portion of, the damages from the negligent employee under section 1 of the Civil Liability (Contribution) Act 1978. Since vicarious liability is a form of joint liability, the Act will apply permitting such recovery.[223] Hence, the negligent driver, if for whatever reason not sued by the victim in the first place, is not off the hook by virtue of the claimant pursuing a vicarious liability claim against Uber, though of course the practical impact of this will be limited. If Uber is sued under vicarious liability, it is most likely indicative that the driver was not worth suing (or not capable of being sued), and so is unlikely to be later chased by Uber itself.

5.1.3 Uber's Liability in the Rest of the UK

The above analysis is focused on the situation in England and Wales, but the process would be similar in Scots Law of Delict.[224] The basic principle is that fault binds only those who cause it,[225] and vicarious liability is an exception to that principle imposed for policy reasons.[226] The bipartite split whereby the relationship has to be that of employment, and the act done in the course thereof is equally present in Scots law,[227] with the distinction that the independent contractor/employee distinction is not as strictly observed as in England.[228] The analysis above is thus equally applicable to Scotland, though our hypothetical litigant faces perhaps a lower hurdle to success.

[223] Civil Liability (Contribution) Act 1978, s 6(1).

[224] Or rather the Scots Law of Reparation, as *delict* is said to be more narrow, since it excludes nuisance or strict liability. *Delict* is used here though to denote the widely known label for damages for civil wrongdoing that is known across the globe in legal jargon, and is most applicable to our case of negligence.

[225] *Culpa tenet suos auctores,* see Stewart (1991).

[226] *Baird v Hamilton* (1826) 4 S. 790, 799 (Lord Robertson).

[227] See for example *Kirby v National Coal Board* [1958] SC 514, 532.

[228] See *Grieve v Brown* (1926) SLT 498, 501 (Lord Sands).

Likewise in Northern Ireland, where the principle of vicarious liability is also subject to the independent contractor exception, whereby 'generally (…) an employer of an independent contractor will not be vicariously liable to an employee of the independent contractor for the negligence of that independent contractor'.[229] The law of vicarious liability is for our purposes the same in Northern Ireland as in England, making the above discussion applicable in that geographic area as well.[230]

In sum, the application of the principles of tortious liability to Uber's activities illustrates the difficulty of applying old concepts to the gig economy, as well as the resulting indeterminacy of the law in this regard. The tentative conclusion drawn here was that it should be the case that vicarious liability in tort is found to satisfy the claims of those who were harmed by the tortious act of an Uber driver. However, it has to be stressed that the chain of reasoning that brought us to that conclusion depended at various crucial steps on our interpretation of the law, rather than any positive norm. The lack of certainty as to whether Uber can be liable in tort under vicarious liability helps to explain why, until the negligent driver is bankrupt, uninsured, unidentifiable, or cannot be brought before the court, it is the driver that will be sued rather than Uber and primary liability will be enough to satisfy the claims of the victims.

6 Conclusion

To reiterate what has been discussed, in this chapter, we provided an overview of Uber's operations in the UK. In the first part of this chapter, we started with the importance of Uber's presence in the domestic context, and we touched upon the tensions arising between Uber and local licensing authorities and Uber's rival in London, Black Cabs. After setting this background, we turned our focus to regulatory issues emerging between local regulators and Uber. We provide an analysis of how the conventional regulatory debates on principle-based regulation vis-à-vis command and control regulation is challenged by Uber's technological apparatus. This analysis is supported by specific examples of interactions between Uber and local licensing authorities in the UK.

The limits of prescriptive regulation are explained by reference to the difficulties that TfL had to deal with when trying to figure out the details of Uber's ride-booking process. The limits of principle-based approaches are discussed by reference to the cross-border hiring problem that local licensing authorities face in their every day duties and the drawbacks of Uber's self-regulatory tool that aimed to contribute to the regulators' efforts. We argue that the fragmentation of the local experience on regulatory issues and the limits of both prescriptive and principle-based approaches

---

[229] *Mackin v S V Drumgath Parish and The RCB and Anor* [2007] NIQB 118, [17].

[230] See for example *Hunter v Department for the Regional Development for Northern Ireland* [2008] NIQB 88, [10–13] where the same authorities are applied, or *Bank of Ireland v McLaughlin* [2015] NIQB 85, [37].

renders the national effort to adopt a homogenous response to regulating a challenging task.

The last three sections on employment law, tax law and tortious liability issues intersecting with Uber's operations in the UK provide us with a practical illustration of how legal blind spots can render national efforts to regulate Uber even more difficult than they already are. The story on how to regulate Uber is still to be continued, this is just the beginning.

References

Adam K, Booth W (2017) In London, black cabs win a battle against Uber. But is the war over? Washington Post. https://tinyurl.com/y9hatwug. Accessed 18 Apr 2020

Ainsworth J (2017) Gig economy. House of Lords Library. Briefing, p 7

Bales K, Bogg A, Novitz T (2018) 'Voice' and 'choice' in modern working practices: problems with the Taylor review. Indus Law J 48(1):46–75

Bennhold K (2017) On London's streets, black cabs and Uber fight for a future. The New York Times. https://tinyurl.com/qsdt4uu. Accessed 18 Apr 2020

Bergin T (2017) Exclusive—loophole allows Uber to avoid UK tax, undercut rivals. https://tinyurl.com/ya6d4mav. Accessed 18 Apr 2020

Bohic C (2018) Les chauffeurs Uber alaries: c'est non pour les prud 'hommes' ('Employed Uber drivers with a right to salary: not for the labour court') IT Espresso. https://www.itespresso.fr/chauffeurs-uber-salaries-non-prud-hommes-183124.html. Accessed 18 Apr 2020

Bolt (2020) Bolt in London. https://bolt.eu/en/cities/london/. Accessed 18 Apr 2020

Business Energy and Industrial Strategy Committee of the House of Commons (2016) The digital economy (second report of session 2016–17). HC 87, 18

Butcher L (2018) Taxi and private hire vehicle licensing in England. House of Commons Briefing Paper, CBP, p 2005

Butler S (2018) Uber loses appeal over driver employment rights. The Guardian. https://www.theguardian.com/technology/2018/dec/19/uber-loses-appeal-over-driver-employment-rights. Accessed 18 Apr 2020

Coghlan A (2018) Delivery giant Deliveroo is now facing a parliamentary inquiry. Eater London. https://london.eater.com/2018/6/19/17479234/deliveroo-parliamentary-inquiry-mp-frank-field-gig-economy. Accessed 18 Apr 2020

Commons Select Committee (2017) Uber, Deliveroo, Hermes and Amazon questioned on 'gig economy'. UK Parliament. https://tinyurl.com/ya76xjyx. Accessed 18 Apr 2020

Department for Transport (2019) Government response; Report of the Task and Finish Group on Taxi and Private Hire Vehicle Licensing: Moving Britain ahead 8. https://tinyurl.com/ydgpcw9l. Accessed 18 Apr 2020

Di Gennaro V, Pavone A (2018) Italian labour court hands down landmark decision on Foodora case with potentially far-reaching implications for any company active in Italy's growing Gig economy. Global Workplace Insider. https://tinyurl.com/ya8ysv6n. Accessed 18 Apr 2020

Dudley G, Bannister D, Schwanen T (2017) The rise of Uber and regulating the disruptive innovator. Political Quarterly 88(3):492–500

Ferrari N (2016) Saving the black cab: why black cabs are vital to London's economy and identity. Policy Exchange 53. https://policyexchange.org.uk/publication/saving-the-black-cab/. Accessed 18 Apr 2020

Gett (2020) Gett. London taxi. https://gett.com/uk/city/london/. Accessed 18 Apr 2020

Grafton-Green P (2018) London taxi protest: Black cab drivers stage demo against TfL and Uber. Evening Standard. https://tinyurl.com/yawmhfam. Accessed 18 Apr 2020

Hatzopoulos V (2018) The collaborative economy and EU Law. Hart Publishing, Oxford
Johnson M (2020) Rowing back on vicarious liability. LSG 117(14):30
Johnston C (2016) Uber drivers win key employment case. BBC News. https://www.bbc.co.uk/news/business-37802386. Accessed 18 Apr 2020
Kabbee (2020) Surprisingly Cheap Airport Rides Whenever You Decide to Go. https://www.kabbee.com/. Accessed 18 Apr 2020
Kapten (2020) Kapten UK. https://www.kapten.com/uk/. Accessed 18 Apr 2020
Katwala A (2019) From Bolt to Kapten: Uber's London rivals are plotting its downfall. Wired. https://www.wired.co.uk/article/uber-alternatives-london-bolt-kapten. Accessed 18 Apr 2020
Lanxon N (2019) Is this the end of the road for Uber in London? Washington Post. https://tinyurl.com/y9humlvu. Accessed 18 Apr 2020
Local Government Association (2017) Taxi and PHV licensing. Councillors' handbook (England and Wales). https://tinyurl.com/y7v32a65. Accessed 18 Apr 2020
London Assembly, 'Questions to the Mayor: Uber Accidents' (May 16, 2019) available online at https://www.london.gov.uk/questions/2019/9003. Accessed 24 Apr 2020
Marique E, Marique Y (2018) Uber in London: Battle between public and private regulation. In: Renders D, Noguellou R (eds) Uber and taxis—comparative law studies Brylant Administrative Law. Bruylant, pp 163–200
Mayor of London (2016) Taxi and private hire action plan 2016 TfL. http://content.tfl.gov.uk/taxi-and-private-hire-action-plan-2016.pdf. Accessed 18 Apr 2020
BBC News (2019) Uber Birmingham: firm 'likely' to have licence Extended. BBC News. https://www.bbc.com/news/uk-england-birmingham-51193314. Accessed 18 Apr 2020
BBC News (2019) Uber loses its licence to operate in London. BBC News. https://www.bbc.com/news/business-50544283. Accessed 18 Apr 2020
OlaRide (2020) Change is Coming, London. https://olaride.uk/. Accessed 18 Apr 2020
Osborne H (2016) Uber loses right to classify UK drivers as self-employed. *The Guardian*. https://www.theguardian.com/technology/2016/oct/28/uber-uk-tribunal-self-employed-status. Accessed 18 Apr 2020
Peel E, Goudkamp J (eds) (2014) Winfield and Jolowicz on tort, 19th edn. Sweet and Maxwell, UK
Phillips J (2018) Changes to where drivers can receive trips. Drivers Announcements. Uber Blog *Blog*. https://www.uber.com/en-GB/blog/changes-to-where-drivers-can-receive-trips/. Accessed 18 Apr 2020
Ratti L (2017) Online platforms and crowdwork in Europe: a two-step approach to expanding agency work provisions. Comp Labor Law and Policy J 38:477–511
Stewart WJ (1991) Reparation: liability for Delict. W. Green
Task and Finish Group on Taxi and Private Hire Vehicle Licensing (2018) Taxi and private hire vehicle licensing: Steps towards a safer and more robust system'. https://tinyurl.com/y3vrfwst. Accessed 18 Apr 2020
Todolli-Signes A (2017) The 'gig-economy': employee, self-employed or the need for a special employment regulation? Transf Eur Rev Labour Res 23:200–205
Tofaris S (2018) Duty of care in negligence: return to orthodoxy? CLJ 77(3):454–457
Topham G (2016) Black cab's driver's Uber protest brings London traffic to a standstill. The Guardian. https://tinyurl.com/y93z7ro8. Accessed 18 Apr 2020
Topham G (2019) 'Uber loses London licence after TfL finds drivers faked identity' The Guardian. https://tinyurl.com/w4y7c7n. Accessed 18 Apr 2020
Topping A (2014) Uber: testing the app driving UK Black cab drivers around the bend. The Guardian. https://tinyurl.com/y9nfkqq9. Accessed 18 Apr 2020
Transport for London (2016) English language requirement. https://tinyurl.com/ydyrcdjb. Accessed 18 Apr 2020
Transport for London (2017) Licensing decision on Uber London Limited. https://tinyurl.com/yc6ry6n4. Accessed 18 Apr 2020
Transport for London (2017) Skeleton argument of Transport for London' in the Magistrates' Court sitting at Westminster. http://content.tfl.gov.uk/tfl-skeleton-argument.pdf. Accessed 18 Apr 2020

Transport for London (2019) Private Hire vehicle drivers topographical skills assessments. Notice 06/19. http://content.tfl.gov.uk/06-19-topographical-skills-assessments.pdf. Accessed 18 Apr 2020
Transport for London (2019) Uber London Limited found to be not a fit and proper to hold a private hire operator licence. https://tinyurl.com/wt47lqv. Accessed 18 Apr 2020
Transport for London (2020) Transport for London guide to taxis and private hire. https://tfl.gov.uk/modes/taxis-and-minicabs/what-to-expect-from-your-journey. Accessed 18 Apr 2020
Uber (2019) Update on Uber in London. https://www.uber.com/en-GB/blog/uber-in-london/. Accessed 18 Apr 2020
Uber (2019) Where does Uber operate in the UK. https://www.uber.com/en-GB/blog/where-does-uber-operate-in-the-uk/. Accessed 18 Apr 2020
Uber (2020) Find Uber in cities around the world. https://www.uber.com/global/en/cities/. Accessed 18 Apr 2020
Uber (2020) Terms and conditions. https://tinyurl.com/y8xc4nmr. Accessed 22 Apr 2020
ViaVan (2020) Solutions. https://www.viavan.com/solutions/. Accessed 18 Apr 2020
Walford J (2017) Uber have been refused a licence to operate in Swansea. Wales Online. https://www.walesonline.co.uk/news/wales-news/uber-been-rejected-license-operate-13976914. Accessed 18 Apr 2020
Wall Street Journal (2014) The London taxi challenge. http://graphics.wsj.com/london-taxi-challenge/. Accessed 18 Apr 2020
Walton CT, Armitage M, Cooper R, Hyde R, Kramer P, Todd S (eds) (2018) Charlesworth and Percy on negligence, 14th edn. Sweet and Maxwell, UK
Watts J (2018) Gig economy: Theresa May promises to improve conditions for millions of workers. Independent. https://tinyurl.com/y9tgv6c4. Accessed 18 Apr 2020
Wheely (2020) https://wheely.com/en?gclid=Cj0KCQiAvc_xBRCYARIsAC5QT9miEhQruj9Fb4Q3pkU7tcYyaK_Cs8ikL7Zsn0gsRRJG62wHbHyn6dQaAppMEALw_wcB. Accessed 18 Apr 2020
Witness statement of Helen Kay Chapman (2018) Westminster Magistrates Court. http://content.tfl.gov.uk/helen-chapman-first-witness-statement-march.pdf. Accessed 18 Apr 2020
Xooox (2020) What is xooox and Why is It Here?. https://xooox.co.uk/about/. Accessed 18 Apr 2020

Chapter 7
The Legal Framework of Uber in Spain

Francisco de Elizalde and Fernando Pastor-Merchante

1 Introduction

Uber started operating in Spain's capital in April 2014 through its UberPop app. Its initial strategy was to open its platform to private drivers without professional license, in the understanding that their services fell outside the scope of both the taxi and the 'lease of vehicles with driver' (VTC) regulatory frameworks. It was a short-lived experience, because the Madrid Taxi Association brought an action for unfair competition and successfully applied for an interim injunction against Uber. In December 2014, a commercial court issued a provisional injunction order prohibiting Uber from offering its platform in Spain.[1] The injunction prompted Uber to quit the Spanish market as of December 30, 2014.

Uber's second landing took place in 2016 through the UberX app. Uber's legal strategy was completely different this time, since the app would only be open to professional drivers with a VTC authorization. Thus, Uber adopted the model that Cabify, its main competitor in the Spanish market, had been using since 2011.[2] The new strategy has allowed Uber to reach more than 50 Spanish municipalities, including large cities such as Madrid, Sevilla and Málaga.[3] However, it has come across regulatory obstacles in other important cities, such as Barcelona. The decision of the Catalan regional government to prohibit VTC holders from picking up

[1]Commercial Court No. 2 of Madrid, Order of 9 Dec 2014. ECLI:ES:JMM:2014:74A.

[2]Doménech Pascual G (2017).

[3]Uber's webpage. https://www.uber.com/global/en/cities. Accessed 16 Apr 2020.

F. de Elizalde (✉) · F. Pastor-Merchante
IE University, Segovia, Spain
e-mail: francisco.deelizalde@ie.edu

F. Pastor-Merchante
e-mail: fernando.pastor@ie.edu

Z. Ayata and I. Önay (eds.), *Global Perspectives on Legal Challenges Posed by Ridesharing Companies*,
https://doi.org/10.1007/978-981-15-7035-3_7

passengers who have not booked up their trips with a minimum 15-min notice has so far kept Uber away from that city.[4]

The purpose of this chapter is to describe the main elements of the legal framework that governs Uber's activities in Spain. The chapter starts with an overview of the legal regime that governs VTC authorizations, for as noted earlier Uber's platform is only open to professional drivers in possession of that administrative permit. The chapter then considers the main challenges faced by Uber from a labor law perspective, before looking into the liability arising from private law.

2 General Regulatory Framework

2.1 Sources of Law and Competences

The regulatory framework that governs private, on-demand transportation services is mostly laid down by the Law on Land Transport and its implementing regulation.[5] The Law on Land Transport is a piece of legislation passed by the central parliament on the basis of the exclusive competence over *inter-regional* land transport that the Spanish Constitution reserves for the central government.[6]

Spain is a quasi-federal country, and it turns out that all of the 17 regions or 'autonomous communities' in which the country is divided have legislative and executive powers over *intra-regional* land transport.[7] This means that their respective legislative bodies could in theory create a parallel VTC regime, whose territorial scope would be limited to the territory of the region in question. However, only two autonomous communities have done so (Cantabria and the Canary Islands)[8]. Given that they do not represent a large share of the Spanish market, the rest of the discussion shall focus on the VTC regime laid down by the *national* Law on Land Transport.

It should be noted though that autonomous communities play an important role under that regime: from a rule-making perspective, because there are certain aspects of the regulation where they are given some leeway;[9] from an executive perspective,

[4]*Decret llei 4/2019, de 29 de gener, de mesures urgents en matèria de transport de viatgers mitjançant el lloguer de vehicles amb conductor.*

[5]*Ley 16/1987, de 30 de julio, de Ordenación de los Transportes Terrestres* (hereinafter, 'Law on Land Transport') and *Reglamento de la Ley de Ordenación de los Transportes Terrestres, aprobado por Real Decreto 1211/1990, de 28 de septiembre* (hereinafter, 'Implementing Regulation on Land Transport'). Unless stated otherwise, all references to the Law on Land Transport and to its implementing regulation are to their respective consolidated versions.

[6]Spanish Constitution, Article 149.1 (21).

[7]Spanish Constitution, Article 148.1 (5) allows autonomous communities to take over competences in this field, which they have all done through their respective by-laws ('*Estatutos de Autonomía*').

[8]On the allocation of competences in this field, see Cano Campos (2009); Velasco Caballero (2009).

[9]E.g. Law on Land Transport, Article 48.3 allows to modify the 1/30 quota discussed below (Sect. 2.4).

because the competence to grant VTC authorizations and to supervise the VTC market has been delegated upon them.[10]

2.2 *The Requirement to Hold an Administrative Authorization*

The Law on Land Transport and its implementing regulation prohibit the provision of passenger transport services without a prior administrative authorization.[11] There are certain exceptions to this rule, but they are not relevant here: private, on-demand passenger transportation services do require a VTC authorization (‘*autorización de vehículos con conductor*’).

The prevailing understanding in Spain is that the obligation to obtain a VTC authorization (and to comply with the VTC regime) falls upon the ultimate providers of the service—that is to say, the owners and drivers of the vehicles used for that purpose. The issue has arisen in the context of the numerous actions based on the Law on Unfair Commercial Practices[12] brought by taxi associations against Uber (and Cabify). The majority of these actions have relied on Article 15, which brings within the definition of unfair commercial practices the competitive advantages obtained by companies as a result of their failure to comply with the legal order. This provision allows market operators to sue their competitors if they fail to comply with the regulatory framework applicable in their sector and to apply for a wide panoply of remedies (including declaratory actions, cessation orders and damages).[13] This type of horizontal litigation unfolds before commercial courts, but the legal controversy often revolves around the interpretation and fulfillment of the regulatory obligations that fall upon the shoulders of defendants.

In general, this type of actions have not been successful, because courts have been reluctant to blame Uber for the infringements of the VTC regulatory framework allegedly committed by VTC owners and drivers. For example, in a dispute between the Professional Federation of Taxi Drivers of Madrid and Cabify, both the first instance and the appeal courts held that the rule banning VTCs from circulating in search of clients binds VTC holders rather than intermediary ride-hailing companies such as Cabify.[14]

---

[10] *Ley Orgánica 5/1987, de 30 de julio, de Delegación de Facultades del Estado èn las Comunidades Autónomas en relación con los transportes por carretera y por cable*, Articles 5 and 6.

[11] Law on Land Transport, Article 42.1 and Implementing Regulation on Land Transport, Article 180.2.

[12] *Ley 3/1991, de 10 de enero, de Competencia Desleal* (‘Law on Unfair Commercial Practices’).

[13] Ibid., Article 32.

[14] Commercial Court No. 12 of Madrid, Judgment of 13 June 2017. ECLI:ES:JMM:2017:3145, confirmed on appeal by the Madrid Court of Appeal, Judgment of 18 Jan 2019. ECLI:ES:APM:2019:3.

This issue was also at stake in the well-known *Asociación Profesional Élite Taxi v Uber* case. A taxi association asked a Commercial Court in Barcelona to order Uber to suspend its activities and to refrain from offering its services in the future. The action was premised on the claim that the drivers operating under Uber platform were in breach of the taxi regulatory framework, because they were actually providing taxi services without an appropriate license, and that Uber was accomplice in that infringement. Uber claimed that its intermediation services fell under the EU directives on services and on electronic commerce, which is why they were not—and could not—be subject to any administrative authorization requirement.[15] In order to clarify this issue, the Commercial Court stayed proceedings and submitted a preliminary reference to the Court of Justice of the European Union (CJEU). The latter held that Uber's services are to be classified as 'services in the field of transport,' which are not covered by either of these directives.[16] Given that the European Union institutions have not legislated in this field, the CJEU further held that transport services are subject to the national regulatory framework of each Member Sate.[17] In light of this answer, the Commercial Court of Barcelona ruled that Uber's services could not be legally characterized as mere 'intermediation' services and that they fell under the ambit of the regulatory framework on transport. However, the Court did not completely spell out the implications that this had, because it dismissed the action on the ground that, even if substantiated, the administrative infringement that the plaintiffs imputed to Uber did not constitute an act of unfair competition and that its imputation to Uber Spain (as opposed to Uber BV, its parent Dutch company) could not be established[18]

Finally, the issue arose again in the context of judicial proceedings instituted by Uber against an administrative sanction imposed by the Catalan regional authorities, on the ground that it lacked an appropriate administrative authorization. Ruling at first instance and prior to the judgment of the CJEU mentioned above, the Administrative Court No 15 of Barcelona quashed the sanction, in the understanding that Uber was not subject to any prior administrative authorization requirement irrespective of its characterization as 'intermediation' or as 'electronic service' provider.[19] The Catalan administration appealed that judgment and the Supreme Court (Administrative Chamber) granted certiorari in order to clarify the regulatory framework to which this kind of platforms were subject. The judgment of the CJEU in the *Asociación Profesional Élite Taxi v Uber* case came out before the Supreme Court rendered its decision and the Supreme Court explicitly relied on it in order to conclude that

[15]Directive 2006/123/EC of the European Parliament and of the Council of 12 December 2006 on services in the internal market (OJ L 376, 27 Dec 2006, p. 36); Directive 2000/31/EC of the European Parliament and of the Council of 8 June 2000 on certain legal aspects of information society services, in particular electronic commerce, in the Internal Market (OJ L 178, 17 July 2000, p. 1).

[16]Court of Justice of the European Union, Judgment of 20 Dec 2017 in *Asociación Profesional Élite Taxi v Uber Systems Spain SL*. ECLI:EU:C:2017:981, para. 40–6.

[17]Ibid., (para. 47).

[18]Commercial Court No. 3 of Barcelona, Judgment of 10 Apr 2018. ECLI:ES:JMB:2018:38.

[19]Administrative Court No. 15 of Barcelona, Judgment of 6 Oct 2016. ECLI:ES:JCA:2016:2579.

Uber's activities fall within the scope of the Law on Land Transport and are therefore subject to the prior authorization requirement laid down by Article 42.1 thereof.[20]

The judgment of the administrative chamber of the Supreme Court is unequivocal as the fact that Uber's activities cannot escape the regulatory framework that governs land transport in Spain and as to the prior administrative authorization requirement that this entails. However, the implications of this judgment have not been fully worked out yet, among other things because the judgment does not clarify the specific regime to which Uber is subject, among the various regulatory frameworks existing in the field of transport. This is an issue that we discuss in more length below.[21] In this section, the rest of the discussion focuses on the legal regime that surrounds the administrative authorizations of VTC owners and drivers.

2.3 *Overview of the Conditions that Govern the Granting of VTC Authorization and the Provision of VTC Services*

In principle, the granting of VTC authorizations is non-discretionary, in the sense that administrative authorities are obliged to give a positive response to any applicant who satisfies the conditions laid down by the Law on Land Transport and its implementing regulation. However, most applications are rejected on the basis of the quantitative restrictions on the number of VTCs explored below.

VTC authorizations are linked to particular vehicles, which is why these conditions concern both the natural or legal person who applies for the authorization and the vehicles that shall be ascribed to the service. On the first front, it is mandatory to be a national of Spain or of another EU Member State, to have a domicile in Spain and an electronic signature and address and to be in compliance with fiscal, labor and social legislation.[22] Additionally, it is necessary to satisfy certain financial and capital requirements.[23] On the second front, vehicles must be registered in Spain, have a maximum of nine seats and satisfy the technical requirements laid down by the implementing regulation.[24] There used to be certain requirements regarding the size of the fleet owned by applicants and the number of employed drivers that they have at their service, but they were quashed by the Supreme Court on ultra vires grounds.[25]

VTC authorizations only allow their holders to offer pre-arranged trips, where the pick up and destination points are agreed prior to the initiation of the journey.[26] It

---

[20] Supreme Court, Judgment of 25 Jan 2018. ECLI:ES:TS:2018:120.

[21] Section 4.

[22] Law on Land Transport, Articles 43.1 and 44.

[23] Law on Land Transport, Articles 45 and 46.

[24] Implementing Regulation on Land Transport, Article 181.1.

[25] Supreme Court, Judgment of 14 Feb 2012. ECLI:ES:TS:2012:1076; Supreme Court, Judgment of 4 June 2018. ECLI:ES:TS:2018:1913.

[26] Implementing Regulation on Land Transport, Article 182.1.

follows that VTCs may not circulate in search of customers and that they may not await customers parked on the street.[27] The walk-up market is thus reserved for taxi-licensees, which are the only ones that may be flagged down on the street or picked up at a public stand. However, unlike taxis, VTCs are not subject to regulated prices, their only obligation being to make their prices public.[28] There are certain ancillary and instrumental rules aimed at ensuring compliance with these conditions. For example, VTC holders are obliged to record all pre-arranged agreements in advance and to make them available to regulatory authorities.[29] Also, VTCs may not have any external sign that could mislead customers into the belief that they are taxis, which is why autonomous communities may additionally require VTCs to display a specific sign identifying them as such.[30] Needless to say, VTCs are obliged to comply with the general legislation on traffic and road safety [31] and to have passengers covered by the appropriate civil liability insurance.[32]

2.4 *Quantitative Restrictions on the Total Number of VTC Authorizations*

One of the most contentious aspects of the VTC regime is the existence of a quantitative cap on the number of authorizations that may be granted (*numerus clausus*).[33] The Spanish regulatory framework has experienced important changes on this front, which is why the rules currently in force cannot be understood without a reference to their precedents.

As originally enacted, the Spanish Law on Land Transport did not contain any specific provision on VTCs. Indeed, the only on-demand service addressed by its chapter on 'urban transport' was the one offered by taxis.[34] For its part, the chapter on 'rental cars' used to be silent on the possibility of leasing cars with a driver.[35] This gap was filled in by the administrative regulation adopted in order to implement that law, which did include a specific section on car-rentals with driver. The regulation made it clear that it was necessary to obtain an administrative authorization in order

[27] Ibid., in fine.

[28] Law on Land Transport, Articles 17.1 and 18; Implementing Regulation on Land Transport, Article 182.3.

[29] See Footnote 26.

[30] Implementing Regulation on Land Transport, Article 182.4.

[31] Law on Land Transport, Article 42.3.

[32] Implementing Regulation on Land Transport, Article 182.6.

[33] Guillén Navarro (2018).

[34] Law on Land Transport (original version), Articles 113–118 which were annulled by the Constitutional Court on jurisdictional grounds in Judgment 118/1996 of 27 June 1996. ECLI:ES:TC:1996:118.

[35] Law on Land Transport (original version), Articles 133–137.

to carry out that activity.[36] Moreover, it included a specific reference to the possibility of rejecting applications for a VTC authorization in case of 'manifest disproportion' between the number of VTC authorizations and the number of potential users within a municipality.[37] The disproportion was deemed 'manifest' where there was more than 1 VTC authorization for every 30 taxi licenses within the territory of the autonomous community where the applicant was based.[38] At the time, this restriction was not very problematic, because VTC services were still very marginal, and the 1/30 quota was rarely if ever reached.

The situation changed completely after the enactment of the legislative package adopted in order to implement the Services Directive.[39] Although transport services fell outside the scope of the directive, the Spanish legislator used the implementation of the directive to introduce a series of liberalizing reforms that went beyond the requirements of Union law. The reform added a specific reference to VTCs in the Law on Land Transport, making it clear that they would not be subject to the legal regime of rental cars but rather of public on-demand services.[40] And, although there was no explicit provision derogating the obligation to obtain an administrative authorization in order to carry out VTC services, the spirit of the reform was to remove regulatory barriers to entry into services markets.[41] It was therefore possible to argue that quantitative restrictions on VTCs and the 1/30 quota had no room in the new regulatory framework.

However, the executive branch of government did not remove these restrictions from the administrative regulations where they were located, despite the fact that it did revise those regulations in order to adapt them to other changes brought about by the implementation of the Services Directive.[42] By the time this happened, demand for VTC authorizations had already begun to grow in regions such as Madrid and Catalonia, where the 1/30 quota had long been reached. The legality of this quota was called into question in the context of the judicial review proceedings brought by applicants whose VTC authorization requests had been rejected. The issue eventually made it to the Supreme Court, which confirmed that the 2009 reform of the Law

[36]Implementing Regulation on Land Transport (original version), Article 180.2.

[37]Implementing Regulation on Land Transport (original version), Article 181.2.

[38]*Orden de 30 de julio de 1998 por la que se desarrolla el Reglamento de la Ley de Ordenación de los Transportes Terrestres*, Article 14.

[39]*Ley 17/2009, de 23 de noviembre, sobre el libre acceso a las actividades de servicios y su ejercicio*; *Ley 25/2009, de 22 de diciembre, de modificación de diversas leyes para su adaptación a la Ley sobre el libre acceso a las actividades de servicios y su ejercicio.*

[40]*Ley 25/2009, de 22 de diciembre, de modificación de diversas leyes para su adaptación a la Ley sobre el libre acceso a las actividades de servicios y su ejercicio*, Article 21.

[41]*Ley 17/2009, de 23 de noviembre, sobre el libre acceso a las actividades de servicios y su ejercicio*, Article 4.1.

[42]*Real Decreto 919/2010, de 16 de julio, por el que se modifica el Reglamento de la Ley de Ordenación de los Transportes Terrestres para adaptarlo a la Ley 25/2009, de 22 de diciembre, de modificación de diversas leyes para su adaptación a la Ley sobre libre acceso a las actividades de servicios y su ejercicio.*

on Land Transport had effectively derogated the quantitative restrictions on VTC authorizations.[43]

Before the judgment of the Supreme Court came out, and in anticipation of that outcome, the legislator had already amended the Law on Land Transport in order to provide quantitative restrictions on VTCs with the legal basis that they lacked.[44] The new wording of Article 48 empowered the executive to impose quantitative restrictions on VTC authorizations where the quantity of taxi licenses is restricted by regional or local regulations. According to the preamble of the reform, the goal behind that measure was to maintain the balance between the two main types of on-demand transport services (taxis and VTCs). It was on the basis of this clause that the administrative regulation on land transport was subsequently reformed, enshrining the 1/30 quota.[45] The Spanish Competition Authority challenged the proportionality of this rule, but its action was dismissed by the Supreme Court.[46] Before the judgment came out, though, the 1/30 quota had been codified in the text of the Law on Land Transport itself, through yet another legislative reform.[47] The quota is now enshrined in Article 48.3, albeit with some flexibility, since the clause allows autonomous communities to alter the quota in order to make it less restrictive for VTCs.

It should be noted, though, that the 1/30 quota only revived after the entry into force of the 2015 reform of the Implementing Regulation on Land Transport. This means that for almost six years—from the entry into force of the legislative package for the implementation of the Services Directive in December 2009 until the reintroduction of the quota in November 2015—the granting of VTC authorizations in Spain was not subject to any quantitative cap. Granted, applications were routinely rejected on this basis prior to the 2014 judgments where the Supreme Court authoritatively confirmed that the 2009 reform had effectively eliminated all quantitative restrictions on VTCs. However, many of these rejections were subsequently set aside, which brought about a surge in the number of new VTC authorizations granted in Spain. However, between 1998 and 2009, the total number of VTS authorizations grew from 1336 to 2665, their number reached 16.489 in 2020.[48]

Thus, the immense majority of the new VTC authorizations granted in recent years have their origin in applications submitted during the six-year 'liberalization window' inaugurated by the reforms inspired by the Services Directive. Given the fact that the total number of taxi licenses has remained stable throughout this time, at around

---

[43]Supreme Court, Judgment of 27 Jan 2014. ECLI:ES:TS:2014:120.

[44]*Ley 9/2013, de 4 de julio, por la que se modifica la Ley 16/1987, de 30 de julio, de Ordenación de los Transportes Terrestres y la Ley 21/2003, de 7 de julio, de Seguridad Aérea.*

[45]Implementing Regulation on Land Transport, Article 181 as amended by *Real Decreto 1057/2015, de 20 de noviembre, por el que se modifica el Reglamento de la Ley de Ordenación de los Transportes Terrestres.*

[46]See Footnote 25.

[47]*Real Decreto-ley 3/2018, de 20 de abril, por el que se modifica la Ley 16/1987, de 30 de julio, de Ordenación de los Transportes Terrestres, en materia de arrendamiento de vehículos con conductor.*

[48]Ministerio de Transportes, Movilidad y Agenda Urbana. https://www.mitma.gob.es/transporte-terrestre/informacion-estadistica/estadisticas-estudio/datos-del-registro-general. Accessed 16 Apr 2020.

70.000,[49] these developments have completely altered the proportion between VTC authorizations and taxi licenses in Spain: whereas in 2009 there were only 1,14 VTC authorizations for every 30 taxi licenses, in 2020 there are 7,7 VTC authorizations for every 30 taxi licenses (although in regions such as Madrid, the proportion is close to 16/30).

2.5 *Territorial Restrictions on the Scope of VTC Authorizations*

Another contentious aspect of the legal regime that governs VTC authorizations is their territorial scope. Recent years have also witnessed important regulatory changes on this front.

The ambitious legislative reforms introduced in the wake of the Services Directive did not only seek to remove regulatory barriers to entry, but also territorial restrictions on the provision of services.[50] One of the measures adopted in order to achieve this goal was the amendment of Article 91 of the Law on Land Transport.[51] Prior to the reform, the text of that provision allowed administrative authorities to limit the territorial scope of authorizations for the provision of on-demand transport services. The reform made it clear that administrative authorizations for the provision of this type of services (and hence of VTC authorizations) would in principle be valid throughout the country. Thus, although the executive competence to grant VTC authorizations lies with the administrative authorities of the autonomous communities, the reform empowered their holders to offer their services nationwide.

However, the new text of Article 91 of the Law on Land Transport left some room for the introduction of this type of territorial limitations via administrative regulation. The government resorted to this option after it became clear that the quantitative cap on VTCs had been removed and that their number was about to soar. Indeed, one of the novelties brought about by the amendments of the regulation on land transport made in 2015 was the introduction of a 'frequency requirement,' according to which VTCs would 'normally' have to be used within the territory of the autonomous community where the authorization was issued.[52] The new text of the regulation also included a legal presumption according to which the 'frequency requirement' would not be met when more than 20% of the fares carried out by a VTC within a period of three months run through the territory of another autonomous community, even if only

[49] Ibid.

[50] *Ley 17/2009, de 23 de noviembre, sobre el libre acceso a las actividades de servicios y su ejercicio*, Article 4.2.

[51] See Footnote 40.

[52] Implementing Regulation on Land Transport, Article 182.5 inserted by *Real Decreto 1057/2015, de 20 de noviembre, por el que se modifica el Reglamento de la Ley de Ordenación de los Transportes Terrestres*.

partially.[53] The '80/20 rule' was challenged by the Spanish Competition Authority on proportionality grounds, together with the 1/30 quota. However, the Supreme Court also dismissed the plea, on the ground that it was suitable and proportionate to protect the balance between different forms of public transport.[54] In any event, before the judgment came out, the 80/20 rule had already been codified into the text of the Law on Land Transport itself.[55]

The regulatory changes in the territorial scope of VTC authorizations do not end here, for a few months later the government (whose political adscription had changed in the meantime) amended the Law of Land Transport again, through another piece of executive emergency legislation.[56] The reform was justified on the ground that the 1/30 and 80/20 rules were not sufficient to address 'the problems of mobility, traffic congestion, and environmental pollution' that the increase in the number of VTCs was causing in the main urban areas. In order to tackle these problems and 'to avoid the general deterioration of transport services, at the expense of users,' the reform amended once again the text of Article 91 of the Law on Land Transport. As a result of the reform, Article 91.1 currently provides that VTC authorizations only allow the provision of 'inter-urban' passenger transportation services (i.e., trips whose route goes across more than one single municipality).

The preamble to the reform acknowledged that most of the services actually offered by VTCs take place within the municipal boundaries of large cities, such as Madrid, and that the new rule may therefore deprive VTC authorizations of most of their commercial value. In order to make up for this, the reform includes a grandfather clause that allows current VTC holders to continue providing intra-urban services up to four years after its entry into force.[57] This four-year period of grace is conceived as compensation for the loss in the commercial value of VTCs caused by the reform, which is meant to pre-empt future state liability claims by VTC holders. The grandfather clause also affects another aspect of the reform that also speaks to the territorial scope of VTC authorizations—namely, the new rule according to which the pickup location of VTC journeys must be located within the territory of the autonomous community which issued the VTC authorization.[58]

The regulatory expulsion of VTCs from intra-municipal markets may have profound consequences for their business model. The constitutionality of this measure is controversial. Leaving aside the doubts raised by the legal instrument chosen to adopt it (an executive piece of emergency legislation), the latest reform of the VTC regime has been criticized on three different grounds: its proportionality is open question; it is not clear whether it falls within the competences of the central

---

[53] Ibid.

[54] See Footnote 25.

[55] See Footnote 47.

[56] *Real Decreto-ley 13/2018, de 28 de septiembre, por el que se modifica la Ley 16/1987, de 30 de julio, de Ordenación de los Transportes Terrestres, en materia de arrendamiento de vehículos con conductor*.

[57] Ibid., *Disposición Transitoria Única*.

[58] Law on Land Transport, Article 91.2 as amended.

government, whose regulatory powers are restricted to interregional transport; finally, and despite some precedents, the validity and sufficiency of the grandfather clause as compensation is also contentious.[59] As a result of its legislative status, neither the Spanish Competition Authorities nor private actors have standing to bring a *direct* action against the prohibition.[60] However, the issue is likely to reach the Constitutional Court *indirectly*, through a preliminary reference of constitutionality submitted by courts reviewing administrative decisions adopted on the basis of the new rule.[61] Time will tell whether the prohibition passes muster.

3 Labor Law Issues

3.1 Overview

This section addresses whether in Spain Uber drivers are in an employment relationship with Uber pursuant to Spanish labor law. If the answer is in the affirmative, Spanish labor law would apply to the employment relationship alongside all protections and guarantees that any other employee would receive.[62] By way of example, Uber drivers would be protected from undue dismissal and would enjoy the right to the corresponding indemnities in the event of a layoff, as well as the benefits from full social security. If the answer is negative, the relationship between Uber and its drivers would be a mere commercial relationship subject to ordinary Spanish contract law, and labor law would not apply.

In Spain, specialist labor courts have jurisdiction to hear disputes between employers and employees in relation to issues of labor law and social security.[63] The labor courts' jurisdiction includes hearing claims for recognition of a labor relationship where none is contemplated by the parties or acknowledged by the employer. Commonly, this occurs where relationships are formalized as contracts for the supply of services. In general terms, a labor relationship is deemed to exist when a worker provides paid services under the direction of its employer.[64] The legal consequence of the recognition of a labor relationship is that the employee qualifies for full social security (and the employer is liable for the outstanding social security payments for the period that is declared to comprise the employment relationship). For an illustrative list of criteria followed by Spanish labor courts in examining whether

[59] Doménech Pascual (2019).

[60] *Ley Orgánica 2/1979, de 3 de octubre, del Tribunal Constitucional*, Article 32.

[61] Spanish Constitution, Article 163 and *Ley Orgánica 2/1979, de 3 de octubre, del Tribunal Constitucional*, Articles 35–37.

[62] *Real Decreto Legislativo 2/2015, de 23 de octubre, por el que se aprueba el texto refundido de la Ley del Estatuto de los Trabajadores* (Spanish Labor Act), Article 1 is the main legal basis pursuant to which labor courts examine whether an employment relationship exists.

[63] *Ley 36/2011, de 10 de octubre, reguladora de la jurisdicción social*, Articles 1–2.

[64] Spanish Labor Act, Article 1.1.

Table 1 Employment disputes against Uber and similar platforms

Court	Judgment	Parties	Cause of action
Second instance labor court, Madrid	ES:TSJM:2019:6642 18 July 2019	Employed driver v. VTC-license holder (Cabify)	Payment of outstanding salaries/indemnities
Second instance labor court, Madrid	ES:TSJM:2019:4296 5 June 2019	Employed driver v. VTC-license holder (Cabify)	Undue dismissal; payment of outstanding salaries/indemnities
Second instance labor court, Madrid	ES:TSJM:2019:10737 29 April 2019	Employed driver v. VTC-license holder (Uber and Cabify)	Payment of outstanding salaries/indemnities
Second instance labor court, Madrid	ES:TSJM:2018:7872 29 May 2018	Employed driver v. VTC-license holder (Uber and Cabify)	Payment of outstanding salaries/indemnities
Second instance labor court, Barcelona	ES:TSJCAT:2017:6920 16 June 2017	Social Security Treasury v. Uber Systems Spain S.L.	Outstanding social security contributions of administrative employees

an employment relationship exists, reference is made to Sect. 3.3 in respect of the *Deliveroo* case.

3.2 Employment Disputes Against Uber (and Other Similar Platforms)

Based on the publicly available judgments as of the date of this chapter, the employment status of Uber drivers in Spain has not been challenged before the labor courts.[65] The following judgments in the below table in respect of Uber and its competitor Cabify have been published. Cabify is included in the sample because it provides the same service as Uber through a competing app with a significant share in the Spanish market. If an employment relationship pursuant to Spanish labor law was deemed to exist in respect of Cabify's drivers, it would most likely apply to Uber (Table 1).

It is notable that in the above published labor cases proceedings were initiated against the VTC holder, and not Uber or Cabify. These cases were initiated by drivers who were already in an employment relationship with the VTC holders, and merely concerned indemnities pursuant to Spanish labor law without the employment status being disputed. Thus, while these drivers operate under the Uber umbrella, their existing employment relationship with the holders of VTC authorizations meant that there was no need to assert an employment relationship with Uber.

[65] CENDOJ judgment database of the Spanish General Council of the Judiciary. http://www.poderjudicial.es/search/indexAN.jsp. Accessed 11 Mar 2020.

3.3 Outlook

It should be noted that the facts of the cases in Table 1 pre-date the judgment of the Supreme Court that abolished the requirement that a VTC holder operates at least seven cars, as explained above.[66] Prior to that judgment, it was necessary to own or to dispose of a fleet of at least seven cars in order to obtain VTC authorizations. This rule prevented self-employed, individual drivers from obtaining VTC authorizations. Most drivers were therefore employed by the natural or legal persons holding VTC authorizations. Given that following this judgment, VTC holders are no longer required to operate at least seven cars, individuals may now hold a VTC license for a single vehicle and operate on a self-employed basis.

In theory, it is therefore possible that the employment status of self-employed VTC-holder-drivers vis-à-vis Uber could be challenged before labor courts in the future. However, the VTC authorization requirement is a likely barrier to the existence of an employment relationship between the drivers and Uber itself on the basis of an express exclusion in the Spanish Labor Act, Article 1.3(g)[67] which in general terms excludes the application of employment law to persons providing transport services that require administrative authorization, and when the vehicle is owned by such person, including when the transport services are provided to a sole client or intermediary. It should be noted that the exclusion in Article 1.3(g) of the Spanish Labor Act was included in 1994 in a very different commercial and technological context, and clearly at a time when the legislator could not have had in mind car sharing applications like Uber. Several disputes were initiated before the labor courts in respect of the existence of an employment relationship of self-employed drivers on the basis of Article 1.3(g), however, in the context of cargo drivers (i.e., proceedings initiated by self-employed van or truck owners who were contracted by logistics agents). The decisions of the labor courts on the application of Article 1.3(g) were contradictory, and the issue was ultimately referred to the Supreme Court which found on the facts of the particular case that an employment relationship existed because the type of vehicle owned by the self-employed driver did not require any authorization to provide transport services, and therefore, Article 1.3(g) did not apply.[68] In its reasoning, the Supreme Court made reference to the Law on Land Transport in examining whether an authorization is required.[69]

Further, the possibility for self-employed individuals to secure VTC authorizations remains limited in most parts of Spain, given the tight quantitative restrictions imposed on the issuing of new authorizations.[70]

An analogous challenge of the employment status of food delivery drivers was brought by the Spanish Social Security Treasury against Roofoods Spain S.L., the operator of the 'Deliveroo' food delivery app. Uber's relationship with its drivers

[66] Section 2.3.

[67] López-Quiroga Teijeiro and Nägele García de Fuentes (2019); Spanish Labor Act, Article 1.3(g).

[68] Supreme Court, Judgment of 23 Nov 1998. ECLI:ES:TS:1998:6970.

[69] Ibid.

[70] Section 2.4.

is analogous to Deliveroo in that, through this app, food delivery drivers attend individual orders from restaurants and deliver the food to their customers. Deliveroo drivers sign up through the app with their own vehicle (commonly a motorbike, e-bike or bicycle) and are paid on a per-trip basis. Until the driver accepts a food delivery order and picks up the food from the restaurant, the information about the trip is withheld from the driver.[71] Deliveroo exercises control over working shifts and distribution areas of its drivers.[72]

One notable difference, however, is that, while from a regulatory point of view, the underlying service that Uber offers is categorized as a transportation (i.e., for human transport), Deliveroo operates formally a messenger service which is not subject to the same regulatory scrutiny. Among others, Deliveroo drivers do not require a VTC license and were from the outset self-employed drivers.

On January 17, 2020, the Madrid Court of Appeal upheld[73] the judgment at first instance that the food delivery drivers are in an employment relationship with Roofoods Spain S.L. (and do not comprise a mere supply of services relationship). The Madrid Court of Appeal's reasoning was that (i) Deliveroo controlled the frequency of the drivers' work which required minimum levels below which drivers were penalized,[74] (ii) the drivers' remuneration was periodic and controlled by Deliveroo,[75] (iii) the drivers were subject to the orders and instructions of Deliveroo, alongside a penalty system for non-compliance,[76] (iv) Deliveroo assumed the business risk and profit of the deliveries,[77] and (v) the drivers provided the service exclusively to Deliveroo.[78] This judgment may be appealed further to the Spanish Supreme Court.

The analysis of the Spanish labor court in the Deliveroo case is broadly consistent with the findings of the International Labor Organization (ILO) as published in its report on 'digital labor platforms' which connect workers with consumers.[79] In respect of Uber specifically, it found that Uber withheld key information from its drivers before a ride is accepted and thereby limiting the decision-making ability of a driver.[80] In particular, '*When a driver accepts a given job, the destination and remuneration are unknown to him or her*',[81] potentially forcing Uber drivers into

[71]Madrid Superior Court of Justice (Social Chamber), Judgment of 17 January 2020. ECLI:ES:TSJM:2020:1, p. 4.

[72]Ibid., (p. 10).

[73]Ibid.

[74]Ibid., (p. 18).

[75]Ibid., (p. 18).

[76]Ibid., (p. 19).

[77]Ibid., (pp. 20–21).

[78]Ibid., (p. 21).

[79]International Labor Organization (2018) The architecture of digital labor platforms: Policy recommendations on platform design for worker well-being.

[80]Ibid., (p. 10).

[81]Ibid., (p. 18).

unprofitable interactions at the drivers' expense.[82] ILO concluded that a greater level of platform control increases the likelihood of worker exploitation:[83]

> Platforms like Uber and Deliveroo set the price for workers; this reduces the worker's power by precluding the possibility of bargaining with consumers over pay [...] Transportation platforms also determine the route that drivers must take, further reducing their free agency. Route setting gives the platform considerable control in that it can require drivers to take a recommended route, even one that is clearly sub-optimal under prevailing weather or traffic conditions. [...] These policies prevent workers from working on their own terms.

As such, it remains to be seen whether the employment status of self-employed Uber drivers will be challenged, notwithstanding the application of Article 1.3(g) of the Spanish Labor Act.

4 Liability Arising from Private Law

In the analysis of the liability of Uber arising from private law, two factual scenarios should be distinguished. On the one hand, the service is rendered to the users of the platform. On the other hand, any liability incurred vis-à-vis third parties, such as that stemming from a car accident.

4.1 The Service

4.1.1 Uber's Terms and Conditions

The type of service that Uber provides to its customers determines the company's liability under private law. Parties are entitled to define the subject matter of contracts,[84] including in standard form contracts, the source of which (as for bargained for contracts) is also deemed to be agreement.[85] On this, Uber's Terms and Conditions that are applicable to Spain define the company's service as one of intermediation in transportation.[86] Additionally, it is denied therein that Uber provides transport services.[87]

Even considering that the term was unilaterally drafted by Uber, it would be part of the contract. The Standard Contract Terms Act, which applies to both B2B and

---

[82]Ibid., (p. 18).

[83]Ibid., (p. 17).

[84]Spanish civil code (CC), Article 1255.

[85]*Ley 7/1998, de 13 de abril, sobre Condiciones Generales de la Contratación* (Standard Contract Terms Act), Articles 5.1 and 7.

[86]Uber's webpage: https://www.uber.com/legal/en/document/?name=general-terms-of-use&country=spain&lang=es-es. Accessed 22 Apr 2020.

[87]Ibid., Clause 2: '*You acknowledge that Uber does not provide transportation services.*'

B2C contracts,[88] provides the general framework for the incorporation of terms into standard form contracts. The law establishes that, for a term to be incorporated, the adherent to the contract should be aware of its existence. Additionally, the term should be transparent, clear, concrete and plain.[89] The Supreme Court has interpreted these requirements to mean *grammatical* (not substantive) transparency of standard terms.[90] Uber's term defining the service, which customers have to accept in order to use the app, seems to meet the requirement of incorporation to the contract as customers should be aware of its existence and it looks grammatically transparent. Therefore, agreeing to Uber's Terms and Conditions by the customer would imply accepting that the subject matter of the contract is intermediation in transport and not a transportation service.

However, in deciding on the legal nature of Uber's services in a contractual dispute, courts would probably apply a long-standing rule on interpretation of contracts: the doctrine of the 'irrelevance of the *nomen iuris*.' Following this doctrine, contracts must be interpreted in accordance to the reality of performance, not by the name that the parties have assigned to their obligations.[91] Therefore, despite the parties' express agreement defining Uber as other than a transport service, courts could find that, in reality, Uber provides transportation.

In the context of B2C contracts, the validity of the term defining the service could additionally be challenged for lack of *substantive* transparency, which is a condition for both main and ancillary terms that is enshrined in Article 80.1 of the Consumer Protection Act.[92] Hence, standard terms in consumer contracts have to meet a double transparency filter (grammatical and substantive) to be valid.[93] The Consumer Protection Act implemented the Unfair Contract Terms Directive (UCTD), [94] the final interpreter of the latter being the Court of Justice of the European Union (CJEU). To this respect, the CJEU has interpreted transparency under the UCTD as the capacity of an average consumer to foresee the legal and economic consequences of a term.[95] Against the backdrop of the relationship of Uber with its clients, courts

---

[88] Standard Contract Terms Act, Article 2.

[89] Standard Contract Terms Act, Article 5.

[90] Supreme Court, Judgment of June 3, 2016. ECLI:ES:TS:2016:2550.

[91] Supreme Court, Judgment of 18 Dec 2019. ECLI:ES:TS:2019:4188.

[92] *Real Decreto Legislativo 1/2007, de 16 de noviembre, por el que se aprueba el texto refundido de la Ley General para la Defensa de los Consumidores y Usuarios y otras leyes complementarias* (Consumer Protection Act).

[93] Supreme Court, Judgment of 9 May 2013. ECLI:ES:TS:2013:1916.

[94] Council Directive 93/13/EEC of 5 April 1993 on Unfair Terms in Consumer Contracts (OJ L 95/29, 21 Apr 1993).

[95] Court of Justice of the European Union, Judgment of 30 Apr 2014 in *Árpád Kásler, Hajnalka Káslerné Rábai v. OTP Jelzálogbank Zrt*. ECLI:EU:C:2014:282, para. 74; Court of Justice of the European Union, Judgment of 26 February 2015 in *Bogdan Matei and Ioana Ofelia Matei v. SC Volksbank România SA*. ECLI:EU:C:2015:127, para. 75; Court of Justice of the European Union, Judgment of 20 Sep 2017 in *Ruxandra Paula Andriciuc and Others v Banca Românească SA*. ECLI:EU:C:2017:703, para. 47.

would have to determine whether an average consumer understands Uber's service in the way that it is defined in the platform's Terms and Conditions.

The following subsections address these two main challenges to the self-characterization that Uber does of its services in the company's Terms and Conditions.

4.1.2 Irrelevance of the *Nomen Iuris*. Lack of Conclusiveness of Case Law

The doctrine of the '*irrelevance of the nomen iuris*' would serve to classify and interpret the contract between Uber and its customers, taking into consideration the actual performances of the parties under the contract. On this, the court rulings that have been rendered to date offer a blurred image.

Uber's activity in Spain and that of the VTC companies has triggered litigation mostly before administrative courts. It is to be recalled that the Supreme Court, Administrative Chamber, decided that the activity of Uber is a substantial part in a transportation service, which exceeds intermediation.[96] However, the court did not give an exact definition of the service.

In the private law jurisdiction, litigation arose in the context of unfair commercial practices, involving Uber and Cabify. It was described before the relevance of these cases for regulation[97], so it is mentioned here their impact on the characterization of the service only. As stated, competitors in the market claimed that Uber or Cabify required an administrative authorization to deploy their activities, which the claimants considered a transportation service. According to them, the lack of such authorization would represent a breach of norms that would grant Uber and Cabify an unfair competitive advantage prohibited in Article 15 of the Law on Unfair Commercial Practices. Those actions were dismissed on a variety of grounds.

In the case that originated the CJEU decision on *Uber Spain*,[98] the commercial court (first instance) agreed with the Supreme Court, Administrative Chamber, in that Uber was not just intermediation and left the door open for the requirement of an administrative authorization. However, it considered that the infringement of administrative regulations does not necessarily entail unfair competition, in line with the prevailing interpretation of Article 15 of the Law on Unfair Commercial Practices.[99] In the dismissal of the action, it was paramount that the defendant was Uber Systems Spain S.L. (incorporated in Spain), while the platform owner and service provider is, in Spain, Uber BV, a Dutch company.

The other case concerns Cabify, and it is important because the company operates under the VTC regime, as Uber currently does. Therein, the first instance court[100]

[96] See Sect. 2.2.

[97] Ibid.

[98] See Footnote 18.

[99] Supreme Court, Judgment of 17 May 2017. ECLI:ES:TS:2017:1922.

[100] Commercial Court No. 12 of Madrid, Judgement of 13 June 2017. ECLI:ES:JMM:2017:3145.

and the Appeal Court of Madrid[101] agreed that the administrative authorization was imposed upon the VTC companies only. It was central in both decisions the understanding that Cabify intermediates in transport services that the VTC companies provide. Therefore, Cabify's activity would not be transportation. Collaterally, the appeal court mentioned the regime of travel agencies, to justify that even if passengers enter into contracts with Cabify and not the VTC company, the platform is still intermediating in transportation (i.e., not transporting). This gives an intriguing leeway from a contract law perspective as travel agencies are, on occasion, liable vis-à-vis the customers for non-conforming services, even when these are provided by a third party. The package travel contract is a good example of this.[102] Therefore, Uber/Cabify could be liable for the transport service even if they do not provide it.

Interestingly, the Appeal Court of Madrid, in a different composition, seems to have reached a different conclusion, i.e., that Uber/Cabify's services would exceed intermediation. The claim was again based in Article 15 of the Unfair Commercial Practices Act. In deciding whether BlaBlaCar, a ride sharing company, performed a transportation service, the court resorted to the criteria that the CJEU set-out in *Uber Spain*.[103] These include: (i) offering transportation services, through an app, that connects customers with drivers; (ii) establishing the fare for the journey which involves algorithmic pricing; (iii) influencing in the supply of services, also with the aid of an algorithm that helps drivers to identify areas of higher demand; (iv) receiving payment from the client; (v) exercising a certain control over the quality of the vehicles and the drivers. In negating that character to BlaBlaCar, the court mentioned Uber (obiter dicta) as an example of a platform also providing the underlying transport service.

Therefore, case law does not offer at this point a classification of Uber's services (and eventually those of Cabify) that could be treated as final for the purposes of the platform-customer relationship. Moreover, the Supreme Court, Private law Chamber, has not dealt with the matter yet so case law is not strictly binding.[104] Additionally, the assessment conducted so far tackles unfair commercial practices between competitors (in the case, a non-contractual B2B scenario), not contract law. Courts were asked to ascertain whether Uber/Cabify had infringed regulation, and because of that, had obtained an unfair competitive advantage. An assessment of a customer-platform relationship, including mandatory consumer contract law, was absent from the court rulings.

Against this backdrop, three alternative contractual frameworks for the client-Uber contract remain possible: (i) that Uber provides transportation; (ii) that Uber intermediates in transportation services between customers and VTCs, without a contractual responsibility for their quality; and (iii) that Uber is an intermediary but remains ultimately responsible for non-conforming transportation services, as it is the case of travel agencies for non-conforming package travels.

---

[101] Madrid Court of Appeal, Judgment of 18 Jan 2019. ECLI:ES:APM:2019:3.

[102] Consumer Protection Act, Article 161.1.

[103] Madrid Court of Appeal, Judgment of 18 Feb 2019. ECLI:ES:APM:2019:1255.

[104] CC, Article 1.6.

4.1.3 Uber and Consumer Contract Law

Uber's activity deserves a specific analysis in respect of B2C contracts. The standard term that defines the subject matter of the contract as intermediation and not transportation (Clause 2 of Uber's Terms and Conditions) is required to meet the benchmark of substantive transparency to be valid. Therefore, an average consumer should be able to foresee the legal and economic consequences of the term, i.e., that Uber is not responsible for the underlying transportation service.

The way in which the consumer relates with Uber could make the term not transparent, especially in the current UberX context in which the service is performed by professional drivers only. Customers access the Uber app 'looking for a transport service offering certain functions and a particular standard of quality. Such functions and transport quality are ensured by Uber.'[105] Throughout the lifecycle of the contract, the customer ignores the identity of the VTC company that performs transportation. The client can learn the name of the driver after confirming the service request, not before. In any case, the driver is an employee of the VTC company, never a counterparty to the contract. Therefore, an average consumer would probably not be able to foresee that a VTC company performs the transportation service that was offered in the Uber app, thus rendering Clause 2 of Uber's Terms and Conditions non-transparent.

In B2C contracts, courts must carry out the transparency assessment *ex officio*[106] as long as they have the legal and factual elements required for that assessment, which can be supplemented by measures of inquiry.[107] A term that lacks transparency is null and void[108] and the gap should not be filled in.[109] Invalidity affects the non-transparent term exclusively, unless the contract cannot continue in existence, which is to be asserted objectively.[110] In that case only and if the dissuasive effect of invalidity may be jeopardized, can the non-transparent term be replaced by non-mandatory law.[111]

Therefore, if Clause 2 of Uber's Terms and Conditions were non-transparent, it is unlikely that the contract could continue in existence without the term as it defines an essential element of the contract (i.e., the subject matter). Based on this, the non-transparent term would most likely render the whole contract invalid. However, if the dissuasive effect of this sanction were to be jeopardized, the contract could continue in existence and the gap should be filled in with default rules. In the scenario under

---

105 Advocate General, Opinion of 11 May 2017 in *Uber Spain*. ECLI:EU:C:2017:364, para. 53.

106 Court of Justice of the European Union, Judgment of 4 June 2009 in *Pannon GSM Zrt. v Erzsébet Sustikné Győrfi*. ECLI:EU:C:2009:350, para. 35.

107 Court of Justice of the European Union, Judgment of 11 March 2020 in *Györgyné Lintner v UniCredit Bank Hungary Zrt*. ECLI:EU:C:2020:188, para. 38.

108 Consumer Protection Act, Article 83.II.

109 Court of Justice of the European Union, Judgment of 14 June 2012 in *Banco Español de Crédito SA v Joaquín Calderón Camino*. ECLI:EU:C:2012:349, para. 73.

110 Court of Justice of the European Union, Judgment of 15 Mar 2012 in *Jana Pereničová and Vladislav Perenič v SOS financ spol. s r. o*. ECLI:EU:C:2012:144, paras. 31–34.

111 Court of Justice of the European Union, Judgment of 30 Apr 2014 in *Árpád Kásler, Hajnalka Káslerné Rábai v. OTP Jelzálogbank Zrt*. ECLI:EU:C:2014:282, paras. 83–85.

analysis, it could be understood that the invalidity of the contract would jeopardize the dissuasive effect of the sanction as consumers would not have an incentive to challenge the term. Indeed, the invalidity of the contract would be onerous for consumers as they would have to claim under tort law which, among others, foresees a shorter prescription period.[112]

If so, the contract should continue in existence and the gap left by the non-transparent term ought to be filled in with non-mandatory law. Thus, default rules would determine the quality of the service to which Uber has committed. To this respect, the answer depends on whether the service is one in which the debtor is obliged to act with due skill and care (*obligaciones de medios*) or, instead, it is committed to achieve a result (*obligaciones de resultado*).[113] Transportation contracts are deemed to generate obligations to achieve a result[114] as the carrier is expected to provide a service that meets the ultimate purpose of the customer (i.e., being safely carried to destination) and not just an activity.

This outcome links with Clause 5 of Uber's Terms and Conditions that excludes all liability for the service, thus assigning the risk of the result to the customer, not even a diligent provision of the carriage being guaranteed. This term would also be controlled *ex officio* by courts, under the Consumer Protection Act. Thereby, the term would be unfair under a variety of grounds as it leaves performance of the contract to Uber's discretion, it restricts liability of the business below what is established in non-mandatory law (obligation to achieve a result), and it establishes obligations on the consumer that are not reciprocal.[115] The unfairness of Clause 5 would result in its invalidity.[116]

4.2 *Tortious Liability*

Beyond the transportation contract, extracontractual liability could arise vis-à-vis third parties, most likely following a car accident. In this scenario, three persons could potentially be liable: Uber, the VTC company and the driver.

Spanish tort law is encroached in the Roman/French tradition of private law. In this sense, liability in tort is established by the negligent infringement of the overarching principle *neminem laedere* (do not harm others). Article 1902 CC dictates: 'The person who, as a result of an act or omission, causes damage to another by his fault or negligence shall be obliged to repair the damage caused.' It is a broad rule that does

[112]Five years for contractual liability (Art 1964.2 CC) v 1 year for extracontractual liability (Art 1968.2 CC).

[113]For a detailed discussion, see de Elizalde F (2014). Important (but not definitive) provisions in this discussion are Article 1104 (negligence) and Articles 1589–91 (work contract) of the Spanish civil code.

[114]Sánchez Calero J, Sánchez Calero F (2015).

[115]Consumer Protection Act, Articles 85–87.

[116]Consumer Protection Act, Article 83.

not require the affection of a protected legal interest nor other further prerequisites. Moreover, tort liability includes pure economic loss. Therefore, the driver would be liable for any damage he causes to a third party by a negligent conduct. The extent of compensation is limited to those damages that were foreseeable to him except in cases of intent in respect of which the foreseeability rule does not apply, and the law demands full compensation.[117]

In addition to direct liability, on occasion tort law makes a third party liable for the damage caused. This is the case of companies for damages that their employees provoke.[118] Against that backdrop, a company is liable unless it is able to prove the absence of negligence in selecting the person who caused the damage (*culpa in eligendo*) or in supervising him (*culpa in vigilando*).[119] Courts have set the bar high for companies to exclude their liability, which is why it has often been defined as 'quasi objective' liability.[120]

Due to the employment relationship that binds VTC companies with drivers, the former would be liable unless it can prove diligence in the selection and supervision of drivers. The action for damages can be filed against the company, i.e., a prior nor a cumulative claim against the employee are required.

The liability of Uber could be more complex to establish as the causal link between its conduct and potential liability vis-à-vis third parties seems less direct than that of the VTC companies. However, liability of businesses in tort is not restricted to employment relationships. Case law has broadened the potentially liable persons to those who supervise the activity of another who, in turn, follows the principal's instructions.[121] The matrix of facts on which some courts have relied to consider that Uber organizes transportation could also serve as a basis of extracontractual liability as they imply that the company has some degree of supervision over the drivers.[122]

Additionally, victims of damages have an action against that who appears to guarantee the activity of another, when the victim relied on that appearance.[123] Although this basis of liability seems less likely to occur as most of the instances of reliance would be covered by contractual liability, it could happen that a victim relied on safe driving of an Uber driver, the lack of which resulted in an accident. It is to be recalled that, in many autonomous communities, Uber cars carry a special label that identifies them. This would make the company responsible for damage.

---

[117] CC, Article 1107. See Morales Moreno (2010).

[118] CC, Article 1903.

[119] CC, Article 1903.6; Ángel (1991).

[120] Ibid., (p. 2013).

[121] Yzquierdo Tolsada (2019).

[122] Ruda (2018).

[123] Ibid., (p. 436).

5 Conclusion

This chapter has analyzed the legal framework that governs Uber's activities in Spain from three different but complementary angles.

The first section has described the general regulatory framework to which Uber's activities are subject, drawing a distinction between the legal regime to which Uber's intermediation services are subject and the legal regime that governs the provision of private, on-demand transportation services. On the first front, the Spanish legal order remains unclear: drawing on the CJEU's ruling in *Asociación Profesional Élite Taxi v Uber*, the Supreme Court has declared that Uber's services are not mere 'intermediation services' and that they fall within the scope of the Law on Land Transport (and hence are subject to the general administrative authorization requirement laid down by that law). However, the implications of this characterization have not been fully worked out, because the Supreme Court has not specified the specific regime to which Uber is subject, among the various regulatory frameworks existing in the field of transport. On the second front, it is clear that the initial strategy deployed by Uber through its UberPop app (which was open to private drivers without professional license) has no room in Spain, where the requirement to hold a VTC authorization in order to offer this kind of service is well-established. However, recent legislative reforms have imposed important quantitative and territorial restraints on these authorizations. These restrictions (and, in particular, the territorial restrictions expelling VTCs from intra-municipal markets) could be a deathblow for Uber and other similar platforms in Spain. However, they are likely to be contested in the future, both in the judicial and the political arenas.

The second section has described the framework that governs the employment status of VTC drivers. Based on the litigation data available, it seems that all employment cases reported so far concern disputes between drivers and VTC authorization holders. In this sense, the VTC authorization requirement may be acting as a shield that prevents the emergence of any kind of employment relationship between Uber and drivers on the basis of an express exclusion in the Spanish Labor Act. In the past, one of the requirements to obtain a VTC authorization was to own or dispose of a fleet of at least seven cars, which may account for the fact that labor law complaints in this field typically target VTC authorization holders. Granted, this requirement was quashed by the Supreme Court, which could have brought about a surge in the number of individual, free-lance VTC drivers. However, it seems that this development has been neutralized by the tight quantitative restrictions to which the granting of new VTC authorizations is subject, so this is unlikely to bring about any significant changes in the future. Also, a recent judgment of a regional court has recognized the existence of an employment relationship between Deliveroo (a food delivery app) and delivery drivers, and some commentators believe that this could have an impact upon VTC drivers.

The third section has conducted a twofold assessment of Uber under private law to tackle the contractual relationship between the company and its customers as well as the liability of Uber vis-à-vis third parties. In respect of the former, Uber's Terms and Conditions describe the platform services' as mere intermediation, while they deny that Uber provides transportation. Even though this term would be incorporated into the contract, its efficacy could be challenged both in B2B and B2C contracts, under different grounds. In the event of a dispute in B2B contracts, the subject matter of the contract would be classified according to the reality of the performances of the parties, ignoring how the parties have labeled them, pursuant to the doctrine of the 'irrelevance of the *nomen iuris.*' However, to date, case law has not rendered a decision that could be treated as final to determine the type of service that Uber provides to its customers. In B2C contracts, consumers could additionally challenge the validity of Uber's Terms and Conditions on the premise of a lack of substantive transparency, as an average consumer might be unable to foresee that Uber does not provide transportation. The second part of the third section has dealt with tortious liability. Therein, it has been concluded that the liability of Uber would eventually be indirect and primarily due to a negligent supervision of the drivers. This claim is more likely to be upheld if, under contract law, it were decided that Uber's activity is transportation.

References

Cano Campos T (2009) El transporte urbano por carretera. In: Carbonell Porras E (dir) Derecho público del transporte en la ciudad. UCM, Madrid, pp 391–447

Doménech Pascual G (2017) La regulación de la economía colaborativa en el sector del taxi y los VTC. In: Pascual JJM (dir) La regulación de la economía colaborativa. Tirant lo Blanch, Valencia, pp 351–401

Doménech Pascual G (2019) Penalty y expulsión. La economía de las plataformas digitales en el sector de los taxis y los VTC. In: Orti Vallejo A, Rubio Gimeno G (eds) Propuestas de regulación de las plataformas de economía colaborativa. Perspectivas generales y sectoriales. Aranzadi, Cizur Menor

de Ángel R (1991) Art 1903. In: Paz-Ares C, Díez-Picazo L, Bercovitz R, Salvador P (eds) Comentario del Código Civil. Ministerio de Justicia, Madrid, II–II: 2003–2034, p 2005

de Elizalde F (2014) Las obligaciones de medios y de resultado en la Propuesta de Código Mercantil. InDret 3:1–40

Guillén Navarro NA (2018) El arrendamiento de vehículos con conductor (VTC) y su entramado jurídico: el avance de Uber, Cabify y la economía colaborativa. Revista de Estudios de la Administración Local y Autonómica 9:128–147

International Labour Organisation (2018) The architecture of digital labour platforms: Policy recommendations on platform design for worker well-being

López-Quiroga Teijeiro C and Nägele García de Fuentes N (2019) La disruptiva en la normativa de transporte y turismo ante las nuevas aplicaciones de movilidad urbana. Actualidad Jurídica Uría Menéndez 52:77–81

Morales Moreno AM (2010) Incumplimiento del contrato y lucro cesante. Civitas, Madrid, pp 172–180

Ruda A (2018) Responsabilidad por hechos ajenos en la economía colaborativa. El caso de Uber. In: Balcells J et al (eds) Collaborative economy: challenges and opportunities. Huygens, Barcelona, pp 424–438

Sánchez Calero J, Sánchez Calero F (2015) Instituciones de Derecho Mercantil, II. Aranzadi, Cizur Menor, pp 479–480

Velasco Caballero F (2009) Transporte urbano por carretera y competencias municipales. In: Carbonell Porras E (dir) Derecho público del transporte en la ciudad. UCM, Madrid, pp 139–149
Yzquierdo Tolsada M (2019) Responsabilidad civil extracontractual. Parte general, Dykinson, Madrid, p 344

EU legislation

Council Directive 93/13/EEC of 5 April 1993 on Unfair Terms in Consumer Contracts (OJ L 95/29, 21 Apr 1993)
Directive 2000/31/EC of the European Parliament and of the Council of 8 June 2000 on certain legal aspects of information society services, in particular electronic commerce, in the Internal Market (OJ L 178, 17 July 2000, p 1)
Directive 2006/123/EC of the European Parliament and of the Council of 12 December 2006 on services in the internal market (OJ L 376, 27 Dec 2006, p 36)

Spanish legislation

Código civil (Spanish civil code [CC])
Constitución española (Spanish constitution)
Decret llei 4/2019, de 29 de gener, de mesures urgents en matèria de transport de viatgers mitjançant el lloguer de vehicles amb conductor
Ley 16/1987, de 30 de julio, de Ordenación de los Transportes Terrestres (Law on Land Transport)
Ley 3/1991, de 10 de enero, de Competencia Desleal (Law on Unfair Commercial Practices)
Ley 7/1998, de 13 de abril, sobre Condiciones Generales de la Contratación (Standard Contract Terms Act)
Ley 17/2009, de 23 de noviembre, sobre el libre acceso a las actividades de servicios y su ejercicio
Ley 25/2009, de 22 de diciembre, de modificación de diversas leyes para su adaptación a la Ley sobre el libre acceso a las actividades de servicios y su ejercicio
Ley 36/2011, de 10 de octubre, reguladora de la jurisdicción social
Ley 9/2013, de 4 de julio, por la que se modifica la Ley 16/1987, de 30 de julio, de Ordenación de los Transportes Terrestres y la Ley 21/2003, de 7 de julio, de Seguridad Aérea
Ley Orgánica 2/1979, de 3 de octubre, del Tribunal Constitucional
Ley Orgánica 5/1987, de 30 de julio, de Delegación de Facultades del Estado en las Comunidades Autónomas en relación con los transportes por carretera y por cable
Orden de 30 de julio de 1998 por la que se desarrolla el Reglamento de la Ley de Ordenación de los Transportes Terrestres
Real Decreto 919/2010, de 16 de julio, por el que se modifica el Reglamento de la Ley de Ordenación de los Transportes Terrestres para adaptarlo a la Ley 25/2009, de 22 de diciembre, de modificación de diversas leyes para su adaptación a la Ley sobre libre acceso a las actividades de servicios y su ejercicio
Real Decreto 1057/2015, de 20 de noviembre, por el que se modifica el Reglamento de la Ley de Ordenación de los Transportes Terrestres
Real Decreto Legislativo 1/2007, de 16 de noviembre, por el que se aprueba el texto refundido de la Ley General para la Defensa de los Consumidores y Usuarios y otras leyes complementarias (Consumer Protection Act)
Real Decreto Legislativo 2/2015, de 23 de octubre, por el que se aprueba el texto refundido de la Ley del Estatuto de los Trabajadores (Spanish Labor Act)

Real Decreto-ley 3/2018, de 20 de abril, por el que se modifica la Ley 16/1987, de 30 de julio, de Ordenación de los Transportes Terrestres, en materia de arrendamiento de vehículos con conductor
Real Decreto-ley 13/2018, de 28 de septiembre, por el que se modifica la Ley 16/1987, de 30 de julio, de Ordenación de los Transportes Terrestres, en materia de arrendamiento de vehículos con conductor
Reglamento de la Ley de Ordenación de los Transportes Terrestres, aprobado por Real Decreto 1211/1990, de 28 de septiembre (Implementing Regulation on Land Transport)

Court of Justice of the European Union cases

Court of Justice of the European Union, Judgment of 4 Jun 2009 in Pannon GSM Zrt. v Erzsébet Sustikné Győrfi. ECLI:EU:C:2009:350, para 35
Court of Justice of the European Union, Judgment of 15 Mar 2012 in Jana Pereničová and Vladislav Perenič v SOS financ spol. s r. o. ECLI:EU:C:2012:144, paras 31–34
Court of Justice of the European Union, Judgment of 14 Jun 2012 in Banco Español de Crédito SA v Joaquín Calderón Camino. ECLI:EU:C:2012:349, para 73
Court of Justice of the European Union, Judgment of 30 Apr 2014 in Árpád Kásler, Hajnalka Káslerné Rábai v. OTP Jelzálogbank Zrt. ECLI:EU:C:2014:282, paras 74 and 83–85
Court of Justice of the European Union, Judgment of 26 Feb 2015 in Bogdan Matei and Ioana Ofelia Matei v. SC Volksbank România SA. ECLI:EU:C:2015:127, para 75
Court of Justice of the European Union, Judgment of 20 Sep 2017 in Ruxandra Paula Andriciuc and Others v Banca Românească SA. ECLI:EU:C:2017:703, para 47
Court of Justice of the European Union, Judgment of 20 Dec 2017 in Asociación Profesional Élite Taxi v Uber Systems Spain SL. ECLI:EU:C:2017:981, para 40–6
Court of Justice of the European Union, Judgment of 11 Mar 2020 in Györgyné Lintner v UniCredit Bank Hungary Zrt. ECLI:EU:C:2020:188, para 38
Advocate General, Opinion of 11 May 2017 in Uber Spain. ECLI:EU:C:2017:364, para 53

Spanish court cases

Administrative Court No 15 of Barcelona, Judgment of 6 Oct 2016. ECLI: ES:JCA:2016:2579
Commercial Court No 2 of Madrid, Order of 9 Dec 2014. ECLI:ES:JMM:2014:74A
Commercial Court No 3 of Barcelona, Judgment of 10 Apr 2018. ECLI:ES:JMB:2018:38
Commercial Court No 12 of Madrid, Judgment of 13 Jun 2017. ECLI:ES:JMM:2017:3145
Constitutional Court, Judgment 118/1996 of 27 Jun 1996. ECLI:ES:TC:1996:118
Madrid Court of Appeal, Judgment of 18 Jan 2019. ECLI:ES:APM:2019:3
Madrid Court of Appeal, Judgment of 18 Feb 2019. ECLI:ES:APM:2019:1255
Supreme Court, Judgment of 23 Nov 1998. ECLI:ES:TS:1998:6970
Supreme Court, Judgment of 14 Feb 2012. ECLI: ES:TS:2012:1076
Supreme Court, Judgment of 9 May 2013. ECLI:ES:TS:2013:1916
Supreme Court, Judgment of 27 Jan 2014. ECLI:ES:TS:2014:120
Supreme Court, Judgment of 3 Jun 2016. ECLI:ES:TS:2016:2550
Supreme Court, Judgment of 17 May 2017. ECLI:ES:TS:2017:1922
Supreme Court, Judgment of 25 Jan 2018. ECLI: ES:TS:2018:120
Supreme Court, Judgment of 4 Jun 2018. ECLI: ES:TS:2018:1913
Supreme Court, Judgment of 18 Dec 2019. ECLI:ES:TS:2019:4188

Chapter 8
The Legal Framework for Ridesharing Businesses and the Case of Uber in Germany

Michael Nietsch and Gregor Schott

1 Introduction

The chapter analyzes Uber's activities in Germany facing strict regulation of the passenger transportation service sector. Uber entered Germany in 2014 and expanded its services accompanied by legal issues right from the beginning (I). The strictly enforced regulations and separation of the different market sectors in Germany (II) created various problems for Uber which culminated in a nationwide ban of UberPop in 2015 (III). UberBlack was subject to court rulings as well (IV). Uber adapted its business models according to the existing regulation, but still faces legal scrutiny (V). Uber's endeavors in Germany provide opportunities to reason about innovation and compliance restraints as well as the legitimacy of German traffic sector regulation (VI).

[1]The UberPop service operated the same as in countries worldwide: Individuals could register to Uber and use their own car to transport passengers whenever they liked and without any governmental approval. The Uber app matched transportation requests to drivers, chose the route to the destination and set the prices. Uber took a percentage of the fee as commission.

M. Nietsch (✉) · G. Schott
EBS Law School, Wiesbaden, Germany
e-mail: Michael.Nietsch@ebs.edu

G. Schott
e-mail: gregor.schott@outlook.com

Z. Ayata and İ. Önay (eds.), *Global Perspectives on Legal Challenges Posed by Ridesharing Companies*,
https://doi.org/10.1007/978-981-15-7035-3_8

1.1 Summary of Uber's Activities in Germany and Court Proceedings

Right from the beginning, Uber's activities in Germany went hand in hand with controversies and legal disputes. Uber started to offer its services "UberPop"[1] and "UberBlack,"[2] as well as "UberTaxi"[3] in Berlin in April of 2014.[4] The same month, the Berlin District Court issued an injunction against the UberBlack service in Berlin following a complaint by a local taxi operator.[5] Regardless, Uber expanded its services to Frankfurt am Main,[6] Munich, Düsseldorf and Hamburg one month later, accompanied by protests from taxi drivers and operators. In September 2014, the District Court in Frankfurt am Main issued a nationwide preliminary injunction against the UberPop service.[7] Uber responded by publicly announcing to ignore the court order and continued to offer its services in the five German cities, claiming that "prohibition of choices never was a good idea" and that "progress could not be stopped."[8] The preliminary injunction was suspended.[9] However in Hamburg, the city administration simultaneously banned Uber's services by executive order, which was upheld by the Hamburg Higher Administrative Court in September 2014.[10] After these rulings, Uber tried to bypass regulation by lowering its prices drastically and claiming they would only constitute the operating costs of a ride, which would exempt the service from regulation.[11]

In March 2015, the District Court in Frankfurt am Main issued a further injunction against UberPop in the principal proceedings for violating the German Passenger Transportation Act.[12] Faced with increasing legal pressure, Uber ceased to operate UberPop in Germany, while launching UberX service in May 2015, offering limousine services with properly licensed drivers (for details on this business model see below Sect. 5) and helping existing drivers to obtain required taxi drivers licenses.[13] Later, Uber stopped all activities in Frankfurt, Düsseldorf and Hamburg, offering only the services UberX and UberTaxi in Berlin and Munich where it had made 70% of its revenue anyway.[14] In June 2016, the Higher Regional Court of Frankfurt am Main upheld the injunction against the UberPop service of the District Court (see

[2]The UberBlack service is Uber's premium service. In Germany, Uber offers transportation services of (properly licensed) professional limousine drivers with more upscale cars via the service.

[3]This service allows ordering regular (licenced) taxis via the Uber app.

[4]Wimmer and Weiß (2015).

[5]Landgericht Berlin, Urteil vom 11.04.2014, 15 O 43/14.

[6]Frankfurter Allgemeine Zeitung (2014a).

[7]Landgericht Frankfurt a.M., Beschluss vom 25.08.2014, 2-03 O 329/14.

[8]Spiegel Online (2014).

[9]Frankfurter Allgemeine Zeitung (2014b).

[10]Oberverwaltungsgericht Hamburg, Beschluss vom 24.09.2014, 3 Bs 175/14.

[11]Wimmer and Weiß (2015, p. 82).

[12]*Personenbeförderungsgesetz* (*PBefG*).

[13]Frankfurter Allgemeine Zeitung (2015a).

[14]Frankfurter Allgemeine Zeitung (2015b).

below Sect. 3), which so far effectively constitutes a permanent ban of the UberPop service in Germany.

Since then, Uber has adapted its business model, complying with regulation, mainly obtaining required licenses for its drivers, and is slowly re-entering the market. As of 2019, Uber operates in eight German cities, providing rentable transportation services under the name UberX and UberBlack (see below Sect. 5 for details).

1.2 The Market for Public Transportation Services

Due to a strict regulation of the public transportation industry, taxis and rentable limousine services (*Mietwagenverkehr*) are the only relevant services offered in the business of non-scheduled transportation services.[15]

1.2.1 Taxis and Similar Services

Taxi services can be offered by independent taxi drivers or larger operators with more taxis available. Furthermore, different providers offer intermediary services. Traditionally, (local) taxi dispatch centers could receive orders for taxis via a hotline or call boxes and pass them to available taxi drivers. Today, such services are increasingly offered via a smartphone app which can be used to book or even pay for a taxi. Competitors in this market are "Free Now" (formerly "myTaxi"),[16] "UberTaxi"[17] or "Taxi.eu" (which is offered by taxi dispatch centers).

Rentable transportation services are oftentimes offered by smaller local and/or specialized (e.g., airport transfer) providers or higher priced limousine services. In this sector, operators like "Blacklane" and intermediaries like Uber (UberX and UberBlack) or Free Now also use smartphone apps for receiving orders.[18]

---

[15]The German Passenger Transportation Act distinguishes between scheduled transportation services between pre-determined stops (*Linienverkehr*) and non-scheduled transportation services (*Gelegenheitsverkehr*). Furthermore, separate provisions are in place for specific vehicle types (e.g., trams and busses). In this context, only the provisions regarding *Gelegenheitsverkehr* (which also includes long distance bus travels) are relevant, Details see below at Sect. 2.1.

[16]MyTaxi was originally founded as a taxi intermediary app. In 2019, it is owned by Daimler and BMW as part of a larger mobility joint venture and changed its name to Free Now. The app now offers rentable limousine services as well, making it similar to Uber's current business model and a de facto competitor. The changes sparked outrage by taxi drivers, many of whom previously cooperated with myTaxi (see TaxiTimes (2019)).

[17]Uber does no longer offer or promote "UberTaxi" as a separate service (e.g., on its website), however, the Uber app still has the option to request a regular taxi for a given destination.

[18]Haucap et al. (2015).

Services with (unlicensed) non-professional drivers offering transportation via an app (the UberPop-model) never gained a larger footing in Germany. "Wundercar" was a local competitor[19] before ending its services in Germany in 2014 (while still operating under "Wunder" in other countries).[20] The injunctions against Uber's services effectively put an end to this business model in Germany. Since then and amidst a debate about a modernization of the law and the industry other mobility start-ups with various business models (different from UberPop's) have launched and been granted local special permits for testing new transportation services.[21]

1.2.2 Ride Sharing Services

Ride sharing services, where *private individuals* share the operating costs for a common ride, are not subject to the above-mentioned regulation. Multiple apps (or websites) offer such services via the internet (e.g., "BlaBlaCar").[22] Commercial ride sharing options, where passengers can share a limousine or taxi, have also emerged, oftentimes short-lived or hindered due to regulatory issues. Recent examples are "Clevershuttle" and "BerlKönig."[23] Like in other countries, Uber itself offers a ride sharing service under the name "UberPool." Although listed on Uber's website, the service is currently not available in Germany due to ongoing legal issues.

2 Regulation of Personal Passenger Transportation Services Under Federal Law

2.1 Public Transportation Services

2.1.1 General Regulation of Public Transportation Service Sector

In Germany, all transportation services using (inter alia) a vehicle are subject to the provisions of the German Passenger Transportation Act (PBefG) if they are offered for payment or run like a business (§ 1 PBefG). Exempted are services where a fee is not charged or amounts are paid only up to and not exceeding the operating costs (§ 1 II Nr. 1).[24]

---

[19] Ingold (2014), pp. 3334–3339, p. 3338.

[20] Die Zeit (2015).

[21] See Haack and Dathe (2019), pp. 81–82 and also below Sect. 5.

[22] Haucap et al. (2015, pp. 18–19).

[23] Compare Haucap et al. (2015, p. 17), e.g., the service "Better Taxi" used to offer taxi sharing.

[24] Other exemptions from the scope of application, excluding, e.g., ambulance services (§ 1 II Nr. 1 PBefG) or transports by public authorities (§ 1 Nr. 2 *Freistellungs-Vorordnung*), do not apply to Uber.

All transportation services falling within the scope of the PBefG require a license (§ 2 PBefG) and are subject to further regulation under the PBefG.[25] However, the law only allows certain defined categories of services. All other forms of transportation falling within its scope but not fitting the categories are generally not admissible. Since 2013, authorities can subject such services to the regulation of the legally defined service category they most closely resemble (see § 2 VI PBefG).[26]

To sum up, the PBefG only allows certain defined transportation services to be offered for a fee. The rationale for this is that transport companies provide public services; the regulation aims to ensure that those services can be offered free from undue market pressure (by competition) therefore safeguarding them to meet public demand long term.[27]

The license requirement applies to the operator of the transportation service. This does not necessarily have to be the driver of the car, but rather the person or business entity which provides the services under its name and for its own account and incurs the responsibility (§ 3 II PBefG). The law also explicitly states that the obligations under the PBefG will still apply if the service provider tries to circumvent its provision (§ 6 PBefG).[28]

Mere intermediary services are not subject to regulation. These are services who match customer orders with offers provided by transportation services, usually charging a fee. In this case, only the provider of the transportation service is subject to the license requirement.[29] Examples of such intermediary services are traditional taxi dispatch centers or apps which refer passengers to taxis and offer payment services[30] or car-sharing agencies.[31]

For non-scheduled transportation services with cars (*Gelegenheitsverkehr*), the law distinguishes between taxi services and rentable transportation services (§ 46 II PBefG). For both services, drivers are required to have a specific driver's license and fulfill further criteria, e.g., being physically and mentally suitable for conducting transportation services (§ 48 IV FeV[32]). Taxi drivers furthermore have to prove their knowledge of the local streets (§ 48 IV Nr. 7 FeV).[33]

---

[25] Wimmer and Weiß (2015, p. 80).

[26] Heinze et al. (2014), § 2 para. 53.

[27] Heinze et al. (2014, § 2 para. 51).

[28] Regarding Uber see Oberverwaltungsgericht Berlin-Brandenburg, Beschluss vom 10.04.2015, OVG 1 S 96.14.

[29] Ingold (2014, pp. 3335–3336).

[30] See above Sect. 1.2.1, further Ingold (2014, p. 3335).

[31] See above Sect. 1.2.2, further Wimmer and Weiß (2015, p. 81).

[32] German Driver's License Regulation (*Fahrerlaubnisverordnung*).

[33] Up until 2017, this requirement existed for rentable transportation services as well; for details see Will and Quarch (2018).

2.1.2 Regulation of Taxi Services

Taxi services are defined in the PBefG as transportation services to a destination chosen by the passenger, with the drivers awaiting orders at authorized taxi stands or picking up passengers on the go (§ 47 I PBefG). Certain rights and obligations follow the classification as a taxi service: Within the municipality where the service is located, taxis are only allowed to wait for passengers at taxi stands (designated areas where no other cars are allowed to park) or at their place of business. However, taxis can also take on orders while in transit, e.g., by hand sign from pedestrians or via communication devices (e.g., radio or phone). In contrast, rentable transportation services are not allowed to do so (see § 49 IV 2, 3 PBefG). They have to return to their designated hub.

Taxis are obliged to transport passengers within their operating area. They cannot reject requests out of inconvenience or for economic reasons (§§ 22; 47 IV PBefG).[34] Taxis are also subject to obligations and regulation regarding prices and payment methods. State legislators are empowered to set prices and payment methods via statutory order (§ 51 I PBefG). The tariffs must be set in such a way that taxi services are economically viable—i.e., (well) above operating costs (§ 39 II PBefG). Most state legislators transfer their legal competence to the municipality.[35] Taxi services are not allowed to alter from the determined tariffs (compare § 39 III PBefG; § 37 BOKraft). Furthermore, technical standards for the vehicles used have to be met (e.g., taxis are marked as a taxi by a certain color and sign, § 26 II BOKraft).

2.1.3 Regulation Regarding Rentable Transportation Services

Taxi services are distinguished in the PBefG from rentable transportation services. They are defined as services, where the passenger books a vehicle to be transported to a defined destination and which are not taxi services (§ 49 IV PBefG). In contrast to taxis, services may only be offered, if orders are only accepted at the operator's place of business and drivers are not allowed to pick up passengers while in transit or to wait for passengers on the streets. The drivers rather have the duty to return to their place of business after completing a trip. As an exemption, orders which are accepted at the operator's place of business can be passed on (via communication device) to drivers, who are returning from a previous trip (§ 49 IV 3 PBefG).[36]

[34]Heinze et al. (2014, § 47 para. 10).

[35]Fromm et al. (2013), 1 PBefG § 52 para. 1.

[36]Drivers can also conduct multiple orders one after another if they have been placed with the operator previous to the trip. The UberX service mainly operates under these exemptions, see below Sect. 5. For details, see ibid., (1 PBefG § 49 para. 8).

2.1.4 Licensing and Concession

Objective and subjective provisions for obtaining a license to operate a transportation service are set out in § 13 PBefG. For all transportation services, a license can only be provided, if the operator can ensure the safety and viability of the business, if there are no indications for a lack of reliability, if the operator is qualified as a service provider and if the operator has its place of business in Germany (§ 13 I PBefG).[37]

For *taxi services*, the PBefG furthermore sets out certain general provisions for obtaining a license (§ 13 IV, V PBefG). A license will only be granted, if the new taxi service is not a threat for the viability of the local taxi industry (§ 13 IV 1 PBefG). Criteria for the viability are especially the demand for transportation via taxi, the density of taxi services provided, the revenue structure and the number and reasons of service providers closing down their business (§ 13 IV 2 PBefG). The license is usually granted for five years, two years for new applicants (§ 13 V 5 PBefG). Licenses can only be transferred if the whole business or independent parts of it are transferred with it (§ 2 III PBefG). For *rentable transportation services*, no such objective criteria have to be met for obtaining a license.

2.2 Consequences for Market Structure

The concession requirement leads to very few new market entries in the taxi sector, especially in bigger cities. New concessions are rarely issued usually coercing new applicants to obtain a license by buying an existing business.[38] One consequence of the high entrance barriers is a significant market concentration: The total number of taxis has remained stable (at around 53.000)[39] while the number of businesses has decreased at the same time (32.000 in 1992 compared to 22.500 in 2016),[40] leading to a higher number of taxis per business (2,35 vehicles used per taxi-business in 2012 compared to 1,61 in 1992[41]). In contrast, the total number of businesses for rentable transportation services in 2012 was around 8.000, operating 35.000 vehicles.[42] Despite a generally high density and some overcapacities in the taxi market, there can still be shortages in supply at peak hours (e.g., at major events) and in rural areas.[43] In large Germany cities, prices for taxis are relatively high

[37] These provisions are further specified in the Ordinance for Entering a Profession in Passenger Transportation (*Personenverkehr-Berufszugangsverordnung*, PBZugV). For example, as proof for the qualification, the operator also has to pass a test about legal and business knowledge (§ 3, Anlage 3 PBZugV).

[38] Haucap et al. (2015, pp. 5, 10); see also: Monopolkommission (2012/2013), p. 114.

[39] Statista (2016).

[40] Statista (2019a).

[41] For figures before 2016, see Haucap et al. (2015, pp. 8–9).

[42] Haucap et al. (2015, p. 15).

[43] Haucap et al. (2015, p. 10).

compared to worldwide standards[44] and compared to the rates for rentable transportation services.[45] The total revenue of the taxi sector was around EUR 3.8 billion in 2014 and is expected to rise to EUR 4 billion by 2020.[46]

Regarding the reception of orders, taxi centers took 74% of all orders in 2014 (the most recent year for which figures are available), while 14% of orders were taken at a taxi stand and 10% were taken while in transit. Only 0,4% of orders were taken via an app in 2014.[47] Taxi dispatch centers can have monopolistic powers in some areas.[48]

2.3 *Sanctions for Compliance Failures*

Operating a business without a (proper) license constitutes a summary offence subject to a fine of up to 20.000€ (§ 61 I Nr. 1, II PBefG) for each violation. A fine of up to 10.000€ can be further imposed if the operator violates his duties under the PBefG (§ 61 I Nr. 2-4; II) as well as the duties under the BOKraft (§ 45 I BOKraft, § 61 I Nr. 4, II PBefG). Subject to sanctions can also be participants to the violation (§ 14 OWiG[49]).

2.4 *Remedies Under German Competition Law*

Under German competition law, unfair competitive practices are forbidden (§ 3 I UWG[50]). Competitors engage in unlawful competition if they violate a law established to protect competition and if the violation is suitable to adversely affect consumers or competitors (§ 3a UWG). The licensing requirement for transportation services as well as the respective duties under the PBefG constitutes such laws.[51]

In the case of an unlawful competitive behavior, competitors have a claim for abatement, removal, or—when there is a risk of repetition—an injunctive relief (§ 8 I, III UWG). Competitors can also have the right for compensation (§ 9 UWG) or the unfairly accumulated profit can be levied (§ 10 UWG).

---

[44] Statista (2019b).

[45] Monopolkommission, (2012/2013, pp. 119 ff.).

[46] Statista (2017).

[47] Current statistics are not available. Given the technical developments and apps available (from third parties and taxi operators alike), the number has likely risen since then.

[48] Haucap et al. (2015, p. 9); Monopolkommission (2012/2013, p. 125).

[49] German Act on Regulatory Offences (*Ordnungswidrigkeitengesetz*).

[50] German Act Against Unfair Competition (*Gesetz gegen den unlauteren Wettbewerb*).

[51] Köhler et al. (2017), UWG § 3a para. 1148.

3 Countrywide Injunction Against UberPop by the Judiciary

As first instance, the District Court of Frankfurt am Main issued a countrywide injunction against UberPop in 2015 in accordance with § 8 III Nr. 1; §§ 3, 3a UWG.[52] The plaintiff, a cooperative of taxi operators, argued that the UberPop service violated the PBefG since Uber's drivers were not in possession of the necessary license (§§ 2 I Nr. 4, 46 PBefG). Uber filed an appeal against the injunction but in June 2016, the court of appeals, the Higher Regional Court of Frankfurt, affirmed the judgment of the trial court.[53]

The court's ruling refers to all the disputed issues concerning the legality of Uber's business model, mainly weather the UberPop transportation services are subject to regulation at all, if Uber was operating transportation services itself or was just an intermediary not subject to any regulation and if the restrictions of the PBefG violate European law or constitutional rights.[54]

3.1 UberPop Subject to Regulation

Dismissing Uber's appeal, the Higher Regional Court held that UberPop's services were subject to regulation under the PBefG; hence, a license to operate a taxi service was required. The service was offered in return for a payment and therefore not exempted under § 1 II Nr. 1 PBefG since the charged fee exceeded the operating costs. Following the injunction of the trial court, Uber had started to declare the payment of the fee as voluntary and drastically lowered the (suggested) prices. However, according to the court, this approach was motivated purely to circumvent the law. In reality, almost none of the customers did make use of "their right" not to pay a fee.[55] The court also held, supported by expert opinions, the fee to be higher than the operating costs. Part of Uber's business model was to offer drivers long-term revenues and profits, which would not be possible if only the operating costs would be charged.[56]

---

[52] Landgericht Frankfurt a.M., Urteil vom 18.03.2015, 3-08 O 136/14.

[53] Oberlandesgericht Frankfurt a.M., Urteil vom 09.06.2016, 6 U 73/15.

[54] While details to those issues were somewhat controversial, the general legal consensus for the most part seemed to be that UberPop is illegal under German law.

[55] Ibid., (paras. 33 ff.).

[56] Ibid., (paras. 33–37).

3.2 Uber as Operator or Aiding and Abetting

Even if Uber itself was not offering the rides as an operator itself, the court held it was still violating competition law: Uber's drivers were not in possession of the required license and did not follow regulation for taxi drivers. Since Uber prompted the respective activities by recruiting drivers through affiliated companies, assigning rides and offering payment services, Uber was liable for the illegal conduct of its drivers.[57] Uber was aware that its drivers were violating the law, at least when its illegality was established by the interpretative rulings of regulatory authorities or other courts. Uber also willingly acted when not requiring its drivers to obtain the necessary license but rather only demanding a normal driver's license and an insured, functioning car.[58] Uber was therefore at least liable for aiding and abetting its driver's unlawful behavior.

In a further *obiter dictum*, the court seconded the finding that Uber itself was the provider of the transportation services. The provider was not necessarily the person who owned the vehicles but rather the person who exercised control over vehicles and employees. The determining factor would be who, in the eyes of the customer, was providing the service. Uber itself was the contractual partner for the customers, which handled the order and payment process and set prices. Uber was furthermore managing the orders and the payment for the drivers. All of this would strongly suggest that Uber was itself the taxi operator.[59]

3.3 Constitutional Rights

Uber claimed, the ban of UberPop service (respectively the strict regulation of the PBefG) violated the constitutional right to free access to a profession (Article 12 Grundgesetz)[60] for itself and its drivers. The Court dismissed these concerns: The guarantee to choose a profession at will could be limited by law to protect legal interests of particular importance. The PBefG aimed to protect the safety of passengers and other road users by regulating the quality of service providers and to ensure the general viability of public transportation services, which constitute important public interests.[61] Uber's defense that it had established an equally effective control mechanism for ensuring the quality and reliability of its drivers,[62] was dismissed by the court. The legislator had the ability to determine whether a private quality control

[57] Ibid., (paras. 43–46).

[58] Ibid., (paras. 46–48).

[59] Ibid., (paras. 40–41).

[60] Guaranteed in Article 12 of the German Constitution (*Grundgesetz*).

[61] Ibid., (paras. 53–54).

[62] Uber required its potential drivers, among others, to present a driving license and a police clearance certificate.

would be equally effective to the provisions of the PBefG, which therefore did not constitute a disproportionate restriction of Uber's constitutional rights.

3.4 Freedom Under EU-Treaty

Concluding its reasoning, the court held that the given interpretation of the PBefG did not violate European law. The freedom to provide services (Article 56 TFEU) was not affected, since it was not applicable to transportation services (Article 58 I TFEU).[63] In a similar case submitted by a Spanish court, the EJC later shared this opinion (see in Detail below Sect. 4).[64]

The freedom of establishment (Article 49 TFEU) was not violated either; this would require Uber to have a branch in Germany. Instead, Uber was only offering its intermediary services cross-border (from the Netherlands), the transportation service itself was not offered across borders.[65]

4 Court Rulings Regarding UberBlack

Similar to UberPop, the UberBlack limousine service faced legal challenges. With this service, Uber is offering limousine services provided by independent local operators via its app. In Berlin, the service was banned by the authorities for violating the PBefG, namely the duty to return to the seat of business after conducting a transport (see above Sect. 2.1.3). The Higher Administrative Court of Berlin-Brandenburg (*Oberverwaltungsgericht*) later upheld the ban.[66] Furthermore, an injunction for the State of Berlin was issued for violating the UWG, following a claim of a local taxi operator.[67]

In both cases, the courts reasoned that the UberBlack service violated the duty to return set out in § 49 IV 1, 2, 5 PBefG. UberBlack would send orders placed via app directly to the nearest UberBlack driver, while at the same time sending the order to the contractor operating the local transportation service. According to the courts, this order placement was not in line with the restriction for rentable transportation services which only allows operators to take orders at their place of business. The direct referral of an order to the closest driver via the app was comparable to a direct communication and order with the driver (which is only allowed for taxis). Under this order placement, it could not be assured that the drivers would return to the place

[63]Ibid., (paras. 65–76).

[64]ECJ, 20.12.2017—C-434/15 (Asociación Profesional Elite Taxi/Uber Systems Spain SL).

[65]Oberlandesgericht Frankfurt (paras. 77–81).

[66]Oberverwaltungsgericht Berlin-Brandenburg, Beschluss vom 10.04.2015, OVG 1 S 96.14.

[67]Landgericht Berlin, Urteil vom 09.02.2015, 101 O 125/14, the injunction was upheld by the Higher Regional Court (Kammergericht): Kammergericht, Urteil vom 11.12.2015, 5 U 31/15.

of business after each order; they could rather wait on the streets for orders from nearby customers.

During Uber's appeal against the injunction to the German Federal Supreme Court (*Bundesgerichtshof*), the court brought the issue to the ECJ, asking whether the duty to return affects the rights awarded by the TFEU[68] and the EU Service Directive[69] and if so, if those restrictions were justified in accordance with Article 16 I of the EU Service Directive because they ensure the viability of the taxi sector.[70] After the ECJ ruled in a similar case regarding Uber's activities in Spain,[71] the German Federal Supreme Court withdrew the request. The ECJ ruled that Ubers mediation services (via app) were so closely connected to the transportation service itself that it constitutes a transportation service rather than a service provision under EU law. Uber's services would therefore not be subject to the EU Service Directive,[72] but rather only national law.[73] The German Federal Supreme Court followed the ECJ[74] in its final ruling, deeming the PBefG's regulations in accordance with EU law.[75] The Court furthermore deemed the PBefG's regulation constitutional, dismissing Uber's arguments that changes in the transportation industry had made the current strict regulation unnecessary and that new market participants would not pose a threat to the overall viability of the non-scheduled transportation sector.[76] Uber later supposedly changed UberBlack's business model to adhere to the ruling.

5 Uber's Market Reentry and Current Regulatory Issues

Following the ban of UberPop and most of Uber's business in Germany in 2015, Uber has slowly re-entered the German market, currently to seven major cities,[77] albeit with a different approach to conducting its business. Uber now explicitly emphasizes its compliance with German regulation.[78] Uber's business in Germany now essentially

[68] Article 56 I TFEU.

[69] Directive 2006/123/EC.

[70] Bundesgerichtshof, Beschluss vom 18.05.2017, I ZR 3/16.

[71] ECJ, 20.12.2017—C-434/15 (Asociación Profesional Elite Taxi/Uber Systems Spain SL).

[72] See Article 2 II c) Directive 2006/123/EC.

[73] For a detailed analysis of the ECJ's ruling, see annotations to ECJ, 20.12.2017—C-434/15 by König (2018) EuZW: 131–135.

[74] Referencing the ECJ's Uber Spain ruling as well as a later similar ruling regarding Uber France (ECJ, 10.4.2018—C-320/16 (Uber France SAS)).

[75] BGH, Urteil vom 13.12.2018—I ZR 3/16 (KG) (paras. 44 ff).

[76] BGH, Urteil vom 13.12.2018 —I ZR 3/16 (KG) (paras. 33 ff.); Uber cited an analysis by the German Monopolies Commission, see Monopolkommission (2012/2013, p. 127); see also below Sect. 8.

[77] Berlin, Düsseldorf, Frankfurt, Hamburg, Cologne, Munich and Stuttgart.

[78] Frankfurter Allgemeine Zeitung (2015c).

consists of two services: UberX and UberBlack. Both are—in their current iteration—similar, with UberX as the standard service and UberBlack acting as a premium version, offering more luxurious cars and better service.[79]

In both cases, Uber acts as a broker for transportation requests, passing them on to local contractors respectively. According to Uber, those contractors fulfill all legal requirements, especially those under the PBefG, as well as, e.g., proper insurance coverage. Uber's drivers (or rather their partnering operators) act as rentable transportation services under the PBefG.

As such, they have a duty to return to their seat of operation after each drive and all orders have to be received there. Only if an order is placed at the operators place of business, it can then be passed along to a driver still returning.[80] In its ruling regarding UberBlack,[81] the German Federal Supreme Court stated that an order can be transmitted to the driver via communication device (such as an app), but has to be placed with the operator first. It is not enough that an order is transmitted to the driver and the operator at the same time or that a driver reports an order he or she has received.[82]

However, Uber still faced criticism by taxi operators claiming Uber would still not comply with the law. The main argument was, that UberX drivers would circumvent the duty to return by idling in traffic or "resting" in strategic places.[83] In June of 2019, the Cologne District Court issued an injunction in the preliminary proceedings against UberX for violations of the duty to return[84]; the court suspected drivers can still accept orders on their own. In December of 2019, the District Court of Frankfurt am Main reinforced those doubts issuing an injunction against UberX.[85] Following the Cologne District Court, the court held that orders were not placed through the operator and Uber did not ensure drivers were at least in the process of returning before accepting a new order. Furthermore, the court determined Uber and not the drivers/local companies to be the provider of transportation services, similar to the obiter dictum of the Higher Regional Court in the UberPop case (see Sect. 3.2). Uber therefore violated the license requirements.

---

[79] See the Uber Website for details. Uber also offers slight variations of the services, like UberX with electric cars (UberGreen) or transports for larger groups (UberXL) as well as further services.

[80] See above II.3.

[81] See above Sect. 4.

[82] BGH, Urteil vom 13.12.2018—I ZR 3/16 (KG) (para. 34). At the time of the trial, the Uber app would transmit an UberBlack order to the nearest driver and at the same time report the order to the operator. Uber claimed to have changed the order process in accordance with the court's ruling.

[83] See Frankfurter Allgemeine Zeitung (2019).

[84] Landgericht Köln—81 O 74/19, the court's ruling has not been published as of February 2020. The court's decision and its broader content has been made public by various German news outlets in October 2019, see, e.g., Legal Tribute Online (2019). The injunction is not final as of February 2020 since Uber has not yet been formally notified by the court. Provider of the German Uber app and therefore the defendant in this case is Uber B.V. a company in the Netherlands. The court therefore has to formally notice the company in Dutch writing.

[85] Landgericht Frankfurt am Main, Urteil vom 19.12.2019, Az.: 3-08 O 44/19.

Uber immediately reacted to the court's issues by changing its order process. The app now shows a warning before each ride that the transportation contract is concluded not with Uber but its local partner. The customer has to explicitly accept this notification. Uber also claimed it has taken technical provisions to ensure compliance with the duty to return. In the short term, Uber can therefore continue its UberX service without major changes. It remains to be seen however, if Uber can remain profitable while being in full compliance with the law. Aside, Uber's business conduct remains controversial and will likely continue to be the target of criticism or further legal challenges, especially by taxi operators.[86]

6 Labor Law Issues

A major point of discussion regarding UberPop was the question if Uber's drivers are *employees* of Uber or *independent contractors*[87] and to what extend Uber therefore must pay taxes and social security payments.[88]

German courts distinguish between employees and independent contractors by examining the overall nature of the relationship to the contracting party. Decisive factors are the actual circumstances in which the service is provided rather than the contractual wording. A person is in particular considered an employee if he or she is subject to instructions by the contracting party concerning the performance of the service, e.g., if the contractor can determine time, place and working methods.[89] Further criteria are whether the contracting party provides equipment, whether the contractual relationship is for a longer period and whether the contractor can offer his activities to others and bears entrepreneurial risks and rewards.[90] If a person is considered an employee, the employer must pay social securities (including health insurance) contributions[91] and forward income taxes to the tax authorities.[92] The employer also must assure compliance with, e.g., working hours restrictions and provide paid sick leave and paid holidays.

Regarding the UberPop service model, no clear consensus or court rulings regarding the status of drivers exists. The fact that drivers could work at any time and use their own vehicles supports the assumption of drivers as individual contractors. However, drivers were also dependent on Uber sending them customers, subject to

[86] Aside from court procedures, taxi operators have started to register violations of the law by Uber drivers, e.g., the duty to return or vehicle safety standards, and passing them to authorities, see Frankfurter Allgemeine Zeitung (2019).

[87] See Lingemann and Otte (2015), 1042–1047; Solmecke and Lengersdorf (2015), pp. 496–497.

[88] See Solmecke and Lengersdorf (2015, p. 496).

[89] See § 611a German Civil Code.

[90] See Lingemann and Otte (2015, p. 1043).

[91] See, e.g., § 7 German Social Insurance Code IV and § 5 German Social Insurance Code V.

[92] See § 38 German Income Tax Act.

regulations regarding their vehicle, routes were determined by the Uber algorithm and drivers had no influence on prices (i.e., no entrepreneurial freedom).[93]

In comparison, taxi drivers are generally considered to be employees if they provide services under the brand of a taxi operator with a concession, who pays them fixed percentages of fees and coordinates working times, especially if they use a vehicle provided by the operator.[94]

With the UberPop service being banned in Germany, those questions are not at issue at this moment. For its remaining services, Uber now collaborates with independent professional companies. Those operators employ drivers and are not only responsible to comply with the PBefG, but also relevant labor and social securities laws.[95]

7 Contractual Issues and Liability

7.1 Insurance Cover for Traffic Accidents

In Germany, vehicle owners are liable for all damages caused by the operation of the vehicle, regardless of fault.[96] In turn, liability insurance is compulsory for road-car owners.[97] Passengers are therefore in a safe position regarding insurance cover. Under the mandatory policy, passengers are covered for any damages they suffer in traffic accidents caused by the driver of the vehicle. If a third party causes the accident, their mandatory insurance covers the damages. Injured passengers can assert their claims directly against the insurance company.[98] These insurance provisions apply regardless of the contractual relationship between the driver, vehicle owner and the passenger (or an intermediary). If and with whom the passenger has a valid transportation contract is irrelevant regarding vehicle owner liability insurance.

For vehicle owners, the general insurance policy usually restricts the vehicle's use to private use. Commercially transporting passengers requires a special insurance. UberPop drivers who did not report the commercial use of their vehicle to their insurance company therefore usually committed a breach of contract toward their insurance. In the event of an accident, an insurance company could terminate the policy and (partially) take recourse against the policy holder for any damages covered.

93 Lingemann and Otte (2015, pp. 1043–1044); Ruland (2019), pp. 690–691.

94 See, e.g., LSG Baden-Württemberg, Urteil vom 18.10.2016—L 11 R 837/16.

95 For details (as well as comparisons to other on-demand-economy companies), see Ruland (2019), pp. 690–691.

96 § 7 *Straßenverkehrsgesetz.*

97 § 1 *Pflichtversicherungsgesetz.*

98 § 115 *Versicherungsvertragsgesetz.*

However, this breach of contract does not affect the insurance company's duty to cover the passengers or other damaged parties.[99]

7.2 General Contractual Issues and Liability

Currently, customers of the Uber app must explicitly accept that Uber's local partners are the provider of the transportation service. A transportation contract therefore is concluded only between the customer and the partner, not Uber. Uber's role is limited to intermediary services. Uber's liability toward the customer is therefore limited to misconduct regarding the intermediary services. For damages arising from the transportation service, the local partner would be liable under general civil liability principles. This means, aside from the above described liability for traffic accidents, the operator is liable for any damages caused culpably within the contract. The operator is also responsible for the actions of its employees or contractors (e.g., drivers).[100]

For its UberPop model, Uber used to state in its general terms and conditions that the transportation service was provided by an independent third party and Uber was merely a mediator. However, due to its overall conduct and marketing,[101] there were strong reasons to consider Uber to be the contractual party for the transportation service. Uber would then be liable for any damages caused by the drivers. However, since the UberPop service violates regulatory law, the transportation contract could be considered void.[102] In this case, aside from claims against the vehicle owner and the insurance, the passenger could still hold the vehicle's driver liable for culpably caused personal or material damages.[103]

8 Regulatory Changes and Lessons Learned

8.1 European Agenda for the Collaborative Economy

The rise of start-ups of the "sharing economy," like Uber, has given impulses to lawmakers in the EU and Germany, to adapt regulation to changing habits and new technologies.

---

[99]See § 28 *Pflichtversicherungsgesetz*, § 117 *Versicherungsvertragsgesetz*. For details see: Bauer and Frießen (2015), pp. 65–67; further Rebler (2014), p. 465.

[100]See §§ 276 f. German Civil Code.

[101]The facts and arguments stated under IV.B. regarding Uber's role as operator apply accordingly.

[102]For details, see Bauer and Frießen (2015, pp. 62 f.).

[103]See § 823 German Civil Code, § 18 *Straßenverkehrsgesetz*.

The EU Commission has published a European agenda for the collaborative economy.[104] With this agenda, the Commission offers non-binding legal guidance and orientation for legislators and help in interpreting existing EU law concerning the sharing economy.[105] Regarding the market access of sharing economy services, like Uber, the Commission's agenda is rather open toward platform providers. The Commission suggests member states should utilize the economic opportunities these new platforms could provide and not suffocate these services with excessive regulation. The Commission therefore asks member states to reconsider existing market entrance barriers taking into account the specific features of the sharing economy's business models.[106] Member states should revise national entry barriers and prohibitions for necessity and commensurability and adopt regulations to this day and age. It is especially advised, to set a threshold for where no commercial activity is assumed if private individuals offer services through intermediary platforms.[107]

The European Agenda for the Collaborative Economy is part of the Commission's overall Digital Market Strategy, which aims to offer better access and market conditions for consumers and businesses to online services and to create the right conditions for digital platforms to grow, therefore strengthening the digital economy.[108]

8.2 The Future of Uber and the Passenger Transportation Market in Germany

The case of Uber is particularly interesting for Germany where Uber's business model, which—according to its critics—builds on gaining unfair competitive advantages bypassing regulation, meets a strictly enforced legal framework. Furthermore, and in contrast to other legal systems, legislation has not been adapted in favor of Uber in Germany. While Uber has made significant changes to its core business model and services, it still faces legal and business challenges that limit its business perspectives and could even threaten its existence in Germany. Courts might compel Uber to further alter its services or to cease its (current) activities entirely. Operating in this regulatory environment will be challenging for Uber altogether:[109] While the local business partners shoulder much of the regulatory weight, they reportedly must

[104]European Commission, SWD (2016) 184 final, with supporting analysis COM (2016) 356 final.

[105]Cauffman (2016).

[106]European Commission, SWD (2016) 184 final, p. 4; see also: Cauffman (2016, p. 236); Wewer (2016), pp. 193–194.

[107]European Commission, SWD (2016) 184 final, p. 8.

[108]Cauffman (2016, p. 235).

[109]Worldwide, Uber is—like many rapidly expanding start-ups—struggling to generate long-term profits; According to its quarterly reports, Uber made a net loss of USD 1.2 bn. in the third quarter of 2019 alone.

forward 25–30% of the revenue to Uber.[110] Retaining its business partners long term and complying with regulation amidst a rise in competitors might prove a difficult challenge, one that Uber was not used to with its UberPop model.

The reluctance to alter the existing regulation of the public transportation sector in Germany stands in line with other shortcomings, e.g., regarding the digitalization of the commercial sector in general.[111] In the case of Uber, public opinion was backing the existing regulatory approach and its enforcement to some extent. In a 2017 survey, 50% of people were in favor of the Uber ban (33% were opposed),[112] and only 27% were open to using a service similar to UberPop.[113] However, a shift toward deregulation seems to be occurring gradually since Uber's market entry. Consumers seem to grow more familiar and confident with Uber amidst a greater number of people having positive experiences (also from traveling abroad). In the light of a gradually changing public opinion and impulses from EU policy makers, e.g., the EU Commission's agenda, German parliamentary groups have issued a request to the government to assess the risk and opportunities of the sharing economy and to examine the need to adapt or implement specific regulation regarding those services.[114] Furthermore, the German Monopolies Commission has raised the question, whether the existing regulation in the taxi and rentable transportation service sector is still suitable in light of technological change and that the existing market entry barriers are not entirely necessary to guarantee a functioning public transportation sector. It therefore recommended to abolish the licensing requirement as well as fixed prices. Furthermore, it suggested dropping the duty for rentable transportation service providers to return to the place of business after every order, allowing those services to better compete with taxis.[115] The current German government followed this trend toward easing regulation in the transportation sector. In its coalition agreement, it promised to modernize the regulation for transportation services and to open the market for new (technology driven) services.[116]

A formal legislative proposal has yet to be released in Germany; however, some key elements were published in a strategy paper by the German Ministry of Transportation.[117] As a first major change, digital operators would explicitly be subject to the PBefG and as such require a license to operate, settling any such disputes. Furthermore, rentable transportation services would be allowed to rent out seats

[110] See Orange by Handelsblatt (2019). Uber's operators also have to deal with tighter checks by authorities and hostility by taxi drivers.

[111] Bundesministerium für Wirtschaft und Energie (2017).

[112] Statista (2019c).

[113] Statista (2017b).

[114] Bt-Drs. 18/11399, pp. 4–5.

[115] Monopolkommission (2012/2013, p. 127).

[116] Coalition Agreement between the Parties CDU, CSU and SPD (2018), p. 121. https://www.bundesregierung.de/breg-de/themen/koalitionsvertrag-zwischen-cdu-csu-und-spd-195906. Accessed 10 Jan 2020.

[117] The paper is available online at the website of the German Taxi Association at https://www.bzp.org/Content/MELDUNGEN/_doc/PBefG-Eckpunkte.PDF. Accessed 10 Jan 2020. For an analysis of the Ministry's plans, see Haack and Dathe (2019, p. 81).

separately and to let an algorithm rather than the customer determine the driving route. The resulting changes aim to legalize ride pooling services, where individual passengers use a shared vehicle and can board at certain stops set by an app. These services are a mixture of scheduled and non-scheduled transportation services and are already tested on a trial basis in some German cities to support scheduled traffic, especially for rural areas.[118] Most importantly, the Ministry plans to let go of the duty to return for rentable transportation services. Additionally, the law would explicitly allow to receive orders digitally (i.e., via app). Therefore, those services would be able to receive orders while in traffic as well, with taxis only keeping privileges like designated lanes or parking zones. As a result, rentable transportation services would increasingly share a market with taxis.[119] Further distinctions, e.g., regarding pricing regulation for taxis, remain unclear. Instead, the Ministry of Transport contemplates to give municipalities the power to ban these rentable transportation services in certain areas, reserving them for taxis altogether.

However, the publishing of the Ministry's paper has also triggered political discourse and backlash by taxi operators. A bipartisan commission has been set in place to debate the changes, with the German Social Democrats opposing liberalization at the expense of social safety.[120] The main innovation of the proposed reform, the abolishment of the duty to return, seems to be in danger. Altogether, the German market might open itself only to some extent to new technology driven transportation services by subjecting them to—adapted—regulation. This seems to fit a general regulatory response to new technologies in Germany. While Uber's disruptive business model (especially UberPop) may have been the trigger to this partial liberalization of the industry, the company itself will have to show that it can compete in a regulated market on a level playing field.

Another unresolved question reaching beyond the specifics of transportation regulation and competition law is how legal systems should deal with challenges by companies' systematic non-compliance. On the one hand, it should be beyond doubt that the implementation of illegal business strategies and business models can not be tolerated as a general line. On the other hand, it has also become clear that encrusted legal structures create hurdles, both to innovation as to competition. In countries with lesser developed standards, it might also affect public health and safety. Whereas it seems right to uphold traditional positions of the law, these arguments may no longer be heard when services provided by emerging providers reach equal (or even higher) standards to this regard. Therefore, in Germany, the ban of Uber lost at least its moral persuasion when the qualification of its drivers and the safty of rides was established. It should come as a big surprise if the ban of Uber would receive a backup by future legislation. It is more likely that amendments will lead to structural changes of the traditional regulation of the transport sector. Despite "zero tolerance" normally being

---

[118]For an analysis of possible changes especially for ride pooling services and their competition with public scheduled transportation, see Haack and Dathe (2019, p. 84); further Linke and Jürschik (2018), p. 502.

[119]Haack and Dathe (2019, pp. 83–84).

[120]Handelsblatt (2019b).

the mantra of every compliance officer, it cannot be denied that without the deliberate non-compliance to transportation laws by Uber, this would have been a highly unlikely scenario. Is this giving renegade strategies legitimacy? It may, at least to a certain level.

References

Bauer C, Frießen S (2015) UberPop – rechtlich top oder eher ein Flop? DAR 61–67

Bundesministerium für Wirtschaft und Energie (2017) Weißbuch Digitale Plattformen

Cauffman C (2016) The Commission's European agenda for the collaborative economy–(Too) platform and service friendly? EuCML 235–243

Die Zeit (2015) Nicht zu bremsen. http://www.zeit.de/2015/18/start-up-wundercar-erfolg. Accessed 10 Jan 2020

Frankfurter Allgemeine Zeitung (2014a) Taxis bekommen neue Konkurrenz. http://www.faz.net/aktuell/rhein-main/app-uber-startet-in-frankfurt-taxis-bekommen-neue-konkurrenz-12961753.html. Accessed 10 Jan 2020

Frankfurter Allgemeine Zeitung (2014b) Taxi Schreck Uber darf weitermachen. http://www.faz.net/aktuell/wirtschaft/taxi-konkurrent-uber-darf-in-deutschland-vorerst-weitermachen-13156626.html. Accessed 10 Jan 2020

Frankfurter Allgemeine Zeitung (2015a) Uber fügt sich deutschen Regeln. http://www.faz.net/aktuell/wirtschaft/unternehmen/uber-startet-neues-angebot-uber-x-in-deutschland-13600407.html. Accessed 10 Jan 2020

Frankfurter Allgemeine Zeitung (2015b) Uber zieht sich aus Frankfurt und Hamburg zurück. http://www.faz.net/aktuell/wirtschaft/netzwirtschaft/fahrdienst-uber-zieht-sich-aus-frankfurt-und-hamburg-zurueck-13885377.html. Accessed 10 Jan 2020

Frankfurter Allgemeine Zeitung (2015c) Uber sucht den Weg in die Legalität. https://www.faz.net/aktuell/wirtschaft/unternehmen/uber-sucht-den-weg-in-die-legalitaet-13511107.html. Accessed 10 Jan 2020

Frankfurter Allgemeine Zeitung (2019) Uber im Visier der Polizei Frankfurt, https://www.faz.net/aktuell/rhein-main/uber-im-visier-polizei-frankfurt-kontrolliert-den-fahrdienst-16497495.html. Accessed 10 Jan 2020

Fromm G et al (2013) Personenbeförderungsrecht, 4th edn. C H Beck, München

Haack TJ, Dathe I (2019) Novellierung des personenbeförderungsrechts. ZRP 81–85

Handelsblatt (2019a) Wie Uber Fahrer die Wut der Taxifahrer zu spüren bekommen. https://orange.handelsblatt.com/artikel/59366. Accessed 10 Jan 2020

Handelsblatt (2019b) Taxi oder Uber: Union und SPD ringen um die Macht auf der Straße. https://www.handelsblatt.com/politik/deutschland/liberalisierung-taxi-oder-uber-union-und-spd-ringen-um-die-macht-auf-der-strasse/24328194.html10.5.2019. Accessed 10 Jan 2020

Haucap J, et al (2015) Chancen der digitalisierung auf märkten für urbane mobilität: Das Beispiel Uber. No. 73 DICE Ordnungspolitische Perspektiven

Heinze C et al (2014) PBefG Personenbeförderungsgesetz, 2nd edn. C H Beck, München

Ingold A (2014) Gelegenheitsverkehr oder neue verkehrsgelegenheiten? NJW 3334

Köhler H et al (2017) Gesetz gegen den unlauteren Wettbewerb, 35th edn. C H Beck, München

Legal Tribute Online (2019) Verbot der UberX-App wirkt nicht. https://www.lto.de/recht/justiz/j/uber-app-lg-koeln-81o7419-taxi-konkurrenz-gerichtsvollzieher-zustellung-ausland/. Accessed 10 Jan 2020

Lingemann S, Otte J (2015) Arbeitsrechtliche fragen der 'economy on demand'. NZA 1045–1047

Linke B, Jürschik C (2018) Analog trifft digital – Neuigkeiten bei den rechtlichen Rahmenbedingungen zum Ride- und Carsharing. NZV 496–506

Monopolkommission (2012/2013) Eine Wettbewerbsordnung für die finanzmärkte, Hauptgutachten 20
Rebler A (2014) Unmoderne regelungswut oder berechtigte kontrolle: Genehmigungspflicht nach PBefG in zeiten von Uber und WunderCar. RdTW 461–467
Ruland F (2019) Beschäftigungsverhältnis oder "neue selbstständigkeit. NZS 681–693
Solmecke C, Lengersdorf B (2015) Rechtliche probleme bei sharing economy. MMR 493–497
Spiegel Online (2014) Uber ignoriert bundesweites Verbot. https://www.spiegel.de/wirtschaft/unternehmen/uber-taxi-konkurrent-ignoriert-urteil-des-landgerichts-frankfurt-a-989459.html. Accessed 10 Jan 2020
Statista (2016) Anzahl der Taxis in Deutschland 2016. http://de.statista.com/statistik/daten/studie/36475/umfrage/anzahl-der-taxen-in-deutschland-seit-1960/. Accessed 10 Jan 2020
Statista (2017a) Taxigewerbe in Deutschland – Umsatzprognose bis 2020. http://de.statista.com/statistik/daten/studie/400445/umfrage/taxigewerbe-in-deutschland---umsatzprognose. Accessed 10 Jan 2020
Statista (2017b) Meinungsumfrage zur Nutzung von Fahrdienstvermittlern in Deutschland 2017. http://de.statista.com/statistik/daten/studie/708661/umfrage/nutzung-von-fahrdienstvermittlern-in-deutschland/. Accessed 10 Jan 2020
Statista (2019a) Anzahl der Taxibetriebe in Deutschland bis 2017. http://de.statista.com/statistik/daten/studie/12498/umfrage/taxibetriebe-in-deutschland-seit-1960/. Accessed 10 Jan 2020
Statista (2019b) Taxitarife in deutschen Städten 2019. http://de.statista.com/statistik/daten/studie/36499/umfrage/taxitarife-in-deutschland-nach-staedten. Accessed 10 Jan 2020
Statista (2019c) Meinungsumfrage zum Verbot Uber in Deutschland 2017. http://de.statista.com/statistik/daten/studie/708681/umfrage/meinungsumfrage-zum-verbot-von-uber-in-deutschland/. Accessed 10 Jan 2020
TaxiTimes (2019) So life die Übergabe der ersten Free Now Massenkündigung. https://www.taxi-times.com/so-lief-die-uebergabe-der-ersten-free-now-massenkuendigung-in-muenchen. Accessed 10 Jan 2020
Wewer G (2016) Faire chance für die kollaborative wirtschaft? ZRP 193–196
Will M, Quarch B (2018) Der Personenbeförderungsschein gem. § 48 FeV für mietwagenfahrer mit D/D1 fahrerlaubnis und die deregulierung des personenbeförderungsrechts. NVwZ 1610–1613
Wimmer N, Weiß M (2015) Taxi-Apps zwischen vermittlertätigkeit und personenbeförderung die verwaltungsgerichtliche entscheidungspraxi zu den Uber-Angeboten. MMR 80–85

Chapter 9
Über Alles or not? the Italian Perspective on the "Uber Case"

Eva R. Desana, Federico Riganti, and Silvana Secinaro

1 Uber and the Legal Context: Some Preliminary Remarks

1.1 Main Issues and Problems

The sharing economy phenomenon, and in particular the "Uber case", is currently triggering broad political, economic and ideological debates throughout Europe and Italy. More specifically, the case at hand has caused great uproar especially if we consider the UberPop service (the equivalent of UberX in the USA), which is the cheapest service offered by Uber.

This particular service, which depends on private amateur drivers, has directly challenged the taxi market in Italy, which is also a key market from a political point of view. To "fight" against Uber, many taxi associations and taxi unions have repeatedly taken direct action against Uber drivers, basing their arguments on the existing national legal framework.

In recent years, several strikes on behalf of taxi drivers and lawsuits have made the "Uber case" a pressing issue that has attracted great attention both in the media and in the highest courts of the country. The problem is still current and interesting, and in some way linked to other players of the so-called "new economy" (like Airbnb and Foodora), which try to develop their own and new business scheme in an "old

E. R. Desana · F. Riganti (✉) · S. Secinaro
University of Turin, Turin, Italy
e-mail: federico.riganti@unito.it

E. R. Desana
e-mail: eva.desana@madlex.it

S. Secinaro
e-mail: silvana.secinaro@unito.it

Z. Ayata and I. Önay (eds.), *Global Perspectives on Legal Challenges Posed by Ridesharing Companies*,
https://doi.org/10.1007/978-981-15-7035-3_9

style" place like Italy. A place where "Permits are a big deal and are literally required for just about everything including driving people around".[1]

1.2 Key Elements of Uber

As well known and mentioned in the previous chapters, Uber could be defined as a technology group of companies with a proprietary technology application (the "UberApp") that provides *inter alia* some kind of on-demand transportation service. Also in Italy, Uber has a huge number of supporters, that emphasize many of its elements, such as (i) reduction of research costs; (ii) a better overview of quality and prices; (iii) presence of Information and Communication Technology (ICT) services to assist drivers who would otherwise not engage in transport services due to the restrictions on entry into the taxi sector, which in Italy is particularly expensive.

On the contrary, there are also a number of allegations, implying that Uber gains its competitive advantage by exploiting loopholes in the EU, national and regional legal frameworks, thus lowering consumer security/privacy standards. These arguments are underlined by Italian Judges in some important judgments.

Moreover, the courts of Milan and Turin have shown common ground to classify the activity undertaken by Uber as unfair competition against the most regulated unscheduled local transport services in Italy and in particular against taxis. Some of the common arguments against Uber are the following: (i) unfair competition; (ii) creation of monopoly; (iii) lack of public safety; (iv) lack of privacy; (v) issues of discrimination; (vi) issues of compensation; and, evidently, (v) tax issues.

As already mentioned, the most problematic service of Uber in Italy has been its cheapest one: UberPop. Nevertheless, UberBlack has been targeted by national courts, but has encountered far fewer challenges than its "cheaper brother" UberPop. The latter has been subject to censorship and numerous court orders in Italy.

2 The Italian Scenario: Regulatory Issues and Legal Impact

2.1 The Italian Legal Framework Within the European Context

Obviously, the Italian legal scenario is strictly connected to the European legal framework, already discussed above in this Volume.[2] With reference to the national

[1] See https://www.wantedinmilan.com/news/uber-in-italy-all-you-need-to-know.html. On the Uber case in Italy see: Amoroso (2016), Dagnino (2016), Iaione (2008), Ingrao (2018), Midiri (2019), Mostacci and Somma (2016), Pollicino and Lubello (2016).

[2] As mentioned above, Uber supporters regard the "Uber system" as an example of Transportation Network Companies (TNCs). This interpretation has been discussed in detail in Italy and Europe,

dispositions, in Italy, transport is regulated by Law No. 21 of 15 January 1992, "*Legge quadro per il trasporto di persone mediante autoservizi pubblici non di linea*" (hereinafter Law No. 21/92), concerning "Public passenger transport through local non-scheduled services". Moreover, national laws give the Regions some important legislative powers in the field of transport: for this reason, most Regions have adopted some additional rules on unplanned public transport.

For example, concerning non-scheduled local transport and on the base of the above mentioned powers of the Regions, the Piedmont Region has sought to regulate the service offered by Uber by means of a Regional Law, in particular Regional Law No. 14 of 6 July 2015 (hereinafter Reg. Law No. 14/2015) on "Urgent measures against unauthorized undertakings in the field of non-scheduled local public transport". The Regional Law provided that the non-scheduled local transport was reserved exclusively for two categories of subjects: taxi drivers and NCCs (*Noleggio con conducente*), another type of professional drivers: In this way the Uber drivers were implicitly excluded: However, in December 2016 the Constitutional Court declared this provision unconstitutional (Decision No. 265/2016). In Court's opinion, in fact,

also given that the "nature" of Uber is strictly connected to some crucial freedoms of the architecture made by the EU Treaties and EU Directives. In fact, a broad interpretation of the fundamental freedoms of the EU legal framework—namely the freedom of establishment (Article 49 TFEU) and the freedom to provide services (Article 56 TFEU)—was requested in connection to the Uber case and in connection to Article 58 TFUE, which prescribes that "Freedom to provide services in the field of transport shall be governed by the provisions of the Title relating to transport". Moreover, the profile under discussion has been related, with problems of coordination and (non)compatibility, to the provisions of the (i) Directive 2006/123/EC of the European Parliament and of the Council of 12 December 2006 on Services in the Internal Market, of the (ii) Directive 2000/31/EC of the European Parliament and of the Council of 8 June 2000 on certain legal aspects of information society services, in particular electronic commerce, in the Internal Market ("Directive on electronic commerce"), and of the (iii) Directive 98/34/EC (especially Article 1) of the European Parliament and of the Council of 22 June 1998 laying down a procedure for the provision of information in the field of technical standards and regulations and of rules on Information Society services, as amended by Directive 98/48/EC of the European Parliament and of the Council of 20 July 1998 (OJ 1998 L 217, p. 18) ("Directive 98/34"). The Directive 98/34 was repealed on 7 October 2015. Nevertheless, it remains applicable *ratione temporis* to the dispute in the main proceedings. On this point, it is well known that at the end of December 2017, the EU Court held that Uber was not a mere platform for intermediary services, but offers, through the recruitment of voluntary drivers, a service which is very similar to the more regulated taxi and NCC service. In other words, as pointed out by the ECJ in December 2017, the service provided by Uber connecting individuals with non-professional drivers "must thus be regarded as forming an integral part of an overall service whose main component is a transport service and, accordingly, must be classified not as 'an information society service' within the meaning of Article 1(2) of Directive 98/34, to which Article 2(a) of Directive 2000/31 refers, but as 'a service in the field of transport' within the meaning of Article 2(2)(d) of Directive 2006/123". Consequently "Directive 2000/31 does not apply to an intermediation service such as that at issue in the main proceedings" and "Such service, in so far as it is classified as 'a service in the field of transport', does not come under Directive 2006/123 either, since this type of service is expressly excluded from the scope of the directive pursuant to Article 2(2)(d) thereof". Moreover, "since the intermediation service at issue in the main proceedings is to be classified as 'a service in the field of transport', it is covered not by Article 56 TFEU on the freedom to provide services in general but by Article 58(1) TFEU, a specific provision according to which 'freedom to provide services in the field of transport shall be governed by the provisions of the Title relating to transport' (see, to that effect, judgment of 22 December 2010, Yellow Cab Verkehrsbetrieb,C-338/09, EU:C:2010:814, the choice of reserving the transport activity to two categories of subjects affected the discipline of competition which is the responsibility of the State.

Actually, it is important to underline the fact that the regulation of competition in the market is a matter of national law according to Article 117 of the Italian Constitution. However, in this regard, the recent decision of the Italian Constitutional Court (Decision No. 56/2020 of 26 March 2020) has stated that Article 117 of the Italian Constitution gives to the State the exclusive power to regulate competition. Such power cannot be so pervasive to absorb, a priori, the subjects under the competence of the Regions. Therefore, State provisions that intend to protect fair competition but through an unproportional and inadequate way—with reference to the transport sector—will be considered illegitimate. The decision concerned Decree-Law No 135 of December 2018 introducing into Law 21 of 1992 certain restrictive requirements for NCCs.

Coming back to the details of the National Law, following Article 1 of Law No. 21/92,[3] there are two types of non-scheduled local transport services:

- taxi service[4];
- car rental with driver (NCC—*Noleggio con Conducente*).[5]

---

paragraph 29 and the case-law cited)". Therefore "Member States can (…) regulate the conditions for providing that service".

[3]Article 1 of L. 21/92 "Public service not on public lines. 1. Public service not on public lines are defined as those which provide collective or individual transport of persons, with a complementary and integrative function with respect to public transport by rail, car, sea, lake and air, and which are carried out, at the request of the transported person, in a non-continuous or periodic manner, on routes and according to timetables established from time to time.

2. Public service not on public lines are:

(a) a taxi service with a car, motor coach, watercraft and animal-drawn vehicles;
(b) the rental service with driver and car, motor coach, velocipede, watercraft and animal-drawn vehicles".

[4]The taxi service is intended to meet the needs of individual transport or small groups of people; it is aimed at an undifferentiated user; parking is in a public place; the fares are determined administratively by the competent bodies, which also establish the modalities of the service; the pick-up of the user or the start of the service takes place within the municipal or district area.

[5]The chauffeur-driven rental service is addressed to the specific user who makes a specific request at the head office or garage for a specific time and/or travel service, also through the use of technological tools. 2. The vehicles must be parked inside the garages or at the docks. 3. The carrier's place of operation and at least one garage must be located in the territory of the municipality, which issued the authorization. The carrier may have further garages in the territory of other municipalities in the same province or metropolitan area in which the territory of the municipality that issued the authorization falls, subject to notification to the aforementioned municipalities, unless otherwise agreed in the Unified Conference by 28 February 2019. By way of derogation from the provisions of this paragraph, due to the specific territorial features and infrastructural deficiencies, only for the regions of Sicily and Sardinia the authorization issued in one municipality of the region shall be valid for the entire regional territory, within which the operational headquarters and at least one garage must be located.

Law No. 21/92 mainly regulates taxis and NCCs with a series of strictly regulatory requirements. To meet these requirements, taxi and NCC drivers must (1) obtain a taxi driver's licence from their district or municipality. In order to acquire such a licence, they must (2) apply for and obtain a qualification certificate from the Provincial Office of Civil Motorization following (3) an examination.

Moreover, to obtain driver qualification, taxi and NCC drivers must (4) obtain a professional qualification certificate (CAP—*Certificato Abilitazione Professionale*) issued by the Ministry of Transport and (5) apply for registration with the local Chambers of Commerce (Article 6 Law. No. 21/1992). Furthermore, it is compulsory for taxi drivers to be (6) insured as professional entrepreneurs, with an insurance covering damages to third parties, much more expensive than a common insurance for users. Taxi services and fares are also (7) fixed and predetermined, and drivers must (8) have a visible taximeter in the vehicle.

When it comes to Uber drivers, the requirements are much less stringent than those mentioned above to become a taxi driver or NCC driver. In fact, the requirements to become an Uber driver are certainly less complex: drivers must be at least (1) 21 years old, (2) only have a driving licence for at least 1 year, (3) have at least 15/20 points on the driving licence, without any prior suspension. Drivers must also have (4) a clean criminal record (5) and a car insurance policy assigned to the driver or a direct relative. (6) The car must be less than 10 years old, 4 doors and 4 seats. That's all.

The matter is also considered in the Legislative Decree No. 285 of 30 April 1992, "New Highway Code". Article 86 of the Code clearly states that whoever designates a vehicle as a taxi service without the required taxi driver's licence, will incur a fine,[6] as well as the suspension and requisition of the driving licence. The activity and service provided by Uber are in contrast with this rule, as drivers do not need to obtain a specific licence to be able to carry out the service and work for the platform.

The taxi driver's licences in question, which are a necessary requirement for unscheduled public transport, are negotiable only with regard to those who are registered with the Chambers of Commerce and, therefore, with regard to registered natural persons, while an Uber driver can be anyone who meets the above mentioned Uber requirements. However, the law does not specify whether taxi services and NCCs are the only services allowed or whether it is possible to carry out the same type of service by different means. Article 1.2 of Law No 21/92 includes taxis and NCCs as two possible options, but it is not clear whether the service is exclusive for the two options. Therefore, if we affirm that Uber and taxis are in substance the same,

[6]Article 86.2 of Legislative Decree. No. 285/92 prescribes that anyone who, without having obtained the licence provided for in Article 8 of Law No. 21 of 15 January 1992 (the taxi driver's licence), uses a street service vehicle with driver or as a taxi is subject to the administrative sanction of payment of a sum ranging from 1.816 to 7264 euros. The violation entails the accessory administrative sanctions of confiscation of the vehicle and suspension of the driving licence from four to twelve months, in accordance with the rules set out in Chap. 2, Sect. 2 of Title 6. Where the same person has committed such an infringement at least twice in a period of three years, the last of which shall entail the accessory sanction of withdrawal of the licence. The same penalties shall apply to those whose driver licence has been suspended or revoked.

then Uber drivers must be regulated as taxi drivers: if not, we could face a breach of Article 2598 of the Italian Civil Code on unfair competition. In fact, given that Uber drivers offer substantially the same services as taxis, but at a lower price thanks to lighter regulation, such services could constitute "unfair competition" pursuant to such Article 2598, par. 3 of the Italian Civil Code. Article 2598 states that "Without prejudice to the provisions concerning the protection of distinctive signs and patent rights, anyone commits acts of unfair competition:

1. uses names or distinctive signs capable of producing confusion with the names or distinctive signs legitimately used by others, or servilly imitates the products of a competitor, or performs any other means capable of creating confusion with the products and with the activity of a competitor;
2. disseminates news and appreciations of a competitor's products and business that could bring it into disrepute, or appropriates the merits of a competitor's products or business;
3. directly or indirectly uses any other means not to comply with the principles of professional fairness and being able to damage other businesses". In other words, Uber would compete, unfairly, with taxi drivers.

The defensive arguments of Uber mainly concern the fact that Uber is not a transport service but simply an intermediate platform, connecting users to drivers, who consider themselves a "community". Uber claims that the company is a TNC, and that drivers voluntarily join the platform in order to become part of a community of drivers. However, it is known that Uber recruits drivers through strong marketing techniques and coordinates drivers through contracts.

Uber, as an example of TNC, is difficult to be included in the pre-existing Italian legislation that regulates taxis with a number of regulatory requirements. In Italy, there is an ongoing discussion on the benefits of regulation and deregulation in this sector. Italian Law No. 21/92 could probably, with some difficulties, be applied to TNC, but the national legislation has not been written taking into account international ICT companies, and is quite obsolete. The closest examples to TNCs have so far been the dispatching centres for telephone taxis (radio-taxis), but also those operating in a significantly different way from UberApp.

However, awaiting a new and updated national legal framework, the first national rulings, decisions and orders have been made.

2.2 The Italian Cases

Unlike other systems, the Italian courts have so far not requested a preliminary ruling from the ECJ, but the conclusions of our judges are similar to those reached by the Court of Justice: Uber is a combination of transport services and intermediation services whose main component is a transport service. Therefore, the Italian transport rules are applicable.

Italian judges have made some important decisions, three of which concerned Uber Pop: the Court of Milan—Business Division (Tribunale Milano—Sezione speciale in materia di imprese) pronounced two investigative measures on 26 May 2015 and 2 July 2015 and the Court of Turin—Business Division (Tribunale Torino—Sezione speciale in materia di imprese) pronounced a ruling on 22 March 2017. The judgements established that Italian Law No. 21/92 and other provisions (Legislative Decree No. 285/1992) must be applied to Uber; since Uber and Uber drivers do not comply with the provisions of Italian law on the matter (such as insurance, driving licence, registration, etc.) Uber and the drivers are responsible for unfair competition. Therefore, the Italian courts have declared that UberPop must cease its activity on national territory.

As mentioned above, the Italian Constitutional Court in December 2016 has declared Article 1 of the Piedmont Regional Law No 14/2015 unconstitutional; according to this provision, public passenger transport for profit must be expressly allowed only to taxi drivers and NCCs. The objective of the Regional Law was obviously to limit the services that Uber drivers offered exclusively to taxis and NCCs. However, the Court classified the matter as a national competence, thus making its regulation at regional level unconstitutional.[7] Therefore, it is also important to remember that, as we have pointed out above, the same Court (Decision No. 56/2020 of 26 March 2020) has designed new perimeters for the distinction between State and Regional competences, de facto affirming that the powers of the State in the area of competition could not automatically and a priori overcome the powers and competence of the Regions in other fields.

2.3 *Labour Law Matters*

The business relationship between Uber and the driver is not part of the classic private employment contracts in Italy, as the only contract between Uber and its drivers is qualified by parties as a "transport service provider" contract. There is therefore no relationship of collaboration and subordination between Uber and customers, nor a real contract/relation of subordination between Uber and the individual driver, which places the drivers in a much less protected working environment. In particular, drivers freely join the community and free themselves from this platform. Once registered and admitted to the community, they are not required to activate the application and, in case of activation, they can freely refuse the request for a ride making it consistent with the optional, occasional and non-professional nature of the activity.

The contract is stipulated between the individual driver and Rasier Operations B.V., a company of the group based in Netherlands which merely provides operational activities and which stipulates the contracts with the drivers.

The payments to the drivers are made through Uber B.V., which is another operational company of the group Uber and which holds the licences for all rights related

[7] The Italian Constitutional Court, judgment of 15 December 2016, No. 265/2016.

to UberApp in Europe. Marketing and consulting services are instead provided by Uber Italy S.r.l. so that these services are more relevant to the Italian community. Both Uber Italy S.r.l. and Raiser Operations B.V. are held by and answer to Uber International Holding B.V. which is controlled by Uber international B.V. The last company (Uber International B.V.) also controls Uber B.V., which pays the drivers and receives the payments from the customers. So, there is more than one company involved in Uber services, but only Rasier Operations stipulates the contracts between the drivers and the management.

Formally, the drivers are to be considered self-employed[8] or, if they have a proper organization, entrepreneurs, even if they are not registered in the national business register. In Italy, drivers can be considered de facto entrepreneurs even if there is no formal registration in the business register (Article 2082 c.c.[9]) in case they have an organized economic activity (Desana 2018).[10]

In any case, the ruling of the Court of Turin clearly clarifies that Uber guarantees drivers full legal assistance and financial support in case of fines. What can this mean? Formally, there is no real employment contract, but Uber protects and assists its drivers (who would not be employees) both legally and financially in case of possible negative accusations. This issue needs to be further expanded and will certainly be in the near future. In the end, it must be underlined that recently Law-Decree No 101/2019 (which amended Legislative Decree No. 81/2015) has addressed some problems of the new economy, defining the notion of the digital platform and recognizing certain minimum levels of compulsory protection to the digital platform workers delivering food and beverages. Concerning the matter, in a famous case, the Court of Appeal of Turin applied the rules contained in Legislative Decree No. 81 of 2015 to drivers delivering food and beverages for the company known as Foodora (Court of Appeal of Turin, judgement No. 26, 4 February 2019). Such an innovative judgement has been confirmed, recently, by the Court of Cassazione, with decision No. 1663 of 24 January 2020.

2.4 *Tax Law and Fiscal Impact*

When it comes to tax law, the issue becomes even more difficult to deal with. The above-mentioned Uber B.V. and Rasier B.V. are based in the Netherlands, which makes them subject to Dutch law and therefore to Dutch taxes.

Moreover, as stated in the judgment of the Court of Turin, Uber's drivers do not print the receipt, as payment is made through the UberApp platform, and therefore there is no real transaction through an Italian entity. Therefore, no taxes seem to have been paid in Italy.

---

[8]Currently, the Legislative Decree No. 81/2015 contains rules applicable to self-employed workers.

[9]Article 2082 of the Italian Civil Code: An entrepreneur is someone who professionally carries out an organized economic activity for the production or exchange of goods or services.

[10]The evolution of the notion of enterprise is analysed by Desana (2018).

A critical issue is how the Italian State Department can investigate transactions between drivers and consumers. Since the transactions take place through Uber B.V., which is Dutch, the money in exchange for the service travels directly to the Netherlands, without contributing to national taxes even if the territory used to run the UberPop service is Italian.

The issue is destined to be further expanded and will certainly be in the near future, as the Uber platform has gained a lot of attention in recent months in Italy.

The main service provided to customers is based on a business model that involves non-professional drivers, equipped with a simple driving licence, who use their own car, providing occasional passages in time.

Business Model

Uber's business model is based on the use of technology to bring together those who need a ride, with potential drivers with a car and time available. In this way, it eliminates all the inefficiencies that the world of "traditional" taxis entails such as: long waits before their arrival, little control over prices and difficulty in estimating the cost of the service in advance.

The first block of the BMC (Business Model Canvas)[11] on which to focus attention is the customer segment. Uber has two macro-groups of customers: passengers and drivers.

The former are distinguished from those of a traditional taxi company because in order to use the platform they must be equipped with a smartphone and a credit or debit card. The drivers, on the other hand, are a segment of customers not present in the world of taxis, as they are traditionally part of the company, inevitably weighing down the structure. To divert this problem, Uber uses freelance drivers, whose common denominators are simply having a smartphone, a car in good condition, being well presented and with the desire to earn extra money occasionally. Using real-time metrics, Uber is able to measure the level of demand, identify the moment when it exceeds the available capacity, and intervene by increasing prices, thus generating an increase in the offer and restoring balance.

There are various versions of Uber in the world and the main ones are:

UberX—Uber's low-cost option, the ride is performed on "normal" cars and is managed as a carpooling service. In Italy, it acquired the name of UberPOP.

UberTAXI—The taxi in the Uber version, currently not present in Italy

UberBLACK—Uber's "original" option, the ride takes place in an elegant sedan

UberSUV—The driver will be driving an SUV.

UberLUX—The ride takes place using a more elegant, expensive and luxurious, representative car.

The version that is most popular is UberPop, the lowest cost and smartest version of the service.

Rates vary from city to city, but are constantly falling as the goal is to reach the costs/km indicated by the ACI for reimbursement of expenses.

However, before each trip you can request an immediate quote through the app.

---

[11]Business Model Canvas is a lean strategic and start-up model for developing new or documenting existing business models.

In particular, UberX business is a low-cost service that allows all drivers with their own private car to join the platform. UberX has become very profitable and has been the "killer app" that has changed the company's market positioning and has sparked its popularity.

The simplified business model therefore provides:

1. Uber, sharing economy platform that connects transport demand and transport offer. Uber collects the service fee, of which 20% is retained.
2. Private motorists, who make their cars and driving skills available to Uber users. They collect 80% of the service fee, through the platform itself.
3. Users who use the service, for a fee.

Taxation in Italy

As for private individuals, their service is part of the sharing economy: In practice, the service offered by Uber allows you to save costs (such as gasoline) as well as allowing less pollution and impact on the environment.

The analysis on direct taxation is focused on two aspects:

1. Taxation of the service operator
2. Taxation of the service provider.

Point 1.

The Uber company, which actually operates on the web through a platform, subjects its profits to foreign taxation according to the principle of permanent establishment, i.e. the tax liability of the territory in which the company has a permanent establishment. The recent U.S. Supreme Court ruling on e-commerce taxation[12] established the principle of taxation on the place where the sale took place, going beyond the concept of permanent establishment. Another tax-relevant aspect is that the taxable profits are defined by recording brokerage revenues, less the costs of the activity. On this point, the European Court of Justice believes, however, that "the brokerage service is an integral part of a global service whose main element is the transport service and, therefore, does not satisfy the qualification of 'service of information society 'but that of a' transport service. It is up to the Member States to regulate the conditions for providing the service, provided that the general rules of the EU Treaty are respected".

Point 2.

With regard to the treatment of the sums paid by Uber to the drivers, there is a belief that for them it is a mere "reimbursement of expenses", devoid of income relevance and therefore not to be declared to the Italian tax authorities. In the Uber blog, we read that the UberPOP service belongs to the "sharing economy" to improve citizens' lives,[13] also allowing "to cover the costs of your car by making your vehicle available to the city and having fun sharing it with other citizens". This presentation, which

---

[12]Court of Cassazione, No. 17-494, of April 17, 2018.

[13]Alfiero et al. (2014), that you can find here: https://emrbi.org/wp-content/uploads/2014/11/euromed-7-2014.pdf.

hinges on the non-profit concepts of ride sharing, sharing, collaborative economy, and so on, however, does not seem totally responsive to the reality of the facts: the non-professional drivers participating in Uber seem in fact not so much of jokers who want to have fun in sharing their car with others, as citizens who wish to round up their (maybe thin) revenues in time.

That said, the thesis according to which drivers would receive mere non-taxable "refunds spent" is questionable. The reference to the ACI[14] tables, which Uber declares it uses to "reimburse" the drivers, involves the conversion of the amount paid by the customer, which is also based on the duration of the ride in minutes, in a translation in terms of distance travelled. In addition, the mileage refund depends on the type of car, while the rates charged to customers do not depend on the vehicle used. Furthermore, the ACI fee is based on a year's use of a single car equal to 15,000 km: it should then be checked whether the parameter of the actual annual distance is taken into account in the reimbursement provided by Uber. It would then be wondering why anyone would have to go around with their car to take passengers from one destination to another, without the prospect of even a small profit (of course, the hypothesis of fun and sharing always remains).

With the "reimbursement", the Transportation Service Providers (as they are called on the Uber website) receive a sum that goes to compensate not only the expenses directly attributable to the journey (such as fuel), but also the other fixed expenses related to the possession and maintenance of the car, and the time dedicated to providing the service. Expenses that would otherwise result in an impoverishment of assets, and which would in any case be borne by the person who, let us not forget, has a car for his own private and family needs and purposes. The "reimbursement" provided by Uber therefore reintegrates the driver from expenses and costs that would otherwise reduce his assets, and which would in any case be largely equally incurred. This differentiates this situation from that of those who, in order to carry out a certain tasks, receive only the reimbursement of expenses which in the absence of that task they would not have suffered (as happens for the pure reimbursement of non-accessory or collateral expenses to a taxable fee, such as those of the lecturers who are reimbursed only for travel expenses). Taxable income emerges from the difference between the amount received in the tax period and the expenses specifically related to their production.

2.5 *Civil and Criminal Liability*

In the event of an accident, the only person held liable would be the driver; the matter depends closely on the employment relationship between Uber and the driver; and since the employment relationship is between two independent contractors, only the driver is held liable to the users. However, after reading the judgement of the Court

[14]ACI is Italian Automobile Club.

of Turin, it can be understood that Uber promises legal and financial assistance in case of sanctions due to violations of Articles 85 and 86 of the Highway Code.

Another hypothesis to be seriously taken into account is when Uber does not examine the certification documents provided by the drivers (driving licence, criminal record, etc.). Uber must verify such documents, since clients and customers rely on Uber's control on its drivers. The details of what would happen if a driver who has clearly loaded false identity documents and records commits an illegal act is not clear and we do not have specific case law on this issue. In this case, Uber could be held civilly liable to third parties for failure to inspect and verify the documents and requirements provided by Uber's drivers. Under Italian Law, this type of liability could constitute, *mutatis mutandis*, a sort of strict liability of Uber, who therefore could be held liable for its position towards the drivers and for the services provided.

Coming, in brief, to the criminal liability profile, in cases such as rape, harassment, kidnapping and other illegal acts, no responsibility should fall on Uber per se. In fact, under Article 27 of the Italian Constitution, the criminal responsibility is strictly personal, and nobody can be held responsible except the person who committed the offence. Therefore, in such cases, only drivers are liable and Uber cannot be invoked and answerable for such crimes.

3 Final Considerations

In conclusion, one point must be strongly underlined with reference to the Italian system: the discrepancy between the regulation followed by Uber and taxis (and NCC) is too wide, considering the fact that the services offered are, in the end, very similar. The above mentioned, taking into account that Italian courts considered Uber not as a community but rather a group of individuals carrying out an activity very similar to that of the taxi driver. More particularly, from the Italian "case law" perspective, UberPop is not to be considered a platform of shared economy, but an application used for profit.

Both Uber and the drivers are profit-seeking entrepreneurs, which is why the judges considered their activity to be part of an unfair competition, on the base that the activity carried out by them is very similar to that one carried out by taxi drivers and NCCs, but without the restrictive and costly rules laid down for public transport services. It is clear that Uber is not welcomed in the Italian system in a friendly way as Uber is not considered as a simple platform service, but an entrepreneur providing transport services.

For sure, an important issue may concern the Italian laws and regulations applied to taxis and Uber in general, which could be entirely too restrictive for both parties. Laws are obsolete for the world of the sharing economy, and therefore need to be adapted to the most modern needs. Both European and national laws tend to open up the market in an attempt to ensure a more balanced legal situation and to guarantee protection from unfair competition for services that fall into a more restrictive category and are currently severely damaged by more frivolous services, which exploit loopholes in the legal system to make a profit. However, the road is still long, and it is very probable that the economy, whether it is "old" or "new", will always be one "step ahead" of the national (or international) legal provisions.

References

Alfiero S, Indelicato A, Rainero C, Secinaro S, Tradori V, and Venuti F (2014) Sharing economy, "crowdsourcing" or crowd-funding" empirical analysis of the Italian Case. In: Paper presented at the 7th annual conference of the EuroMed academy of business Kristiansand, Norway

Amoroso R (2016) Uber: problemi giuridici risolti? www.altalex.com/documents/news/2016/04/26/uber

Dagnino VE (2016) Uber law: prospective giuslavoristiche sulla sharing/on demand economy. Dir Rel Ind 137–163

Desana E (2018) L'impresa fra tradizione e innovazione. Giappichelli, Turin

Iaione C (2008) La regolazione del trasporto pubblico locale. Bus e taxi alla fermata delle liberalizzazioni, Jovene, Napoli

Ingrao A (2018) Uberlabour: l'organizzazione "uberiana" del lavoro in Brasile e nel mondo. Il driver è un partner di Uber o un suo dipendente? Diritto delle relazioni industriali 705–713(28):2

Midiri M (2019) Nuove tecnologie e regolazione: il "caso Uber". Rivista trimestrale di diritto pubblico 1017–1038(68):3

Mostacci E, Somma A (2016) Il caso Uber La sharing economy nel confronto tra common law e civil law. Egea, Milano

Pollicino O, Lubello V (2016) Un monito complesso ed una apertura al dibattito europeo rilevante: Uber tra giudici e legislatori. Giurisprudenza Costituzionale 2479–2497:61

Chapter 10
Disruptive Technologies and Taxi Rides in South Africa: What Is the '*Uber*' Uproar About?

Sylvia Papadopoulos and Stefan van Eck

1 Disruptive Technologies and Uber in South Africa

There has not been extensive discussion in the broader South African legal literature on the import and effect that disruptive technologies have had on existing regulatory frameworks, in South Africa.[1] The focus of this discourse will mainly be on the taxi hailing services introduced into South Africa by Uber which has caused some consternation among domestic regulators and the powerful lucrative taxi industry in South Africa.[2] The aim of this article is to investigate the fundamentals of this technology and the law in the taxi industry and to highlight some of the regulatory challenges posed. The main challenges found in the South African jurisprudential landscape include issues around public transport and passenger carrying licensing, the position of Uber drivers within the domestic employment context, liability for passenger injury and possible anti-competitive behaviour. As an auxiliary aim, the article will also cursorily consider the idea posited by MacGann that national rules and regulations are being used by established companies to protect themselves from

[1]Except in the employment law context. See for example, Mokoena (2016, pp. 1574–1583, 2018, pp. 1453–1463), Van Eck and Nemusimbori (2018, pp. 473–483), Du Toit (2019, pp. 1–11) 'Disruptive innovation' was an idea introduced by Bower and Christensen (1995, pp. 43–53), where they described it as a process where a smaller company with fewer resources is able to successfully challenge established businesses through innovation. A disruptive innovation '…creates a new market by providing a different set of values, which ultimately (and unexpectedly) overtakes an existing market'. *Cf.* Hayward (2018, p. 51).

[2]Apart from Uber, Taxify was also launched as a transport network app-based taxi ride hailing service in South Africa in 2016, *cf.* Taxify 2018).

S. Papadopoulos (✉) · S. van Eck
University of Pretoria, Pretoria, South Africa
e-mail: sylvia.papadopoulos@up.ac.za

S. van Eck
e-mail: stefan.vaneck@up.ac.za

Z. Ayata and I. Önay (eds.), *Global Perspectives on Legal Challenges Posed by Ridesharing Companies*,
https://doi.org/10.1007/978-981-15-7035-3_10

new and innovative services like Uber, to the detriment of consumers and therefore regulations need to be adapted to the digital age to allow for innovation.[3] The question (perhaps rhetorical?) is how to regulate without stifling innovation? On the regulatory side, there have been several developments in South Africa that have direct relevance to the taxi e-hailing services that are of interest to those curious about the challenges raised by technology and the taxi e-hailing industry.

2 Legal and Regulatory Challenges

2.1 Market Regulation: Public Transport and Passenger Carrying Taxi Licensing

In South Africa, public transport is regulated by the National Department of Transport (DoT) in terms of the National Land Transport Act 5 of 2009 (NLT Act). The NLT Act establishes a number of entities across the three spheres of government, namely national, provincial and municipal level.[4] These entities play various functions from licensing to transport planning.[5] The DoT's core functions are to assign certain functions across government entities, to monitor and oversee public transport and develop policies for the effective functioning of the public transport in the country.[6]

The NLT Act defines a 'metered taxi service' as a '*...public transport service operated by means of a motor vehicle which is available for hire by hailing while roaming, by telephone, may stand for hire at a rank, and is equipped with sealed meter in good working order to determine fare payable, that is calibrated for such fare or complies with any other requirements applicable to such meters*'.[7] According to the NLT Act, these metered taxi service operators are required to apply for an area-based permit.[8] A detailed description of the route or routes (or radius) as well as allocated taxi ranks, terminal, pickup and drop-off points must be specified before obtaining the operating licence.[9] However, the metered taxi may pick up passengers outside of its respective area specified in the operating licence if the fare is pre-booked and the passenger will return to such area.[10] The fares can be determined by the sealed

---

[3]Teffer (2015).

[4]See for, e.g. ss9–10 on the functions of MEC's, s11 on the responsibilities of the three spheres of government and s12 on intergovernmental relations.

[5]Ss11(1)(b)–(c) and ss17–18 NLT Act.

[6]S11(1)(a) NLT Act.

[7]S1 NLT Act.

[8]S50 NLT Act.

[9]S50(3), s54, s66 NLT Act.

[10]S66(c) NLT Act.

meter or by negotiation between the driver and the passenger.[11] In addition to these, the metered taxis are required to have special markings.[12]

The land-based public passenger transport sector is highly fragmented in nature and is dominated by the minibus taxi industry accounting for approximately 70% of total transport usage.[13] The remaining 30% share of land-based public passenger transport industry in South Africa is captured by bus and rail, accounting for 20.1% and 9.9%, respectively.[14] Of the 70% taxi total, the minibus taxi industry accounts for approximately 63% while the metered taxi industry accounts for 7% of the total transport usage.[15] The taxi industry in South Africa is largely informal but subjected to public transport regulations. The taxi industry comprises different types of taxis, namely the (1) minibus taxis,[16] (2) metered taxis,[17] (3) app-based taxis[18] and (4) other niche players in the market such as 'tuk-tuks' and 'four-plus-ones'.[19] The South African Parliament officially passed the National Land Transport Amendment Bill B7D-2016 (NLT Amendment Bill) on 20 March 2018, which among other amendments, seeks to ensure that taxi e-hailing services are regulated.[20] Under the Bill, the definition of a 'electronic hailing service' or 'e-hailing service' means a public transport service operated by means of a motor vehicle, which (1) is available for hire by hailing while roaming, (2) may stand for hire at a rank and (3) is equipped with an electronic e-hailing technology-enabled application, as contemplated in section 66A.[21] The effect is that every vehicle being used to provide an e-hailing public transport service such as Uber will have to do so under a valid operating licence issued by the relevant authority. They will also have to comply with the requirements for special markings and provide specified information to passengers.[22]The amendments give the Minister of Transport the authority to make additional regulations for e-hailing

[11]S66(d) NLT Act.

[12]S66(4)(c) NLT Act.

[13]Organisation for Economic Co-operation and Development (OECD) 2018).

[14]Ibid.

[15]Ibid. (p. 4).

[16]'Minibus taxi' refers to a vehicle designed or modified solely or principally for conveying between 9 and 16 seated persons, including the driver. A minibus taxi-type service is an unscheduled public transport service operated on a specific route or routes. Ibid. (p. 4).

[17]See s1 NLT Act definition above.

[18]Described as technological platform that provides private operators or drivers with a platform to source passengers using Global Positioning System (GPS) technology to connect the nearest active linked driver to a passenger who demands the service. OECD (2018, p. 4).

[19]Tuk-tuk refers to a three-wheeled motor vehicle designed conveying not more than three-seated persons, including the driver. Four-plus-one taxi-type services refer to transport services provided by sedan motor vehicles and must carry not more than five passengers including the driver. The services provided are unscheduled services with no timetables. OECD (2018, p. 4).

[20]*Cf.* Sabinet (2018). The NLT Amendment Bill was amended and passed by the National Council of Provinces (NCOP) on 28 March 2019 and returned to the National Assembly for concurrence. The Portfolio Committee is scheduled to meet on 11 February 2020 for a briefing on the Bill. *Cf.* Sabinet (2020).

[21]Inserted definitions as per s1 NLT Amendment Bill B7D-2016, amending s1 of the NLT Act.

[22]S10 and s66 NLT Act.

services, including possible changes to the smartphone app to allow for a clearer idea of who exactly is driving the vehicle, the route it is taking and how much it will cost. Section 40 of the NLT Amendment Bill aims to insert a new section 66A into the NLT Act. Under the new section 66A, vehicles that are hailed or pre-booked electronically using e-hailing or technology-enabled applications are subject to rules such as those set by a regulatory entity granting an operating licence. These can also specify the area for picking up passengers.[23] The vehicle may not operate an e-hailing service where the application for the vehicle is not working properly.[24]

Furthermore, the e-hailing or technology-enabled application must[25]:

1. have the facility to estimate fares and distances, taking into account distance and time, and must communicate the estimate to passengers in advance electronically;
2. communicate the final fare to the passenger or passengers at the conclusion of the trip electronically and
3. provide the prescribed details of the driver of the vehicle to the passenger or passengers electronically.

In addition, the Minister may make regulations prescribing[26]:

1. measures to ensure accurate readings of the e-hailing or technology-enabled application;
2. information regarding the driver and the vehicle that must be communicated to passengers;
3. other information that the e-hailing or technology-enabled application must provide to passengers,
4. any other matter affecting the standard or quality of operation of e-hailing services and
5. special markings or other requirements for vehicles used for e-hailing services.[27]

Where a person conducts a business providing an e-hailing software application (such as Uber), that person may not permit an operator to use that application for a vehicle for which the operator does not hold a valid operating licence or permit for the vehicle, or whose operating licence or permit has lapsed or been cancelled, and must disconnect the e-hailing application forthwith and keep it disconnected until a valid operating licence has been obtained for the vehicle.[28] A person who fails to comply with these requirements commits a criminal offence.[29]

The NLT Amendment Bill introduces new penalties against e-hailing companies such as Uber. Under the Bill, e-hailing companies must deactivate the accounts of operators who do not have an operating licence or else face a fine of up to R100,000.[30]

---

[23]New s66A(1) to be inserted into NLT Act, s40 of the NLT Amendment Bill B7D-2016.

[24]New s66A(2) ibid.

[25]New s66A(3) ibid.

[26]New s66A(4) ibid.

[27]New s66A(4) ibid.

[28]New s66A(6) ibid.

[29]New s66A(7) ibid.

[30]S90(2) NLT Act.

The penalties in the NLT Act against individuals who operate without a valid operating licence remain the same. The potential penalties are severe and can amount to up to two years imprisonment or a fine of up to R100,000 or up to two years' imprisonment.[31]

Effectively, this means that the 'e-hailing' drivers will be regulated in the same way that other metered taxi drivers are, across South Africa.

2.2 *Labour Law Perspectives: Uber Drivers as Employees*

Labour law is underpinned by the realisation that employees are generally in a weaker social, economic and welfare position than their counterpart employers. At its core, this field of study aims to establish a more equal balance between the underdog in the relationship, the employee, and the bearer of social power, the employer.[32] It is the underlying philosophy of labour law to protect workers against exploitation. The main mechanisms for such protection most often emanate from legislation that establishes floors of rights, such as minimum wages and protection against unfair dismissal[33] and the recognition of trade unions and the institution of collective bargaining.[34]

South Africa is a member of the International Labour Organisation (ILO) that was established directly after the First World War in 1919 by the Treaty of Versailles. This is the oldest United Nations agency, and it is founded on the principle that universal and lasting peace can be accomplished only if it is based on social justice.[35] The ILO's founding principles are reaffirmed through its Declaration of Philadelphia, 1944 that states that '…poverty anywhere is a threat to prosperity everywhere'.[36] As a member of this agency, South Africa is bound to implement ratified conventions of the ILO.

---

[31] S90 NLT Act, s50 NLT Act Amendment Bill B7D-2016.

[32] The classic statement of this perspective remains the often-cited passage: '…The main object of labour law [is] to be a countervailing force to counteract the inequality in bargaining power which is inherent and must be inherent in the employment relationship'. See Davies and Freedland (1983, p. 18).

[33] So, for example, the basic conditions of Employment Act 75 of 1997 makes provision for maximum hours of work, minimum paid leave and notice periods prior to termination of contracts of employment. Added to this, the National Minimum Wage Act 9 of 2018 has since 2019 made provision for a national minimum wage. The Labour Relations Act 66 of 1995 also regulates unfair dismissal law and provides that no employment relationship may be terminated without a fair reason and a fair procedure being followed.

[34] The registration and recognition of trade unions, the right to strike and the binding effect of collective agreements are all regulated in terms of the Labour Relations Act 66 of 1995. *Cf.* Van Niekerk et al. (2019, p. 4).

[35] Office of the Secretary General's Envoy on Youth *International Labour Organization (ILO)* available at https://www.un.org/youthenvoy/2013/08/ilo-international-labour-organization/. Accessed 2 Feb 2020.

[36] Article 1(c) of the Declaration of Philadelphia.

The ILO's aspirations that place human rights and the well-being of humans at the forefront are truly inspirational. The architects of the South African Constitution have expressly recognised that international instruments that give effect to international standards serve as points of reference for the interpretation of labour and other legislation.[37] However, these goals could also stifle the development of new forms of work that could potentially create new jobs and that would nurture any growing economy. Such a smothering effect could be brought to bear through the fear of disruptions to traditional forms of work where labour and social security protective measures generally prevail.

The gateway to labour and social security protection is through the existence of an employment relationship.[38] However, the vague dividing line between instances where there is an employment relationship and one where there is independent contracting has long been debated.[39] Labour law in its narrowest sense does not apply to the self-employed and independent contractors. It follows that should persons engaged in modern forms of work, like crowdsourcing or on-demand platform work not be classified as employees, they would fall beyond the protective reaches of labour law.

Could the solution to the eroding effect of new forms of work, like Uber, lie in the mere extension of the definition of employee? The ILO has recognised that the traditional mechanisms aimed at affording employee's protection against exploitation will not suffice during the modern world of work. In 2019, the ILO Global Commission on the future of work published its landmark report in which it examined how to achieve a better future of work for all at a time of unprecedented change and exceptional challenges in the world of work.[40] We return to this later, but the answer was not found in the mere extension of the definition of employee.

In South Africa, like many other countries of the world, Uber drivers have resorted to relying on labour law protection on the premise that they are employees. In *Uber South Africa Technology Services (Pty) Ltd v NUPSAW and SATAWU obo Tsepo Morekure*,[41] the Commission for Conciliation, Mediation and Arbitration (CCMA) held that Uber drivers are employees for the purposes of the Labour Relations Act 66 of 1995 (LRA). In this initial proceeding, the matter that was considered was

[37] S233 of the Constitution of South Africa Act 108 of 1996 (the Constitution) provides that '…when interpreting any legislation, every court must prefer any reasonable interpretation of the legislation that is consistent with international law over any other interpretation that is inconsistent with international law.'

[38] Van Niekerk et al. (2019, p. 59). *Cf.* Thompson (2003).

[39] Brassey (1990) refers to *National Labour Relations Board v Hearst Publications* (1944) 322 US 111 at 121 where an American court said more than 60 years ago that '…[f]ew problems in the law have given greater variety of application and conflict in result than cases arising in the borderline between what is clearly an employer-employee relationship and what is clearly one of independent entrepreneurial dealing'.

[40] ILO Global Commission (2019).

[41] *Uber South Africa Technology Services (Pty) Ltd v NUPSAW and SATAWU obo Tsepo Morekure* unreported case WECT12537-16 7 July 2017.

whether several drivers who were all 'deactivated' by Uber were employees of Uber SA and were eligible to refer their 'unfair dismissal' disputes to the CCMA.

On review to the Labour Court in the case of *Uber South Africa Technology Services (Pty) Ltd v National Union of Public Service and Allied Workers*[42], it was held that Uber drivers are not employees. There were three main reasons for this. Firstly, the court held that the existence of a contractual relationship between an employee and an employer is a necessary precondition to the existence of an employment relationship.[43] Secondly, the court held that the CCMA was incorrect in ignoring any material distinctions between Uber SA and Uber BV when it applied the different indicators of the reality test to Uber as a whole.[44] Thirdly, the court held that had the CCMA applied the Uber drivers' relevant factors, for the existence of an employment relationship on Uber SA only, the commissioner should, on the drivers' own version, have found that they had failed to prove the existence of an employment relationship.

It is submitted that the South African Labour Court may have opened itself for criticism in the way it approached the matter. Firstly, it is argued that it would have been appropriate for the Labour Court to consider the lessons learnt elsewhere in the world regarding the question whether Uber drivers should be classified to be employees. Section 23(1) of the Constitution accords 'everyone' with the right to 'fair labour practices' and section 39(1)(b)–(c) of the Constitution makes it clear that when interpreting the Bill of Rights, courts and tribunals 'must consider international law… and may consider foreign law'.

Uber has been held to be the employer in several other countries of the world. For example, in 2015, the Californian Labour Commission in *Barbara Ann Berwick v Uber Technologies, Inc, A Delaware Corporation and Rasier*[45] ruled that an Uber driver was an employee and not an independent contractor. In *Uber Technologies, Inc v Barbara Berwick*[46], the US Supreme Court of Appeal upheld the Labour Commission's ruling.

Following these decisions, California's Labour Commission, the Bureau of Labour and Industries of the State of Oregon (BOLI) in October 2015 released an advisory opinion regarding the employment status of Uber drivers.[47] The opinion relied on the economic realities test, as set out by the US Department of Labour in determining worker classification under the Fair Labour Standard Act.[48] Having

[42]*Uber South Africa Technology Services (Pty) Ltd v National Union of Public Service and Allied Workers* (2018) ILJ 903 (LC).

[43]Ibid. (paras. 49–51).

[44]For criticism of this case, see Van Eck and Nemusimbori (2018, pp. 473–483).

[45]*Barbara Ann Berwick v Uber Technologies, Inc, A Delaware Corporation, and Rasier* 11-46739 EK.

[46]*Uber Technologies, Inc v Barbara Berwick* CGC-15-546378.

[47]California's Labour Commission, the Bureau of Labour and Industries of the State of Oregon (BOLI) (2015) *Advisory Opinion of The Commissioner on The Employment Status of Uber Drivers* (14 October 2015).

[48]Fair Labour Standard Act 1938 29 USC.

analysed the facts under each factor as applied to Uber drivers, BOLI declared that '…under Oregon law… Uber drivers are employees'.[49]

Uber drivers have also been categorised as workers in the UK. Uber drivers in the London area brought several claims in the Employment Tribunal, which required them to be 'workers' in terms of the Employment Rights Act, 1996, of the Working Time Regulations, 1998 and of the National Minimum Wages Act, 1998. On appeal before the Employment Appeal Tribunal in *Uber BV, Uber London Ltd and Uber Britannia Ltd v Aslam, Farrar*[50] (*Uber BV* (EAT)), it was argued that there was no contract between the Uber drivers and Uber London Ltd. There were only agreements between the drivers, the holding company Uber and the passengers. *Uber BV* (EAT) dismissed the appeal and held that, based on the factual reality of the situation, the court *a quo* was correct to conclude that there was an agreement between Uber London Ltd and the drivers who personally undertook work for Uber London Ltd as part of its business of providing transportation services to passengers in the London area.[51]

Secondly, the Labour Court in South Africa missed an opportunity to open a whole new paradigm for workers engaged in the world of work during the Fourth Industrial Revolution. The South African Courts have over the past number of years been engaged in a movement to extend, rather than to limit, the scope of who is an employee. So, for example, in 1999 the Constitutional Court in *SA National Defence Union v Minister of Defence*[52] held that uniformed soldiers are 'akin' to employees and that they have the right to establish trade unions. This was followed by *Discovery Health v CCMA*[53] that held that irregular migrants may be classified as employees for the purpose of labour law protection. The court held that even if the contract with the worker was invalid, the definition of 'employee' does not necessarily presuppose a valid contract of employment and that they fell under section 23(1) of the Constitution's right to fair labour practices.

The decision was followed by *State Information Technology Agency (SITA) (Pty) Ltd v CCMA*[54] that held that the focus has shifted from the actuality of a formal contract of employment to the existence of an employment relationship. In finding that the LRA did apply, the court abridged the tests to three primary principles for the employment relationship, namely an employer's right to supervision and control, whether an employee forms part of the employer's organisation and whether the employee is economically dependent upon the employer.

[49]See Keeton (2017, pp. 207–277 at p. 259).

[50]*Uber BV, Uber London Ltd and Uber Britannia Ltd v Aslam, Farrar* UKEAT/0056/17/DA (hereafter Uber BV (EAT)).

[51]Ibid. para 116.

[52]*SA National Defence Union v Minister of Defence* (1999) *ILJ* 2265 (CC).

[53]*Discovery Health v CCMA* [2008] 7 BLLR 633 (LC) para 42.

[54]*State Information Technology Agency (SITA) (Pty) Ltd v CCMA* [2008] 7 BLLR 611 (LAC) para 12.

Finally, in 2008 the Labour Appeal Court in *Kylie v CCMA*[55] held that even though Kylie was a sex worker with no valid contract of employment, she was entitled to unfair dismissal protection under the LRA. This, the court held, is vindicated in the constitutional framework which establishes a right to fair labour practices for 'everyone' in terms of section 23(1) of the Constitution. It resolved that Kylie was in an employment relationship even though there was no valid contract of employment.

Intuitively, and in law, it is clear that the Labour Court in the first Uber case was not willing to extend the definition of employee to bring Uber drivers within the protective reaches of labour legislation as had been done in a number of other cases. In the Uber case, the court placed particular emphasis on the existence of a contractual relationship rather than merely determining whether there was an employment relationship in place.

The main shortcoming of the argument that the definition of employee should be extended in order to provide Uber drivers with labour law protection is the fact that the identification of the employment relationship will remain a moving target during the modern era. New forms of work are destined to sprout during this era of innovation, and labour law will find itself in a position of playing an endless game of catch-up to redefine the concept of the employment relationship to remain relevant. For this reason, the ILO's 2019 Global Commission Report did not include the suggestion to extend the definition of employee.

In its stead, the Global Commission suggested three pillars of action: The first is to increase investment in people's capabilities among others lifelong learning. The second is to increase investment in the institutions of work. This pillar envisages the establishment of a universal labour guarantee. This floor of human rights would apply to everyone engaged in work and would not be limited to those persons in traditional employment relationships. By means of labour inspection, collective bargaining and employment contracts pathways to formalisation need to be forged that would reduce working poverty and secure a future of work with dignity, economic security and equality. The third pillar relates to increased investment in decent and sustainable work that involves transforming economies to embrace technology, but to remain human-centred. Countries should prioritize long-term, sustainable investments that favour human development and in line with the UN 2030 Agenda for Sustainable Development.

2.3 Liability

According to Visser and Potgieter, the law of damages is that part of the law which indicates how the existence and extent of damage, as well as the proper amount of damages or satisfaction (*solatium*) are to be determined in the case of delict, breach of contract and other legal principles providing for the payment of damages.[56]

[55] *Kylie v CCMA* [2010] 7 BLLR 705 (LAC).

[56] Potgieter et al. (2012, p. 1).

2.3.1 Claims Based in Delict

The general basis and approach of South African law to claims based on delict is to follow the Roman Dutch Law approach in the continental rather than in the English system, because in general, all damage caused unjustifiably (*injuria*) is actionable, whether caused intentionally (*dolo*) or through negligence (*culpa*).[57] Therefore, the South African law of delict is founded on the basic principle that all harm caused by wrongful and blameworthy (or culpable) conduct can be recovered through a delictual action.[58] To claim compensation in respect of patrimonial loss, for example, a plaintiff must show that he or she sustained harm (*damnum*), which was wrongfully and culpably (*iniuria*) caused (*datum*) by the defendant, while an *iniuria* is the wrongful and intentional infringement of an interest of personality.[59] A delict is therefore the wrongful, culpable conduct of a person that causes harm to another.[60] The broad basis of the law of delict provides flexible and adaptable principles of liability.[61]

Vicarious liability exists where a person or business entity is liable, not for a delict committed by themselves, but for a delict committed by another person. It is a claim based on strict liability, or liability without fault, on the part of the defendant.[62] The question of vicarious liability rests on two legs, the first by inquiring whether or not a relationship exists between the person who commits the delict and the person purportedly liable and, secondly, by establishing a link between the delict and either the latter's instruction or his or her work. In other words, liability is based upon a relationship which is capable of establishing liability and an activity which can be linked to the person who is sought to be held liable. Vicarious liability is not limited to an employment relationship but has been found in mandate contracts and that between an owner and driver of a motor vehicle. This list of parties who may be held vicariously liable is not a closed list; however, if one seeks to add to it, depending upon the circumstances, either a relationship that is similar to an employment relationship or a right of control needs to be present.

Damages include both patrimonial (pecuniary) loss and non-patrimonial loss. One's patrimony is the monetary value (market value) of the sum total of a person's rights and duties.[63] To determine the loss, a comparative method known as the 'sum-formula' approach is applied. This is where the complainant's hypothetical patrimonial position prior to commission of the wrongful act is compared to his

---

[57] *Perlman v Zoutendyk* 1934 CPD 151, *Minister of Justice v Hofmeyr* 1993 (3) SA 131 (A) 154; Midgley (2016), paras. 7, 26.

[58] Midgley (2016, para. 26); *Universiteit van Pretoria v Tommie Meyer Films (Edms) Bpk* 1977 (4) SA 376 (T) 383.

[59] Midgley (2016, para. 26).

[60] Nagel et al. (2015, p. 26), Neethling et al. (2005, p. 1), Roos (2003, p. 540).

[61] Midgley (2016, para. 26).

[62] Midgley (2016, para. 38); *cf. De Beer v Sergeant* 1976 (1) SA 246 (T), *Godfrey v Campbell* 1997 (1) SA 570 (C) 577.

[63] Midgley (2016, para. 44), Nagel et al. (2015, p. 37); *Government of the RSA v Ngubane* 1972 (2) SA 601 (A), *Guardian National Insurance Co Ltd v Van Gool* 1992 (4) SA 61 (A), *Rudman v Road Accident Fund* 2003 (2) SA 234 (SCA) 241.

or her current position after the wrongful act.[64] Non-patrimonial loss is a value allocated for the harm suffered due to the impairment of personality interests such as a persons impaired reputation, dignity, feelings, physical integrity and includes pain and suffering, shock, disfigurement, loss of amenities of life or shortened life expectancy. In South Africa, the courts are conservative in their awards for non-patrimonial losses and make the determinations using comparative methodologies with emphasis on awards made in previous cases with similar circumstances.[65]

In the claim for damages, the 'once and for all' maximum is applied which means that the complainant must claim all damages stemming from a specific delict, in a single action.[66] This is not without some practical difficulties. It is usually difficult to determine prospective losses such as loss of future income as well as proving the certainty of a future loss occurring.[67] The claimant likewise has a reciprocal duty to mitigate damages and any benefit or compensating advantage the complainant receives is set off against the claim for damages.[68]

The party claiming damages may institute three possible actions against the person liable, namely *actio legis Aquiliae, actio iniuriarum* and the action for pain and suffering. The *actio legis Aquiliae* is instituted to claim damages for pecuniary loss caused by all forms of culpable conduct. Sentimental damages as a *solatium* for an injury to the personality are formally claimed under the *actio iniuriarum*, while pain and suffering associated with physical injury are formally redressed by the award of general damages under action for pain and suffering. The same conduct may establish a claim in respect of all three actions, provided that the different forms of harm arose.[69]

In delictual actions, there are defences directed at the wrongfulness element and defences which serve to exclude fault.[70] A ground of justification excludes the wrongfulness of the defendant's conduct. Grounds of justification are typical circumstances which occur regularly in practice and indicate conclusively that interference with the plaintiff's legally protected interests was reasonable, and therefore, lawful.[71] Interference with a legally protected interest, for example, the object of a subjective right, is *prima facie* wrongful, and the existence of a recognised ground of justification conclusively rebuts the *prima facie* inference of wrongfulness. In other words, conduct which ordinarily would have been unlawful is considered to be lawful.[72]

---

[64]Nagel et al. (2015, p. 37), Potgieter et al. (2012, pp. 71–78); *Transnet Ltd v Sechaba Photoscan (Pty) Ltd* 2005 (1) SA 299 (SCA).

[65]Nagel et al. (2015, p. 38), Potgieter et al. (2012, pp. 103–120).

[66]Dendy (2018, para. 28), Potgieter et al. (2012, pp. 155–168).

[67]Nagel et al. (2015, p. 38), Potgieter et al. (2012, pp. 139–149); *Transnet Ltd v Sechaba Photoscan (Pty) Ltd* 2005 (1) SA 299 (SCA).

[68]Nagel et al. (2015, p. 39), Potgieter et al. (2012, pp. 295–301).

[69]Midgley (2016, para. 44), Nagel et al. (2015, p. 39).

[70]Ibid. para. 110.

[71]Midgley (2016, para. 110), Nagel et al. (2015, pp. 29–32).

[72]*Le Roux v Dey (Freedom of Expression Institute and Restorative Justice Centre as Amici Curiae)* 2011 (3) SA 274 (CC), *Argus Printing & Publishing Co Ltd v IFP* 1992 (3) SA 579 (A) 588,

Thus, insofar as Uber or the driver has caused loss or damage in a culpable way, they could be held liable through a delictual action. Nonetheless, the issue of holding Uber vicariously liable viz-a-viz its drivers has not been settled through case law or statutory regulation and since Uber drivers are not employees, a claimant would have to show that the relationship is similar to an employment relation or that there is an element of control.

2.3.2 Claims Based in Contract

According to the terms and conditions published by Uber, '*...[T]hese Terms of Use ("Terms") govern the access or use by you, an individual, from within any country in the world ... of applications, websites, content, products, and services (the "Services") made available by Uber B.V., a private limited liability company established in the Netherlands, ... ("Uber")...Your access and use of the Services constitutes your agreement to be bound by these Terms, which establishes a contractual relationship between you and Uber... The Services constitute a technology platform that enables users of Uber's mobile applications or websites provided as part of the Services (each, an "Application") to arrange and schedule transportation and/or logistics services with independent third party providers of such services, including independent third party transportation providers and independent third party logistics providers under agreement with Uber or certain of Uber's affiliates ("Third Party Providers"). ... you acknowledge that Uber does not provide transportation or logistics services or function as a transportation carrier and that all such transportation or logistics services are provided by independent third party contractors who are not employed by Uber or any of its affiliates*'.[73]

These Uber terms and conditions warrant a cursory analysis. It appears that there are at least three contracts in the use of the app and services. The first would be through the use of the app (according to Uber) a digital 'service' that arranges and schedules transportation. The second an agreement between Uber and 'Third-Party Providers' (drivers) who will meet the app users' request for transport (transport providers) and the third between the passenger and driver for the actual trip. A detailed analysis of each of these contractual relations falls outside the scope of this chapter. However, the principles discussed below must be applied to each of these, as relevant.

Contracts are the primary vehicles of commerce and although a full analysis of the applicable common law relating to contracts falls outside the scope and purpose of this chapter, the validity of a contract in South Africa is still largely governed by principles established in the common law. The same general principles apply

---

Gardener v Whitaker 1995 (2) SA 672 (E) 686, *S v Adams; S v Werner* 1981 (1) SA 187 (A) 220. *Cf.* Midgley (2016, para. 110), Nagel et al. (2015, pp. 40–41).

[73]Uber B.V. (2020).

whether the contract is formed electronically or through traditional oral or paper-based methods.[74]

Under the South African common law, a contract can only be validly concluded where it is based on consensus, either real or ostensible, between the parties.[75] Furthermore, the parties must have the capacity to contract,[76] the contract must be lawful[77], and it must be physically possible to complete or adhere to, with certainty.[78] Most contracts are concluded without adhering to formalities but there are limited instances where either legislation or the parties themselves set specific formal requirements for the validity of the contract.[79]

Due to the methodology employed by Uber,[80] all the transactions are concluded electronically. This, in turn, means that the South African Electronic Communications and Transactions Act 25 of 2002 (ECT Act) is applicable to each transaction.

This act has been in force since 30 August 2002[81] and is applicable to any electronic transaction or data message.[82] An 'electronic transaction' as a phrase is not defined in the ECT Act, but a 'transaction' is either of a commercial or non-commercial nature, and it includes the provision of information and e-government services.[83] A 'data message' on the other hand is data[84] generated, sent, received or stored by electronic means and includes voice, where the voice is used in an automated transaction and a stored record.[85]

Chapter III of the ECT Act is enabling legislation founded on the E-Commerce Model Law,[86] which confirms the South African common law principles of contract for electronic transactions by establishing the 'functionally equivalent' criteria for

---

[74]Eiselen GTS in Van der Merwe DP et al. (2016, p. 157), Papadopoulos et al. (2012, pp. 43–44), Pistorius (1999, pp. 285–287); *Jafta v Ezemvelo KZN Wildlife* [2008] 10 *BLLR* 954 (LC).

[75]Christie and Bradfield (2016, pp. 28–31), Nagel et al. (2015, pp. 48–56), Van der Merwe et al. (2012, pp. 7, 19–22), Pistorius (1999, pp. 285–287).

[76]Christie and Bradfield (2016, pp. 265–292), Nagel et al. (2015, pp. 77–90), Pistorius (1999, pp. 285–287).

[77]Christie and Bradfield (2016, pp. 392–447), Nagel et al. (2015, pp. 92–100), Pistorius (1999, pp. 285–287).

[78]Christie and Bradfield (2016, pp. 155–173 and 468), Nagel et al. (2015, pp. 100–102) Van der Merwe et al. (2012, pp. 160–164, 192–221), Pistorius (1999, pp. 285–287).

[79]Christie and Bradfield (2016, pp. 123–154), Van der Merwe et al. (2012, pp. 129–147), Nagel et al. (2015, pp. 104–106).

[80]See Uber (undated).

[81]Came into effect in terms of Proc R68 *GG* 23809 of 30 August 2002 (*Reg Gaz 7449*).

[82]S4(1) ECT Act.

[83]S1 ibid.

[84]S1 ibid. Data is an electronic representation of information in any form.

[85]S1 ibid.

[86]UNCITRAL Model Law on Electronic Commerce Guide to Enactment with 1996 with additional article 5 as adopted in 1998.

contracting electronically.[87] Chapter III of the ECT Act is dedicated to facilitating electronic transactions and addresses aspects of online communications and online contracting. The chapter is divided into two parts. The first sets out the legal requirements for data messages and the second for the communication of data messages. The distinction is important because the first part of Chapter III creates mandatory provisions (in sections 11–20), while the second part provides a default position in law that parties to an agreement are free to vary (in sections 21 to 26).[88]

In the formation and validity of an agreement, section 11 of the ECT Act pertinently gives legal recognition to data messages and stipulates that a data message is not without legal force and effect merely because it is wholly or partly in the form of a data message. In other words, it is confirmed that using data messages to negotiate and conclude a contract can result in a legally enforceable act ensuring functional equivalence is entrenched.[89] Working in tandem with this is section 22(1) of the ECT Act, which confirms that legal effect will be given to a contract concluded by means of data messages. This section provides the default position that applies should parties to a contract not specifically agree differently.[90]

In the absence of express agreement by the parties to a contract, section 22(2) of the ECT Act sets out a rule (a default position) for determining when and where the contract was concluded. The section states that an agreement concluded between parties, by means of data messages, is concluded at the time when and at the place where the acceptance of the offer was received by the offeror, thereby, adopting the reception theory for the time and place of conclusion of an e-contract.[91] It must also be noted that the provisions of section 22 are only applicable where parties have not by express agreement indicated a different method of determining time and place of conclusion of the contract.[92]

Several theories are used to determine the place and time for conclusion of a contract. In South Africa, the information theory is the de facto theory used for this purpose. The information theory sets out that the contract is concluded at the place where and at the time when the person who has made an offer is informed (becomes aware) that the offer has been accepted. The use of the reception theory in the ECT

---

[87] Eiselen in van der Merwe et al. (2016, p. 155), Pistorius (1999, pp. 285–287), Papadopoulos et al. (2012, p. 41).

[88] Papadopoulos et al. (2012, p. 46).

[89] See *Jafta v Ezemvelo KZN Wildlife* [2008] 10 BLLR 954 (LC) where it was held that a valid contract of employment was concluded via SMS messages, *Sihlali Mafika v South African Broadcasting Corporation Ltd* [2010] 5 BLLR 542 (LC) where it was held that an employee had resigned from his employer via SMS and in *Spring Forest Trading 599 CC v Wilberry (Pty) Ltd t/a Ecowash and Another* 2015 (2) SA 118 (SCA) where it was held that the typed name for a sender of an email was sufficient for an ordinary e-signature and that the contract had been validly amended in writing through the emails sent between the parties.

[90] S21 ECT Act.

[91] Christie and Bradfield (2016, p. 94), van der Merwe et al. (2012, pp. 62–64), Nagel et al. (2015, p. 58). For criticism, see Lötz and Du Plessis (2004a, pp. 15, 1–20, 2004b, 224–243). For reasoning in support, see Pistorius (2006, pp. 178–213).

[92] S21 ECT Act; Christie and Bradfield (2016, p. 94), van der Merwe et al. (2012, pp. 62–64), Nagel et al. (2015, p. 58), Papadopoulos et al. (2012, p. 53).

Act is an exception to the general rule and a contract via data messages would be concluded once that acceptance data message is received by the party who made the final offer even if the recipient has not opened and read it or is unaware of the acceptance in a data message.[93] Consequently, section 23(b) of the ECT Act states that a data message is regarded as having been received, when the data message enters the information system[94] designated or used by the addressee and is capable of being retrieved and processed implying the point that all data packets are assembled into a whole message that can be retrieved.[95] Receipt is also regarded as being at the offeror's (addressee's) usual place of business or residence.[96]

Sections 11(2) and 11(3) are intended to remove the prevailing uncertainty about whether click-wrap and browse-wrap agreements are enforceable on the basis of actual or *quasi*-mutual assent. Considered an innovation in the ECT Act, these sections recognise that information, which is merely referred to in a data message (that is, not actually part of such message) can have legal force and effect and that for it to be incorporated into a website or an agreement:[97]

1. The information must be referred to in a way in which a reasonable person would notice it; and
2. It must be accessible in a format that may be read, stored or retrieved either electronically or as a computer printout.[98]

When would a reasonable person notice it? The courts use an objective test based on reasonableness, and the nature of the document itself will be important in the court's considerations. It has been suggested that the link should be eye-catching, and the font should at a minimum, be as big as the rest of the text on the webpage,

[93] Christie and Bradfield (2016, p. 94); Eiselen in van der Merwe et al. (2016, pp. 159–160), van der Merwe et al. (2012, pp. 62–62), Nagel et al. (2015, p. 58).

[94] An 'information system' is defined in s1 of the ECT Act as a system for generating, sending, receiving, storing, displaying or otherwise processing data messages and includes the Internet.

[95] S23(b) ECT Act. S23(a) determines that a data message, used in the conclusion or performance of an agreement must be regarded as having been sent by the originator when it enters an information system outside the control of the originator or if the originator and addressee are in the same information system, when it is capable of being retrieved by the addressee.

[96] S23(c) ECT Act.

[97] S11(1)–(2) ECT Act. S11(1) states that '…information is not without legal force and effect merely on the grounds that it is wholly or partly in the form of a data message' and s11(2) that '…information is not without legal force and effect merely on the grounds that it's not contained in the data message purporting to give rise to such legal force and effect, but is merely referred to in such data message'. Further s24(2) confirms that an expression of intent or other statement can validly be made in the form of a data message and that an expression of intent or other statement can be validly made through means other than an electronic signature. *Cf.* s13(5) ECT Act where it confirms that '…an expression of intent or other statement is not without legal force and effect merely on the grounds that (1) it is in the form of a data message, or (2) it is not evidenced by an electronic signature but is evidenced by other means from which such person's intent or other statement can be inferred'. *Cf*. Pistorius (2004, pp. 574, 568–576).

[98] S11(3)(a)–(b) ECT Act.

possibly even displayed in a bright colour. The link should also be displayed where a reasonable person would expect to find the terms and conditions for the transaction.[99]

On accessibility, Pistorius lists several factors that could be considered. These include the ease of access to the target text, the availability of the linked information, data integrity (verification of content, authentication of sender and mechanism for correcting communication errors) and the extent to which the terms and conditions are subject to later amendment (with or without notice).[100]

Outside of the general electronic contracting provisions detailed above, of importance for this chapter are the provisions on automated transactions in section 20 of the ECT Act. Under the ECT Act, an 'automated transaction' is an electronic transaction conducted or performed, in whole or in part, by means of data messages and where the conduct of one or both parties, are not reviewed by a natural person within the ordinary course of such a person's business or employment.[101]

An automated transaction therefore is a transaction where one or both of the parties make use of automated systems, that is, software that communicates with or responds to third parties without any human intervention. The ECT Act uses the concept of an 'electronic agent' to describe the non-human actors. An 'electronic agent' is defined to mean a computer program or an electronic or other automated means used independently to initiate an action or respond to data messages or performances in whole or in part, in an automated transaction.[102] As automated transactions are completed by interactions with software or technology requiring no human interventions, section 20 provides very specific rules to ensure that the resulting agreement will be fair and effective. The provisions on automated contracts are mandatory, and it is not possible to contract out of complying with them.[103]

Section 20 of the ECT Act reads as follows:

'…*In an automated transaction*

1. *an agreement may be formed where an electronic agent performs an action required by law for agreement formation;*
2. *an agreement may be formed where all parties to a transaction or either one of them uses an electronic agent:*
3. *a party using an electronic agent to form an agreement is, subject to paragraph (d), presumed to be bound by the terms of that agreement irrespective of whether that person reviewed the actions of the electronic agent or the terms of the agreement;*
4. *a party interacting with an electronic agent to form an agreement is not bound by the terms of the agreement unless those terms were capable of being reviewed by a natural person representing that party prior to agreement formation.*

---

[99]Ibid. These principles were applied by the Supreme Court of Appeal in *Durban's Water Wonderland (Pty) Ltd v Botha & another* 1999 (1) SA 982 (SCA). See also *King's Car Hire (Pty) Ltd v Wakeling* 1970 (4) SA 640 (N).

[100]Pistorius (2004, p. 574), Jacobs (2004, pp. 558–559).

[101]S1 ECT Act, Eiselen in van der Merwe et al. (2016, p. 164).

[102]S1 ECT Act.

[103]Eiselen in van der Merwe et al. (2016, pp. 164–165), Papadopoulos et al. (2012, p. 55).

5. *no agreement is formed where a natural person interacts directly with the electronic agent of - another person and has made a material error during the creation of a data message and-*
   (a) *the electronic agent did not provide that person with an opportunity to prevent or correct the error;*
   (b) *that person notifies the other person of the error as soon as practicable after that person has learned of it;*
   (c) *that person takes reasonable steps, including steps that conform to the other person's instructions to return any performance received, or, if instructed to do so, to destroy that performance; and*
   (d) *that person has not used or received any material benefit or value from any performance received from the other person*'.

In terms of this provision, a party on whose behalf software or an electronic agent has been programmed to respond in concluding contracts will be bound to the pre-programmed actions of the technology deployed. Section 20(c) provides that a party using an electronic agent to form an agreement is, subject to paragraph (d), presumed to be bound by the terms of that agreement irrespective of whether that person reviewed the actions of the electronic agent or the terms of the agreement.[104]

Section 20 has created a strict statutory regime for the validity and enforceability of automated transactions where section 20(d) provides a party contracting with an electronic agent the right to review the transaction as a whole prior to the formation of a contract. There is some criticism of this subsection because the legal effect of non-compliance is not clearly stated.[105]

According to Pistorius as far as attribution is concerned, section 20(c) is in line with the South African common law, where contract formation through automated means was recognised long before electronic commerce became a reality.[106] At common law, it followed that where mistakes occur in an electronic communication through the malfunction of an electronic agent, the party that installed the malfunctioning electronic agent must assume the risk of any defects or delays in the transmission.[107] As such, section 20(e) provides a procedure to be followed by an aggrieved consumer to have the transaction set aside due to a reasonable material mistake (*iustus error*)[108]

---

[104]Eiselen in van der Merwe et al. (2016, pp. 164–165).

[105]Ibid. (p. 165).

[106]Pistorius (2008, p. 9). *Cf*. Olmesdahl (1984, pp. 545–553, 551–553); *S v Swanepoel* 1980 (1) SA 144 (NC). Eiselen in Van der Merwe et al. (2016, p. 165) states that s20(a) to (c) restates the common law position to some extent but that s20(d) introduces new consequences where contracts are concluded via electronic agents.

[107]Pistorius (2008, p. 10), Kerr (1998, pp. 110–111) where he discusses 'electronic wizardry' and fault on the part of the offeror and the equipment used.

[108]Eiselen in Van der Merwe et al. (2016, p. 170). For a discussion of how mistake and *iustus* error influence consensus, see Christie and Bradfield (2016, pp. 379–383), Van der Merwe et al. (2012, pp. 22–26), Nagel et al. (2015, p. 67).

where the requirements of subsections (i)–(iv) are met. The onus is on the customer to prove all these requirements, which are cumulative.[109]

With section 20(e), the legislature has set out when a mistake will be justifiable and reasonable (a *iustus error*) and when the contract will be binding, or when the customer may not rely on his or her mistake to set the contract aside.[110] When a contract is void due to a mistake, the ordinary contractual remedies are available to the parties entitling the prejudiced party is entitled to reclaim any performance with an enrichment action.[111]

Chapter VII of the ECT Act introduced a number of important protective measures for consumers in an electronic transaction over and above those that were typically available for offline consumers.[112] The consumer protection provisions of the ECT Act place seven duties on the supplier (*not defined*), who offers goods or services for sale, hire or exchange by way of an electronic transaction.[113] These main duties are to:

1. disclose the listed minimum information to consumers on the website where the goods or services are offered[114];
2. provide an opportunity to the consumer to review, correct and withdraw from the electronic transaction[115];
3. provide a secure payment system[116];
4. execute the order within 30 days of receiving the order unless otherwise agreed; and[117]
5. ensuring that the consumer is made aware that in applicable circumstances they are entitled to exercise a right of withdrawal (cooling-off).[118]
6. comply with rules on sending unsolicited commercial electronic communications.[119]
7. ensure the retention of rights under the ECT Act.[120]

A failure to make the listed information available to the consumer gives the consumer the right to cancel the transaction within fourteen days of receiving the goods or services.[121] If the transaction is terminated in this manner, the only charge

[109] Eiselen in Van der Merwe et al. (2016, p. 170), Pistorius (2008, p. 4).
[110] Eiselen in Van der Merwe et al. (2016, p. 170), Pistorius (2008, p. 4).
[111] Nagel et al. (2015, p. 58).
[112] Buys and Cronje (2004, p. 140).
[113] Jacobs (2004, p. 557).
[114] S43(1)(a)–(r) ECT Act.
[115] S43(2).
[116] S43(5).
[117] S46(1)–(3).
[118] S42(l)–(r) and s44.
[119] S45.
[120] S48.
[121] S43(3) ECT Act.

that may be levied against the consumer is the direct charge of returning the goods.[122] The consumer is obliged to return all goods received or cease using the services offered, and the supplier must return all other amounts received.[123]

The supplier's second duty is to provide a consumer with an opportunity to review a summary of the entire electronic transaction, correct any mistakes and withdraw from the transaction, before it is finalised or complete or before any order is placed.[124] With the confirmation process, the consumer should be given an opportunity to identify the goods or services they wish to purchase, to identify and to correct any errors and to express an informed and deliberate consent to the transaction.[125] While the shopping cart ordering/confirmation mechanism is often used, there are many different ways for consumers to place or confirm their orders.[126] The requirement is that consumers be offered all the elements that is, the ability to identify what they have ordered, the ability to cancel or modify their order, the ability to see the total cost, the ability to express consent to the order and the ability to retain an accurate record.[127]

The ECT Act does not state at what stage or how this confirmation process should be afforded, only that it be completed before finally placing any order. Buys suggested that the consumer be given a complete summary of his or her purchases once the consumer has indicated a readiness to effect payment.[128] For example, the consumer may put various items in his or her shopping basket and then click on a 'confirm order' icon. The summary should specify the goods or services purchased, the cost, any applicable taxes, any delivery costs applicable, a delivery address, personal details of the consumer, payment details and the total amount due. The consumer should then be prompted to either change the information, withdraw from the transaction or proceed with payment.[129]

If the consumer elects to change information, a new summary should be created incorporating the amended information. If the consumer decides to withdraw from the transaction before it is finalised, the withdrawal cannot carry any costs or penalties.[130] If the supplier fails to allow the consumer the opportunity to confirm the transaction in a process as detailed above, the consumer may elect to cancel the transaction within fourteen days from receipt of the goods or services.[131] In case of cancellation, the consumer must return the goods or cease using the services, and the supplier must refund all payments made by the consumer minus the direct cost of returning the goods.[132]

---

[122] S43(4) ibid.

[123] Ibid.

[124] S43(2) ECT Act.

[125] Eiselen in Van der Merwe et al. (2016, pp. 203–204), Papadopoulos et al. (2012, p. 76).

[126] Ibid.

[127] Ibid.

[128] Buys and Cronje (2004, p. 149).

[129] Ibid.

[130] Ibid.

[131] S43(3) ECT Act.

[132] S43(4).

On payment security, section 43(5) of the ECT Act requires a supplier to utilise a sufficiently secure payment system that is aligned with accepted technological standards at the time of the transaction and with the type of transaction concerned. The determination of a sufficiently secure payment system is a factual question that must be answered by examining the general technological security standards used at the time of the transaction, for the specific type of transaction employed in the specific industry.[133]

If the supplier's payment system is not secure, they could be held liable for damages suffered by a consumer.[134] However, to succeed with a damages claim against the supplier for damages, the consumer would have to allege delictual liability and prove that:

1. There was a breach of security during or after the payment process that relates to the consumer's payment or payment information;
2. The breach was due to a failure or refusal by the supplier to use or maintain a sufficiently secure payment system in accordance with the latest available technology or systems or that the supplier or its employees acted negligently with the consumer's payment or payment information; and
3. That the consumer suffered damages because of the supplier's actions/inaction.[135]

The Protection of Personal Information Act 4 of 2013 (POPIA) is data protection legislation in South Africa that regulates the processing of personal information by public and private individuals and ensures that the processing of personal information takes place according to internationally accepted data protection principles.[136] Although the act in its entirety has far-reaching implications for consumer protection and Uber services and transactions, the most important provisions for payment are the provisions relating to security in sections 19–22 and the provisions on 'unlawful acts in connection with an account number' in section 105–106. These sections will play an important role in deciding if the system is sufficiently secure under the ECT Act.[137]

When detailing aspects of consumer protection in South Africa, it is pertinent to note that the ECT Act concurrently regulates consumer contracts with the extensive Consumer Protection Act 68 of 2008. The Consumer Protection Act (CPA) is designed to enhance the consumer's choice and rights and to provide effective redress for grievances. It therefore prohibits various unfair business practices and sets a range of obligations on suppliers and service providers with corresponding rights for a consumer. Determining the scope of application starts with section 5(1) of the CPA, which states that this act applies to:

1. Every transaction occurring within the Republic, unless it is exempted;

---

[133] Papadopoulos et al. (2012, p. 77).

[134] S43(6) ECT Act.

[135] Papadopoulos et al. (2012, p. 77), Buys and Cronje (2004, pp. 156–157). A comprehensive discussion of payment protection is excluded from the scope of the chapter.

[136] Preamble and s2 of POPIA. A comprehensive discussion of POPIA is excluded from the chapter.

[137] Nagel et al. (2015, pp. 473–478).

2. The promotion of any goods or services, or of the supply of any goods or services, within the Republic;
3. Goods or services that are supplied or performed in terms of a transaction to which this act applies, irrespective of whether any of those goods or services are offered or supplied in conjunction with any other goods or services, or separate from any other goods or services; and
4. Goods that are supplied in terms of a transaction that is exempt from the application of this act.[138]

In the context of electronic transactions, it is also important to consider the implications of the requirement that the transaction (or promotion, supply or performance) 'occurs within South Africa' before the CPA applies to it. De Stadler indicates that this could either be at the place of:

1. conclusion of a contract;
2. delivery of goods; or
3. supply of services.[139]

In order to determine the place of conclusion of a contract, it is necessary to refer either to the common law principles applicable to contracts[140] or in the case of an electronic transaction to the statutory provisions of the ECT Act.[141] In most instances, the terms and conditions of transactions via a website will be constructed in a way that it will be the consumer who makes an offer, which is then accepted by the e-trader (supplier).[142] This could mean that the consumer's place of residence or business will

[138]Under s5(1)(d) and 5(5), if any goods are supplied within the Republic to any person in terms of a transaction that is exempt from the application of the Consumer Protection Act 68 of 2008 (CPA), the goods and importer or producer, distributor or retailer are still subject to s60 and 61 which relate to safety monitoring, recall and strict product liability. The exemptions are listed in s5(2) and relate to goods and services promoted to the state, where the consumer is an exempt juristic person, transactions exempted by the minister, credit agreements under the National Credit Act 34 of 2005 (NCA), services under an employment contract, etc.

[139]De Stadler (2018 section 5, para. 5.22).

[140]If parties do not conclude a contract while in each other's physical presence, various theories are applied in order to determine the time and place of conclusion of a contract. The predominant theory applied in South African law is the information theory. According to this theory, the contract is concluded where the offeror receives notification (takes cognisance of the fact) that his offer has indeed been accepted by the offeree. This theory is applied in all situations where contracts are concluded in person, by telephone or fax. If the methods of communication are mixed (i.e. telephone and fax), the information theory is applied. The other theory that sometimes finds application in South Africa in so-called true or real postal contracts is the expedition theory. In terms of the expedition theory, the contract is concluded at the time when and the place that the acceptance is dispatched (posted) to the offeror. A real postal contract is a contract where both the offer and the acceptance are made via the postal services. Nagel et al. (2015, pp. 57–58), Christie and Bradfield (2016, pp. 92–96), Van der Merwe et al. (2012, p. 62). *Cf. Cape Explosive Works Ltd v South African Oil and Fat Industries, Cape Explosive Works Ltd v Lever Bros(South Africa)* 1921 CPD 244, *Kergeulen Sealing and Whaling Co v Commissioner of Inland Revenue* 1939 AD 487, *Smeiman v Volkersz* 1954 (4) SA 170 (C).

[141]*Cf.* detailed discussion in para II.C.2 above and ss11, 22, 23 ECT Act.

[142]Fitzgerald et al. (2011, pp. 744–745).

determine the place of conclusion of contract and if the transaction is one occurring within South Africa. The default rule of the ECT Act can be expressly changed in the terms or conditions of the contract and web traders will often exercise this option with a clause setting out the applicable law or jurisdiction.[143] 'Choice-of-law' or 'choice-of-jurisdiction' clauses are particularly problematic in consumer contracts as the choice is not always valid and enforceable.[144]

De Stadler contends that under regulation 44(3)(z)(bb) read with regulation 44(1) of the CPA,[145] a choice-of-law clause in a contract will be presumed to be unfair if the consumer was residing in the Republic at the time when the agreement was concluded and the consumer entered into an agreement for the purposes wholly or mainly unrelated to his or her business or profession. Therefore, these clauses cannot oust the mandatory application of the CPA to transactions occurring within the Republic.[146] While this may be so and in agreeing that suppliers should not unfairly be able to evade the provisions of the CPA through choice-of-law clauses, it is in enforcement that consumers will face their greatest challenges. Space and limited word count dictate that this legislation cannot be discussed in any further detail in this chapter.[147]

In general, the remedies in the event of a breach of contract are aimed at performance and fulfilment of contractual obligations, at cancellation or at compensation

---

[143]Eiselen in Van der Merwe et al. (2016, p. 188). The determination of jurisdiction and related trans-border issues such as applicable law fall outside the scope of this chapter, but it is acknowledged that this is an almost inextricable component of Internet or electronic-based trading. 'Choice-of-law' or 'choice-of-jurisdiction' clauses are particularly problematic in consumer contracts as the choice is not always valid and enforceable. In addition, the rules established in private international law need to be applied. *Cf.* Eiselen in Van der Merwe et al. (2016, pp. 182–195).

[144]The applicable law has to be determined through domestic rules on the time and place of conclusion of the contract (jurisdiction) together with the principles of private international law. *Cf.* Eiselen in Van der Merwe et al. (2016, pp. 182–195).

[145]Regulation 44(1) reads that '*...a term of a consumer agreement between a supplier operating on a for-profit basis and acting wholly or mainly for purposes related to his or her business or profession and an individual consumer or individual consumers who entered into it for purposes wholly or mainly unrelated to his or her business or profession is presumed to be unfair if ...*' and Regulation 44(3)(z)(bb) states that '*...imposing a limitation period that is shorter than otherwise applicable under the common law or legislation for legal steps to be taken by the consumer (including for the making of a written demand and the institution of legal proceedings); ... (bb) providing that a law other than that of the Republic applies to a consumer agreement concluded and implemented in the Republic, where the consumer was residing in the Republic at the time when the agreement was concluded...*'.

[146]De Stadler (2018, para. 5.23).

[147]Papadopoulos (2019) Selected Aspects of E-Commerce, Digital Content And Consumer Protection in South Africa, LLD Thesis, University of Pretoria, conducted an analysis of the current consumer protection regulatory environment in South Africa, and its application to online consumers, engaged in e-commerce and their acquisition of digital content (intangible goods and services). The study found that online digital content transactions are not effectively subject to consumer protection legislative frameworks, leaving online consumers less protected than offline consumers, thus eroding trust in e-commerce-based transactions. The thesis made substantial recommendations for the amendment of consumer protection legislation in South Africa that could improve the position of online consumers in their digital content and e-commerce transactions.

(damages) for loss caused by the breach of contract. A claim for damages may be instituted together with remedies aimed at fulfilment or cancellation, where damages are required, in addition to performance in order to place the plaintiff in the financial position in which the plaintiff would be, had there not been a breach of the contract.[148] Consumers with contracts subject to the Consumer Protection Act also have a number of remedies at their disposal.[149]

2.3.3 Claims Based on Statutory Third-Party Insurance

The Road Accident Fund Act 56 of 1996 (RAF Act) creates a statutory fund, the Road Accident Fund (RAF), financed from levies on fuel in sold in South Africa, which is then applied in terms of the act's provisions, to the payment of compensation for claims based on bodily injury or certain prescribed patrimonial losses resulting from a motor vehicle accident.[150] According to section 17 of the RAF Act, the fund is '*…obliged to compensate any person (the third party) for any loss or damage which the third party has suffered as a result of any bodily injury to himself or herself or the death of or any bodily injury to any other person, caused by or arising from the driving of a motor vehicle by any person at any place within the Republic, if the injury or death is due to the negligence or other wrongful act of the driver or of the owner of the motor vehicle or of his or her employee in the performance of the employee's duties as employee: Provided that the obligation of the Fund to compensate a third party for non-pecuniary loss shall be limited to compensation for a serious injury …and shall be paid by way of a lump sum*'.

The RAF Act does not in itself prescribe the requirements of liability of the RAF. Fundamentally, it does no more than to substitute the RAF as wrongdoer in order to achieve security of recovery of damages by a road accident victim which may have a proven legal claim and proven damages against the common law wrongdoer but may find that the wrongdoer is unable to pay his or her damages. Therefore, the actual legal basis for and principles of liability of the RAF are to be found in common law, that is, in delictual liability.[151]

The requirements for liability where the identity of a driver or the owner of motor vehicle is known are set out in section 17(1)(a) of the RAF Act, where the claimant (being 'any person whomsoever' or a 'third party', i.e. not the driver but the road accident victim or dependents) must prove that:[152]

[148]Dendy (2018, para. 47).

[149]See e.g. ss 10, 16, 17, 20, 21, 40–43, 51, 52, 54–61 (and others) CPA.

[150]Klopper (2019), para. 7.3.2.

[151]This principle is established by s21 read with s19(a) RAF Act. See also Klopper (2019, para. 7.3.2 at A-22); *Rose's Car Hire v Grant* 1948 (2) SA 466 (A) 472 474–475, *Da Silva v Coutinho* 1971 (3) SA 123 (A), Klopper (2016, pp. 19–20). For discussion on delict please refer to above II.C.1.

[152]Klopper (2019, para. 7.3.5 at A-31); *Smith v Road Accident Fund* 2006 (4) SA 590 (SCA). In order to succeed with a claim against the RAF in circumstances where the identity of neither the driver nor owner can be established, the claimant must be able to show that: (1) he or she is a person

1. They have suffered damage or loss in the form of bodily injury to him- or herself or by virtue of the death of another person;
2. There was the negligent driving of a motor vehicle or another unlawful act resulting in;
3. Damage or loss flowing from personal injury or loss of maintenance to the third party;
4. The damage or loss must have been caused by or arisen from the negligent driving of a motor vehicle; and
5. The collision must have occurred within the borders of the Republic of South Africa.[153]

Not all damage caused by the unlawful and negligent driving of a motor vehicle can be recovered from the RAF. Only damage specifically referred to in section 17(1) of the RAF Act can be claimed. Patrimonial loss actually incurred, such as medical and hospital expenses, assistants' salaries, costs of artificial limbs and medical and paramedical aids, past loss of earnings and, in appropriate circumstances, past loss of support or maintenance, constitutes actual patrimonial loss and is treated as special damage.[154] Material damage to property, such as luggage, clothing, a motor vehicle and other personal effects, cannot be recovered from the RAF, since the act limits its liability to damages resulting from bodily injuries or the death of any person.[155] Damages of this nature must be claimed from the wrongdoer by separate delictual action.[156] Loss in respect of pain and suffering, disfigurement, diminished earning capacity and loss of the amenities and expectation of life constitutes non-patrimonial loss, and together with prospective patrimonial loss (i.e. a loss which has not yet been incurred or suffered but which will be incurred or suffered in the future, such as future hospital and medical expenses and loss of earnings) considered general damages.[157] A claim for emotional shock does not lie against the RAF but against the wrongdoer.[158] Where loss of support is claimed, the dependent has a direct claim,

---

(third party) who has suffered damage or loss as a result of bodily injury or the death of another person, (2) the bodily injury or death was caused by or arose out of the negligent driving of a vehicle of which the identity of the driver or owner is unknown or that the injury or death was caused by another wrongful act, and (3) he or she must lodge a claim in terms of regulation 1(a), (s17(1)(b) RAF Act). Klopper (2019, para. 7.4 at A-64).

[153]For a summary of the requirements for liability of the RAF, see *MS v Road Accident Fu*nd [2019] 3 *All SA* 626 (GJ).].

[154]Klopper (2019, para. 7.3 at C-5- C-10).

[155]Ibid. (para. 3.1 at C-4.).

[156]*Oberholzer v Santam Insurance Co Ltd* 1970 (1) SA 337 (N).

[157]*Guardian National Insurance Co Ltd v Van Gool NO* 1992 (4) SA 61 (A) 63D–G, *Zondo v MEC for Health of the Gauteng Provincial Government* (25644/2014) [2016] ZAGPJHC 243 (2 September 2016).

[158]S19 RAF Act states that liability excluded in certain cases and in particular s19(g) states that the fund or an agent shall not be obliged to compensate any person in terms of s17 for any loss or damage suffered as a result of an emotional shock sustained by that person when that person witnessed or observed or was informed of the bodily injury or the death of another person as a result of the driving of a motor vehicle.

enforceable in his or her own name. That right is not derived from the deceased or from the deceased estate but is conferred upon the dependant members of the family. It is *sui generis.*[159]

From 1 August 2018, all Uber driver partners and Uber Eats delivery partners using the Uber app in South Africa were automatically covered with injury insurance at no cost to the drivers.[160]

2.4 Uber and Anti-competitive Market Practices

A complaint was filed by the metered taxi industry in 2015 against Uber.[161] The metered taxi industry alleged that Uber was (1) conducting unfair business practice as it secures partnerships with multinational companies that have exposure to its client base and ultimately giving it unparalleled market access (2) non-compliant with the South African public transport rules and regulations in that it does not pay any permit renewal, rank fees and licensing fees as do other traditional metered taxis and (3) charging below cost rates to the detriment of traditional metered taxi operators.[162] The Competition Commission of South Africa investigated the complaint under abuse of dominance provisions (predatory pricing) and found that Uber driver partners were not charging prices below cost in any of the cities in which Uber operated. The Competition Commission decided not to refer the complaint to the Tribunal for prosecution. With the other allegations, the Competition Commission was of the view that advocacy engagements with the relevant regulators within the transport industry might lead to better outcomes.[163]

---

[159] Klopper (2019, para. 7.3.5 at A-50).

[160] See Uber Blog (2018). It is stated that drivers and delivery partners will have access to the following benefits: (1) emergency medical treatment: if an accident happens on-trip, this cover reimburses drivers for emergency medical treatment costs they have incurred in the first 48 h following the accident up to a capped sum. In addition, this cover reimburses ambulance service costs and provides drivers with an immediate small lump sum payment to cover their basic expenses following the accident, (2) death and final payments: in the unfortunate event that a driver dies as a result of an accident on-trip, their dependents or heirs will benefit from a lump sum payment. They will also obtain an additional lump sum amount which can be used as they deem fit, (3) permanent disability payments: in the unfortunate event that a driver suffers a permanent disability as a result of an accident on-trip, they will benefit from a lump sum payment. The amount depends on the severity of the disability, as determined by the insurer, (4) daily confinement payment: if a driver is hospitalised for more than 24 h, they will receive a daily payment for up to 30 days for each day that they have to remain in the hospital. This is non-medical expense cover as a result of hospitalisation and not a substitute for medical aid cover, (5) daily payment benefit (injury): if a driver is hospitalised for more than 48 h as a result of an accident that happened on-trip and are thereafter unable to drive because of those injuries, they will receive a daily payment for up to 30 days while they are medically certified by a doctor as unfit to work.

[161] OECD (2018, p. 5).

[162] Ibid.

[163] Ibid.

Given the number of complaints and diversity of allegations the Competition Commission decided to conduct a market inquiry into the land-based public passenger transport.[164] This was done because there was reason to believe that there were features or a combination of features in the industry that could prevent, distort or restrict competition, contrary to the purposes of the Competition Act.[165]

Some of the preliminary findings of the Competition Commission showed that traditional metered taxis' prices remain higher than app-based prices. Based on the pricing analysis conducted on few routes, the base price charged by the traditional metered taxis is between 33 and 42% higher than that charged by app-based taxis.[166]

Evidence at the Competition Commission's disposal indicated that the traditional metered taxi industry is responding to the introduction of app-based taxi services. Traditional metered taxis are also gravitating towards app-based services. It was noted that the traditional metered taxis are modernising their business in response to competitive constraints imposed by app-based services by developing its own e-hailing apps. The members of South African Metered Taxi Association designed a full e-hailing service called 'Yookoo' to connect users with metered cab drivers in their close proximity.[167]

In their *Market Inquiry Into Land-Based Public Passenger Transport Metered Taxis And E-Hailing Services Report* of 19 February 2020, the Competition Commission of South Africa made the following findings:[168]

1. Area restrictions contained in section 66 of the NLT Act are inefficient and distort competition between e-hailing operators and metered taxi operators.
2. On fare determination for metered taxis—despite the existing legislative framework providing guidelines on how metered taxis can set their fares, neither the Minister nor the MEC regulates fare structure as alluded by the metered taxis.
3. Substantial backlogs in the application of operating licences at various 'provincial regulatory entity's' exist due to the inefficiencies and capacity constraints experienced. This has led to a significant proportion of e-hailing operators and metered taxi operators operating without valid operating licences, and thus operating illegally.
4. The commission has observed that the relationship between e-hailing companies and e-hailing operators is not governed by any labour laws.

[164]On 10 May 2017, the Competition Commission under its powers in s43B1 of the Competition Act 89 of 1998 published a notice that it would conduct a market inquiry into land-based public passenger transport sector.

[165]Competition Commission of South Africa (2020).

[166]Ibid. (pp. 36–37).

[167]Ibid. (pp. 13–14). E-hailing companies in South Africa include Uber, Bolt plus new entrants such as inDriver, Ntuza Digital TaxiCab app (launched in East London), YoTaxi app (Launched in Durban by 12 metered-taxi associations), YooKoo Passenger, Hailer (launched in Kimberly) and inDriver app (available in Port Elizabeth, Cape Town, Johannesburg and Pretoria). YooKoo Passenger (a newly developed e-hailing app) announced its partnership with the metered taxi industry with the aim of challenging both Uber and Bolt.

[168]Ibid. (p. 63).

5. The commission has also observed that metered taxis' operators are currently fragmented without a nationally recognised body advancing the interests of the industry.[169]

3 Conclusion

Although it is generally understood that innovation is essential for growth, it is also imperative that regulatory frameworks within various industries should not unjustifiably curtail disruptive entrants. Innovation should be the catalyst for development and push incumbents to innovate such as the taxis that are migrating to app-based ride hailing.

South Africa has taken the first steps regarding the recognition and regulation of taxi e-hailing services. It is a positive development that steps are being taken to harmonise regulation rather than follow the examples set in other countries to ban Uber with the view of protecting existing taxi industries. The encouragement of healthy competition is to be supported.

There is still some clarification needed on the nature of the relationship between the drivers (actual transport providers), Uber BV (which is incorporated in the Netherlands and owns and operates the Uber App) and Uber SA which is a subsidiary company of Uber BV rendering defined services to Uber BV especially in so far as it relates to the status of the drivers as employees. This would require an in-depth multifaceted analysis.

References

Books and Theses

Buys R, Cronje F (eds) (2004) Cyberlaw@SAII: the law of the internet in South Africa, 2nd edn. Van Schaiks Pretoria

Christie RH, Bradfield GB (2016) Christies law of contract in South Africa. LexisNexis South Africa

Davies PL, Freedland MR (eds) (1983) Kahn-Freund's labour and the law volume 24 of Hamlyn lectures. Stevens

Dendy M (2018) Law of South Africa (LAWSA) damages, vol 14, no 1, 3rd edn. LexisNexis, South Africa

De Stadler E, Du Plessis J, Eiselen GTS (managing ed), Feris L, Loubser MM, Melville N, Naudé T (managin ed), Reid E, Sharrock R, Stoop P, van Heerden CH, van Zyl E; Woker T; Yeats JL (2018) Commentary on the consumer protection act updatable loose-leaf. Juta, South Africa

Fitzgerald B, Fitzgerald A, Clark E, Middleton G, Lim YF (2011) Internet and e-commerce law, business and policy, 2nd edn. Thomson Reuters Legal Australia

Hayward S (2018) The agile leader: how to create an agile business in the digital age. Kogan Page Publishers, London

[169]Ibid.

Kerr AJ (1998) The principles of the law of contract, 5th edn. Butterworths Durban
Klopper HB (2016) The law of third-party compensation. LexisNexis, South Africa
Klopper HB (2019) RAF practitioners guide. LexisNexis, South Africa
Midgley JR (2016) Law of South Africa (LAWSA) delict, vol 15, 3rd edn. LexisNexis, South Africa
Nagel CJ (editor), Barnard J, Boraine A, Delport P, Kern KN, Lotz DJ, Otto JM, Papadopoulos SM, Prozesky-Kuschke B, Roestoff M, Van Eck BPS, Van Jaarsveld SR (2015) Commercial law, 5th edn. LexisNexis, South Africa
Neethling J, Potgieter JM, Visser PJ (2005) Neethling's law of personality, 2nd edn. LexisNexis, Butterworths, South Africa
Papadopoulos S, Snail S (eds) (2012) Cyberlaw@SA III: the law of the internet in South Africa, 3rd edn. Van Schaiks, South Africa
Papadopoulos S (2019) Selected aspects of e-commerce, digital content and consumer protection in South Africa. LLD thesis, University of Pretoria
Potgieter JM, Steynberg L, Floyd TB (2012) Visser and Potgieter's law of damages, 3rd edn. LexisNexis, South Africa
Roos A (2003) The Law of data (privacy) protection: a comparative and theoretical study. LLD thesis, UNISA
Van Niekerk A, Christianson M, McGregor M, Smith E, Van Eck BPS (2019) Law@Work, 5th edn. LexisNexis, South Africa
Van der Merwe DP, Roos A, Pistorius T, Eiselen GTS, Nel S (2016) Information and communications law, 2nd edn. LexisNexis, South Africa
Van der Merwe SWJ, Van Huyssteen LF, Reinecke MFB, Lubbe GF (2012) Contract: general principles, 4th edn. Juta, Cape Town

Case Law

Argus Printing & Publishing Co Ltd v IFP 1992 (3) SA 579 (A)
Barbara Ann Berwick v Uber Technologies, Inc, A Delaware Corporation, and Rasier 11-46739 EK
Cape Explosive Works Ltd v South African Oil and Fat Industries, Cape Explosive Works Ltd v Lever Bros (South Africa) 1921 CPD 244
Da Silva v Coutinho 1971 (3) SA 123 (A)
De Beer v Sergeant 1976 (1) SA 246 (T)
Discovery Health v CCMA [2008] 7 BLLR 633 (LC)
Durban's Water Wonderland (Pty) Ltd v Botha & another 1999 (1) SA 982 (SCA)
Gardener v Whitaker 1995 (2) SA 672 (E)
Godfrey v Campbell 1997 (1) SA 570 (C)
Government of the RSA v Ngubane 1972 (2) SA 601 (A)
Guardian National Insurance Co Ltd v Van Gool 1992 (4) SA 61 (A)
Jafta v Ezemvelo KZN Wildlife [2008] 10 BLLR 954 (LC)
Kergeulen Sealing and Whaling Co v Commissioner of Inland Revenue 1939 AD 487
King's Car Hire (Pty) Ltd v Wakeling 1970 (4) SA 640 (N)
Kylie v CCMA [2010] 7 BLLR 705 (LAC)
Le Roux v Dey (Freedom of Expression Institute and Restorative Justice Centre as Amici Curiae) 2011 (3) SA 274 (CC)
MS v Road Accident Fund [2019] 3 All SA 626 (GJ).]
Minister of Justice v Hofmeyr 1993 (3) SA 131 (A)
National Labour Relations Board v Hearst Publications (1944) 322 US 111
Oberholzer v Santam Insurance Co Ltd 1970 (1) SA 337 (N)
Perlman v Zoutendyk 1934 CPD 151

Rose's Car Hire v Grant 1948 (2) SA 466 (A) 472 474–475
Rudman v Road Accident Fund 2003 (2) SA 234 (SCA)
S v Adams, S v Werner 1981 (1) SA 187 (A)
S v Swanepoel 1980 (1) SA 144 (NC)
SA National Defence Union v Minister of Defence 1999 ILJ 2265 (CC)
Sihlali Mafika v South African Broadcasting Corporation Ltd [2010] 5 BLLR 542 (LC)
Smeiman v Volkersz 1954 (4) SA 170 (C)
Smith v Road Accident Fund 2006 (4) SA 590 (SCA)
Spring Forest Trading 599 CC v Wilberry (Pty) Ltd t/a Ecowash and Another 2015 (2) SA 118 (SCA)
State Information Technology Agency (SITA) (Pty) Ltd v CCMA [2008] 7 BLLR 611 (LAC)
Transnet Ltd v Sechaba Photoscan (Pty) Ltd 2005 (1) SA 299 (SCA)
Universiteit van Pretoria v Tommie Meyer Films (Edms) Bpk 1977 (4) SA 376 (T)
Uber South Africa Technology Services (Pty) Ltd v NUPSAW and SATAWU obo Tsepo Morekure unreported case WECT12537-16 7 July 2017
Uber South Africa Technology Services (Pty) Ltd v National Union of Public Service and Allied Workers 2018 ILJ 903 (LC)
Uber B.V., Uber London Ltd and Uber Britannia Ltd v Aslam, Farrar UKEAT/0056/17/DA
Uber Technologies, Inc v Barbara Berwick CGC-15-546378
Zondo v MEC for Health of the Gauteng Provincial Government (25644/2014) [2016] ZAGPJHC 243 (2 September 2016)

Journals

Bower JL, Christensen CM (1995) Disruptive technologies: catching the wave. Harvard Bus Rev 73(1):43–53
Brassey M (1990) The nature of employment. Ind Law J Juta 11:889–937
Du Toit D (2019) Platform work and social justice. Ind Law J Juta 40:1–11
Jacobs W (2004) The electronic communications and transactions act: consumer protection and internet contracts. SA Merc LJ 16(4):556–567
Keeton (2017) An Uber dilemma: the conflict between the Seattle rideshare ordinance, the NLRA and for-hire driver worker classification. GLR 52(2):209–277
Lötz DJ, Du Plessis C (2004a) Elektroniese koopkontrakte: 'n tegnologiese hemel of hel (Deel 1) De Jure 37(1):1–20
Lötz DJ, Du Plessis C (2004b) Elektroniese koopkontrakte: 'n tegnologiese hemel of hel (Deel 2) De Jure 37(2):224–243
Mokoena K (2016) "Are Uber drivers employees? A look at emerging business models and whether they can be accommodated by South African Labour Law. Ind Law J Juta 37:1574–1583
Mokoena K (2018) Are Uber drivers employees or independent contractors? A comparative analysis. Ind Law J Juta 39:1453–1469
Olmesdahl MCJ (1984) Unheralded demise of Wolmer versus Rees. South African Law J 101(3):545–553
Pistorius T (1999) Formation of internet contracts: an Analysis of the contractual and security issues. South African Mercantile Law J 11(3):282–299
Pistorius T (2004) Click-wrap and web-wrap agreements. South African Mercantile Law J 16(4):568–576
Pistorius T (2006) From snail mail to e-mail—A south african perspective on the web of conflicting rules on the time of e-contracting. Compar Int Law J Southern Africa 39(2):178–213

Pistorius T (2008) The legal effect of input errors in automated transactions: The South African Matrix. J Inf Law Technol (JILT) 2008(2):1–21. https://warwick.ac.uk/fac/soc/law/elj/jilt/2008_2/pistorius2/pistorius2.pdf. Accessed on 31 May 2020
Thompson C (2003) The changing nature of employment. Ind Law J Juta 24:1793–1815
Van Eck BPS, Nemusimbori NE (2018) Uber drivers: Sad to say, but not employees of Uber SA. Tydskrif vir Hedendaagse Romeins-Hollandse Reg. J Contemp Roman-Dutch Law LexisNexis S Afr 81(3):473–483

Legislation

South Africa
Basic Conditions of Employment Act 75 of 1997 (BCEA)
Competition Act 89 of 1998
Constitution of South Africa Act 108 of 1996 (The Constitution)
Consumer Protection Act 68 of 2008 (CPA)
Electronic Communications and Transactions Act 25 of 2002 (ECT Act)
National Credit Act 34 of 2005 (NCA)
National Minimum Wage Act 9 of 2018
National Land Transport Act 5 of 2009 (NLT Act)
National Land Transport Act Amendment Bill B7D-2016 (NLT Amendment Bill)
Labour Relations Act 66 of 1995 (LRA)
Protection of Personal Information Act 4 of 2013 (POPIA)
Proclamation R68 *Government Gazette* 23809 of 30 August 2002 (*Regulation Gazette nr. 7449*)
Road Accident Fund Act 56 of 1996 (RAF Act)

International

Employment Rights Act, 1996 (UK)
Fair Labour Standard Act. 1938 29 USC (USA)
National Minimum Wages Act,1998 (UK)
UNCITRAL Model Law on Electronic Commerce Guide to Enactment with 1996 with additional article 5 as adopted in 1998
Working Time Regulations, 1998 (UK)

Treatise

Declaration of Philadelphia, 1944
Treaty of Versailles, 1919

Reports and/or Internet

California's Labour Commission, the Bureau of Labour and Industries of the State of Oregon (BOLI) (October 2015) Advisory Opinion of The Commissioner on The Employment Status of Uber Drivers (14 October 2015)

Competition Commission of South Africa (2020) Market Inquiry into Land Based Public Passenger Transport Metered Taxis And E-Hailing Services Report 19 February 2020 iii-iv. http://www.compcom.co.za/wp-content/uploads/2020/02/PROVISIONAL-REPORT-ON-E-HAILING-AND-METERED-TAXIS-19February2020-NON-CONFIDENTIAL-VERSION1.pdf. Accessed 25 Feb 2020

International Labour Organisation (ILO) Global Commission on the Future of Work (2019) Work for a brighter future. https://www.ilo.org/wcmsp5/groups/public/—dgreports/—cabinet/documents/publication/wcms_662410.pdf. Accessed 28 May 2020

Office of the Secretary General's Envoy on Youth *International Labour Organization (ILO)* available at https://www.un.org/youthenvoy/2013/08/ilo-international-labour-organization/. Accessed 2 Feb 2020

Organisation for Economic Co-operation and Development (OECD) Directorate for Financial and Enterprise Affairs: Competition Committee Working Party No. 2 on Competition and Regulation (2018) Taxi, ride-sourcing and ride-sharing services—Note by South Africa. https://one.oecd.org/document/DAF/COMP/WP2/WD(2018)21/en/pdf. Accessed on 16 Feb 2020 (OECD 2018)

Sabinet (2018) National land transport amendment bill sent to NCOP. https://legal.sabinet.co.za/articles/national-land-transport-amendment-bill-sent-to-ncop/. Accessed on 16 Feb 2020

Sabinet (2020) Bill tracker. https://discover-sabinet-co-za.uplib.idm.oclc.org/document/BTD10816. Accessed on 10 Feb 2020

Taxify (2018) 2 Years of taxify in South Africa. https://blog.taxify.eu/en-za/2018/04/2-years-of-taxify-in-south-africa/. Accessed on 10 Feb 2020

Teffer P (2015) EU court to classify Uber: taxi or information company? https://euobserver.com/digital/129709. Accessed 25 Feb 2019

Uber BV (2020) Terms and conditions available at https://www.uber.com/legal/en/document/?name=general-terms-of-use&country=south-africa&lang=en. Accessed on 25 Feb 2020

Uber (undated) A guide for how to use Uber. https://www.uber.com/za/en/ride/how-it-works/. Accessed on 02 Jan 2020

Uber Blog (2018) Introducing Partner Injury Protection for more peace of mind. https://www.uber.com/en-ZA/blog/introducing-partner-injury-protection-chubb/. Accessed on 02 Feb 2020

Chapter 11
A Legal Perspective on Uber's Activities in Turkey

Işık Önay and Emek Toraman Çolgar

1 Introduction

Uber started providing services in Turkey in June 2014[1] and was active in the three cities of Istanbul, Muğla, and İzmir. In the latter two cities, Uber's activities remained limited to the popular summer destinations of Bodrum and Çeşme.[2] During the first three years of Uber's operations in Turkey, there was extensive coverage in the Turkish media of the problems Uber was facing in both local and global contexts. Discussion on Uber in the legal literature, however, was almost non-existent. The reasons for that may have been twofold: first, there were no reported court decisions regarding Uber until the end of 2016, and second, Uber's UberPop (UberX) service, the one that is most prone to legal challenges, was not introduced in Turkey.[3] Instead, Uber mostly provided its UberXL service, using vehicles with licenses to engage in touristic transportation.

The discussion on Uber became heated in 2017, when drivers operating within Uber's system and their passengers were increasingly subjected to fines. Some of those fines were criticized for being against the principle of certainty[4] and some were challenged in court. A significant number of decisions were made by administrative courts on the issue. In 2018, the administration responded with changes in

[1] Yetim (2015, p. 626), Kaya (2019b, pp. 289–322, 290).

[2] Kaya (2019b, p. 296), also see DigitalAge (2017).

[3] See the July 2015 interview with Uber's then current operations manager Austin Kim, where he states that UberPop will not be offered in Turkey: Cumhuriyet (2015).

[4] Türkiye Büyük Millet Meclisi Kamu Denetçiliği Kurumu (Ombudsmanlık) (2018).

I. Önay (✉) · E. Toraman Çolgar
Koç University Law School, Istanbul, Turkey
e-mail: ionay@ku.edu.tr

E. Toraman Çolgar
e-mail: ecolgar@ku.edu.tr

Z. Ayata and I. Önay (eds.), *Global Perspectives on Legal Challenges Posed by Ridesharing Companies*,
https://doi.org/10.1007/978-981-15-7035-3_11

regulation, introducing sanctions for out-of-purpose use of certain licenses. A second blow to Uber's Turkish operations came with lawsuits brought by the United Taxi Drivers Association (*Birleşik Taksiciler Derneği*) and Istanbul Artisanal Chamber of Motorists (*İstanbul Otomobilciler Esnaf Odası*).

This chapter will first describe the services that are being offered by Uber in Turkey and will then give an overview of the regulations pertaining to transportation services. This is followed by the regulatory challenges faced by Uber, a discussion of the legal nature of Uber's relationship with passengers and drivers, the issues that may arise due to civil liability, and an analysis of Uber's activities within the context of unfair competition as well as information on the ongoing legal dispute.

2 Services Offered by Uber

Uber used to offer UberTAXI[5] and UberXL[6] services in Turkey. In the UberTAXI service, Uber merely acted as an intermediary between the taxi driver and the passenger. The fare was calculated by the taximeter and was usually paid directly to the driver. Uber required its drivers to submit their driving licenses, vehicle licenses, and clearance certificates indicating the lack of a criminal record.[7] This service was already being offered by a local service provider, BiTaksi,[8] before Uber's entry into Turkey. Uber initially offered this service free of charge.[9]

A passenger could also opt for the UberXL service. In this case, Uber provided an SUV for six people.[10] The vehicle in question was not a registered taxi and was subject to regulations for transportation services. Uber required the vehicles registered in its system to have the so-called D2 license,[11] which is granted for commercial but non-scheduled transportation with buses or automobiles fulfilling certain requirements.[12] In this service, the fare was calculated by Uber's dynamic pricing algorithm. The passenger would make the payment directly to Uber, who then charged a 20% commission fee[13] and forwarded the payment to the driver.

---

[5]http://uberturkiye.com/taksi/. Accessed 21 Jun 2017.

[6]A similar service offered was UberFAMILY, where the vehicle in question has a child safety seat and therefore offers safe travel for families with children: http://uberturkiye.com/aile/. Accessed 21 June 2017. It seems that Uber also offered the UberBOAT service in Istanbul in June 2015: https://www.uber.com/tr/blog/uberboat/. Accessed on 26 Mar 2020. However, this service seems to have been discontinued soon thereafter.

[7]http://uberturkiye.com/taksi/. Accessed 21 Jun 2017.

[8]http://www.bitaksi.com/en/. Accessed 26 Mar 2020.

[9]İnci (2018, pp. 33–39, 37).

[10]https://www.uber.com/us/en/ride/uberxl/. Accessed 7 Apr 2020.

[11]Kaya (2019b, p. 296, n.32).

[12]By-Law on Road Transport Arts. 6 (4) b and 24 (2) m (Official Gazette, 08.01.2018, No. 30295).

[13]İnci (2018, p. 36).

Uber's XL service had competition from companies such as YOLO,[14] OLEV,[15] GelGit,[16] Careem,[17] and Scotty.[18] As of February 2020, only Scotty, which offers transportation services with motorcycles, remains active in Turkey. Uber announced that it stopped its UberXL service in Turkey as of 31.05.2019. It was stated in Uber's announcement that it had over 4 million registered users and about 12,000 registered Uber XL drivers.[19] Uber continued to offer its UberTAXI service for a while but then announced on 07.01.2020, via its official Twitter account, @Uber_Turkiye, that access to this service would also be blocked due to the court decision in the unfair competition case,[20] although that case only pertained to the UberXL service.

3 Regulatory Framework for Passenger Transportation Services and Legal Challenges Faced by Uber

3.1 Overview of the Regulatory Framework

Under Turkish law, the authority to coordinate transportation services is bestowed on municipalities (Art. 15/p of the Municipality Law[21]). In provinces where there is a metropolitan municipality, it possesses the authority to coordinate transportation (Art. 7/f of the Metropolitan Municipality Law[22]). Within the boundaries of the metropolitan area, it is the metropolitan municipality that has the authority to issue licenses for land and sea vehicles offering public transportation including taxis and shuttles (Art. 7/p of MML).[23] In metropolitan municipalities, the so-called transportation coordination centers (Turkish acronym: UKOME) are established, which are tasked with the coordination of transportation services within the metropolitan area (Art. 9 of MML). Decisions by the UKOME enter into force upon the approval of the mayor (Art. 9 para. 3 of MML).

[14]http://www.yolo.com.tr/. Accessed 21 Jun 2017.

[15]https://www.olev.com.tr/. Accessed 21 Jun 2017.

[16]http://www.gelgit.com.tr/. Accessed 21 Jun 2017.

[17]https://drive.careem.com/tr-tr. Accessed 26 Mar 2020. Careem was later acquired by Uber for $3.1. billion (Uber 2020) and then announced that it would exit the Turkish market as of 31 Jan 2020 (Capital Online 2020).

[18]https://www.scotty.app/. Accessed 26 Mar 2020.

[19]CNN Türk (2019).

[20]Access to Uber's website and application was blocked in December 2019 based on the decision by the 10th Civil Court of First Instance in Istanbul, dated 16.10.2019, No. 2016/1082.

[21]Law No. 5393 (OG, 13.07.2005, No. 25874); hereafter referred to as ML.

[22]Law No. 5216 (OG, 23.07.2004, No. 25531); hereafter referred to as MML.

[23]Yetim (2015, pp. 638–639).

Each municipality imposes different standards for taxis and taxi drivers. An example is the Directive on Commercial Taxis and Commercial Shuttles[24] issued by the Istanbul Metropolitan Municipality. Art. 9 of the directive contains rules of conduct for taxi and shuttle drivers. For example, it requires drivers of commercial taxis and shuttles to possess a document authorizing them to drive public transportation vehicles (*Toplu Taşıma Aracı Kullanım Belgesi*), to be properly dressed and clean, and to have a properly functioning taximeter in the vehicle, which is visible to the passenger. Art. 10 of the directive lists the qualifications to be a taxi or shuttle driver. Accordingly, the driver is required to have graduated from primary school, to complete the driver training coordinated by the Istanbul Metropolitan Municipality and the Ministry of Education, to receive a clean bill of health on a yearly basis, to not have been convicted of certain crimes and misdemeanors, to have a Social Security Institution document issued in the name of the transporter, etc. Finally, Art. 11 of the directive contains technical specifications for the vehicle.

The Law on Road Transport[25] (*Karayolları Taşıma Kanunu*) regulates transportation of passengers and goods. Art. 5 of the law requires those who will provide transportation services to get an authorization document from the Ministry of Interior Affairs. It should also be noted that this law allows the administration to leave the regulation of local transport services performed within a province and interprovincial transportation not exceeding 100 km to provincial authorities, whereas local transport performed within municipal boundaries can be entrusted to municipalities (Art. 2 para. 3); indeed, municipalities are entrusted with certain authorities pursuant to the By-Law on Road Transport (*Karayolları Taşıma Yönetmeliği*).[26] A second important rule found in the Law on Road Transportation is Art. 10, which bans acting as a commissioner in passenger transportation. This article does not preclude persons from acting as agents in passenger transportation but requires such persons to have a license for agency.[27]

Another important piece of legislation concerning transportation services is the Law on Road Traffic (*Karayolları Trafik Kanunu*),[28] as it imposes sanctions on those not abiding by the regulations on transportation services. For example, taxi drivers who operate without a taximeter are sanctioned with a monetary fine and vehicles in an improper state are banned from traffic by traffic officers (Art. 31 of the Law on Road Traffic). More importantly for Uber, Additional Art. 2 of the Law on Road Traffic regulates the consequences of the use of vehicles for purposes other than their registered ones. Accordingly, transporting passengers with a commercial purpose in the borders of a municipality without the necessary license from the relevant

[24]İstanbul Büyükşehir Belediyesi Ticari Taksi Ve Taksi Dolmuş Yönergesi. https://tuhim.ibb.gov.tr/dosyalar/taksi%20taksi%20dolmu%C5%9F%20y%C3%B6nerge.pdf. Accessed Mar 26, 2020.

[25]Law No. 4925 (OG, 19.07.2003, No. 25173). An unofficial English translation is available on the International Labor Organization's website: ILO (2013).

[26]Ekşi (2019, pp. 283–346, 296).

[27]The license for acting as an agent is called the F license. An F1 license entitles persons to act as agents in domestic passenger transportation, whereas an F2 license allows both international and domestic passenger transportation [By-Law on Road Transport Art. 6 (5)].

[28]Law No. 2918 (OG, 18.10.1983, No. 18195).

municipality is subject to administrative fines and the vehicle may be banned from traffic. The current version[29] of the article imposes administrative fines for the drivers for use of vehicles for purposes other than their registered ones and to the owners, provided that they have permitted such use. The operator or the owner of the vehicle is also required to take necessary precautions and to make sure that the vehicle is not used without necessary permits even if he/she is not the driver. Failing to do so results in the vehicle being banned from traffic for a time period depending on the violation (Law on Road Traffic Additional Art. 2/IV).

3.2 *Uber's Regulatory Challenges*

In December 2016, there was extensive press coverage of an instruction issued by the General Directorate of Security.[30] According to reports, the instruction referred to the Constitutional Court's decision cited above and urged traffic divisions in all provinces to fine Uber drivers operating without the necessary license, as well as the passengers traveling with Uber. Drivers who were first-time offenders were to be fined 2,532 and a repeated offense incurred a fine of 4,220. Passengers who traveled using Uber were fined 281. In cases where the driver was also the owner of the vehicle, the vehicle was banned from traffic.[31] It has been reported that 1227 drivers were fined between 01.01.2017 and 10.04.2017.[32]

Following extensive media coverage in December, Uber announced that it was operating legally and that all vehicles providing transportation services via Uber were

---

[29]The article has undergone two recent amendments. With the first amendment [Law No. 7145, Art. 26 (OG, 26.10.2018, No. 30577)], administrative fines were increased and the scope of persons subject to them were widened [Ekşi (2019, p. 297)]. The second amendment [Law No. 7166, Art. 5 (OG, 22.02.2019, No. 30694)] was merely cosmetic, changing the order of the paragraphs [Ekşi (2019, p. 302)].

Prior to the Constitutional Court's decision on 11.09.2014 [Turkish Constitutional Court, 11.09.2014, 52/139 (OG, 09.04.2015, No. 29321)], the mentioned monetary fine was applicable to the driver, the owner of the vehicle, and persons in charge of the enterprise or business with which the vehicle was affiliated. The Constitutional Court partially annulled Additional Art. 2/III of the Law on Road Traffic by emphasizing the principle of individual criminal responsibility (Turkish Constitution Art. 38/VII). According to the Constitutional Court, it is only the driver who would be expected to know whether the vehicle has the necessary permits and licenses required to transport passengers with a commercial purpose. Therefore, the court concluded that the fine envisaged for the driver is constitutional. On the other hand, the parts of the article imposing sanctions on other persons (the owner of the vehicle and the persons in charge of the enterprise or business with which the vehicle is affiliated), irrespective of whether they had permitted or knew of the unlicensed use of the vehicle, were found to be unconstitutional and annulled [Yetim (2015, pp. 639–640)].

[30]Aykanat (2017); Sol Gazete (2016); NTV (2016); Can (2016); Habertürk (2016); Kurt (2016).

[31]The president of the Association of United Taxi Drivers announced that according to the statistics provided by the General Directorate of Security, 912 vehicles were banned from traffic in four months [NTV (2016)].

[32]Akıllı Gündem (2017).

licensed,[33] further asserting that they should not be fined pursuant to Additional Art. 2 of the Law on Road Traffic.[34] A few days later, Uber released a press statement explaining that the instruction issued by the General Directorate of Security targeted vehicles operating without a license and therefore would not concern Uber. Uber announced that all vehicles operating within its auspices were licensed to transport passengers. It was also stated in the press release that Uber's name was not mentioned in the instruction issued by the General Directorate of Security.[35] In an interview,[36] the general manager of Uber Turkey, Neyran Bahadırlı, stated that vehicles registered with their platform belonged to tourism companies, offered VIP transportation, and had the necessary licenses. Upon being asked about the sanctions imposed on drivers and passengers, Bahadırlı responded that it was not Uber but the tourism companies who were subjected to those fines and that they were challenging said fines in court.

The licenses in question were the so-called D2 licenses issued by the Ministry of Transport, Maritime Affairs, and Communication,[37] holders of which have the right to engage in commercial and unscheduled transportation services (By-Law on Road Transport, Art. 6/4/b). The vehicles also had a permit for the itineraries of tourism service shuttles (*Turizm Servis Aracı Güzergâh İzin Belgesi*) issued by municipalities.[38]

In cases where the imposed fines were challenged, decisions by first instance courts were not uniform. Some annulled the fines, whereas others approved them. The Regional Administrative Court (*Bölge İdare Mahkemesi*) of Istanbul, on the other hand, ruled in most of its decisions that use of the said licenses for transportation via Uber's application did not violate Additional Art. 2 of the Law on Road Traffic. Where first instance courts annulled the fines imposed pursuant to this article, the Regional Administrative Court approved those decisions.[39] On the other hand, in cases where

[33] It is argued that this statement alone could constitute unfair competition pursuant to Art. 55/1(a)(2) [Eroğlu (2019, pp. 371–440, 395]; see Sect. 6 below for more on unfair competition.

[34] Yamak (2017), Sol Gazete (2016), NTV (2016).

[35] Milliyet (2016), DigitalAge (2016).

[36] Mumay (2017).

[37] As of 09.07.2018, the organizational structure of the Ministry was changed along with its name. It is now called the Ministry of Transport and Infrastructure.

[38] The Council of State (*Danıştay*) ruled that the existence of a D2 license per se does not render transportation within municipality borders lawful. Permissions from the relevant municipality are also required (Council of State, 15th Chamber, 04.12.2015, 6728/8471; Council of State, 15th Chamber, 06.11.2015, 5047/7089).

[39] Regional Administrative Court of Istanbul, 8th Chamber, 24.04.2017, 739/631; Regional Administrative Court of Istanbul, 8th Chamber, 31.05.2017, 766/875; Regional Administrative Court of Istanbul, 8th Chamber, 31.05.2017, 876/876; Regional Administrative Court of Istanbul, 8th Chamber, 28.03.2017, 428/488; Regional Administrative Court of Istanbul, 8th Chamber, 28.03.2017, 379/485; Regional Administrative Court of Istanbul, 8th Chamber, 26.04.2017, 651/675; Regional Administrative Court of Istanbul, 8th Chamber, 10.02.2017, 132/157; Regional Administrative Court of Istanbul, 8th Chamber, 11.01.2017, 2016/396, 2017/39; Regional Administrative Court of Istanbul, 8th Chamber, 21.03.2017, 349/395; Regional Administrative Court of Istanbul, 8th Chamber, 24.04.2017, 756/635; Regional Administrative Court of Istanbul, 8th Chamber, 18.04.2017, 346/609. The court quashed a decision by the first instance court indicating

fines were approved by the first instance court, the Regional Administrative Court quashed those decisions, emphasizing the existence of the license.[40]

In most of these decisions, a dissenting opinion existed, emphasizing that the said permit was issued for tourism services and that its existence per se did not render the service in line with Additional Art. 2 of the Law on Road Traffic. Accordingly, a driver should be able to present a contract concluded with a hotel, travel agent, or tourism company and an approved list of passengers. Since these documents were not presented by UberXL drivers, the dissenting opinions concluded that the annulment by the court of first instance was unlawful and the sanctions should be upheld.

Some of the decisions by the same court[41] stated that only sanctions regarding the permit for the itineraries of tourism service shuttles could be imposed in these cases. Those sanctions are regulated by the Directive on Service Shuttles (*Servis Araçları Yönergesi*)[42] issued by the Istanbul Metropolitan Municipality. In a decision by the UKOME on 31.10.2017 (No. 2017/7-7),[43] it is explicitly stated that any issued permit does not grant all of the vehicle's operations the permission of the municipalities, as required by Additional Art. 2 of the Law on Road Traffic. The issued permit shall cover the operation in question. Accordingly, taxi or personnel transportation cannot be carried out with a permit issued for tourism service transportation. With this decision, the UKOME decided to add a new sanction to the Directive on Service Shuttles. Pursuant to Art. 10/h of the directive, use of the permit for the itineraries of tourism service shuttles beyond the specified purpose of the issued permit will result in the cancelation of the permit, and the same permit cannot be issued to that person again for six months.

As these developments show, the compliance of Uber's activities with regulations for transportation services was uncertain for some time. Although the vehicles hailed from Uber's application were licensed, the D2 license and the permit for the itineraries of tourism service shuttles were not meant to be a service equivalent to services provided by commercial taxis,[44] and, therefore, the transportation activities facilitated by Uber could be construed as illegal.[45] The use of vehicles for purposes other than their registered one, as regulated by Additional Art. 2 of the Law on Road Traffic, constitutes a misdemeanor under Turkish law.[46]

---

that the permit for the itineraries of tourism shuttles had expired on the day the fine was imposed (Regional Administrative Court of Istanbul, 8th Chamber, 26.04.2017, 740/669).

[40]E.g., Regional Administrative Court of Istanbul, 8th Chamber, 16.05.2017, 935/796. Exceptional case, wherein the court approved the first instance court's decision to approve the fine imposed upon the driver: Regional Administrative Court of Istanbul, 8th Chamber, 17.10.2017, 2214/1691.

[41]E.g., Regional Administrative Court of Istanbul, 8th Chamber, 20.06.2017, 1092/1077; Regional Administrative Court of Istanbul, 8th Chamber, 26.09.2017, 1290/1452; Regional Administrative Court of Istanbul, 8th Chamber, 08.11.2017, 2246/1998; Regional Administrative Court of Istanbul, 8th Chamber, 08.11.2017, 2231/2000.

[42]İstanbul Büyükşehir Belediyesi (2007).

[43]İstanbul Büyükşehir Belediyesi (2017).

[44]İnci (2018, p. 37).

[45]Ekşi (2019, pp. 299–301).

[46]Yenerer Çakmut (2019, pp. 347–369, 355–358).

Finally, in the second half of 2018, a series of events took place that made the government's stance regarding Uber's compliance with transportation regulations clear. Art. 30/4 of the By-Law on Road Transport was amended twice, first to include new sanctions for those persons who let others use their licenses for activities falling outside the scope of the purpose and then later to reduce those sanctions.[47] After the first amendment,[48], the licenses of persons violating this rule twice within a calendar year were to be revoked and such persons shall not be granted the same license again for two years. It has been reported that this amendment was intended to curb Uber's activities[49] and was passed upon Prime Minister Binali Yıldırım's instruction.[50] Just a day before that, President Erdoğan had stated that Uber was not different from "pirate" (unlicensed) taxis and would not be allowed under their governance.[51] On 01.06.2018, President Erdoğan clearly stated that providing an alternative service to commercial taxis with a D2 license is illegal under Turkish law.[52] These developments, coupled with the unfair competition suit brought against Uber, which is analyzed below, eventually forced Uber to withdraw its UberXL service from Turkey. The aforementioned sanctions were recently loosened with a second amendment.[53]

4 Identifying Uber's Legal Relationship with the Driver and the Passenger: What Is Uber? An Employer, a Transportation Service Provider, or Merely an Intermediary?

Identifying the legal nature of Uber's relationships with the passenger and the driver is important for determining both Uber's compliance with transportation regulations and grounds for potential liability toward its drivers, passengers, and third parties.

---

[47] Ekşi (2019, p. 295), Yücel (2019, pp. 461–516, 465).

[48] By-Law Amending the By-Law on Road Transport, Art. 5 (OG, 25.05.2018, No. 30431).

[49] Ekşi (2019, p. 299).

[50] T24 (2018), Hürriyet (2018).

[51] T24 (2019a).

[52] T24 (2019b).

[53] By-Law Amending the By-Law on Road Transport, Art. 10 (OG, 15.11.2019, No. 30949).

4.1 *Uber: A Transportation Service Provider or an Intermediary?*

Uber has always claimed that it does not offer transportation services but merely provides a platform for bringing the parties of a transportation contract together.[54] If this argument was to be accepted, Uber would be acting as an intermediary. If that were the case, as an intermediary Uber could qualify as a broker (*simsar, tellal*), a commissioner (*komisyoncu*), or an agent (*acente*) for passenger transportation.[55]

Uber's argument that it is merely an intermediary is rejected by most scholars.[56] The fact that Uber can determine an essential element of the transportation contract, i.e., the fare, constitutes the main argument for rejecting it. The statement in Uber's user terms is also not of significance, since pursuant to Art. 19 of the Turkish Code of Obligations,[57] the nature of a contract is determined by the real intentions of parties, not by the words used. Accordingly, Uber should be regarded as a transportation service provider or shortly a carrier (*taşıyıcı*).[58]

4.2 *Uber as an Employer?*

Another debated issue about Uber's legal status concerns its relationship with its drivers (or the licensed companies that carry out the transportation). The contract between Uber and the drivers can either be classified as an employment contract or a transportation contract. In the latter alternative, the driver would be a subcarrier (*alt taşıyıcı*).[59] To our knowledge, there are no reported cases decided by Turkish courts on the nature of the relationship between Uber and the drivers.

The main element distinguishing employment contracts from other contracts where a service is provided is subordination (dependency).[60] In a typical employment relationship, the subordination element is very dominant. The employee is

[54]The following statement is included in Uber's user terms: "For the avoidance of doubt: Uber itself does not provide transportation services, and Uber is not a transportation carrier. It is up to the transportation provider to offer transportation services, which may be requested through the use of the Application and/or the Service. Uber only acts as an intermediary between you and the transportation provider. The provision of the transportation services by the transportation provider to you is therefore subject to the agreement (to be) entered into between you and the transportation provider. Uber shall never be a party to such agreement" (https://www.uber.com/legal/tr/document/?name=general-terms-of-use&country=turkey&lang=tr. Accessed 17 Mar 2020).

[55]For a more detailed discussion on whether Uber is merely an intermediary, see Sect. 6 of this chapter.

[56]Kaya (2019b, p. 305), Yücel (2019, p. 471), İnci (2018, p. 36).

[57]Law No. 6098 (OG, 04.02.2011, No. 27836).

[58]For a more detailed discussion on whether Uber qualifies as a carrier pursuant to TCC, see Sect. 6 of this chapter.

[59]Kaya (2019b, p. 311), Yücel (2019, p. 472).

[60]See Centel (2017, p. 69).

bound by orders and instructions issued by the employer and is constantly under supervision. The degree of dependency is not necessarily this high in all employment relationships. Atypical employment relationships have become more common, with technological and economic developments[61] gradually influencing the concept of dependency.[62] Due to this development, an accessorial criterion is adopted. Accordingly, it is sufficient for a person to qualify as an employee if they work for the benefit of another person (employer) under the latter's organization.[63] The relationship between Uber and its drivers could therefore be qualified as an employment relationship, as it fulfills this accessorial criterion.[64] It has also been argued that a case-by-case analysis is necessary for determining the nature of the relationship.[65] Where the vehicle is owned by a company or where the owner's activities are not labor-intensive, the relationship would not be one of employment due to lack of dependency.[66] If this distinction is adopted, Uber cannot be regarded as an employer due to lack of dependency, as in Turkey, it was mostly tourism companies that owned the vehicles operating within Uber's system.[67]

5 Uber's Liability for Damages Caused During the Provision of Transportation Services

5.1 Contractual Liability

If Uber is deemed a transportation service provider (carrier), which, as explained, is the prevailing opinion under Turkish law, it may be held liable if the passenger incurs damages due to a contractual breach. Pursuant to Arts. 6/3 and 7/1 of the Law on Road Transport, the carrier is obliged to provide secure and comfortable transportation for passengers. Liability of carriers in passenger transportation is regulated under Arts. 914–916 of the Turkish Commercial Code (TCC).[68] TCC Art. 914/2 states that the carrier shall compensate damages incurred by passengers due to an accident. In the case of death, those who are deprived of the passenger's support can also claim damages. The carrier can only avoid liability if they prove that the damage occurred due to a reason that was unavoidable even if they and their auxiliaries acted with utmost care. The TCC also contains special rules on carrier liability in cases

[61] Ibid. (p. 69).

[62] Erol (2019, pp. 69 ff).

[63] Centel (2017, p. 69), Yücel (2019, pp. 474–475).

[64] Yücel (2019, p. 474), Erol (2019, p. 176 n. 536, pp. 181–183): The author gives Uber's operation as an example of zero-hour contracts, where he concludes that the dependency element is present.

[65] Kaya (2019b, p. 317).

[66] Ibid.

[67] Ibid.

[68] Law No. 6102 (OG, 14.02.2011, No. 27846).

of cancelation, delay, or interruption of transportation (TCC Art. 907 ff.). For the carrier's liability in the case of damaged or lost baggage, TCC Art. 912/1 refers to rules on the transportation of goods (TCC Arts. 875–886).[69] It should be noted that the exemption clauses in Uber's user terms are legally insignificant, as TCC Art. 854 deems provisions exempting the carrier of liability invalid.[70]

Another significant issue as to Uber's contractual liability pertains to consumer protection law. Uber's contract with the passenger undoubtedly qualifies as a consumer transaction, as Art. 3/l of the Law on Consumer Protection (LoCP)[71] lists transportation contracts as an example of consumer transactions. Furthermore, the passenger party to such a contract would usually be a consumer as per Art. 3/k of the LoCP, defining a consumer as any real (natural) or legal (juridical) person acting outside the scope of a commercial and professional activity, and Uber would qualify as a service provider pursuant to LoCP Art. 3/ı.[72] Therefore, the question arises of whether the rules on liability for supplying defective services (LoCP Arts. 13–16) would be applicable to transportation contracts. According to case law[73] and the prevailing opinion in the doctrine,[74] the rules on the liability of the carrier regulated in the TCC preclude the application of the rules on defective services in the LoCP. The question of whether these disputes are to be resolved by commercial or consumer courts is also problematic. Case law on this issue is not uniform. Pursuant to LoCP Art. 73/1, consumer courts have competence on all disputes arising out of consumer transactions, and LoCP Art. 83/2 states that the existence of special provisions on a transaction does not per se preclude the competence of consumer courts if one of the parties is a consumer. Based on these provisions, in most of its decisions, the Court of Cassation (*Yargıtay*) ruled that these cases would be heard by consumer courts.[75]

[69] For a detailed explanation on these rules and their application to Uber's services, see Yücel (2019, pp. 487–492).

[70] Kaya (2019b, p. 310), Yücel (2019, pp. 487–488).

[71] Law No. 6502 (OG, 28.11.2013, No. 28835).

[72] Yücel (2019, pp. 482–484).

[73] E.g., Court of Cassation, 11th Civil Chamber, 12.09.2018, 2016-13994/2018-5222; Court of Cassation, 11th Civil Chamber, 06.02.2017, 2016-890/2017-586.

[74] Aksoy (2015, pp. 305–334, 321–326), Bahtiyar and Biçer (2016, pp. 395–436, 417–418), Baş Süzel (2018, pp. 966-998, 973–974), Yücel (2019, pp. 500–502).

[75] E.g., Court of Cassation, 11th Civil Chamber, 20.08.2018, 2016-12033/2018-4586; Court of Cassation, 11th Civil Chamber, 04.10.2017, 2016-7393/2017-5025; Court of Cassation, 11th Civil Chamber, 11.04.2016, 2015-15205/2016-3941; Court of Cassation, 20th Civil Chamber, 02.06.2016, 4303/6248. An exceptional decision by the Court of Cassation, where the commercial court was found to be competent. The legal grounds of this decision are not ascertainable from its text (Court of Cassation, 20th Civil Chamber, 21.11.2016, 11654/11009). Also see for analysis of this decision Aksoy (2017, pp. 295–301, 295–296).

5.2 Quasi-contractual Liability: Liability Based on Reliance

It must be noted that a contractual claim would most likely fail if Uber's argument to be a mere intermediary were accepted. In that case, Uber's obligations would be limited to providing a platform and facilitating the formation of a contract between the passenger and the driver, who would be the carrier. In this legal construction, Uber's contractual liability could only arise if a breach of said obligations led to a damage on the passenger's part. A quasi-contractual[76] claim may, however, be available due to liability on reliance (*güven sorumluluğu*). A general[77] regulation on liability based on reliance is not present under Turkish law (cf. § 311/III of the German Civil Code) but is recognized by the doctrine and case law[78] as an extension of the good faith and fair dealing principle regulated under Art. 2 of the Turkish Civil Code. The requirements for such liability are as follows: (1) a person shall influence the formation of a contract between others; (2) such a person needs to have an interest in the formation of that contract; (3) at least one of the contracting parties should have relied on this person while forming the contract.[79] A textbook example is the second-hand car dealer, who brings interested parties together and does not become party to the sales contract.[80] If the buyer suffers damage due to malfunctioning brakes of the second-hand car, it is argued that the car dealer can be held liable, because the buyer entered into the contract with the seller relying on the car dealer and the requirements above have been met. Uber's position is not that different. It does indeed create a reliance among passengers by emphasizing that it offers a safe travel option using driver profiles.

5.3 Tortious Liability

Uber's liability for damages may also arise out of tort. This would be the case, for example, if the driver is regarded as an employee of Uber.[81] In this case, TCO Art. 66 would be applicable and Uber would be held responsible as an employer provided that the damage occurred during (or in relation to) the work, i.e., transportation service.[82]

---

[76]Although the nature of liability based on reliance is a debated issue, the prevailing opinion is that in such cases, rules on contractual liability are applicable. It should also be noted that Turkish legal doctrine perceives the liability based on reliance as a tool to create liability in cases where contractual, tortious, and other accepted forms of liability (e.g., *culpa in contrahendo*) prove to be insufficient for the protection of a person who rightly relied on another and suffered loss due to a breach of this reliance [Kocayusufpaşaoğlu (2008, § 49N. 27, n. 50), Serozan (2014, § 19N. 3)].

[77]TCC Art. 209 regulates liability based on reliance in a group of companies.

[78]Court of Cassation, 13th Civil Chamber, 26.01.2012, 2011-16549/ 2012-1177.

[79]Serozan (2014, § 19N. 3).

[80]Ibid.

[81]See 4.2. above.

[82]Yücel (2019, pp. 506–507).

Uber may only escape this liability by proving that it has shown the utmost care in selecting, instructing, and supervising the driver and also that it has taken every necessary step in its working organization to ensure that such damages do not occur.

Even if the driver is not regarded as Uber's employee, Uber's tortious liability may be based on Art. 85/1 of the Law on Road Traffic. Accordingly, the so-called "operator" and "the owner of the enterprise, with which the operator is affiliated" are strictly liable for pecuniary damages suffered due to the operation of motor vehicles. The operator of the vehicle is in principle the owner. However, if the vehicle is leased, borrowed, or given as a pledge for a long period of time, the leasee, the borrower, or the pledgee is deemed to be the operator (Art. 3 of the Law on Road Traffic).[83] Since Uber is usually not the owner of the vehicle and it neither leases nor borrows it, it could not be held liable as an operator. However, it is an interesting question whether Uber would qualify as the owner of the enterprise with which the operator is affiliated. This concept is defined under Art. 3 of the Law on Road Traffic as the owner of the enterprise that issues tickets or the owner of the enterprise whose title is used during the issuance of the tickets. Although Uber does not issue any tickets, it could qualify as the owner of the enterprise with which the operator is affiliated, as the fare is directly paid to Uber.[84] Based on previous case law, it seems that this approach may also be adopted by Turkish courts. In a case decided by the Turkish Court of Cassation, a vehicle operating under the name of a cargo company had caused damages in an accident. The Court of Cassation held the cargo company liable for damages as the owner of the enterprise with which the operator was affiliated, although the cargo company was neither the owner of the vehicle nor the employer of the driver.[85]

It should be noted that strict liability based on Art. 85 of the Law on Road Traffic could arise in relation to damages incurred by both the passenger and third parties. Uber can only avoid this liability by proving that the accident occurred due to an act of God (force majeure) or gross fault on the damaged person's or third party's part, without the influence of a defect in the vehicle or fault on Uber's or its auxiliaries' part (Art. 86 of the Law on Road Traffic).

---

[83] For more on the concept of operator, see Oğuzman and Öz (2020, N. 601–605), Nomer (1992, pp. 36–89, 49 ff).

[84] Yücel (2019, p. 93).

[85] Court of Cassation, 4th Civil Chamber, 28.04.2009, 2009-3997/2009-6066.

6 United Taxi Drivers Association and Istanbul Artisanal Chamber of Motorists Versus Uber: Is the Ride-Sharing Company an Unfair Competitor?

6.1 In General

Similar to many other countries that have adopted a liberal economic system, the Turkish Constitution has also ensured the right to carry on commerce under fair and free competitive market conditions. While Art. 48 of the Turkish Constitution allows everyone to establish private enterprises freely, Art. 167 expressly states the duty of the state to prevent the formation of cartels as a result of agreements or de facto practices.[86]

However, it should be emphasized that the right to carry on commerce and competition has its limitations and restrictions.[87] First of all, Law No. 4054 on the Protection of Competition (Competition Act) imposes rules to prevent collusions that restrict competition and ban the abuse of dominant position.[88] Another important source allowing and protecting fair competition is the unfair competition law. The rules regarding unfair competition aim to regulate the restrictions on the right to engage in commercial activity and to identify the legal actions to be taken in the case of violation of these rules.[89] Although unfair competition is regulated in both the TCO[90] and the TCC, it is widely accepted that the applicable provisions are solely set in the TCC.[91]

Pursuant to Art. 54/1 of the TCC, the general purpose of the provisions regarding unfair competition set in this section is to ensure fair and inviolate competition for the sake of all parties involved. Art. 54/2 of the TCC gives an indirect definition[92] of unfair competition by stating "*Any behavior or commercial practices which are misleading or against good faith in any other way, that affect the relationship between competitors, or between suppliers and consumers, are deemed unfair and against*

[86] Teoman (2006, pp. 449, 450), Kendigelen (2018, p. 112).

[87] Kendigelen (2018, p. 112).

[88] Nomer Ertan (2019, pp. 545–623, pp. 547–548). Art. 54 of the TCC defines unfair competition broadly, leading to an overlap between competition law and unfair competition law [Yasaman (2012, pp. 33–44, p. 33)].

[89] Nomer Ertan (2019, p. 547).

[90] Circulating false information or making such declarations or acting against good faith is accepted as unfair competition under Art. 57 of the TCO, leading to a false interpretation stating that the articles of the TCC on unfair competition are reserved for commercial affairs, so the articles of the TCO will be applicable to non-commercial affairs and the articles of the TCC will be applicable to commercial affairs. However, since the TCC does not make a distinction between commercial and non-commercial affairs, it should be accepted that only the rules in the TCC are applicable to unfair competition. See Teoman (2006, pp. 451–453).

[91] Teoman (2006, pp. 452–453), Poroy and Yasaman (2004 p. 281); Nomer Ertan (2016, p. 27); see also Court of Cassation, 11th Civil Chamber, 21.02.2010, 2008-9072/2010-591.

[92] Kendigelen (2018, p. 113).

the law." Since this paragraph expressly states so, it is not necessary for the parties of unfair competition lawsuits to be competitors.[93] In most of its decisions, the Court of Cassation has also ruled in the same way.

For instance, in a case before the court, a trade association of hairdressers and manicurists claimed that the defendant was providing services for a price below the official fee tariff and therefore asked for the declaration and prevention of unfair competition. The court of first instance ruled that the defendant was not under an obligation to follow the fee tariff set by the plaintiff since the defendant was a merchant and not an artisan. However, the Court of Cassation stated that trade associations can bring lawsuits against anyone based on "violation of business conditions" and reversed the decision of the court of first instance since it failed to evaluate whether or not the act in question constituted unfair competition.[94]

Art. 55 of the TCC sets forth the most commonly observed examples of unfair competition. Accordingly, if an act carries one of the qualities provided in Art. 55, it unquestionably constitutes unfair competition. On the other hand, if the act does not fall under the examples provided in Art. 55, either directly or through analogy,[95] then an assessment should be made in accordance with the general provision given in Art. 54.[96] Since fault is not a requirement for an act to constitute unfair competition[97] under Turkish law, the examples given in Art. 55 must be interpreted with caution. For instance, according to Art. 55/1, b-1, guiding a customer to violate his/her contract with another party in order to conclude a contract with that customer himself/herself particularly constitutes unfair competition. It is obvious that termination of an agreement is a legal right for everyone and also that it is necessary for there to be competition between enterprises offering similar goods or services. For this provision to be applicable, it is not sufficient to give some information about the products and services and the customer's right to terminate the agreement.[98] Directing a party of the contract to breach can only constitute unfair competition if the directing party is aware of the contract's existence and shows a conscious effort to have the contract breached or terminated.[99]

The most relevant example listed under Art. 55 is the violation of business conditions. Pursuant to Art. 55/1(e), "*violating business conditions, especially the ones imposed on competitors by law or an agreement or the business conditions that are common in a certain profession or field*" constitutes unfair competition. Business

[93] Yasaman (2012, p. 35); Okutan Nilsson (2014, p. 111–120, p. 113). Even though the former TCC did not contain a specific provision like that, it was also accepted by the doctrine that the parties could be non-competitors. See Teoman (2006, p. 455), Kendigelen (2012, p. 80).

[94] Court of Cassation, 11th Civil Chamber, 08.05.2018, 2016-11557/ 2018-3347; see also Court of Cassation, General Assembly of Civil Chambers, 11.12.2018, 2017-117/2018-1883.

[95] Teoman (2006, p. 457).

[96] Kendigelen (2018, p. 82).

[97] Teoman (2006, p. 456).

[98] Nomer Ertan (2016, p. 290).

[99] Paksoy (2018, pp. 196–197).

conditions do not necessarily have to be stipulated through written rules[100]; it is possible to accept customary rules and professional rules of conduct as business conditions as well.[101] Defining highly strict business conditions and accepting the violation of these rules as unfair competition would prevent new entries into the market, which is against the aim of rules concerning unfair competition and competition law. On the other hand, it should be noted that since taxi services are regulated by administrative authorities, there are restrictions on entering the market, prices are regulated, and there are rules in order to ensure the safety of the trip,[102] it is already not possible for any actor who wishes to do so to freely enter the market.[103] Therefore, when evaluating whether Uber violated business conditions, attention should be paid to these two points, especially when commercial customs and professional rules are to be recognized as business conditions.

Some examples of unfair competition as a violation of business conditions in judicial decisions are as follows: producing unlabeled chili pepper containing aflatoxin above the maximum allowed amount without a food permit and a production permit, which is against the Turkish Food Codex[104]; selling bread at a price below the price set by trade associations[105]; selling cosmetics that lack instructions for use in Turkish in their packaging and therefore are against cosmetics regulations[106]; going off-route and setting a price below the fare while carrying passengers in a minibus, which is against the By-Law on Road Transport[107]; starting a business without the required license[108]; employing workers without social insurance[109]; violating the

[100] Although the provision only mentions violation of the law as unfair competition, in the literature, it is accepted that regulations, by-laws, and communiqués are also within the scope of the provision, and the rules can be found in regulations concerning labor law, tax law, and environmental law. See Nomer Ertan (2019, p. 597).

[101] Court of Cassation, 11th Civil Chamber, 21.11.2017, 2016-4741/2016-6386.

[102] Art. 4 of the By-Law on Road Transport states that drivers operating a motor vehicle on the road must have the relevant professional competence certificate. See Ekşi (2019, p. 297) on Uber drivers failing to meet this condition. In our opinion, Art. 5 of the Law on Road Transport obligates all drivers using commercial vehicles in order to transport goods and passengers to obtain professional competence certificates without making any distinctions. On the other hand, in order to eliminate the uncertainty regarding whether taxi drivers are subject to this obligation, the Ministry of Interior sent a letter to all governorships stating that drivers who are transporting passengers within municipality borders will not be required to have competence certificates (SRCs). In 2018, there were news stating that taxi drivers were no longer subject to the SRC obligation. See https://www.guneydoguekspres.com/gundem/src-belgesi-zorunlugu-kalkti-taksiciler-sevindi-h2369.html and http://www.sanalbasin.com/yuk-ve-yolcu-tasimaciliginda-src-zorunlulugu-kalkti-28313649/.

[103] See Ekşi (2019, p. 289) for American law.

[104] Court of Cassation, 11th Civil Chamber, 09.12.2003, 2003-5014/2003-11697.

[105] Court of Cassation, 11th Civil Chamber, 11.12.2017, 2016-8790/2017-7058; 26.11.2018, 2017-1916/2018-7379.

[106] Court of Cassation, 11th Civil Chamber, 08.07.2013, 2012-14895/2013-14465.

[107] Court of Cassation, 11th Civil Chamber, 17.02.2016, 2015-7249/2016-1583.

[108] Can (2007, pp. 151–176, 165).

[109] Teoman (2006, pp. 466–467).

rules regarding working hours set in the Labor Law[110]; and Booking.com, a website acting as an intermediary in marketing hotels in Turkey, carrying out its activities without paying taxes in Turkey.[111]

6.2 *Unfair Competition Case Against Uber in Turkey*

As explained above, the services being provided under the name UberTAXI have not been challenged in terms of violating unfair competition law since the UberTAXI system only uses taxis with a license and UberTAXI could only be accepted as an intermediary. However, the United Taxi Drivers Association and Istanbul Artisanal Chamber of Motorists filed a suit against Uber in the 10th Commercial Court of First Instance where the Consumer Protection Association became an intervener-plaintiff for UberXL's service.

The plaintiff claimed that the systems used for calling a taxi or an UberXL vehicle are not different and that the UberXL system does not contain information on all passengers or information on the users and their national identity numbers. It was argued that, although the defendant claimed that the operated vehicles have D2 licenses, based on Art. 40/3 of the By-Law on Road Transport, these vehicles cannot operate in such a system, and therefore, the service provided by UberXL is against the law. The plaintiff also asked the court to decide on an interim injunction preventing access to the UberXL system.

The defendant stated that there are significant differences between the services provided by taxi operators and UberXL D2 operators. For example, UberXL D2 operators do not pick up passengers from the side of the road, only accepting passengers through the application or via established companies; the service significantly differs from the service provided by taxi operators in terms of quality, luxury, comfort, and pricing; UberXL D2 operators use large and usually newer and more luxurious cars such as the Mercedes Vito or Volkswagen Caravelle instead of small sedan vehicles; the vehicles of D2 operators must be at least $9 + 1$ pursuant to the relevant regulation; the law does not set forth a specific fare or pricing method, and unlike with taximeters, passengers who use UberXL D2 can see the price they are going to pay before the trip; and UberXL D2 operators possess D2 licenses and permits for the itineraries of tourism service shuttles. Thus, it was asked that the court rejects the interim injunction request.

The court of first instance rejected the interim injunction request, stating that the injunction decision would provide the same legal benefit as the final decision, that the plaintiff tried to gain the legal benefit to be awarded as a result of the trial with an injunction request, and that interim injunctions cannot award the same results as the trial itself.

---

[110]Nomer Ertan (2019, p. 597).

[111]For the analysis of the decision, see Eroğlu (2019, pp. 400–401).

In its appeal application, the plaintiff stated that UberXL services do not follow the mandatory working standards in the market (i.e., they do not obtain a taxi license/plate); they do not follow the legal taxi meter fare and they apply price policies of their own liking; unlike touristic transportation, the UberXL service allows passengers whose identities are unknown at the beginning of the trip to call a ride at any given time through the mobile application and the UberXL vehicle will pick such passengers up from their location, which means that the service is identical to licensed taxi transportation; the defendant was trying to benefit from the D2 license outside of its intended purpose, while with the aim of preventing such unlawful use the Ministry of Transport, Maritime Affairs, and Communication has established new regulations that require the names and national ID numbers of passengers to be transported with a D2 license to be entered into the Ministry's system at least one hour before the start of the trip; Art. 61 of the TCC includes a special provision with regard to interim injunction requests and allows the party that is subject to unfair competition to request the prevention of unfair competition, and since this is a special provision concerning interim injunctions, it shall have priority; various penalties concerning the Uber application are already being implemented; and with the interim injunction, the plaintiff is not trying to gain the legal benefit to be awarded at the end of the trial beforehand, but rather aims to prevent the loss that thousands of taxi drivers would endure during the course of the trial, amounting to millions of Turkish lira.

The regional court of justice (i.e., the court of second instance functioning as a court of appeal) rejected the appeal application of the plaintiff unanimously, stating that pursuant to Art. 389 of the Code of Civil Procedure and the following articles, an interim injunction is a precautionary measure; the claims of the plaintiff require adjudication and the court of first instance, which is authorized to rule on the merits of the case, used its discretionary power in light of the submitted evidence to reject the interim injunction request; and the decision of the court of first instance was not against the law or public order.

The court appointed five experts on 20.02.2019 to determine whether the services provided by UberXL were related to taxi services. While the case was pending, Uber declared that it stopped its operations in Turkey on 31.05.2019. The expert report stated that no significant difference was found between the services provided by taxis and UberXL. In particular, when the operations of UberXL are taken into account, the experts argued that the service cannot be deemed as an information technology service; rather, the service can only be accepted within the transportation service sector due to its combination of transportation and IT elements, since finding customers is crucial for the service. The expert report also noted that D2 operators were used to provide taxi services, which require a license, and without that license, the carrying out of such services should be accepted as a violation of the "business conditions," an example of unfair competition under Art. 55/1(e) of the TCC. Finally, Uber's operations were stopped by the court on 16.10.2019.[112]

[112]Diken. http://www.diken.com.tr/ubere-erisim-engellendi/. Accessed 10 Mar 2020.

6.3 Assessment of the Case

The main debate surrounding this case is about determining the nature of the service that UberXL provides. Determining the service is important in order to identify the relevant regulations concerning that service and therefore to evaluate whether business conditions have been violated. The main argument raised by Uber is that their operations cannot be accepted as a transportation service and they should be deemed as an intermediary that provides information technology services. However, the legal experts appointed by the court were not convinced. Therefore, the service provided by UberXL should be discussed first, and after that, the question of whether identifying the service makes any difference in terms of violation of unfair competition provisions must be answered.

TCC defines a carrier as the person who undertakes transportation of goods or passengers (TCC, Art. 850/1). In cases where more than one person is involved in the transportation service, the Turkish Court of Cassation also regards those who have the authority to control and supervise the transportation service as carriers.[113] As the party determining and collecting the fare, it can easily be argued that Uber has significant control over the transportation service and should therefore be regarded as a transportation service provider.[114]

Were Uber to be qualified as a carrier, a second question arises whether its services are identical or similar to taxis. If the answer is affirmative, then Uber operating without the necessary license would be in violation of a business condition. Since Uber carries out the same service without obtaining the license and therefore gains a cost advantage, the transportation services of Uber will undoubtedly constitute unfair competition. Another important issue is the differences in pricing policy between taxis and UberXL services. In order to secure the financial accessibility of the service for average citizens, taxis are subject to maximum price limitations set by tariffs. However, Uber is able to achieve high profits with the price model it uses where supply is low and demand is high.[115] Additionally, obligations under tax and labor laws also increase the costs of taxi services.[116]

The ECJ[117] and courts in Germany[118] identified Uber's service as a transportation service since Uber is introducing itself to customers as a provider of taxi services,

---

[113]Court of Cassation, General Assembly of Civil Chambers, 27.06.2018, 504/1258: In this case, the court ruled that a foundation operating a school is the transportation service provider, where students were being transported in a rented vehicle, because the foundation had the authority to control and supervise the transportation service. Court of Cassation, 11th Civil Chamber, 02.12.2003, 4767/11386: In this case, the court quashed the decision by the first instance court stating that it should have investigated whether a transportation cooperative (one of the defendants) had the authority to control and supervise the transportation service and decided accordingly. Also see Kaya (2019b, pp. 302–303).

[114]Ibid. (p. 310).

[115]Mudrić (2019, pp. 57–83, 70).

[116]Ekşi (2019, p. 293).

[117]See ibid. (pp. 308–320) for the ECJ decision.

[118]See ibid. (p. 292) for the Berlin and Hamburg Federal Administrative Courts' decisions.

Uber's system prohibits customers from paying the driver directly, and the payment is made directly to Uber, which pays the driver after making a commission deduction.

On the other hand, Kişi, who evaluated Uber in terms of the sharing economy, listed the differences between Uber and traditional taxi services as follows: unlike traditional taxis, with Uber it is possible to make reservations through a smartphone and learn about drivers before they arrive; drivers who get low points in the scoring system are removed from the system; and payments via cash or credit card and also online payments are accepted.[119] The author also argued that since empty vehicles do not have to drive around in order to find customers, Uber is favorable in terms of traffic and fuel consumption, and also allows inactive licenses to be used efficiently.[120]

If we accept the fact that UberXL activities and taxi services differ significantly in terms of quality, luxury, comfort, and pricing and that UberXL services therefore cannot be replaced by taxi services, then Uber would not be violating the relevant business conditions applicable to taxis and unfair competition would thus not exist under Art. 55/1(e).[121] However, there would still be the need to make an assessment pursuant to the general provision under Art. 54. As explained above, the parties of unfair competition do not necessarily have to be competitors because the aim of unfair competition provisions is not to protect the economic interests of competitors, but rather to protect the economic order based on competition.[122] The Court of Cassation, in its decision where it ruled that collecting, marketing, and reselling glass packaging constituted unfair competition, stated that the parties do not have to be competitors. The court stated that the defendant who collected and marketed empty bottles both violated regulations on waste management and also reduced the market share of the plaintiff bottle producer, causing the plaintiff loss of profits. The court also decided that the act of the producer who filled empty bottles with its own juice was unfair competition, since it lowered its costs compared to its competitors against good faith.[123]

In order to make an assessment of this matter, it is necessary to determine the scope of the D2 license and whether or not it is possible to carry out UberXL services with a D2 license. D-type licenses are given to real or legal persons who carry out scheduled or unscheduled domestic passenger transportation services with a bus or personal transportation services, while a D2 license is given for commercial and unscheduled transportation. In one of its decisions, the Council of State stated that a D2 license does not authorize commercial passenger transportation within municipality borders

[119] Kişi (2018, pp. 57–68, 61). For a general evaluation on the benefits of Uber, see Yetim (2015, pp. 634–637).

[120] Ibid. See also Mudrić (2019, p. 150).

[121] For a view stating that the parties must be competitors in order for Art. 55/1 of the TCC to be implemented, see Eroğlu (2019, pp. 396–397).

[122] Court of Cassation, 11th Civil Chamber, 01.05.2001, 1828/3862.

[123] Ibid.

and does not eliminate the necessity to obtain a license and permit from the relevant municipality.[124]

The biggest legal challenge for Uber's use of D2 licenses in its operations is the 2018 amendment to Art. 30/4 of the By-Law on Road Transport. This provision introduced sanctions on D2 license owners who use their vehicles for purposes outside of the scope of the license, or let their vehicles be used for activities by other persons who do not hold a license. The provision states that in cases of violation, the license will be canceled. Additionally, pursuant to Art. 9/2 of the same regulation, transferring the license is also prohibited. This prevented Uber from carrying out its operations by using licenses belonging to other people.

The abovementioned provisions prevent the transfer and leasing of D2 licenses to persons without a license, and therefore, the question of whether Uber can obtain the necessary licenses must be answered. At this point, it is important to determine whether Uber acts as an intermediary or a transporter.[125] As an intermediary Uber could either qualify as a broker (*simsar, tellal*),[126] a commissioner (*komisyoncu*), or an agent (*acente*)[127] for passenger transportation.

First of all, Uber should not be considered a broker, since brokerage is distinguished from agencies by the temporary nature of the relationship with a specific client (here, the driver). Where such a relationship is of a continuous nature, the contract is qualified as one of an agency.[128]

Second, in the literature, it has been claimed that pursuant to Art. 10/3 of the Law on Road Transport,[129] Uber cannot carry out intermediacy services.[130] However,

[124]Council of State, 15th Chamber, 06.11.2015, 5047/7089. See also Regional Administrative Court of Istanbul, 8th Chamber, 13.03.2018, 2017-2596/2018-448. For the view evaluating UberXL carrying out its activities with a D2 license as unfair competition see Eroğlu (2019, p. 410).

[125]In 2014, when Uber was still preparing to enter the Turkish market, the Competition Authority stated in its decision regarding BiTaksi (which provides services similar to those of Uber, but taxis with licenses are used) that since the BiTaksi application does not require the phone number of the user, the user does not have to be close to a taxi stand and the location of the user is not required, the route to the destination is predetermined, it is possible to see which taxi is being used, and there is an English version of the application, "mobile taxi requesting applications could qualify as a market." [02.07.2014, 14-23/ 462-200].

[126]The following authors state that the relationship between Uber and the driver would be a contract of brokerage subject to Arts. 520 ff of the TCO if Uber's argument is accepted: Kaya (2019b, p. 304), Yücel (2019, p. 470). Also see Üçyıldız (2019, p. 54), where the author characterizes Uber as a broker.

[127]The following authors argue that providers of online platforms can generally be qualified as agents [Baş (2017, pp. 115–153, p. 133), Eroğlu (2019, pp. 406–407)]. However, he states that since most of the time the client is not a merchant, the articles of the TCC on agency cannot be implemented. See Eroğlu (2019, p. 407).

[128]Kaya (2019a, pp. 723–918, 788), Arkan (2019, pp. 220–221), Ansay and Önay (2014, pp. 47–58, 55).

[129]"*Commissioning is not allowed in passenger transportation.*".

[130]Ekşi (2019, p. 299).

in our opinion, the article in question prevents "commissioning"[131] in passenger transportation. The Law on Road Transport defines three separate activities under Art. 2, namely transportation, agency, and commissioning for transportation, thus Art. 10/3 of the Law on Road Transport does not ban acting as an agent in transportation.

Therefore, the question whether Uber qualifies as an agent still merits discussion. Uber's argument that it legally operates as an intermediary is only possible if Uber is an agent.[132] It must however be noted that Art. 10/1 of the Law on Road Transport requires agencies to have a transportation license if they are carrying out transportation services on their own behalf or make another party carry out these services on behalf of them.[133] It is also possible for agents to merely act as an intermediary. In that case agents would need a different license, regulated under Art. 6/5 of the By-Law on Road Transport. These so-called F-type licenses are given to real and legal persons who carry out agency services in passenger transportation for commercial purposes.

Thus, if the activities of Uber are deemed as agency activities, then the applicable provisions of the legislation will be different. In order for Uber's activities to be in line with the legislation, Uber must acquire the F-type license for acting as a mere agent. If Uber is providing transportation services on its own behalf, it must also obtain a transportation license. According to Art. 5 of the Law on Road Transport, an agency license is given to persons who possess professional reputability, as well as financial and professional competency. It must be noted that in principle, these licenses can only be granted to Turkish nationals or legal persons pursuant to Turkish law.[134] Foreigners can obtain the necessary licenses provided that they fulfill the conditions set forth by the Law on Direct Foreign Investments[135] and the conditions in the By-Law for Road Transport. Pursuant to the abovementioned legislation, there is no difference between the establishment of companies with foreign partners and capital and the establishment of companies with domestic partners and capital;[136] so, only companies established under the laws of the Republic of Turkey can obtain the license. Therefore, it is not possible for Uber Technologies Inc. or Uber BV to

[131] According to Art. 917 of the TCC, in commissioning agreements, the commissioner undertakes the transportation of objects. Therefore, concluding a commissioning agreement in passenger transportation is not possible due to the TCC. Similarly, Art. 2 of the Law on Road Transport defines transportation commissioners as persons who transport objects for a fee using their names but on behalf of clients.

[132] Agent, in the context of road transportation is defined as persons who constantly act as an agent in contracts concerning one or multiple transporters or make contracts on behalf of them in a certain place or region based on a contract as their profession without having a dependent relationship such as commercial representative, commercial agent, salesman, or employee (Art. 2 of Law on Road Transport).

[133] "*Persons who have an agency or transportation commissioning license cannot carry out transportation services on their own behalf or make others carry out these services on their own behalf without a transportation license.*".

[134] By-Law on Road Transport Art. 13/a–b; Ekşi (2019, pp. 298–299).

[135] Law No. 4875 (OG, 17.06.2003, No. 25141).

[136] Ekşi (2019, p. 300).

obtain a license.[137] The only way Uber could have operated in accordance with the law in Turkey was if it had established a subsidiary with a registered office in Turkey and this subsidiary obtained a license.

In short, even if Uber's activities are accepted as intermediary services, as claimed by Uber, there would still be a violation of the law since, as mentioned above, this service cannot be provided without an "agency license" and in some cases "transportation license." Even if the provisions that have been violated cannot be accepted as business conditions under Art. 55/1(e), there would still be unfair competition due to the violation of Art. 54 of the TCC, since such violation would reduce taxis' market share.

Another relevant example of unfair competition provided under Art. 55 of the TCC, worthy of discussion, concerns the determination of price. Since Uber's application utilizes the dynamic price increase model based on the nexus of supply and demand, it is possible to charge even lower prices compared to taxis.[138] In this case, the question is whether or not Uber is violating Art. 55/1(a)(6) of the TCC.[139] It must be noted that everyone has the right to determine the price of products and services they are offering. Even selling a product below its production cost cannot be deemed a violation of the unfair competition rules.[140] However, if a store creates the impression that it sells all its products at lower prices in order to make customers shop there, then this provision will be relevant. For this provision to be applicable, there should be regular sales at a price below the supply price, this fact should be emphasized in advertisements, and, in this manner, the customers should be misled.[141] It is not possible to state that these conditions have taken place in Uber's case.

Finally, regarding the decision on the interim injunctions, it is not possible to agree with the reasoning of the court. Art. 61 of the TCC includes a special provision for interim injunctions in cases of unfair competition. According to this provision, the court can rule for the "*elimination of the current situation caused by unfair competition, prevention of unfair competition and correction of the false or misleading declarations.*" This rule constitutes an exception to the general principle of procedural law[142] that forbids interim injunctions that award the same result as the final judgment would. However, in cases of unfair competition, the doctrine argues that irreversible injunctions, such as the destruction of products violating trademark or

---

[137] Ibid.

[138] See Mudrić (2019, p. 70).

[139] "*Presenting some goods, business products and activities below their supply price more than once, emphasizing this fact in advertisements and therefore misleading customers about the ability of itself and its competitors; if the sale price is lower than the supply price of similar goods, business products and activities purchased at similar volumes, then the existence of misleading is accepted as a presumption; if the defendant proves the real supply price, then this price will be taken into consideration.*"

[140] Nomer Ertan (2016, p. 223).

[141] Court of Cassation, 11th Civil Chamber, 11.12.2017, 2016-8790/ 2017-7058. For the dissenting opinion: Can (2007, pp. 151–175, 161–162), Yasaman (2012, pp. 38–39).

[142] For an overview of this principle and its exceptions, see Deren Yıldırım (2002, pp. 9–11).

execution proceedings of pecuniary claims, should not be ruled.[143] Since Uber will be able to continue its activities if the court decides that UberXL activities do not constitute unfair competition, the interim injunction is not irreversible in this case.

7 Conclusion

One of the main debates concerning Uber is the legal nature of the services that it offers. Uber's argument, that it operates as an intermediary, seems valid for Uber's UberTAXI service. However as far as UberXL is concerned, the Turkish doctrine rejects Uber's claim that it merely operates as an intermediary. If Uber's argument were also to be accepted for the UberXL service, it could only legally qualify as an agent for two reasons. First, the continuous relationship with license holders precludes the characterization of this agreement as a brokerage contract. Second, Art. 10 of the Law on Road Transport prohibits commissioning in passenger transportation. The remaining option, i.e., agency, would only be compliant with transport legislation provided that Uber had a license for agency.

This shows that, irrespective of this debate, Uber's activities were not compliant with the legislation in force at the time of Uber's entry into the Turkish market. Following a period of uncertainty, the Turkish legislator/administration responded to Uber by introducing further regulations making its noncompliance with the legislation clearer. Whether to incorporate Uber within the legal system or not was a political question, and Turkey has decided not to. An alternative could have been to amend legislation to include Uber within the system, taking its benefits for society into account.[144]

The question whether the relationship between Uber and the drivers is one of employment has not yet been answered by Turkish courts. Nonetheless, legal scholars argue for a less strict criterion instead of subordination. It must however be noted that, in Turkey, Uber was operating in collaboration with tourism companies, which employed drivers. In such a scenario, drivers would be employees of the said companies.

Uber finally succumbed to pressures and announced that it would exit the Turkish market on 31.05.2019, following the legislator's reaction and the unfair competition case brought by the United Taxi Drivers Association and the Istanbul Artisanal Chamber of Motorists. To our knowledge, there are currently pending cases brought against Uber, where drivers claimed damages, due to Uber's exit from Turkish market.

[143] Deren Yıldırım (2002, p. 78), Kendigelen (2018, p. 131), Okutan Nilsson (2014, p. 117).

[144] Kişi (2018, p. 65), Eroğlu (2019, p. 413), Colangelo and Maggiolino (2017, pp. 47–68, 66).

References

Akıllı Gündem (2017) İstanbul Emniyeti'nden 1227 UBER sürücüsüne ceza! https://www.akilligundem.com/istanbul-emniyetinden-1227-uber-surucusune-ceza/. Accessed on 26 Mar 2020

Aksoy S (2015) 6502 sayılı tüketicinin korunması hakkında kanunun taşıma hukukuna müdahalesi. Banka ve Ticaret Hukuku Dergisi 31(2):305–334

Aksoy S (2017) Yargıtay 20. Hukuk Dairesi'nin taşıma sözleşmesinden doğan davalarda görevli mahkemeye dair yargı yeri belirleme kararının değerlendirilmesi. Banka ve Ticaret Hukuku Dergisi 33(1):295–301

Ansay T, Önay I (2014) Agency. In: Ansay T, Schneider EC (eds) Introduction to Turkish business law, 2nd edn. Kluwer, Dordrecht, pp 47–58

Arkan S (2019) Ticarî işletme hukuku, 25th edn. Seçkin Yayıncılık, Ankara

Aykanat A (2017) Uber Türkiye'de resmen yasaklandı. Webtekno http://www.webtekno.com/uber-turkiye-de-resmen-yasaklandi-h23385.html. Accessed 26 Mar 2020

Bahtiyar M, Biçer L (2016) Adi iş/ticari iş/tüketici işlemi ayrımı ve bu ayrımın önemi. Marmara Üniversitesi Hukuk Fakültesi Hukuk Araştırmaları Dergisi 22(3):395–436

Baş K (2017) Online platformların acentelik niteliği ve bu platformlar özelinde Türk Ticaret Kanunu'nun acenteliğe ilişkin hükümlerin uygulanması. Banka ve Ticaret Hukuku Dergisi 33(4):115–153

Baş Süzel E (2018) Tüketici hukukunda iş görme (hizmet) sözleşmelerinde ayıplı ifa. Marmara Üniversitesi Hukuk Fakültesi Hukuk Araştırmaları Dergisi 24(2):966–998

Can A (2016) Yolcusu da ceza yiyor. Hürriyet. http://www.hurriyet.com.tr/yolcusu-da-ceza-yiyor-40312736. Accessed on 26 Mar 2020

Can M (2007) Türk Ticaret Kanunu tasarısına göre haksız rekabet. TBB Dergisi 69:151–175

Capital Online (2020) Careem de Türkiye'ye veda etti. https://www.capital.com.tr/haberler/tum-haberler/careem-de-turkiyeye-veda-etti. Accessed 26 Mar 2020

Centel T (2017) Introduction to Turkish labour law. Springer, Berlin

CNN Türk (2019) Uber, Türkiye'de sarı ve turkuaz taksi ile hizmet verecek. https://www.cnnturk.com/turkiye/uber-xl-faaliyetlerini-turkiyede-sonlandirdi. Accessed on 22 Feb 2020

Colangelo M, Maggiolino M (2017) Uber: a new challenge for regulation and competition law? Market Competition Law Rev 1(2):47–68

Cumhuriyet (2015) Dünyada taksicileri çok kızdırdı ama bizde kullanıcı memnun. Bu ulaşım çok suber. http://www.cumhuriyet.com.tr/haber/sokak/320971/DUNYADA_TAKSiCiLERi_COK_KIZDIRDI__AMA_BiZDE_KULLANICI_MEMNUN_Bu_ulasim_cok_suber_.html. Accessed on 26 Mar 2020

Deren Yıldırım N (2002) Haksız Rekabet Hukuku ile Fikri Mülkiyet Hukuku'nda ihtiyati tedbirler, 2nd edn. Alkım Yayınevi

DigitalAge (2016) Uber'den yasaklamalara yanıt geldi. http://digitalage.com.tr/uber-turkiyeden-yasaklama-iddiasina-yanit-geldi/. Accessed 26 Mar 2020

DigitalAge (2017) Uber şimdi Bodrum ve Çeşme'de. http://digitalage.com.tr/uber-simdi-bodrum-cesmede/. Accessed 16 Jan 2020

Ekşi N (2019) Milletlerarası özel hukuk gözüyle Uber. Uluslararası Ticaret ve Tahkim Hukuku Dergisi 8(2):283–346

Eroğlu M (2019) Uber uygulaması ve rekabet sorunları. Uluslararası Ticaret ve Tahkim Hukuku Dergisi 8(2):371–440

Erol A (2019) Mukayeseli hukuk ve Türk Hukuku'nda iş sözleşmesinin bağımlılık unsuru. Dissertation, Istanbul University

Habertürk (2016) Emniyet tüm illere talimat gönderdi: "Uber'e korsan cezası kesin!" http://www.haberturk.com/ekonomi/teknoloji/haber/1341401-emniyet-tum-illere-talimat-gonderdi-ubere-korsan-cezasi-kesin. Accessed 26 Mar 2020

Hürriyet (2018) Uber'e şok… Başbakan Yıldırım talimat verdi yönetmelik değişti. https://www.hurriyet.com.tr/ekonomi/ubere-sok-basbakan-yildirim-talimat-verdi-yonetmelik-degisti-40851901. Accessed 26 Mar 2020

İnci E (2018) Sarı taksiler ve gri sulardaki Uber. İktisat ve Toplum Dergisi 90:33–39
Kaya A (2019a) Tacir yardımcıları. In: Ülgen H, Helvacı M, Kaya A, Nomer Ertan F (eds) Ticari işletme hukuku, 6th edn. Vedat Kitapçılık, İstanbul, pp 723–918
Kaya A (2019b) Araç çevirme uygulaması üzerinden gerçekleştirilen yolcu taşıma faaliyetleri kapsamında uber, yolcu ve sürücü arasındaki ilişkinin hukuki niteliği. Türkiye Barolar Birliği Dergisi 141:289–322
Kendigelen A (2012) Yeni Türk Ticaret Kanunu değişiklikler, yenilikler ve ilk tespitler, 2nd edn. On İki Levha Yayıncılık, İstanbul
Kendigelen A (2018) Hukukî mütalâalar, C. XIV: 2014–2016. On İki Levha Yayıncılık, İstanbul
Kişi N (2018) Paylaşım ekonomisinin ulaşım sektörüne yansımaları: Uber örneği. J Int Manage Soc Res 5(10):57–68
Kocayusufpaşaoğlu N (2008) Borçlar hukuku genel bölüm, birinci cilt: borçlar hukukuna giriş, hukuki işlem, sözleşme, 4th edn. Filiz Kitabevi, İstanbul
Kurt S (2016) Turkey bans Uber. Macreports. http://macreports.com/turkey-bans-uber/. Accessed 26 Mar 2020
ILO (2013) Road transport act. http://ilo.org/dyn/natlex/docs/MONOGRAPH/79928/86155/F82326389/TUR79928%20English.pdf. Accessed 19 May 2020
Milliyet (2016) Uber'den yasaklamalara yanıt geldi. http://www.milliyet.com.tr/uber-den-yasaklamalarla-ilgili-teknoloji-haber-2368752/. Accessed 26 Mar 2020
Mudrić M (2019) Public interest and regulatory approach. In: Marin J, Petrović S, Mudrić M, Hrvoje Lisičar H (eds) Uber—Brave new service or unfair competition: legal analyses of the nature of Uber services. Springer, Berlin, pp 57–83
Mumay C (2017) Uber genel müdüründen ses getirecek açıklamalar. Sözcü. https://www.sozcu.com.tr/2017/ekonomi/uber-genel-mudurunden-ses-getirecek-aciklamalar-2054953/. Accessed 26 Mar 2020
Nomer Ertan F (2016) Haksız rekabet hukuku. On İki Levha Yayıncılık, İstanbul
Nomer Ertan F (2019) Haksız rekabet. In: Ülgen H, Helvacı M, Kaya A, Nomer Ertan F (2019) Ticari işletme hukuku, 6th edn. Vedat Kitapçılık, İstanbul, pp 545–623
Nomer HN (1992) 2918 sayılı karayolları trafik kanununa göre araç işletenin sorumluluğu. İstanbul Barosu Dergisi 2:36–89
NTV (2016) Uber, kullanan yolculara 281 TL para cezası kesildi. http://www.ntv.com.tr/ekonomi/uber-kullanan-yolculara-281-tl-para-cezasi-kesildi,49bC0RIwuEOHZZFSfoecQA. Accessed 26 Mar 2020
Oğuzman MK, Öz T (2020) Borçlar hukuku genel hükümler, vol 2. 15th edn. Vedat Kitapçılık, İstanbul
Okutan Nilsson G (2014) Unfair trade law. In: Ansay T, Schneider EC (eds) Introduction to Turkish business law, 2nd edn. Kluwer, Dordrecht, pp 111–120
Paksoy MS (2018) Sözleşmeyi ihale yöneltme. On İki Levha Yayıncılık, İstanbul
Poroy R, Yasaman H (2004) Ticarî işletme hukuku, 10th edn. Vedat Kitapçılık, İstanbul
Serozan R (2014) Borçlar hukuku genel bölüm, üçüncü cilt: ifa, ifa engelleri, haksız zenginleşme, 6th edn. Filiz Kitabevi, İstanbul
Sol Gazete (2016) Türkiye'de Uber uygulaması yasaklandı: araçlara ve yolculara ceza kesilecek. http://haber.sol.org.tr/toplum/turkiyede-uber-uygulamasi-yasaklandi-araclara-ve-yolculara-ceza-kesilecek-180341. Accessed on 21 June 2017
T24 (2018) Taşıma Yönetmeliği değişti: Uber'e tırpan vurulacak. https://t24.com.tr/haber/tasima-yonetmeligi-degisti-ubere-tirpan-vurulacak,639327. Accessed on 26 Mar 2020
T24 (2019a) Erdoğan: Uber konusu bizim hükümetimizde yoktur, bitmiştir. https://t24.com.tr/haber/erdogan-uber-konusu-bizim-hukumetimizde-bitmistir-boyle-bir-sey-yok,822923. Accessed 26 Mar 2020
T24 (2019b) Cumhurbaşkanı Erdoğan: Uber işi bitti, artık öyle bir şey yok. https://t24.com.tr/haber/cumhurbaskani-erdogan-uber-isi-bitti-artik-oyle-bir-sey-yok,641713. Accessed 26 Mar 2020
Teoman Ö (2006) Ticari işletme hukuku. Vedat Kitapçılık, İstanbul

Türkiye Büyük Millet Meclisi Kamu Denetçiliği Kurumu (Ombudsmanlık) (2018) No. 2017/1243. https://www.ombudsman.gov.tr/wp-content/uploads/2018/03/karar-2017–12143.pdf. Accessed 20 Jan 2020

Uber (2020) Uber completes acquisition of Careem. https://www.uber.com/en-JO/newsroom/uber-careem-close-jo/. Accessed on 26 Mar 2020

Üçyıldız H (2019) Simsarlık sözleşmesi. Thesis (LLM), Selçuk University

Yamak M (2017) Türkiye'de Uber ile seyahat edenlere 281 TL para cezası kesildi! Webtekno. http://www.webtekno.com/turkiye-de-uber-ile-seyahat-edenlere-281-tl-para-cezasi-kesildi-h23231.html. Accessed on 26 Mar 2020

Yasaman H (2012) 6102 sayılı yeni Türk Ticaret Kanunu'nun haksız rekabet ile ilgili getirdiği yenilikler. In: Teoman Ö, Ok B (eds) Yeni Türk Ticaret Kanunu'nun ticari işletme hukuku alanında getirdiği yenilikler. Seçkin Yayıncılık, Ankara, pp 33–44

Yenerer Çakmut Ö (2019) Ceza hukuku açısından Uber'in Türkiye'deki faaliyetleri hakkında genel değerlendirme. Uluslararası Ticaret ve Tahkim Hukuku Dergisi 2:347–369

Yetim S (2015) Uber, hukuki sorunlar ve çözüm önerileri. Uyuşmazlık Mahkemesi Dergisi 6:621–666

Yücel Y (2019) Uber, sürücü ve yolcu arasındaki hukuki ilişki ve bu çerçevede Uber'in ve sürücünün, taşıma hizmetinin gereği gibi ifa edilememesi nedeni ile yolcuya karşı hukuki sorumluluğu. Galatasaray Üniversitesi Hukuk Fakültesi Dergisi 18(1):461–516

Cases

All cases were accessed on 01.05.2020 through http://www.lexpera.com

10th Civil Court of First Instance in Istanbul, dated 16.10.2019, No. 2016/1082
Council of State, 15th Chamber, 06.11.2015, 5047/7089
Council of State, 15th Chamber, 04.12.2015, 6728/8471
Court of Cassation, 4th Civil Chamber, 28.04.2009, 3997/6066
Court of Cassation, 11th Civil Chamber, 01.05.2001, 1828/3862
Court of Cassation, 11th Civil Chamber, 02.12.2003, 4767/11386
Court of Cassation, 11th Civil Chamber, 09.12.2003, 5014/11697
Court of Cassation, 11th Civil Chamber, 21.02.2010, 2008/9072, 2010/591
Court of Cassation, 11th Civil Chamber, 08.07.2013, 2012-14895/2013-14465
Court of Cassation, 11th Civil Chamber, 17.02.2016, 2015-7249/2016-1583
Court of Cassation, 11th Civil Chamber, 11.04.2016, 2015-15205/2016-3941
Court of Cassation, 11th Civil Chamber, 06.02.2017, 2016-890/2017-586
Court of Cassation, 11th Civil Chamber, 04.10.2017, 2016-7393/2017-5025
Court of Cassation, 11th Civil Chamber, 21.11.2017, 4741/6386
Court of Cassation, 11th Civil Chamber, 11.12.2017, 2016-8790/2017-7058
Court of Cassation, 11th Civil Chamber, 8.5.2018, 2016-11557/2018-3347
Court of Cassation, 11th Civil Chamber, 20.08.2018, 2016-12033/2018-4586
Court of Cassation, 11th Civil Chamber, 12.09.2018, 2016-13994/2018-5222
Court of Cassation, 11th Civil Chamber, 26.11.2018, 2017-1916/2018-7379
Court of Cassation, 13th Civil Chamber, 26.01.2012, 2011-16549/2012-1177
Court of Cassation, 20th Civil Chamber, 02.06.2016, 4303/6248
Court of Cassation, 20th Civil Chamber, 21.11.2016, 11654/11009
Court of Cassation, General Assembly of Civil Chambers, 27.06.2018, 504/1258
Court of Cassation, General Assembly of Civil Chambers, 11.12.2018, 2017-117/2018-1883
Regional Administrative Court of Istanbul, 8th Chamber, 11.01.2017, 2016-396/2017-39
Regional Administrative Court of Istanbul, 8th Chamber, 10.02.2017, 132/157
Regional Administrative Court of Istanbul, 8th Chamber, 21.03.2017, 349/395

Regional Administrative Court of Istanbul, 8th Chamber, 28.03.2017, 379/485
Regional Administrative Court of Istanbul, 8th Chamber, 28.03.2017, 428/488
Regional Administrative Court of Istanbul, 8th Chamber, 18.04.2017, 346/609
Regional Administrative Court of Istanbul, 8th Chamber, 26.04.2017, 651/675
Regional Administrative Court of Istanbul, 8th Chamber, 24.04.2017, 739/631
Regional Administrative Court of Istanbul, 8th Chamber, 24.04.2017, 756/635
Regional Administrative Court of Istanbul, 8th Chamber, 16.05.2017, 935/796
Regional Administrative Court of Istanbul, 8th Chamber, 31.05.2017, 766/875
Regional Administrative Court of Istanbul, 8th Chamber, 31.05.2017, 876/876
Regional Administrative Court of Istanbul, 8th Chamber, 20.06.2017, 1092/1077
Regional Administrative Court of Istanbul, 8th Chamber, 26.09.2017, 1290/1452
Regional Administrative Court of Istanbul, 8th Chamber, 17.10.2017, 2214/1691
Regional Administrative Court of Istanbul, 8th Chamber, 08.11.2017, 2231/2000
Regional Administrative Court of Istanbul, 8th Chamber, 08.11.2017, 2246/1998
Regional Administrative Court of Istanbul, 8th Chamber, 13.03.2018, 2017-2596/2018-448
Regional Administrative Court of Istanbul, 8th Chamber, 26.04.2017, 740/669
Turkish Constitutional Court, 11.09.2014, 52/139 (OG, 09.04.2015, No. 29321)

Legislative Materials

By-Law on Road Transport (*Karayolu Taşıma Yönetmeliği*), Arts. 6 (4) b and 24 (2) m (OG, 08.01.2018, No. 30295)
By-Law Amending the By-Law on Road Transport, Art. 5 (OG, 25.05.2018, No. 30431)
By-Law Amending the By-Law on Road Transport, Art. 10 (OG, 15.11.2019, No. 30949)
İstanbul Büyükşehir Belediyesi (2007) Servis Araçları Yönergesi. https://tuhim.ibb.gov.tr/media/2145/servis-ara%C3%A7lar%C4%B1-yoenergesi.pdf. Accessed on 11 Mar 2020
İstanbul Büyükşehir Belediyesi (2017) https://application2.ibb.gov.tr/tulasim/UKOME/2283.pdf. Accessed 11 Mar 2020
İstanbul Büyükşehir Belediyesi Ticari Taksi Ve Taksi Dolmuş Yönergesi. https://tuhim.ibb.gov.tr/dosyalar/taksi%20taksi%20dolmu%C5%9F%20y%C3%B6nerge.pdf. Accessed on 26 Mar 2020
Law No. 2918 (OG, 18.10.1983, No. 18195)
Law No. 4875 (OG, 17.06.2003, No. 25141)
Law No. 4925 (OG, 19.07.2003, No. 25173)
Law No. 5216 (OG, 23.07.2004, No. 25531)
Law No. 5393 (OG, 13.07.2005, No. 25874)
Law No. 6098 (OG, 04.02.2011, No. 27836)
Law No. 6102 (OG, 14.02.2011, No. 27846)
Law No. 6502 (OG, 28.11.2013, No. 28835)
Law No. 7145, Art. 26 (OG, 26.10.2018, No. 30577)
Law No. 7166, Art. 5 (OG, 22.02.2019, No. 30694)

Chapter 12
Policy Implications of the Comparative Findings

Işık Önay and Zeynep Ayata

1 Introduction

Individual contributions from the countries within the scope of our study have shown that the legal challenges posed by Uber are diverse. This chapter aims to provide an overview and a comparison of the identified challenges within a subject-based framework. The first section deals with market access, a challenge common to all countries studied here and elsewhere. This section shows how regulators in different jurisdictions responded to Uber in the context of taxi and transportation regulations. The second section of this chapter focuses on the relationship between Uber and its drivers and questions whether this is an employment relationship. This was an important topic of debate in many of the jurisdictions included in this study. Consumer protection and civil liability issues are also relevant for Uber's activities, as most users of the app qualify as consumers, and whether or not Uber's contractual and tortious liability for damages caused during the ride can be established is a topic worthy of investigation. These issues, which are dealt within the third section of this chapter, are followed by a discussion on whether Uber's activities constitute unfair commercial practices. Uber has faced litigation regarding this issue in Spain and Turkey. The next section is on antitrust issues, where it is discussed whether Uber bypassing the requirements to get expensive authorizations or licenses and being able to determine its fares constitutes a problem in terms of market structure and barriers to entry. This discussion is based on reports from our contributors in Spain, the USA, South Africa, and Germany. Finally, the last section of this chapter is dedicated to tax issues. This discussion concerns value-added taxes, employment taxes, and

I. Önay (✉) · Z. Ayata
Koç University Law School, Istanbul, Turkey
e-mail: ionay@ku.edu.tr

Z. Ayata
e-mail: zayata@ku.edu.tr

Z. Ayata and I. Önay (eds.), *Global Perspectives on Legal Challenges Posed by Ridesharing Companies*,
https://doi.org/10.1007/978-981-15-7035-3_12

revenue taxes. Taxation issues regarding Uber's activities seem to be caused mainly by Uber operating through its company in the Netherlands and denying its status as an employer.

2 Market Access Requirements and Regulatory Responses to Uber

It should first be noted that our study has revealed that, in all the countries that have been examined, urban transportation services and specifically taxi services are heavily regulated. The regulatory authority is usually the municipality. Interestingly, even in federal systems, urban transportation services appear to be regulated at city level rather than regional level. Thus, the challenges posed by Uber have shown the importance of local authorities and their regulatory powers but have also been very diverse and different even within the same country. There are also some examples of specialized authorities that regulate urban transportation services. Transport for London (TfL) is one such example as it is the competent authority for different types of transportation services, including taxis, in the city of London.[1]

Regulations encompass several aspects of the service. The most significant feature of these regulations lies in their detailed definitions of various services. Indeed, it can also be observed that there are several types of urban transportation services in most countries and cities; taxi services appear as one among many. Although the services may be very similar, they usually have to comply with separate sets of comprehensive rules. The historical division between London's black cabs and private hire vehicles (PHVs) illustrates such differences in normative frameworks well.[2] Although they are both regulated by the same authority, these services are defined separately in legal norms and the scope of each service is clearly distinguished. Another example of diversity in services is seen in South Africa, where four different types of urban transportation services can be identified: minibus taxis, metered taxis, app-based taxis, and additional niche services.[3] Metered taxis, for instance, are subject to various distinctive rules regarding issues such as price regulation and pick-up locations.

These well-defined and comprehensive normative frameworks show how rigid urban transportation services are in most cities. Although many cities provided specific rules for app-based services or private hires, the entrance of Uber into the market has shown that these rules are not flexible enough to encompass the platform's activities. The USA, for example, has gone through a significant wave of deregulation, starting in the 1970s, in sectors such as telecommunications and electricity.[4] This is the reason why the disruption caused by Uber eventually led to deregulation in the sector. A sharp contrast can be seen in Germany, where, so far, the response

[1]Chapter 6: UK, Sect. 1.

[2]Chapter 6: UK, Sect. 2.1.

[3]Chapter 10: South Africa, Sect. 2.1.

[4]Chapter 3: USA, Sect. 2.

to Uber's services has been in the form of outright bans by courts and legislators have been very reluctant to amend the rules. The case law in Germany has shown the significance accorded to the protection of legal interests such as the safety of passengers.[5] Socioeconomic factors, legal traditions, and related policy considerations seem to have played an important role in these countries when tackling the legal challenges posed by Uber.

In all the countries examined in this volume, the providers of taxi or equivalent services have to obtain a license or authorization. The license system serves several purposes. First, it enables authorities to ensure that certain qualifications and standards are met by the driver and the vehicle. These rules pertaining to the vehicle and the driver come in the form of background checks for obtaining the license as well as regular controls for keeping the license. Second, licenses allow for the control of the supply of taxi services. Most cities aim to limit the number of taxis for reasons such as congestion and pollution. They accordingly tend to limit the number of available licenses in order to restrain the supply. Third, licenses reinforce geographical limitations established for taxis. As will be discussed later in this section, authorities place restrictions on the geographical areas within which taxis can operate. Licenses also help to clarify the geographical scope assigned to the service and thus facilitate its control.

On the downside, licenses raise barriers to entry. Barriers to entry will obviously be particularly high when regulators aim to restrain the number of taxis in the market. However, all requirements with regard to the vehicle and the driver will constitute barriers and will deter potential entry into the market. These requirements are generally justified through the protection of the passenger or the driver, road safety, etc. Such requirements may be costly in themselves, but the crucial problem is that authorities may charge very high sums for the license itself. Examples of such expensive license policies can be seen in the USA.[6] Lastly, licensing will increase the transaction costs for taxi service suppliers.

Another noteworthy characteristic of the taxi services market is price regulation. Our study has shown that countries such as Turkey,[7] Germany,[8] and the UK[9] not only impose the use of taximeters but also interfere with prices to a significant extent. Regulating price may serve two distinct purposes. First, it may protect the interests of the public and passengers by ensuring that drivers do not overcharge. For instance, in Mexico City, taxi services from the airport to the city charge fixed rates to different areas.[10] Second, authorities may wish to keep taxi fare rates high in order to allow the operators to recuperate their initial investments and costs. In Germany, for example, taxi fare rates are reported to be particularly expensive.[11] A similar

[5]Chapter 8: Germany, Sect. 3.3.

[6]Chapter 3: USA, Sect. 4.1.

[7]Chapter 11: Turkey, Sect. 6.3.

[8]Chapter 8: Germany, Sect. 3.1.

[9]Chapter 7: Spain, Sect. 2.3.

[10]Chapter 4: Mexico, Sect. 2.

[11]Chapter 8: Germany, Sect. 2.2.

observation has also been made for the black cabs in London.[12] However, these high rates obviously lead to a negative perception of taxi services among consumers.

Finally, an interesting characteristic of taxi services that has been identified by the authors is the distinction between hailing taxis and ordering taxis. In most cities, we can encounter both taxis (though the nomenclature may change among different cities or countries) and private hire services. The normative structure usually allows taxis to accept passengers who hail them from any pick-up location, whereas private hires are banned from doing so. Private hires appear to be only allowed to provide pre-booked fare services. This distinction has been of particular importance in London, where the authorities have tried to pinpoint exactly when an order was placed was accepted by Uber drivers in order to establish the correct classification of its services. This aspect was also an important factor in the judicial assessment of Uber in Germany, where the Federal Supreme Court ruled that, similarly to rentable transportation services, all orders for UberBlack must be placed with the operator and the driver has to return to his or her seat of operation after each ride.[13] In fact, a few years later, the Cologne District Court ordered an injunction because the app did not allow the drivers to return to their stations before accepting a new order.[14] The service was therefore not in line with rentable car services and more closely resembled a taxi service.

All of the characteristics of taxi markets described above were incompatible with Uber's operations. However, Uber's operations usually did not fit into the category of legally defined private hire services, either. Generally, providers of private hire services have to be registered. Furthermore, they need to have a station at which they are based and to which they return after each fare. Also, as has already been stated, private hires are not allowed to accept customers who try to hail a service from the street. They are only allowed to provide pre-booked services.

Uber defines itself as an intermediary platform and claims that it does not provide a transportation service. However, in several of the jurisdictions examined in this book, authorities or taxi service providers have challenged this claim. The common trend has been to classify Uber as a provider of a transportation service. For EU member states, the preliminary ruling delivered by the Court of Justice of the European Union (CJEU) has played an important role.[15] Faced with the question of whether Uber's operations should be qualified as an information service or a transportation service, the CJEU opted for the latter, which has significant consequences for Uber in EU countries not only because it lost its claim as an intermediary platform but also because the ruling meant that each EU country was now competent to regulate Uber without harmonization within the internal market. In Spain, the Commercial Court of Barcelona as the addressee of the preliminary ruling held that Uber's services

[12]Chapter 6: UK, Sect. 1.1.2.

[13]Chapter 8: Germany, Sect. 4.

[14]Chapter 8: Germany, Sect. 5.

[15]Judgment of 20 Dec 2017 in *Asociación Profesional Élite Taxi v Uber Systems Spain SL*. ECLI:EU:C:2017:981.

could not be qualified as mere intermediation and thus were subject to the regulatory framework of transportation services.[16] On the other hand, the German Federal Supreme Court also requested a preliminary ruling from the CJEU on the qualification of the services provided by Uber but withdrew its request after the court's preliminary ruling for Spain.[17] In Germany, several following court decisions held that Uber should be subject to the same regulation as taxi services.[18] In Italy, court decisions adopted a similar approach, ruling that Uber's services had elements of intermediation services but that it was essentially a transport service.[19]

In Mexico, despite comprehensive reports stating that such services should be seen as belonging to a different category, the competent public authority ruled that Uber was a private transportation service.[20] The authority displayed an interesting reasoning, drawing a distinction between platforms that connect passengers with taxis and those that connect passengers with private drivers, Uber belonging to the latter group and hence constituting a private transportation service. The Supreme Court of Mexico also later ruled that Uber provided a transportation service.[21] The court decided that it was not possible to separate the functioning of the platform from the transportation services it provided.

As can been seen from these examples, Uber has been unsuccessful in many countries in convincing authorities and courts that it is merely an intermediation platform. Furthermore, in some of these countries, such as Germany[22] and Italy,[23] Uber has faced outright bans through administrative or judicial decisions. In Germany, courts have ordered many injunctions for various different characteristics of Uber's operations. Today, only UberX can legally operate in Germany, and other Uber services in the form that courts allow are probably no longer profitable.[24] In Italy, the Constitutional Court dismissed hopes of regional regulation for Uber by declaring that the matter must be regulated at the national level.[25] The regional regulation, which had tried to allow Uber's activities to a certain extent, was declared unconstitutional by the court. Thus, in these countries, although there have been some minor attempts to introduce new rules to include Uber, the tenacity of existing norms has prevailed over concerns for economic progress.

One of the most important purposes of our study was to examine and analyze the ways in which Uber and similar platforms have affected and transformed policies and regulations applicable to transport services. Many of the countries studied in this volume yield interesting examples of changes and reactions aimed at adapting

[16]Chapter 7: Spain, Sect. 2.2.

[17]Chapter 8: Germany, Sect. 3.1.

[18]Chapter 8: Germany, Sect. 3.1.

[19]Chapter 9: Italy, Sect. 2.2.

[20]Chapter 4: Mexico, Sect. 2.

[21]Chapter 4: Mexico, Sect. 2.

[22]Chapter 8: Germany, Sect. 3.

[23]Chapter 9: Italy, Sect. 2.2.

[24]Chapter 8: Germany, Sect. 5.

[25]Chapter 9: Italy, Sect. 2.2.

to disruption and novelty. Even in countries where the courts have banned or limited Uber's services, some authorities have called for a more inclusive approach and changes in the legislation.

As stated before, the reaction to Uber in the USA eventually reflected the deregulation trend that had been seen in many other sectors. Uber was initially banned in certain cities, and its activities were significantly restricted in many others. For instance, in 2016 many cities did not allow Uber to provide services from airports.[26] California was the first state to adopt new legislation that directly regulated transportation network companies, providing rules similar to those applicable to taxi services but without significant control over price.[27] The scope of the legislation covered all platforms or online apps that connected drivers to passengers and thus included Uber's services. Taxi drivers and operators challenged local regulations, mostly under right to property claims. Their main motive was the sharp decline in the value of taxi medallions and the problem of barrier to entry created by licensing rules. Their legal claims before courts have been mostly unsuccessful. Richard Posner, US Appellate Judge and former law professor known for his seminal work on law and economics, has opined that the licensing system does not aim to guarantee a property, i.e., a license, that is free of competition for taxi operators.[28]

Brazil also displays an interesting example of how legislators have tried to adapt to the disruption caused by Uber. Although, according to our authors, the taxi services market was highly regulated, a federal law aiming to regulate the ridesharing industry was adopted in 2018.[29] The new legislation set forth the minimum requirements and allowed local authorities to regulate transportation services provided by apps and platforms according to its guidelines. The requirements focused on setting standards for the vehicles and the drivers but also imposed significant insurance rules. A year later, the Brazilian Supreme Court ruled that decisions by local authorities banning Uber's activities were altogether unconstitutional and that, although they could regulate Uber's activities to a certain extent, they should not enforce outright bans.[30] In line with this legal framework, the city of Sao Paulo established enrollment procedures for app-based transport service operators and, in addition to standards for vehicles and drivers, they imposed geographical limitations.

South Africa was another country that introduced new rules for electronic hailing services in 2018.[31] The new framework required that companies providing these services obtain a license from the relevant authority. According to the amended legislation, Uber and similar applications must comply with strict rules relating to information provided for the passengers about the fare and the driver.[32] Under the amended law, operators or applications that fail to obtain a license and/or continue

[26]Chapter 3: USA, Sect. 4.1.

[27]Chapter 3: USA, Sect. 4.1.

[28]Chapter 3: USA, Sect. 4.1.

[29]Chapter 5: Brazil, Sect. 2.

[30]Chapter 5: Brazil, Sect. 2.

[31]Chapter 10: South Africa, Sect. 2.1.

[32]Chapter 10: South Africa, Sect. 2.1.

to provide service with an expired license will have committed a criminal offence. Indeed, the new penalties for non-compliance are very severe, ranging from very high pecuniary penalties to two years of imprisonment.[33]

Uber's path in the UK has been somewhat different as the classification of Uber's services in London has taken a few interesting turns. Uber was initially granted a PHV license, although its contract with the drivers included a clause stating that Uber does not provide transportation services. The initial license policy of the city of London was due, according to our authors, to the expected rise of demand during the Olympic Games in 2012.[34] After that period, Uber lost its PHV license and the TfL refused to grant it again on several occasions and for different reasons.[35] Uber had limited victory before the courts. However, it also changed and adapted its terms of service numerous times in order to at least appear in line with the applicable legislation.[36] These adjustments included changes such as setting better safety standards for vehicles and better background checks for drivers. As a response, the TfL added new requirements for PHVs, which meant that the legal framework for PHVs and black cabs became increasingly similar.[37] There was also a very interesting inquiry into whether it was Uber or the driver accepting the request from the passenger, which was of crucial importance to determine whether Uber should hold an operator's license.[38] This query, during which the TfL outsourced studies and research to private parties, lasted more than three years. Throughout the process, there were also problems with regard to Uber's disclosure of data. Comprehensive study showed that bookings took place at the same time that the drivers were notified of the booking, but only after a driver accepted a request was the booking confirmed by the app's algorithm.[39] After this query, the TfL still refused to grant Uber the necessary license.[40] Thus, we see in the example of London a very proactive regulator whose responses to Uber's activities have been almost entirely negative. It is therefore possible to observe in the UK an example of a responsive regulator who has used its prerogatives to restrain Uber even when courts have at times been more permissive. Furthermore, the London regulator has made serious efforts to better understand the operations of Uber as an app. Although the TfL has been very reluctant to allow the operations of Uber in all of its aspects, it has tried to understand its functioning in order to better classify its activities.

These examples highlight the different interests and concerns that legislators have had to face while dealing with Uber (Fig. 1). The majority of court decisions in our study have been unfavorable to Uber. However, legislators in many countries have tried to strike a balance between various stakes, such as protection of the consumer,

[33]Chapter 10: South Africa, Sect. 2.1.

[34]Chapter 6: UK, Sect. 1.1.1.

[35]Chapter 6: UK, Sect. 1.1.1.

[36]Chapter 6: UK, Sect. 1.1.1.

[37]Chapter 6: UK, Sect. 1.2.

[38]Chapter 6: UK, Sect. 2.1.

[39]Chapter 6: UK, Sect. 2.3.

[40]Chapter 6: UK, Sect. 2.3.

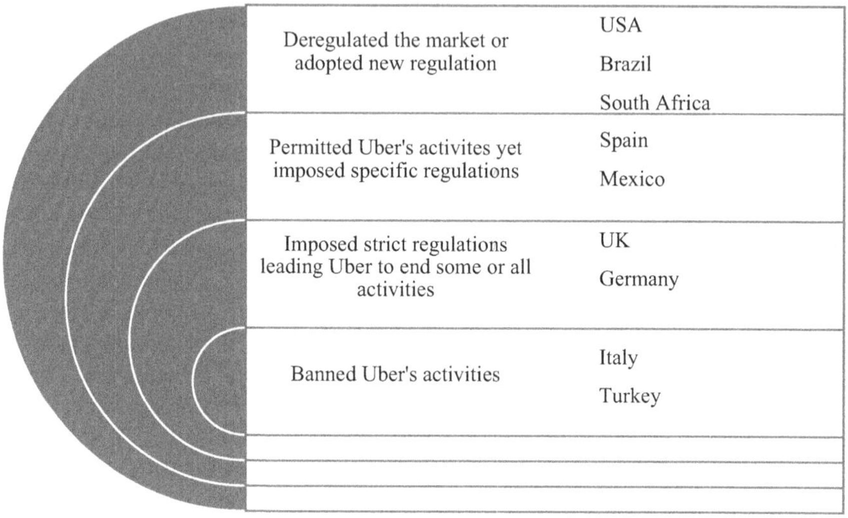

Fig. 1 Regulatory responses to Uber's activities

safety measures, the interests of taxi operators and drivers, and the benefits provided by Uber's low prices and use of technology, while addressing the company's social, legal, and economic challenges.

3 Uber Drivers: Employees or Independent Contractors?

The reports by the contributors of this study show that one of the significant legal challenges faced by Uber concerns labor law. Uber has always claimed that its drivers are independent contractors. Nonetheless, in some jurisdictions such as Brazil,[41] South Africa,[42] and the UK,[43] Uber has faced litigation over its alleged employer status. This issue is of utmost importance for Uber, because being classified as an employer would mean that it would be subject to mandatory rules on the labor law of the country in which it is operating. For example, as an employer, Uber would be required to make social security payments and to comply with the minimum wage and maximum hours prescribed by law.

This challenge is not unique to Uber; it concerns most business models of the sharing economy operating through digital platforms. The challenge lies within the traditional dichotomy between employees and independent (self-employed) contractors. Most jurisdictions still distinguish between these two alternatives based on

[41]Chapter 5: Brazil, Sect. 3.

[42]Chapter 10: South Africa, Sect. 2.2.

[43]Chapter 6: UK, Sect. 3.

several criteria, which usually prove inadequate in classifying the nature of the legal relationship between the parties in the context of the sharing economy.

Before moving on to the differences between approaches adopted by the jurisdictions examined within this study (see Fig. 2. for an overview), a common feature must be emphasized. In almost all jurisdictions, the contractual wording used by Uber is disregarded in characterizing the legal nature of the relationship.[44] This is consistent with paragraph 9 of the ILO's recommendations on employment relationships[45]: "For the purposes of the national policy of protection for workers in an employment relationship, the determination of the existence of such a relationship should be guided primarily by the facts relating to the performance of work and the remuneration of the worker, notwithstanding how the relationship is characterized in any contrary arrangement, contractual or otherwise, that may have been agreed between the parties."

In some jurisdictions, drivers have been classified as independent contractors because they failed to fulfill the classical criteria for qualifying as employees. An example is Brazil, where contradictory court decisions exist but the judicial trend is to deny Uber drivers the status of employees. In recent decisions, where courts have decided in favor of Uber, the main argument was the lack of subordination. The drivers' flexibility in determining when to work and the lack of a fixed payment were influential factors for arriving at this conclusion.[46] Italy[47] and Mexico[48] are other examples of jurisdictions qualifying the drivers as self-employed contractors, emphasizing the lack of subordination. Nonetheless, recent legislation granting a minimum level of protection for those delivering food and beverages through digital platforms in Italy signals further development along these lines. The South African Labour Court held in an Uber case that Uber drivers are not employees due to the lack of a contractual relationship. The court's stance on the issue was deemed as open to criticism for both ignoring the developments elsewhere in the world and contradicting the court's prior approach in favor of extending the scope of the employee concept.[49]

Other jurisdictions have stretched the concept of the employment relationship in a way that may include the relationship between Uber and the driver. For instance, in Spain, the operator of a food delivery application was found to be in an employment relationship with drivers. Spanish courts have not ruled on Uber yet, but this decision shows that it is likely for Spanish courts to qualify Uber as an employer. Nonetheless, a possible obstacle for this outcome is found in Article 1.3(g) of the Spanish Labor Act, which excludes the application of the act to persons providing transport services that require administrative authorization.[50] In countries like Germany and Turkey, where UberPop/UberX service is not offered, the issue is not of practical importance at the

[44] E.g., Chapter 8: Germany, Sect. 6; Chapter 4: Mexico, Sect. 3.

[45] ILO (2016).

[46] Chapter 5: Brazil, Sect. 3.

[47] Chapter 9: Italy, Sect. 2.3.

[48] Chapter 4: Mexico, Sect. 3.

[49] Chapter 10: South Africa, Sect. 2.2.

[50] Chapter 7: Spain, Sect. 3.3.

moment and the courts did not have to deal with this problem.[51] Nonetheless, legal scholars in Turkey seem to favor the approach that classifies Uber as an employer, emphasizing the inadequacy of the traditional subordination criterion.[52] The UK seems to be the jurisdiction where Uber's status in labor law was at the heart of the discussion surrounding Uber's legal challenges. Unlike other jurisdictions, a third intermediary category called "workers" is present in the UK in addition to employees and independent contractors. Workers are subject to employment law, albeit protected to a lesser extent when compared to employees. In its landmark decision in the Aslam, Ferrer v. Uber case,[53] the Employment Tribunal ruled that Uber drivers are workers, emphasizing the degree of control imposed by Uber. Uber's arguments identifying itself as an intermediary were promptly rejected: "... it is, in our opinion, unreal to deny that Uber is in business as a supplier of transportation services. Simple common sense argues to the contrary".[54]

The question of Uber drivers' status in the USA seems to be far from settled. Two important events took place in 2019, which went in different directions. In April 2019, the General Counsel of the National Labor Relations Board classified UberX and UberBLACK drivers as independent contractors in an advice memorandum. This was justified by the degree of control the drivers exercised over the work they performed. On the other hand, in September 2019, a law passed in California classified all drivers working through ridesharing platforms as employees.[55]

It must be noted that even in jurisdictions where Uber is identified as an employer, its status may change depending on the particularities of the case. For instance, where the owner of the vehicle and the driver are different persons,[56] especially where Uber operates by collaborating with professional companies,[57] the drivers would be the employees of said companies. Whether Uber may still be qualified as an additional employer due to the control it imposes on the service in such scenarios is a question yet to be answered.[58]

Based on the reports by our contributors, it seems clear that almost all jurisdictions are struggling to place Uber within the traditional labor law rules. Therefore, labor law seems to be an area that needs to adapt to the needs of persons operating in a sharing economy. Keeping Uber completely outside of the scope of labor law does not seem to be the ideal solution. The pitfall there is obvious: It would leave Uber drivers

[51] Chapter 8: Germany, Sect. 6.

[52] Chapter 11: Turkey, Sect. 4.2.

[53] *Aslam v Uber BV* (2017).

[54] *Aslam v Uber BV* (2017), p. 89; see Footnote 43; Prassl (2018), pp. 98–99, Mudrić (2019), pp. 24–26.

[55] Chapter 3: USA, Sect. 4.4.

[56] Chapter 4: Mexico, Sect. 3.

[57] Chapter 8: Germany, Sect. 6; Chap. 11: Turkey, Sect. 4.2

[58] For challenges regarding multiple persons exercising different traditional employer functions in the gig economy, see Prassl (2018), pp. 103–104.

in a precarious position, i.e., without social protection.[59] In the Report on Digital Labour Platforms and the Future of Work, the ILO warns that "[w]orkers should not be misclassified as self-employed if they are employees in practice".[60] Prassl, who criticizes the contractual misclassification of the legal relationship between digital platforms and gig workers[61] and argues for a functional concept of the employer, sees ridesharing platforms as a fitting example where the platform owner is an employer.[62] A recent study on Uber also concluded that Uber drivers should be qualified as employees due to the overwhelming influence of Uber over drivers.[63] Indeed, the fact that such control and influence are exerted through algorithms in a digital platform should not deprive Uber drivers of benefits and rights they would otherwise enjoy.

Looking beyond what has happened so far, this issue may become even more relevant with the increase in the number of persons whose main source of income is work through digital platforms.[64] On the other hand, the emergence of driverless cars to offer such services may render this discussion obsolete.

4 Consumer Protection and Uber's Liability for Damages Occurring During Transportation

It is not only the drivers who are the weaker party in their contractual relationship with Uber. Uber's contract with the passengers is a B2C contract and is subject to national laws of consumer protection. At the EU level, the Unfair Contract Terms Directive[65] and Unfair Commercial Practices Directive[66] are relevant.[67] It should be noted that the Consumer Rights Directive[68] is of limited significance, as Article 3/3/k excludes contracts for passenger transport services.

At the national level, our contributors from Spain, Mexico, and South Africa have elaborated on the validity of the provisions in Uber's standard terms, which is questionable pursuant to Consumer Protection Law. The Spanish contributors report that Uber's terms and conditions are problematic in terms of grammatical and substantive transparency.[69] In Mexico, the city of Tijuana requires pre-formulated

[59] On social protection of digital platform workers, also see Eurofound (2018), pp. 22–24 (cited as Eurofound Report hereafter).

[60] ILO (2018).

[61] Prassl (2018), pp. 91 ff.

[62] Ibid., (pp. 101–102).

[63] Mudrić (2019), p. 54.

[64] For empirical estimates of the extent of work on digital platforms, see Eurofound Report (2018), pp. 22–24.

[65] Council Directive 93/113/EEC (OJ L 95, 21.4.1993).

[66] Directive 2005/29/EC (OJ L 149, 11.6.2005).

[67] Marin (2019), p. 205.

[68] Directive 2011/83/EU (OJ L 304, 22.11.2011).

[69] Chapter 7: Spain, Sects. 4.1.1 and 4.1.3.

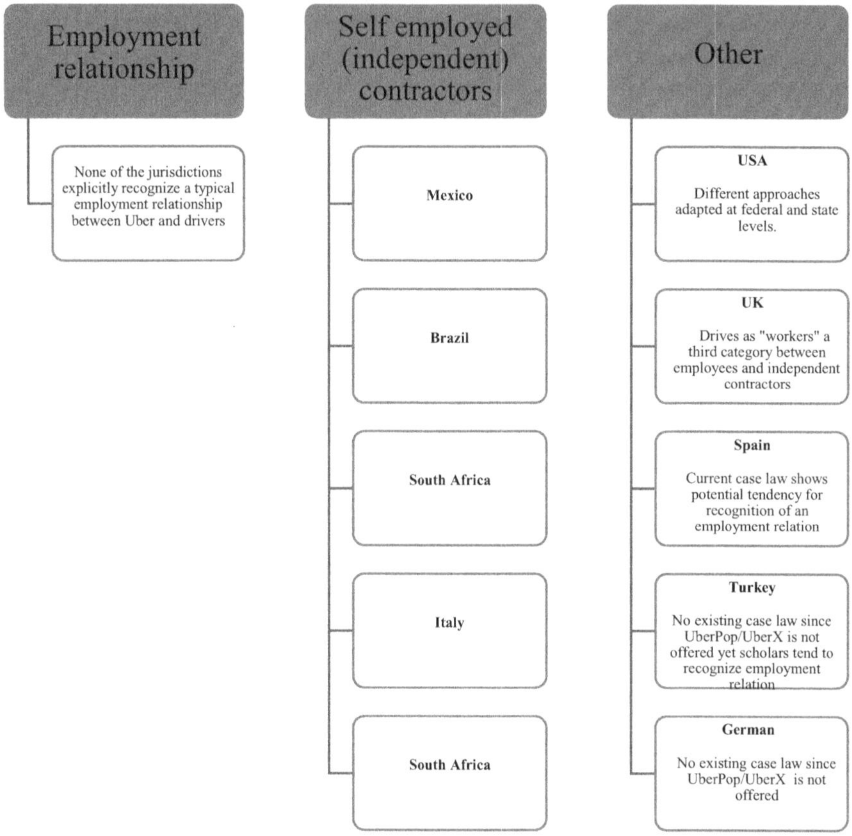

Fig. 2 Nature of the legal relationship between Uber and drivers

standard contracts to be approved by the Bureau of Consumer Protection.[70] The Federal Consumer Protection Law of Mexico also bans unfair commercial practices and imposes duties on service providers to provide information. Furthermore, clauses imposing disproportionate, unfair, and abusive obligations on consumers are deemed invalid.[71] In South Africa, duties are imposed on persons who supply goods or services by way of an electronic transaction.[72] The choice of law and the choice of jurisdiction clauses in Uber's standard terms and conditions also seem problematic in light of mandatory rules on consumer protection in South Africa.[73]

The basis of Uber's liability for damages that occur during the ride depends on several factors. If the passenger is injured, contractual liability may arise provided that a contractual breach has occurred. Whether there is a breach on Uber's part

[70]Chapter 4 : Mexico, Sect. 2.

[71]Chapter 4: Mexico, Sect. 4.

[72]Chapter 10: South Africa, Sect. 2.3.2.

[73]Chapter 10: South Africa, Sect. 2.3.2.

would depend both on facts and the legal nature of the contract between Uber and the passenger. If Uber is deemed to be a transportation service provider rather than an intermediary, it would be easier to establish its liability in most cases.

Brazil seems to be the only jurisdiction among the ones included in this study where extensive case law exists on the issue of Uber's civil liability. The State Court of São Paulo held Uber liable for damages suffered by the passenger during the ride on many occasions. Uber's liability in Brazil is based on the strict liability regime regulated under the Federal Consumer Protection Code.[74] Despite the lack of reported cases, establishing Uber's contractual liability also seems possible under Turkish law pursuant to rules governing transportation contracts under the Turkish Commercial Code, considering that the prevalent view in the doctrine perceives Uber as a transportation service provider. Even in the case that Uber is considered a mere intermediary, one could still argue for its liability on a quasi-contractual basis.[75] Under Spanish law, Uber's contractual liability can be established if it qualifies as a provider of transportation services, and such a qualification was made by the Madrid Court of Appeal[76] in a decision concerning BlaBlaCar. Even in the case that Uber is considered an intermediary, another decision by the same court[77] creates the impression that it may still be held liable for non-confirming transportation service. This, however, is far from being clear, as the mentioned decisions did not directly address private law issues but were rather on whether these companies infringed the regulation and therefore gained unfair competitive advantage.[78]

Uber's contractual liability seems more difficult to establish under German,[79] South African,[80] and Mexican law, as Uber is not considered a party to the transportation contract; it is nonetheless reported for Mexico that Uber may be held liable for damages due to its abusive commercial practices toward consumers.[81] In these countries, a breach of the intermediation contract would of course lead to Uber's contractual liability.[82] This would be the case, for example, if Uber fails to verify documents provided by the drivers during registration.[83]

In the absence of a contractual breach vis-à-vis the injured passenger or where a third party (e.g., a pedestrian) is injured during the ride, Uber's liability should be discussed within the framework of tort law. Most jurisdictions[84] hold a person liable for damages caused by their employees during the course of the work. Thus, for

[74]Chapter 5: Brazil, Sect. 4.

[75]Chapter 11: Turkey, Sects. 5.1 and 5.2.

[76]Madrid Court of Appeal, Judgment of 18 Feb 2019. ECLI:ES:APM:2019:1255.

[77]Madrid Court of Appeal, Judgment of 18 Jan 2019. ECLI:ES:APM:2019:3.

[78]Chapter 7: Spain, Sect. 4.1.2.

[79]Chapter 8: Germany, Sect. 7.2.

[80]Chapter 10: South Africa, Sect. 2.3.2.

[81]Chapter 4: Mexico, Sect. 4.

[82]Chapter 8: Germany, Sect. 7.2.

[83]This example is given by our Italian contributors (Chapter 9: Italy, Sect. 2.5).

[84]E.g., Chapter 6: UK, Sect. 5.1.2.2; Chapter 11: Turkey, Sect. 5.3; Chapter 9: Italy, Sect. 2.5; Chapter 8: Germany, Sect. 7.2.

vicarious liability to be established, reference has to be made to the earlier discussion on whether the drivers are Uber's employees or independent contractors.[85] For example, in South Africa, where drivers are classified as independent contractors, Uber's tortious liability is unlikely to be established.[86] In Brazil, where drivers are classified as independent contractors, courts have dismissed the claims for damages by pedestrians directed at ridesharing companies, especially in cases where the driver was not carrying a passenger at the time of the accident. Our Brazilian contributors report that it is uncertain whether courts would hold Uber liable for damages suffered by third parties during a ride or on the way to a pick-up. They submit that a rule in the Consumer Protection Code holding service providers liable for damages suffered by bystanders could be used to establish liability.[87] Also, in Mexico, another jurisdiction where drivers are considered self-employed, many states have issued laws establishing tortious liability of transportation network companies for damages caused by drivers during the ride.[88] In Germany, Uber in its current operation collaborates with local partners that are party to the transportation contract, and those partners would be liable for damages caused by drivers.[89]

In Turkey, Uber's vicarious liability would be established if the driver is deemed Uber's employee. Other grounds for Uber's tortious liability under Turkish law could be found in the Law on Road Traffic, which holds the owner of the enterprise with which the operator is affiliated along with the operator strictly liable for damages occurring due to the operation of the motor vehicle.[90] As previously explained, drivers are considered workers in the UK, an intermediate category between employees and independent contractors. Tort law, however, adopts a binary distinction between employees and independent contractors, and it is currently unclear where Uber drivers fall within this distinction. Our contributors from the UK submit that in terms of both policy and law, it seems sound to consider Uber drivers employees for the purposes of vicarious liability.[91] They also raise two interesting questions: First, should the fact that a driver keeps multiple ride-hailing apps open change the status?[92] Second, would an accident be considered as having taken place during the course of employment if the driver was not carrying a passenger but merely driving around with the app activated?[93] Both of these questions remain unanswered and would probably need case-by-case analysis.

[85]See Sect. 3 of this chapter.

[86]Chapter 10: South Africa, Sect. 2.3.1.

[87]Chapter 5: Brazil, Sect. 4.

[88]Chapter 4: Mexico, Sect. 2.

[89]Chapter 8: Germany, Sect. 7.2.

[90]Chapter 11: Turkey, Sect. 5.3.

[91]Chapter 6: UK, Sect. 5.1.2.2.

[92]Chapter 6: UK, Sect. 5.1.2.2.

[93]Chapter 6: UK, Sect. 5.1.2.3.

5 Uber's Activities in Terms of Unfair Competitive Practices

Uber has often been accused of providing a taxi service or a similar car hire service. The platform has consistently denied these claims, but many aspects of its services have indeed resembled existing services defined in regulations. These similarities have caused significant incumbents, specifically taxi drivers, to take legal action against Uber. These actions were often taken on grounds of unfair competitive practices. Many jurisdictions prohibit deceptive or wrongful practices by companies in an attempt to gain a competitive advantage. Often, unlike antitrust law, not only direct competitors but also consumers or associations will have an interest in bringing an action against unfair competition, and such a right will be recognized by law. In many jurisdictions, taxi operators or professional associations have challenged Uber's activities on grounds of unfair competition.

The infamous CJEU preliminary ruling on Uber originated as an unfair competition action brought by a professional taxi drivers' association in Barcelona against the platform.[94] The association claimed that the platform should only be allowed to operate with licenses and authorizations required for taxis. Otherwise, the association argued, Uber would be gaining a competitive advantage by failing to comply with a regulation that is obviously very costly.[95] After the CJEU ruling, the national commercial court decided that Uber's operations and the lack of legal authorization for these services did not constitute an unfair competitive practice. In Italy, however, national courts reached a different conclusion in light of the authority recognized by the CJEU to consider the matter under national law rather than EU law. The courts ruled that Uber's failure to comply with national rules applicable to taxi services amounts to unfair competitive practices and thus ordered Uber to cease its activities.[96]

There has also been significant discussions and actions based on allegations of unfair competitive practices in Turkey. The claim that was brought before a commercial court in Istanbul was instituted by a taxi drivers' association and a professional chamber. The claimants argued that Uber was providing a taxi service and should therefore be subject to taxi regulation and, most importantly, should be required to obtain the necessary authorizations. Interestingly, Uber claimed that its services were dissimilar to taxis, arguing that vehicles and pick-up locations were different instead of relying on the platform and intermediary model.[97] The case is still pending before the court; however, expert reports have stated that, given the essentiality of finding passengers for transport, Uber's services should be classified not as an information technology service but as a taxi service.

---

[94] Judgment of 20 Dec 2017 in *Asociación Profesional Élite Taxi v Uber Systems Spain SL*. ECLI:EU:C:2017:981.

[95] Chapter 7: Spain, Sect. 2.2.

[96] Chapter 9: Italy, Sect. 2.2.

[97] Chapter 11: Turkey, Sect. 6.2.

6 Antitrust Claims Against Uber

Uber has the ability to provide transport services at much lower prices than taxi rates. Taxi prices are often regulated. More importantly, there are high barriers to the entry in the taxi markets that are marked by expensive authorizations or licenses and costly transactions. Uber did not have to bear these costs, at least initially, while it operated in a regulatory loophole. Hence, Uber was able to provide a transport service similar to taxis at a much lower price and quite often at better quality. Taxi drivers and national authorities have thus also seen Uber's activities as a problem in terms of market structure and barriers to entry and thus antitrust.

For instance, Spain's regulatory reactions to Uber have led to many intersections with antitrust law. In light of the CJEU's ruling, Spanish courts qualified Uber as a transportation service. The judgement of the Supreme Court also confirmed that Uber was subject to rules applicable to land transport and therefore should have authorization to operate. However, the court did not specify the regime that should govern Uber's activities.[98] In Spain, the preexistent service most similar to Uber was the leasing of vehicles with driver (VTCs). Before these legal challenges, when Spain was adopting measures in order to implement the Services Directive, the Spanish legislator adopted certain measures that concerned VTCs, qualifying them as public on-demand services.[99] This amendment meant that VTCs would no longer be subject to a quantitative restriction that provided that within the same territory only one VTC authorization could be granted for every thirty taxi authorizations.[100] However, despite legislative reforms, restrictions were not removed from administrative measures. The legislator amended the law in 2009, allowing the executive to impose such quantitative restrictions when necessary, but most authorities chose not to regulate VTCs. For many years, there had been a significant increase in the number of authorizations granted in Spain and their ratio to taxi numbers was multiplied by seven. Thus, the legislator in Spain had liberalized markets many years before Uber made an entry in order to include alternatives to taxi services. Another restriction that concerned VTCs was also removed by implementing the measures adopted in 2009 for the Services Directive: geographical restrictions.[101] With the amendment, the legislator provided that authorizations issued by the administration would be valid throughout the country but again delegated the authority to the executive to impose restrictions when necessary. Since then, there have been two amendments with regard to geographical restrictions. The first, in 2015, provided that eighty percent of fares should be within the territory of the granted authorization. This rule was removed by another amendment in 2018, going back to the initial position of restricting VTCs' activities to inter-urban services. Both restrictions, quantitative and territorial, had in fact been challenged by the Spanish Competition Authority before the Supreme

[98] Chapter 7: Spain, Sect. 2.4.
[99] Chapter 7: Spain, Sect. 2.4.
[100] Chapter 7: Spain, Sect. 2.4.
[101] Chapter 7: Spain, Sect. 2.5.

Court. The Competition Authority argued that these restrictions were not proportionate. However, the Supreme Court ruled that there were adequate measures for striking a balance between different types of public transport.[102]

In the USA, some of the most significant legal challenges to Uber's activities were also in the field of antitrust. In some cities, such as Philadelphia, taxi operators claimed that allowing Uber's entry into the market could lead to an attempt to monopolize the market through predatory pricing, forbidden under Sect. 2 of the Sherman Act. The court in Philadelphia rejected these claims, stating that Uber had been increasing competition by creating an alternative that was more advantageous for consumers on many grounds.[103] The court furthermore stated that Uber's entry and fast success demonstrated that, contrary to common opinion, barriers to entry were not very high in the relevant market.[104] Thus, monopolizing the market would not be very easy either.

A similar claim was made in South Africa, where the taxi industry alleged that Uber was abusing its dominant position through predatory pricing.[105] The matter was brought before the South African Competition Commission, which found that Uber's prices were not below cost and thus did not constitute predatory pricing. However, these claims led the commission to launch a sectoral inquiry into the transport industry.[106] In the report presenting its findings, the Competition Commission clearly observed that the competition created by Uber has had a significant impact on traditional taxi services.[107] Although prices of taxis remained considerably higher than Uber's fares, taxis have started to develop electronic app-based services. The expansion of e-hailing in traditional metered taxis shows that, although it has not triggered price competition most likely due to price regulation in the sector, Uber has increased competition in terms of quality.[108] Traditional taxis have adopted app-based systems in order to improve the quality of their service and thus better compete with Uber. This finding clearly demonstrates that Uber's disruption and entry into the market have had positive competitive effects on incumbents.

The German Monopolies Commission also stated its position on the activities of Uber and its effects on market competition. The Monopolies Commission questioned not only the effects created by Uber but also the market structure created by existing rules for taxi services.[109] It was argued that, as Uber has demonstrated, licenses for taxi operators have now become an unnecessary intervention in the public transportation sector. According to the Monopolies Commission's opinion, the existing regulation, which clearly creates barriers to entry, has become obsolete in the face

[102]Chapter 7: Spain, Sects. 2.4. and 2.5.

[103]Chapter 3: USA, Sect. 4.1.

[104]Chapter 3: USA, Sect. 4.1.

[105]Chapter 10: South Africa Sect. 2.4.

[106]Chapter 10: South Africa Sect. 2.4.

[107]Chapter 10: South Africa Sect. 2.4.

[108]Chapter 10: South Africa Sect. 2.4.

[109]Chapter 8: Germany, Sect. 8.2.

of new technology.[110] Its recommendation stated that Uber should be allowed to compete with taxis under similar terms and new rules such as returning to a particular station should not be imposed. Rejecting the idea that public services should be free of pressures creating market competition, the Monopolies Commission opined that new technology-driven operators such as Uber and the advantages they offer should be more welcomed in order to allow for modernization and improvement of services.[111]

7 Uber's Tax Liability

Uber has often been accused of tax evasion, and this claim is one of the sources of the uproar against it. Three major problems arise with regard to Uber's tax obligations. First, as a service provider, Uber's activities should be subject to a sales tax or what is commonly called value-added tax. Value-added tax is a tax applied by the state for the provision of a good or service and comes in the form of a predetermined percentage. If the value of a good or service surpasses a certain threshold, the buyer will have to pay the tax, which would be included in the final price. However, commonly, the providers would also have to pay a value-added tax if their incomes exceed a certain threshold. The second type of tax that may be problematic in the case of Uber is employment taxes.[112] Uber refuses to qualify the platform's drivers as employees. This implies that Uber does not have to pay a portion of income tax based on the drivers' revenue and is not liable for their social security and insurance payments. Finally, in some countries, Uber does not establish companies or operates in the name of a parent company based in another country. This model creates problems for the collection of revenue tax in the country where it actually offers services.

These tax-related issues have been raised by some of our authors. In Italy and the UK, revenue tax evasion could be clearly observed. In fact, Uber could easily avoid its tax obligations in many EU countries due to an EU rule called reverse charging.[113] Uber has established its headquarters in the Netherlands for its EU operations. All its subsidiaries in Europe are owned by this parent company, which benefits from the favorable Dutch incorporation rules. Incorporating in one member state while operating entirely in another is allowed by EU freedom of establishment rules according to a long-standing set of CJEU decisions.[114] Furthermore, in order to lower transaction costs, EU norms allow for the value-added tax to be collected in the member state where the provider of the good or service operates. As Uber

[110] Chapter 8: Germany, Sect. 8.2.

[111] Chapter 8: Germany, Sect. 8.2.

[112] Prassl (2018), pp. 125–126.

[113] Chapter 6: UK Sect. 7.

[114] CJEU Case C-212/97, 9 March 1999, *Centros Ltd v Erhvervs-og Selskabsstyrelsen*; CJEU Case C-208/00, 5 November 2002, *Überseering BV v Nordic Construction Company Baumanagement GmbH (NCC)*.

claims that it is not itself the provider of the service, the value-added tax has to be collected by the drivers. However, a great majority of Uber drivers do not surpass the threshold set for being liable for VAT collection. This is often the case, for instance, for Uber drivers in the UK.[115] Therefore, value-added tax is not collected in the UK or the Netherlands, allowing the platform to evade VAT collectable under EU rules. Furthermore, Uber BV is a Dutch company and thus has to pay corporate taxes in the Netherlands and not in Italy.[116] Finally, it has also been argued that by not accepting that the drivers are the platform's employees, Uber evades social security contributions, which are a significant concern in European countries. Hence, through its corporate scheme and business model, Uber minimizes its tax liability and creates economic and social problems.

8 Conclusion

This study has clearly shown the inadequacy of existing norms in many areas of law for framing and regulating Uber's activities. It appears that the most important difficulty for public authorities has been categorizing Uber and its activities, which often did not fully fit into existing definitions. Elements or even the entirety of Uber's activities does not fit into categories defined in regulatory frameworks, allowing the platform to claim to be free of such liabilities. This is the major disruption that Uber, like many other sharing economy companies, has caused for legal systems.

However, this study has also shown that the courts, regulatory authorities, and stakeholders in many countries have worked against these claimed regulatory loopholes. There are no jurisdictions in this study where Uber has not faced a significant legal challenge, ranging from authorization refusals to outright bans. This finding signifies that legislators are not yet willing to give up entirely on certain standards and protections provided in the law. This resistance has been stronger in some countries, such as Germany, than in others, such as the USA. As our comparative study has shown, legal traditions and trends play an important role in such differences. In the USA, where there has been a trend for decades toward the deregulation of certain sectors, regulators and courts have chosen a less interfering approach. On the other hand, in Germany, where the importance of protecting certain social interests is strongly embedded in the legal tradition, a more dismissive approach has been adopted by courts. In the context of labor law, many jurisdictions such as Italy or Mexico have accepted Uber's position qualifying drivers as self-employed, as the relationship between the platform and the drivers could not really be considered an employment contract. There are further examples where a more progressive approach was preferred. The traditional dichotomy between employees and independent contractors, and the criteria applicable for distinguishing between them seem to have grown stale. Considering the degree of control exercised by digital platforms

[115] Chapter 6: UK Sect. 4.

[116] Chapter 9: Italy, Sect. 2.4.

on the services provided, establishing intermediary categories (as is the case in the UK) or updating the requirements for the recognition of an employment relationship seems to be possible solutions.

Nevertheless, Uber has led legislators in many countries to adapt to changing circumstances in the economy and in society. Our study has shown that legislators could be anything but indifferent to Uber. This is perhaps the most important policy implication that may be drawn from this research. Some, like in Brazil, have chosen to create a new normative category to regulate Uber. Others, like in South Africa, have amended existing legislation in order to include Uber in the regulatory framework. Even in countries where there have been more prohibitive reactions to Uber, regulators have made attempts to reconcile with these new market forces. In the UK, the regulator has gone through a lengthy quest to better grasp the functioning of the platform. In Germany, in a report on Uber's impact on competition in markets, a public authority has questioned the necessity of extensive regulation in the transport sector. Thus, whether it has brought negative reactions or tides of change, Uber has been a significant legal phenomenon on a global scale. Its impact has affected both sides of the dilemma: Regulation could not be indifferent to Uber just as Uber could act freely of regulation.

References

Eurofound (2018) Non-standard forms of employment: recent trends and future prospects. Eurofound, Dublin (Cited as: Eurofund Report)

ILO (2016) Recommendation No. 98. https://www.ilo.org/dyn/normlex/en/f?p=NORMLEXPUB:12100:0::NO::P12100_INSTRUMENT_ID:312535. Accessed 20 May 2020

ILO (2018) Digital labour platforms and the future of work: towards decent work in the online. World International Labour Office-Geneva. https://www.ilo.org/wcmsp5/groups/public/—dgreports/—dcomm/—publ/documents/publication/wcms_645337.pdf. Accessed 23 May 2020

Marin J (2019) Passengers' rights and consumer protection. In: Marin J et al. (eds.) Uber—brave new service or unfair competition. Ius Gentium: Comparative Perspectives on Law and Justice, vol 76. Springer, Berlin, pp 199–211

Mudrić M (2019) Nature of Uber services. In: Marin J et al (eds.) Uber—brave new service or unfair competition. Ius Gentium: Comparative Perspectives on Law and Justice, vol 76. Springer, Berlin, pp 15–56

Prassl J (2018) Humans as a service. Oxford University Press, Oxford

Cases

Aslam v Uber BV (2017) I.R.L.R.4 (ET). https://www.judiciary.uk/wp-content/uploads/2018/12/uber-bv-ors-v-aslam-ors-judgment-19.12.18.pdf. Accessed 23 May 2020

Asociación Profesional Élite Taxi v Uber Systems Spain SL. ECLI:EU:C:2017:981

CJEU Case C-208/00, 5 November 2002, *Überseering BV v Nordic Construction Company Baumanagement GmbH (NCC)*

CJEU Case C-212/97, 9 March 1999, *Centros Ltd v Erhvervs-og Selskabsstyrelsen*

Madrid Court of Appeal, Judgment of 18 Jan 2019. ECLI:ES:APM:2019:3
Madrid Court of Appeal, Judgment of 18 Feb 2019. ECLI:ES:APM:2019:1255

Legislative Materials

Council Directive 93/113/EEC (OJ L 95, 21.4.1993)
Directive 2005/29/EC (OJ L 149, 11.6.2005)
Directive 2011/83/EU (OJ L 304, 22.11.2011)

Chapter 13
Looking Ahead...

Zeynep Ayata

Part of this edited volume was written during the COVID-19 crisis, which was marked by the rise and significance of digitalization and digital platforms. In the course of that crisis, the demand for Uber rides in the USA saw a notable decline, and there were reports that Uber would be laying off thousands of its employees.[1] On the other hand, there have also been reports that Uber Eats, Uber's food delivery service, has seen a substantial rise in demand.[2] UberEats was a service developed by Uber amid prohibitions of services such as UberPOP in some countries. It allowed for a continuation of Uber, giving the drivers a different task but operating essentially in the same way. Such incidents underline the flexibility and the adaptability of digital platforms and more importantly of innovators and disruptors.

The COVID-19 crisis has also emphasized once again the importance of data and their use. Many states have introduced applications that track the movements and interactions of individuals. These developments have obviously raised serious privacy concerns and heated debates on balancing public security and personal rights. However, this unusual state of affairs has also led states to collaborate with digital platforms. Not only the data collected and stored by digital platforms but also their software and their models have proven to be valuable for individuals and public authorities.[3] Thus, we have seen once again the importance and potential benefits of collaboration between policy-makers and public authorities and private stakeholders.

[1] Heater (2020). https://techcrunch.com/2020/05/06/uber-is-laying-off-3700-as-rides-plummet-due-to-covid-19/. Accessed 28 May 2020.

[2] Chiapetta (2020).

[3] Waltz (2020).

Z. Ayata (✉)
Koç University Law School, Istanbul, Turkey
e-mail: zayata@ku.edu.tr

Z. Ayata and I. Önay (eds.), *Global Perspectives on Legal Challenges Posed by Ridesharing Companies*,
https://doi.org/10.1007/978-981-15-7035-3_13

As this study has shown, Uber, like many other digital platforms and especially sharing economy platforms, has built a business model and an operation that disrupts, among other things, the legal system. Most of its elements do not fit into the normative framework that is expected to be applied. This often leads enforcers to give a prohibitive response to Uber's activities. However, Uber, similarly to all innovators and especially digital platforms, has one major advantage: flexibility. Our study has shown many examples where, in the face of interdiction, Uber has changed its system, its standards, or its functions. Hence, Uber does not merely provide flexibility for users; because of its business model and its dynamic nature, it is in itself adaptable.

This characteristic is in sharp contrast with regulations. Norms are often rigid, but more importantly, they are not easy to change. Amending rules or adopting new legislation is a process that takes a long time and requires extensive expertise. Furthermore, if these processes are going to be democratic, which is evidently desired, various stakeholders need to be involved. Such democratic processes that need to be inclusive not only require more time but also necessitate the reconciliation of conflicting interests. Additionally, these features create transaction costs, making these processes all the more costly and time-consuming.

It is also often argued that the lack of norms creates flexible spaces where innovation thrives.[4] For instance, Uber was one of the first companies to test driverless cars. The initiative led to the killing of a pedestrian in Arizona in 2018, and although Uber was not incriminated, there were reports stating that its software had flaws.[5] However, only two years later, Uber's self-driving cars were allowed again in certain states in the USA.[6] Uber could thus be the first corporation to deploy and commercialize this new technology. Driverless cars could eventually eliminate Uber's labor law challenges, which were discussed at length in this volume. It would also make Uber the pioneer of yet another new service through the use of sophisticated technology and software in an area that is not fully regulated.

Whether innovation necessitates regulation-free zones or not, we can probably identify a pattern where such innovators, or at least sharing economy platforms, often emerge within or perhaps even choose such loopholes.[7] On the other hand, this study has shown that operating in these loopholes is not sustainable due to legal and social reactions. Regulators, competitors, consumers, and other stakeholders want to ensure that these disruptors also act within a specified framework. It is only the extent of regulatory intervention that varies. The real controversy is between dynamic and adaptable disrupters and rigid and resistant rule-makers. Hence, the essential question before us is how to overcome this incongruity.

One noteworthy answer that may be found in the literature is, of course, flexible regulation. Several concepts and methods have been suggested by scholars as

---

[4]Fleischer (2010, pp. 227–290).

[5]Shepardson (2019).

[6]BBC (2020).

[7]Katz (2015, pp. 1067–1092).

a solution to the stringency and slowness of law making.[8] These theories suggest a more flexible law-making that takes actors of the market generally and innovators specifically as more heavily than just stakeholders. According to these approaches, innovators should be included among the rule-makers. Such theories underline the importance of inclusive processes for democracy and transparency, but more importantly for ensuring compliance with the law. Moreover, some authors have even argued that corporations should be able to self-regulate their activities[9] and that along with other actors of the market, such as professional organizations, they should be able to determine their own principles of control and governance.[10]

To what extent is self-regulation reliable and sufficient? Warnings against the limits of self-regulation can be found in the literature. In her seminal work, Ford argues that although flexible regulation presents many advantages such as transparency and inclusiveness, it also bears significant risks.[11] According to Ford, these processes may be dominated by the economically more powerful actors of the market and create problems in terms of equality before the law. Prassl argues, on the other hand, that some intervention will always be necessary in order to protect weaker parties, such as workers or consumers.[12] As the platforms will always have more bargaining power than these weaker parties, they will have more influence over policy-makers and legislative processes.

Could Uber's rating and complaint system be trusted to provide enough protection for passengers, for instance? Our study has shown that most regulators were not convinced that it could. Indeed, legislators and courts in most countries are still reluctant to rely entirely on systems created by private parties to safeguard individual rights. Platforms are corporations that seek to reduce their transaction costs in order to sustain lower prices, and higher standards of protection may increase transaction costs and restrict their sphere of action. Thus, they may not necessarily have incentives to provide better protection, unless there is a pressing demand from users. However, users may not always be in a power position to exert such pressures on platforms.[13] In other words, market dynamics may not suffice for adequate control and protection.

On the other hand, identifying the shortcomings of self-regulation should not lead to the conclusion that traditional regulation and regulatory processes should remain untouched. Sharing economy platforms such as Uber do offer benefits that should not be undermined. These platforms offer services at a lower price, have the ability to reduce information asymmetry, can utilize idle assets, and may offer higher quality. In the face of these benefits, outright bans do appear disproportionate. Thus,

---

[8]Ayres and Braithwate (1991), Gunningham and Graborski (1998), Lobel (2004, pp. 342–470), Parker (2002).

[9]Sundajaran (2014).

https://economix.blogs.nytimes.com/2014/03/03/trusting-the-sharing-economy-to-regulate-itself/?smid=tw-share. Accessed 28 May 2020.

[10]Gunningham and Grabosk (1998).

[11]Ford (2017).

[12]Prassl (2018).

[13]Hill (2016).

the emergence and expansion of platforms call for dynamism and change on the regulation side. Policy-makers have to reconcile these interests in order to encourage and sustain a variety of services in the market.

Platforms also have to assume more responsibility and relieve social concerns. This requires not only active collaboration with regulators but also substantial changes in their policies. For instance, Uber may have to acknowledge that a driver who works forty hours a week may no longer be considered as self-employed, and the information with regard to his/her generated income is perhaps not his/her personal data. Although they may increase transaction costs, certain safety controls for drivers and vehicles are necessary in order to provide adequate protection of passengers. Uber should also accept its tax liability because tax evasion not only causes significant damage to the welfare system but also creates social disturbance. Concerns over congestion and pollution are crucial social and environmental problems, and thus, Uber should comply to a certain extent with local transport regulations.

On July 28, 2018, I had to go from central Madrid to Barajas International Airport. I was returning from a conference at IE University, where I had chaired a seminar on legal challenges posed by Uber with presentations by several authors from this volume. On the day of my flight, Madrid's taxi drivers were on strike against Uber. Unable to call a taxi, I had to wait three hours for an Uber ride, which I shared with two other guests from the hotel. On our way to the airport, our immigrant Uber driver told us stories of the disputes and at times violent clashes between Uber drivers and taxi drivers in the city. This ironic anecdote shows how it is necessary for Uber, regulators, incumbents, and other market actors to find middle ground where the platform can survive without damaging individual rights and public interest. This volume, which provides comparative insights on these challenges, will hopefully contribute to the building of such an environment and the sustainability of the benefits of dynamic market forces.

References

Ayres I, Braithwate J (1991) Responsive regulation: transcending the deregulatory debate. Oxford University Press, New York

BBC (2020) Uber self-driving cars allowed back on California roads. BBC. https://www.bbc.com/news/technology-51393808. Accessed on 28 May 2020

Chiapetta M (2020) Uber eats demand soars due to COVID-19 Crisis. Forbes. https://www.forbes.com/sites/marcochiappetta/2020/03/25/uber-eats-demand-soars-due-to-covid-19-crisis/#4b2d47ad580c. Accessed on 28 May 2020

Fleischer V (2010) Regulatory arbitrage. Texas Law Review 89(2):227–290

Ford C (2017) Innovation and the state: finance, regulations and justice. Cambridge University Press, New York

Gunningham N, Graborski PM (1998) Smart regulation: designing environmental policy. Oxford University Press, New York

Heater B (2020) Uber is laying off 3700 as rides plummet due to COVID-19. Tech Crunch
https://techcrunch.com/2020/05/06/uber-is-laying-off-3700-as-rides-plummet-due-to-covid-19/. Accessed 28 May 2020

https://economix.blogs.nytimes.com/2014/03/03/trusting-the-sharing-economy-to-regulate-itself/?smid=tw-share. Accessed 28 May 2020

Hill S (2016) The California challenge. Friedrich Ebert Stiftung. https://steven-hill.com/wp-content/uploads/2016/10/Hill-FES-paper-California-Challenge-How-not-to-regulate-disruptive-business-models.pdf. Accessed on 28 May 2020

Katz V (2015) Regulating the sharing economy. Berkeley Technol Law J 30(4):1067–1092

Lobel O (2004) The renew deal: the fall of regulation and the rise of governance in contemporary legal thought. Minnesota Law Rev 89(2):342–470

Parker C (2002) The open corporation: effective self-regulation and democracy. Cambridge University Press, New York

Prassl J (2018) Humans as a service: the promise and perils of work in the Gig economy. Oxford University Press, Oxford

Shepardson D (2019) In review of fatal Arizona crash, U.S. agency says Uber software had flaws. Reuters. https://www.reuters.com/article/us-uber-crash/in-review-of-fatal-arizona-crash-us-agency-says-uber-software-had-flaws-idUSKBN1XF2HA. Accessed 28 May 2020

Sundajaran A (2014) Trusting the 'sharing economy' to regulate itself. New York Times

Waltz E (2020) How Facebook and google track public's movement in effort to fight COVID-19. IEEE Spectrum. https://spectrum.ieee.org/the-human-os/telecom/wireless/facebook-google-data-publics-movement-covid19. Accessed 28 May 2020

The manufacturer's authorised representative in the EU is Springer Nature Customer Service Centre GmbH, Europaplatz 3, 69115 Heidelberg, Germany. If you have any concerns regarding our products, please contact ProductSafety@springernature.com

Printed and bound by CPI Group (UK) Ltd, Croydon, CR0 4YY
30/09/2026
02225497-0014